GEORGE III., 1819.

SOCIAL ENGLAND

UNDER

THE REGENCY

BY

JOHN ASHTON

AUTHOR OF

'SOCIAL LIFE IN THE REIGN OF QUEEN ANNE,' 'FLORIZEL'S FOLLY,' ETC.

A NEW EDITION

WITH NINETY ILLUSTRATIONS

With an Introduction and Bibliography
by
LESLIE SHEPARD

LONDON

CHATTO & WINDUS

1899

Now Reissued by
Singing Tree Press
1249 Washington Blvd., Detroit, Michigan 1968

Library of Congress Card Number: 67-23940

INTRODUCTION

John Ashton compiled some thirty works, mainly in the fields of social history and folklore, but never received proper biographical notice. There are stray bibliographical notes in Allibone's *Critical Dictionary of English Literature* and Cousin's *Short Biographical Dictionary of English Literature* (Appendix to 1910 edition) but there are no details of his life, and even his death was not recorded in any standard reference work. The present reissue of a group of his books is a good opportunity to list the few facts it has been possible to discover about this interesting author.

John Ashton was born in London, September 22, 1834, son of Thomas and Isabella Ashton. Thomas Ashton was a shipbroker in the city of London and his wife followed the specialized trade of gun maker in the Goodman's Fields 'area. In addition to John Ashton there were two sisters and one brother. Thomas Ashton died in 1851 at his residence in Lewisham, Kent, and Isabella Ashton in 1875. We have no details of the early education and employment of John Ashton, but by the age of 40 he had settled down to regular research at the British Museum, London. In 1882 he published three books: *The Earliest Known Printed Ballad. A ballade of the Scottysshe King* (a facsimile of the first printing of Skelton's ballad, with introductory notes), *Chap-books of the Eighteenth Century*, and *Social Life in the Reign of Queen Anne*—the latter book was the first of a series of valuable compilations on social history. Ashton read steadily at the British Museum for more than thirty years, producing a new book about once a year.

In 1895 he lived at 4 Middleton Road (now Grove), Islington, in north west London, a rather dreary area near Camden Road. It was in this district that novelist

George Gissing lodged his character Alfred Yule in *New Grub Street*, and John Ashton must have been one of many struggling authors contemporary with Gissing, living frugally in a furnished room and making his way each day to the British Museum by omnibus, studying under the great glass dome of the Reading Room. It is doubtful whether Ashton made much money out of his books. Although they sold well, the rewards of authors in those days were modest, especially for non-fiction books. But clearly Ashton studied the kind of subjects that interested him—curiosities of history, and manners, modes and customs of past times. Living in an uninspiring district of endless rows of houses, he plodded away at his books, living in a romantic past. He had some skill in sketching, and embellished his books with many copies of old prints. Two of his books—*The Old Bailey and Newgate* [1902] and *Old-Time Aldwych, Kingsway and Neighbourhood* [1903] were published under the pseudonym "Charles Gordon", possibly to avoid complications on a publishing contract.

Ashton wrote little in his last few years and his death on July 29, 1911 seems to have passed unnoticed. Between 1906 and 1913 *Who's Who* had noted his works and it continued to list him until 1913 (though he does not appear in *Who Was Who*).

Ashton did not claim to be more than a compiler, but his compilations were thorough and entertaining, avoiding the extremes of heavy scholarship or over popularisation. He was a typical dedicated researcher with a keen delight in the everyday customs and traditions of ordinary people of former times. His books are not dated, and more than half a century after his death they remain as interesting and instructive as when they were first published.

London, England   Leslie Shepard
1967

BIBLIOGRAPHY OF WORKS WRITTEN OR EDITED
BY JOHN ASHTON

(Publication dates are for British editions; American editions sometimes vary.)

Chap-books of the Eighteenth Century; with facsimiles, notes, and introductions. 1882.

[SKELTON, John] *The Earliest known printed English Ballad. A ballade of the Scottysshe King* (facsimile reprint without introduction). 1882.

Social Life in the Reign of Queen Anne, taken from original sources. 1882.

The Adventures and Discourses of Captain John Smith, sometime President of Virginia. 1883.

Humour, Wit, and Satire of the Seventeenth Century. 1883.

Lord Mayor's Show in the Olden Times [Drawings by F. C. Price] [1883].

English Caricature and Satire on Napoleon I 2 vols. 1884; new edition 1888.

Old Times: a picture of social life at the end of the Eighteenth Century. 1885.

The Dawn of the XIXth Century in England. A social sketch of the times. 1886 [1885]; Popular edition 1886.

The Legendary History of the Cross. A series of sixty-four woodcuts from a Dutch book published by Veldener, A.D. 1483. Introduction by J. Ashton; Preface by S. Baring-Gould. 1887 [1886].

Romances of Chivalry told and illustrated in facsimile. 1887. [1886].

A Century of Ballads . . . Edited, and illustrated in facsimile of the originals. 1887.

[MANDEVILLE, Sir John] *The Voiage and Travayle of Sir John Maundeville* (Edited, annotated and illustrated by J. Ashton). 1887.

The Fleet: its River, Prison, and Marriages. 1888. [1887].

Eighteenth Century Waifs [essays]. 1887.

Modern Street Ballads. 1888.

Men, Maidens and Manners a Hundred Years Ago. 1888.

Curious Creatures in Zoology. 1890. [1889].

Social England under the Regency, 1890; New edition 1899.

[HOOD, Thomas] *The Poetical Works of T. Hood* [with memoir and notes by J. Ashton] [1891].

Real Sailor-Songs. Collected and edited. 1891.

[with MEW, James] *Drinks of the World.* 1892.

A History of English Lotteries. 1893.

Charles Letts's Date Book and Chronological Diary, or record of important events in English history [1893].

A Righte Merrie Christmasse!!! The story of Christmastide [1894].

Varia [essays]. 1894.

Hyde Park from Domesday-Book to date. 1896 [1895].

When William IV was King. 1896.

The Devil in Britain and America. 1896.

The History of Gambling in England. 1898

Florizel's Folly. George IV and Brighton. 1899.

[under pseudonym of GORDON, Charles] *The Old Bailey and Newgate.* 1902.

[under pseudonym of GORDON, Charles] *Old-Time Aldwych, Kingsway and Neighbourhood.* 1903.

Gossip in the First Decade of Victoria's Reign. 1903.

The History of Bread from prehistoric to modern times. 1904.

PREFACE.

CERTAINLY, it is not the least part of an Author's reward for all his pains and trouble, to find that the Public appreciates his efforts, and purchases and reads his books. I am thus emboldened to continue my work, and sketch the men and manners of the Regency. Most books of this class deal mainly with the great ones of the land, but I have only done so where necessary to illustrate the history of the times, my aim being more to delineate the social condition of England and her people. I may add, that this work will be found perfectly reliable as history, nothing being taken at second-hand, but all compiled, even down to the illustrations, from original and contemporaneous authorities.

JOHN ASHTON.

CONTENTS.

CHAPTER I.

CHAPTER VI.
1812.

CONTENTS

CHAPTER XXXIV.

CHAPTER XXXV.

ILLUSTRATIONS.

SOCIAL ENGLAND UNDER THE REGENCY.

CHAPTER I.

The King's Malady—Former preparations for a Regency—King's
recovery—The King at home—His love of music—Severe frost
—Lucien Buonaparte a prisoner of war—French obstructions to
commerce—A gallant merchantman.

'STATE OF HIS MAJESTY'S HEALTH.

'Windsor Castle, January 1, 1811.
            'His Majesty has passed a quiet night, without
much sleep, and continues the same as he was yesterday.
                                    'H. HALFORD.
                                    'W. HEBERDEN.
                                    'R. WILLIS.'

SUCH was the announcement contained in *The Times* of 2nd of
January, 1811, and, for some time, the subjects of George III.
were fed with daily news of the King's health. By and by,
as his mental disease was confirmed, they grew fewer, until
they were furnished just once a month, and then only the
very scantiest intelligence of his condition was vouchsafed to
his people.

This was not the first time that his mind had given way.
In the early part of October, 1788, he had decided symptoms
of mental aberration, and was totally incapable of undertaking
any of the affairs of State ; but his physicians were hopeful

1

of his recovery—and their hopes were gratified. But the
Ministry thought differently, and, after suggesting that the
Government should be carried on by a Commission, on the
30th of December, 1788, Pitt wrote a letter to the Prince of
Wales, stating that his Majesty's Ministers had come to the
conclusion to offer him the Regency of the kingdom under
certain restrictions.

The Prince of Wales replied at once, expressing his sorrow
at the occasion of his proposed elevation, but accepting the
trust. Of course, this suggestion of the Government could
not be acted upon without mature deliberation, and it was
not until the 30th of January, 1789, that the following
resolutions of the Lords and Commons were presented to the
Prince of Wales—'That his Royal Highness be empowered
to exercise the royal authority under the title of Regent.'
'That the power given, should not extend to the granting of
any peerage, except to the Royal issue.' 'Nor to the grant
of any office in reversion, or any office, salary, or pension,
than during his Majesty's pleasure ; or to the granting his
Majesty's real or personal estates.' 'That the Care of his
Majesty be committed to the Queen, who should nominate all
persons to the offices in the household.'

Needless to say, the Prince made no objections, and by the
12th of February, the Regency Bill had gone through all its
stages in the House of Commons, and was ordered to be sent
to the Lords. But the proverbial 'slip 'twixt cup and lip'
occurred. On the 19th of February the Lord Chancellor
informed the House of Lords that, according to the report
of his physicians, the King's health was steadily mending, and
they therefore abstained from further consideration of the
Regency Bill.

The physicians' hopes were fully justified ; the King got
better rapidly, and, on the 27th of February, his perfect
recovery was announced, the prayer for the same was discontinued, and a form of prayer of thanksgiving for his
restoration to health, was ordered to be read in all Churches
and Chapels throughout England and Wales. Rejoicings and
illuminations were the order of the day, and, on the 23rd of
April, the day of general thanksgiving, the King, Queen, and
Royal family went in state to St. Paul's Cathedral, to return
thanks to God for His mercy in giving the King his reason
and health once more.

Years went on, and the King did not suffer from mental

disease, until the year 1810, when to bodily illness of his own, was added the death of his daughter, the Princess Amelia. This shock his intellect, perhaps never too strong, could not stand, and, although his condition was concealed for some little time from the people—under the pretence that he had a cold—the truth was obliged to come out ; and we read in *The Morning Post* of October 31st—'It is with heartfelt sorrow we announce that His Majesty's indisposition still continues.   It commenced with the effect produced upon his tender parental feelings on receiving the ring* from the hand of his afflicted beloved daughter, the affecting inscription upon which, caused him, blessed, and most amiable of men, to burst into tears, with the most heart-touching lamentations on the present state, and approaching dissolution of the afflicted and interesting Princess.   His Majesty is attended by Drs. Halford, Heberden, and Baillie, who issue daily bulletins of the state of the virtuous and revered monarch, for whose speedy recovery the prayers of all good men will not fail to be offered up.'

This time the physicians held out no hopes of the King's recovery, or if they did, it was at some vague, indefinite future, the date of which none could prognosticate, and Parliament found itself in a serious situation.   It met on the 1st of November, to which date it had been prorogued, only to find that there was no King to open the session, and no Commission for so doing had been named.   So, in default of any other recognized authority, the Lord Chancellor, and the Speaker, took the lead in their different assemblies, and after vainly trying to find out how they should act, an Order in Council cut the Gordian Knot, adjourning Parliament to the 29th of November, a decision which was confirmed in the House of Commons by a majority of 285.   When they again met, they, after discoursing of the King, set to work to concoct a Regency.

But that may wait for a while, and come in its proper place, for King George is passing away from this history, and the full blaze of the Regency leaves very little room for the

* The Princess Amelia, when dying, ordered a valuable stone she possessed, to be set in a ring, for a keepsake of her to her father, and so urgent was she that it might be made before she died, that a jeweller was sent for, express, from London to make it.   It contained a lock of her hair, and, on it, was her name, and, ' *Remember me when I am gone.*

1—2

shadow of the old King to show : yet, before he disappears altogether, it may be as well if we can recall a reminiscence of him, as late as possible, before his sad malady overtook, and mastered him.   Not in his public capacity, but as it were *en famille,* let us see him ; and we get a good view of him through the medium of the Rev. John Evans, LL.D., of Islington, who wrote ' An excursion to Windsor,' and thus describes what he saw on the 10th of July, 1810 :—

' We entered Windsor about six o'clock, and, having refreshed ourselves at the inn with a cup of tea, hastened to *The Terrace,* where we found a considerable portion of genteel company.   Intent on the gratification of a laudable curiosity, we felt peculiarly happy in joining them on this occasion. It was seven o'clock, and the good old King soon made his appearance with his accustomed punctuality.

' A little door in the Castle was thrown open, when two attendants were seen leading this *venerable personage* with great care down a flight of steps till he safely alighted upon the terrace.   Then the Princesses *Elizabeth* and *Augusta,* who were present, accompanied him, one on each side, or rather took hold of his arm ; they paced backwards and forwards for an hour, two bands of music playing alternately ; and the fine tones of the several instruments being heightened by the stillness of the closing day.

' The King was dressed neatly : blue coat with gilt buttons and blue star, white waistcoat and small clothes, white stockings, and gold buckles in his shoes.   His hat somewhat resembled that worn by the clergy, with the addition of a gold button and loop, mounted by a black cockade, which marks him out conspicuously from the rest of the company. His Majesty looked ruddy and full ; his voice is sonorous, and he converses with cheerfulness, though, when he attempts to speak rather hastily, it is with hesitation.

' His want of sight is very apparent, for his hat is drawn over the upper part of his face, and he feels about with his cane, especially ascending or descending a step.   It is affecting to see him, though he appears cheerful when he speaks, and seems as if nothing were the matter with him.   He now and then stops to converse either with the officers, or with the nobility and gentry.   We saw him several times on the Terrace ; but on this first evening there was a more than ordinary degree of conversation.   He was full of inquiries respecting the *installation* of Lord Grenville as Chancellor of the University of Oxford, which had taken place during the week. He inquired also about the *balloon* in which Mr. Sadler* had ascended on this occasion, and was particularly anxious to know how long it continued in the air, and where it had alighted; Harrow-on-the-Hill was mentioned, though the spot had not then been ascertained. He conversed at all times on a variety of topics with the utmost freedom and even hilarity.

'This daily promenade must benefit both his mind and body: while the presence, as well as the attention, of so many of his subjects, some coming from distant parts, must yield him no inconsiderable gratification. The countenances of the Princesses are replete with good nature, and most exemplary is their attention to their aged parent. . . .

'It should be mentioned that the King, in returning back to his apartments in the Castle, passing by the *band of musicians* on the steps, always touched his hat, and said, in an audible voice, "*Gentlemen, good-night, I thank you.*" Indeed, his Majesty, during the whole time, seemed in perfect good humour with all the company.

'The only etiquette observed on *the Terrace* is, that when the King passes, the ladies and gentlemen withdraw on either side, the latter merely uncovering the head; bows and curtsies being dispensed with on the occasion. A police officer is in attendance, who, with a little switch, keeps individuals from pressing too much on the *King*, when he stops to converse; but this is done with the greatest urbanity. Owing to a slight indisposition, the Queen did not make her appearance on the Terrace; but we saw her on other occasions. His Majesty was regular in his attendance at Chapel every morning, and seemed seriously engaged in his devotions.

'About ten o'clock, when the weather is fine (Sundays excepted), the King rides out on horseback; and, considering his age, he mounted his horse with wonderful agility. He is, in his ride, accompanied by two of the Princesses, who have some of their *maids of honour* following in a landau or phaeton. The King has several attendants, two of whom are close by him, and one has a little stick, the crooked end of which catches that part of the bridle nearest the curb, so that, should the animal on which his Majesty rides stumble, instant assistance might be given.'

* Then the principal aëronaut in England.

Music was his greatest solace from his latter seizure till his death, and we learn of him in the beginning of the year 1811 (*Morning Chronicle*, Jan. 8th):—

'Windsor, January 6th.—The Bulletin of to-day is of a very cheering nature, and for these five days past his Majesty has been gradually improving, both in mental and bodily strength. His Majesty has become more tranquillized in his general deportment, and there are daily visible signs that his malady is on the decline. His Majesty now uses the sitting-room in the Blenheim Tower; takes his meals regularly, and at intervals amuses himself with playing the most familiar tunes, on the harpsichord, with a correctness surpassing the most sanguine expectations. As a striking proof of this fact, on some very recent occasions, when his Majesty, in consequence of his defective sight, struck a wrong key, he instantly corrected the error by modulating the tune, and finishing it with his accustomed science and judgment. . . .

'The Harpsichord on which his Majesty plays, formerly belonged to the great Handel, and is supposed to have been manufactured at Antwerp in the year 1612. Handel's music is highly esteemed by his Majesty, and many of his most favourite compositions are now played by his Majesty from recollection.' And so let us leave him, for a while, to be soothed by his music.

The year 1811 came in bitterly cold, and sad were the tales told in consequence. As to the Coaches, they suffered severely. On the 4th of January the fall of snow was so great, that the Northern roads were all but impassable, and the Mail Coach from Boston could only be dragged four miles through the snow, the guard having to do the best he could, on horseback, with the mails, and the mails from London to Boston had to be conveyed in the same manner. The Leicester Coach, on the way to Stamford, was upset in the snow at Burton-Lazarus, and several of the passengers were hurt; the Carlisle Mail was dug out of the snow at Tickencote, and with difficulty got to Stamford with eight horses, three hours later than usual; but it could not proceed further than Thornhaugh, whence the guard was obliged to take the letter-bags on horseback. Three coaches from the north lay all night in the snow about a mile from Stamford, and as many near Winsford. Oh! for the good old Coaching days! when Pullman's Cars were unknown, and people with slender purses had to ride outside in all weathers—and it was recorded that on the 5th of January, 1811, on the arrival of the Carlisle Coach in London two poor women, outside passengers, were frozen to death. The Coachman supposed them to be asleep, and did not attempt to disturb them until he arrived at his destination, when they were found stiff in death. Two persons near Lincoln perished in the snow, and the cold was so great, even so far south as London, that the Thames was nearly frozen over.

Tender hearts felt for the Poor Debtors, and those in Ludgate record their thanks to M. A. Taylor, Esq., M.P., for his annual benevolent gift of two Chaldrons of Coals, 158 lbs. Beef, and 23 half-peck loaves; and to Alderman Wood, the friend of Queen Caroline, for his present of £5; and an unknown donor for 40 lbs. Beef. The poor debtors in Newgate had very many large sums to acknowledge, and were duly grateful for the kindly and thoughtful assistance thus rendered them. Sad, however, is it to find that during the Severe Frost, on the 7th of January, a poor prisoner died of Cold and Want in the Marshalsea prison. At this time we learn there were about 320 debtors in Newgate alone; and those that were without private means, had to subsist on the prison allowance of 2d. worth of bread (the quartern loaf being, in January, 1s. 3d.), so that their relief during the inclement winter, was a work of necessity, as well as of benevolence.

In 1811 was living amongst us an illustrious Prisoner of War, no less a person than Lucien Buonaparte, Prince de Canino (his son, Prince Louis Lucien, also afterwards lived with us), who, not altogether falling in with his brother's policy, was on his way to the United States, when, on the 1st of August, 1810, he was taken and made prisoner by a British Cruiser. After some detention at Malta, he was sent on to England, and Ludlow was assigned as his place of detention; and there he lived for some time, inhabiting Dinham House, the seat of the Earl of Powis. He seems to have accepted the inevitable cheerfully, according to *The Times* of Friday, January 4th:—

'Lucien Buonaparte arrived at Ludlow about 4 o'clock on the evening of Wednesday, sen'night, accompanied by his nephew, an interpreter, secretary, Mr. Mackenzie, and a few servants. He drove to the Angel Inn, where he dined and slept. On Thursday morning he walked about the town, viewed the Castle, and some of the principal streets; but, as

the weather was rather unfavourable, and public curiosity
great, he did not stay long. On that evening, one of the
Winter Dancing Assemblies took place, which Lucien, his
nephew, and some of his friends attended. Some of the
latter danced, but Lucien did not. He continued in the
room till supper was announced ; he then attended Countess
Powis to the supper rooms, and sat at her Ladyship's right
hand during supper : after which he returned to the ball and
card rooms. On Saturday he went to Stone-house, a seat of
Lord Powis, about five miles from Ludlow, where Lucien is in
future to reside, and from thence proceeded to Walcot, the
principal residence of his Lordship, where he stayed a day or
two, and returned to Ludlow.'

The next day's *Times* says : ' Madame Lucien Buonaparte,
with her family, and a numerous train of servants, occupying,
in all, four carriages, arrived at Ludlow on Wednesday ;
having performed the journey from Plymouth, in a week.
Lucien removed, on the preceding day, from the Inn to Lord
Powis's residence in that town, called Dinham-house ; his
Lordship's seat in the neighbourhood (Stone-house) being
found too small for the reception of so numerous a suite.'

In another Newspaper the ladies are described with almost
American frankness : ' Madame Buonaparte is extremely
handsome and fascinating ; Lucien's daughter, of whom so
much has been said, has great claims to a genteel figure, and
elegant demeanour, but she is not beautiful. The motto on
Lucien's carriage is an extraordinary one, *Luceo, non uro,* " I
shine without burning," ' On this motto the following
Epigram was made :—

> ' A Wag, requested to translate
> The Motto, on the Coach of State
>   That sets all Wales into a wonder.
> " It means," said he, and scratcht his pole,
> " It means *I shine*, with what I stole ;
>   My foolish brother *burns* his plunder.'

He afterwards, bought the estate of Thorngrove, near
Worcester, and there lived until the restoration in 1814,
when he went to Rome.

Some explanation is needed, to elucidate the last line of
the above epigram. Napoleon was determined to do the
utmost damage to England, and endeavoured to injure her in
her most vulnerable part, her commerce—so, whenever the

goods of Great Britain, or her Colonies, were found, they were burnt. That this was not an idle threat is shown by the following excerpts from *The Times* of January 7th and 8th :—

'A Gentleman who has arrived within these three days from the Continent, and has been present at several burnings of British manufactures, informs us that in every place where the decrees to that effect were put in force, it was done at the point of the bayonet: French Soldiers being always present to prevent tumult and disorder, which, on such occasions, manifested themselves everywhere.'

'At the beginning of December, a number of French Officers of the Customs, with a detachment of the 17th regiment of Infantry, arrived at Brandenburg, to make searches for Colonial produce, which they immediately began with great strictness.'

'Parma, December 12th. Yesterday, there were burnt in this town 24 bales of spun cotton, 150 pieces of cotton handkerchiefs, and 74 pieces of stuffs of the same manufacture ; the whole being English manufactures, and seized by the Custom House agents on the frontiers of the department of the Po.'

But, at sea, sometimes a Merchantman could look after its cargo itself, without need of the strong arm of a Convoy, as in the case of the good ship *Cumberland*, Barrett, master, bound from Quebec to England. On the 13th of January, 1811, she arrived in the Downs under a jury foremast and bowsprit, having lost both foremast and bowsprit in a heavy gale of wind off the banks of Newfoundland.

This, one would have thought, would have been sufficient excitement for one voyage, but no ! when close home, between Deal and Folkestone, about seven and eight in the morning, she was attacked by four French lugger privateers, who approached under the pretence of knowing whether Captain Barrett wanted a pilot. But he was wary, and replied in the negative, whereupon the privateers declared themselves in their true colours, and poured in a volley of musketry.

Captain Barrett ordered his men down below, arming them with boarding pikes, and as soon as about twenty of the enemy were aboard, his crew attacked them, and cleared the decks, killing most of them ; the others jumping overboard. Five times were they boarded, (the Frenchmen ceasing firing, for fear of hurting their own men), and five times the enemy experienced a crushing defeat. Captain Barrett then discharged three of his Carronades, loaded with round shot and Canister. One shot carried away the mainmast of one of the privateers; the second, the bowsprit of another, and doubtless injured some of their men, as there was a great cry heard. This proved enough for 'Mounseer,' and the four luggers sheered off.

The Crew of the *Cumberland* was twenty-six men, and the force of the enemy was estimated at two hundred and seventy according to the statements of the prisoners taken. The loss to the *Cumberland* was one man killed, and the chief mate wounded; the French loss is set down as about sixty. And what think you was the reward of the gallant crew? 'The Lords of the Admiralty have, as a mark of their satisfaction at the gallantry exhibited on this occasion, expressed their intention *to grant to each of the crew of the* Cumberland, *a protection from the impress, for the space of three Years.'* !!!

CHAPTER II.

A Regency inevitable—Prince of Wales waited on—He undertakes the Regency—French and English prisoners of war—Roman Catholic soldiers—Roughness of manners—Passing of Regency Bill—The Prince's companions—Inauguration of the Prince as Regent—Improvement in the health of the King.

ALL the year the Lords and Commons had been incubating a Regency, and matters were so far advanced, that on the 8th of January, the House of Commons received a message from the Lords that they had ' ordered the Lord President, and the Lord Privy Seal to attend his Royal Highness the Prince of Wales with the several Resolutions agreed to by the Lords and Commons, for the purpose of supplying the defect of the personal exercise of the royal authority during his Majesty's illness, on the part of their lordships, and desired that that House would appoint a proportionate number of their members to go with them. Also that they had ordered Earl Harcourt, and Earl Morton, to attend her Majesty with the Resolution and Address agreed to by the Lords and Commons respecting the care of his Majesty's royal person, and the direction of such part of his Majesty's household as may be requisite for the comfort of his Majesty, and for the maintenance of the Royal dignity ; and desired that the House would appoint a proportionate number of their members to go with them.'

The Commons chose, as under, to go with the Lords to wait upon the Prince of Wales : The Chancellor of the Exchequer (the Right Hon. Spencer Perceval), the Secretary of State for the Home Department (the Right Hon. Richard Ryder), the President of the Board of Control for the affairs of India (the Right Hon. Robert Saunders Dundas, afterwards Lord Melville), and Sir William Grant, the Master of the Rolls ; whilst the members chosen to wait upon the Queen were Lord John

Thynne, Lord Palmerston (Secretary at War), Lord Clive, and Colonel Desbrowe.

On the 11th of January these two deputations went in great state, the one to the Prince, the other to the Queen. The Prince received them in the grand drawing-room of Carlton House, standing with his Chancellor, William Adam, Esq., and Earl Moira on his right hand, the Duke of Cumberland and Mr. Sheridan on his left ; whilst behind him were four officers of his household, Mr. Tyrwhitt, Colonel M'Mahon, General Bloomfield, and General Turner.

The Lord President, as chief of the deputation, then read a paper, informing the Prince that 'they were a Committee appointed to attend his Royal Highness with the resolutions which had been agreed to by the Lords and Commons, for the purpose of supplying the defect of the personal exercise of the royal authority, during his Majesty's illness, by empowering his Royal Highness to exercise that authority in the name and on the behalf of his Majesty, subject to such limitations and restrictions as shall be provided.

'And that they were directed to express the hope which the Lords, spiritual and temporal, and Commons entertain, that his Royal Highness, from his regard to the interests of his Majesty, will be ready to undertake the weighty and important trust proposed to be invested in his Royal Highness, as soon as an Act of Parliament shall have been passed for carrying the said resolutions into effect.'

The Lord President first read and then delivered to the Prince the Resolutions, and he replied :

'My Lords and Gentlemen,

'I receive the communication which the two Houses have directed you to make to me of their joint Resolutions, on the subject of providing for "the exercise of the Royal Authority during his Majesty's illness," with those sentiments of regard which I must ever entertain for the united desires of the two Houses.

'With the same sentiments I receive the expressed hopes of the Lords and Commons, that from my regard for the interest of his Majesty and the Nation, I should be ready to undertake the weighty and important trust proposed to be invested in me, under the Restrictions and Limitations stated in those Resolutions.

'Conscious that every feeling of my heart would have

prompted me, from dutiful affection to my beloved Father and Sovereign, to have shown all the reverential delicacy towards him inculcated in those Resolutions, I cannot refrain from expressing my regret, that I should not have been allowed the opportunity of manifesting to his afflicted and loyal subjects that such would have been my conduct.

'Deeply impressed, however, with the necessity of tranquillizing the public mind, and determined to submit to every personal sacrifice, consistent with the regard I owe to the security of my Father's Crown, and the equal regard I owe to the welfare of his people, I do not hesitate to accept the office and situation proposed to me, restricted as they are, still retaining every opinion expressed by me upon a former and similar distressing occasion.

'In undertaking the trust proposed to me I am well aware of the difficulties of the situation in which I shall be placed ; but I shall rely with confidence upon the Constitutional advice of an enlightened Parliament, and the zealous support of a generous and loyal people. I will use all the means left to me to merit both.

'My Lords and Gentlemen,
        'You will communicate this my answer to the two Houses, accompanied by my most fervent wishes and prayers, that the Divine Will may extricate us, and the nation, from the grievous embarrassments of our present condition, by the speedy restoration of his Majesty's health.'

The Queen gave an answer, couched in a similar spirit to the deputation which waited upon her.

Whilst the Lords and Commons are debating on the Regency Bill (and they took the whole of January to do it), let us see what was happening in England.

There was a subject that touched many, and all over Britain, from the highest to the lowest, and that was the British prisoners of war in France. Truly we had many more French prisoners in England than there were English in France ; *The Morning Post*, October 15th, 1810, placing the numbers respectively at 50,000 and 12,000. The French prisoners here were not treated too well ; but the English prisoners in France were treated worse, and many thousands of hearts must have yearned towards those poor Captives, and many thousands were willing to part with their means, although there were then many, and urgent, calls upon their purses, in order to alleviate their lot.

Lloyd's was then the Centre of benevolence, as the Mansion House now is ; and the leading Merchants and Bankers issued an advertisement in *The Times* of January 7th, saying that their means of helping these prisoners were exhausted, and they appealed for fresh funds.

'The Committee beg to state that there are upwards of 10,000 British Prisoners in the different Prisons in France, for the most part in great distress, and that the subscription is intended for the alleviation of their sufferings in some degree, by assisting them with articles of clothing, bedding, fuel, and such other necessaries as they stand in most need of.

' They think it proper to add that the relief from the last subscription was intrusted to the care of some of the most respectable persons detained in France, among whom were Clergymen, and several officers both Naval and Military, and that they have made so satisfactory a distribution of the funds, and rendered such particular details thereof, as to entitle them to the highest credit. The same Gentlemen, there is reason to expect, will kindly undertake the distribution of a new subscription.'

Needless to say that the appeal was nobly responded to.

Scant courtesy seems to have been paid to the prisoners on either side, almost degenerating into pettiness : for, this month, an Order was issued from Whitehall that no French women should be allowed to land in this country, who might have left France to see their husbands. The reason assigned for this very peculiar proceeding was, that the French Government would not permit Lady Lavie and family to join her husband, Sir Thomas, who was a prisoner at Verdun.

But pettiness in official circles seems to have obtained. Can we barely imagine, at a time when every soldier was wanted, and it might be thought that good treatment, at all events, might have allured men to the ranks, that they trod upon their tenderest feelings? Yet so it was, and it was mainly owing to the exertions of *The Dublin Evening Post* that the following ' General Order' was issued :

' ADJUTANT GENERAL'S OFFICE, DUBLIN,
' *January*, 1811.

' Reports have been circulated, that Catholic soldiers have been prevented from attending Divine worship, according to the tenets of their religion, and obliged, in certain instances, to be present at that of the Established Church; the Commanding Officers of the several Regiments are to be attentive to the prevention of such practices, if they have, in any instance, existed in the Troops under their command, as they are in *violation* of the Orders contained in the Circular letter of the 14 May, 1806, and, since, *repeated to the Army*. And the Catholic soldiers, as well as those of other Sects, are to be allowed, *in all cases*, to attend the Divine Worship of the Almighty according to their several persuasions, when duty does not interfere, *in the same manner, and under the same regulations*, as those of the Established Church.

> 'WM. RAYMOND, Dep. Adjt. Gen.
> 'N. RAMSEY, Maj. Assist. Adjt. Gen.'

The Morning Chronicle, commenting upon this, says: 'So late as Friday morning last, some of the artillery, privates and drivers, quartered in Enniskillen, continued to do duty with *turned coats*, the most mortifying punishment ever inflicted on a brave man, and this, merely for having attended, *according to law*, to the Worship of their Church; but on the evening of that day, the scene was somewhat changed, the General Order arrived, and on the following morning, the officer accused of the oppression departed for Dublin, and on Sunday, the Catholic soldiers of the garrison were marched to the Roman Catholic Chapel, accompanied by the officers of that religion.'

It would seem that all parties were trying to make the Services unpopular: the navy, especially, by impressment—and even the Militia did not escape—for in January, a number of farmers and others were summoned before the magistrates at Stafford for making deductions from the wages of those servants who were enrolled in the Militia, and who had been absent for their training. It must be remembered that in those days farm labourers were hired at Statute fairs, for a twelvemonth, and the 15th clause of 48 Geo. III., cap. 3, had to be shown to those summoned, whereby they learned that no ballot, enrolment, or service under the Act should make void or in any manner affect, any indenture of apprenticeship, or contract of service. And so they had to pay their men.

They were rather a rough lot in the Country, and this anecdote is thus recorded in *The Times* of January 31, 1811 :—

'The following *ludicrous** circumstance occurred on Tuesday week at Bristol :—A couple of Jews being apprehended in the act of stealing several articles from the stables of the White Hart Inn, were hauled into the yard by two stout fellows, whither the whole fraternity of the currycomb were immediately summoned. The long beards of these disciples were then stuck together with pitch (their hands being previously tied behind them) ; and, whilst thus face to face, a profusion of snuff mixed with hellebore, was administered, which caused them to sneeze in such a manner, that by the frequent and violent bobbing of noses one against the other, a copious stream of blood issued from either nostril, whilst the enraged Culprits were kicking and capering about in all directions.'

Chronologically, we must now turn to the Prince of Wales, who, one would imagine, was desirous of emulating the Squires of old, who spent the eve of their knighthood in vigil, prayer, fasting, and watching their armour—so before he became Prince Regent, he must needs partake of the Holy Eucharist, and did so at the Chapel Royal, St. James's, on Sunday the 27th of January ; *the sole object of which was to obtain a certificate that he was in the Communion of the Church of England.* This public act of worship was a stately affair. The Prince was in the Royal Closet during the major portion of the service, the Bishop of London and sub-dean duly bowing to the royal presence, at their entrance. Afterwards, attended by the Earl of Moira, and Lords Dundas and Keith, he went up to the Altar, took his seat under a canopy, made his offering in a gold dish, and then the Dean, the Prince, and the three Lords Communicated.

On the 5th of February the Lords and Commons had their final conference over the Regency Bill, they agreed to the interpolation of two words 'and Commons,' and the thing was all but finished. It only wanted what was done immediately afterwards, the Royal Commissioners to give the Royal Assent, the Deputy Clerk of the Crown to read the title of the Act, the Clerk Assistant of the Parliaments to utter the words ' Le Roi le veult '—and the Prince of Wales was *de facto* Regent.

Knowing his proclivities, it was imagined that he would give places to all his *entourage*, and, accordingly, we have the caricature of ' Robeing the Prince, or the Road to Preferment.'

* The italics are mine.—J. A.

Grey. Whitbread. Grenville. Sheridan.   Geo. Bloomfield.   Regent.   Col. McMahon.   Adam.   Perceval.   Sir John Douglas.
    G. Hanger.

ROBEING THE REGENT; OR, THE ROAD TO PREFERMENT.

(*Published February 1, 1811, by Walter and Knight, Cornhill.*)

To the extreme left is Earl Grey, who says ' A bason of *Grey* pease soup is better than porter for your Highness,' but Whitbread is of opinion that ' If his Highness should want any refreshment, here's a pot of my best brewing.' Grenville offers his services to the Prince. Sheridan hopes ' your Royal Highness will not forget *Old Sherry;* pray allow me to brush the Royal shoes, they seem quite mouldy with lieing by so long.' Colonel Bloomfield is tying his garter. Whoever is holding the looking-glass exclaims, ' What an honour this is ! but I hope for greater.' The Regent tells Sheridan, ' Fear not, my friend, all in good time.' Col. McMahon says, ' Why ! can't you see you have given him the wrong sleeve ; do give it to me, you'll make a fine figure of him !' But the person holding the robe replies, ' Don't push so, Col., you won't let any one come near his Highness but yourself.' Mr. Adam, the Prince's Chancellor, soliloquises thus, ' A dam good prospect now, however.' Sir John Douglas calls out, ' Who wants me ?' and Col. Geo. Hanger, hopes ' you won't forget poor Georgy.'

Perhaps the three best known of these Companions of the Prince are Sheridan, Col. McMahon, and George Hanger. The first belongs to history, and the second will be noticed by and by. Col. Hanger came of a noble Irish family, but in his youth led a wild harum scarum life. Of course he entered the army, and whilst holding the King's Commission he fell in with, and joined a gang of gipsies, when he fell in love with a dusky beauty, and married her according to the customs of her tribe, which, probably, only involved the jumping over a broomstick. He introduced her to his brother officers, and all went well for about a fortnight, when she eloped with a bandy-legged tinker. His tastes were congenial to those of the Prince, and he made himself useful, bought horses for him, looked after his racing arrangements, and was one of his equerries, which post he kept until he was, by his extravagance, compelled to resign it. He was more than once imprisoned for debt, but turned steady after the death of his brother Lord Coleraine (called *blue Hanger,* from the colour of his garments) in 1814, when he succeeded to the title, which became extinct on his death in 1824.

Meanwhile, all was being prepared for the assumption of the Regency, Carlton House was being brushed up, chandeliers cleaned, &c., a congenial task for its occupier, the Hanoverian creams were publicly exercised, and made to pass between files

of soldiers, and, at last, the 6th of February, the day appointed
for the Prince to take the oaths, arrived. The following is
probably an official *communiqué*, as it appears in all the Newspapers of the period :—

'The 6th of February being the day appointed for swearing
in the Prince of Wales as Regent, before his taking upon
himself that important office, about twelve o'clock a party of
the flank companies of the grenadiers, with their Colours, the
band of the first regiment, drums and fifes, with white gaiters
on, marched into the courtyard of Carlton House, where the
colours were pitched in the centre of the grand entrance ; the
band struck up " God save the King," and continued playing
that national piece alternately with martial airs during the
day, until near five o'clock. Colonel Bloomfield, one of the
Prince's principal attendants, having written to the Earl of
Macclesfield, the Captain of his Majesty's yeomen of the
guard, informing him it was his Royal Highness' command
that as many yeoman of the guard should attend at Carlton
House, as usually attended upon councils being held by the
King in state, the noble Earl not being in London, the letter
was opened by the person in waiting, who ordered six yeomen
and an usher to attend at Carlton House, which they accordingly did ; and they, together with the Prince's servants in
state, lined the grand hall and staircase : several of the life-
guards men were also in some of the rooms, in a similar
manner as on Court-days at St. James' Palace. About a
quarter before two o'clock, the Duke of Montrose arrived,
being the first of the privy councillors who attended ; he was
followed by all the royal dukes, and a very numerous assembly
of privy councillors, who had all arrived by a quarter before
three o'clock. The whole of the magnificent suite of state
apartments were opened, and the illustrious persons were
ushered into the Gold Room (so called from the style of the
ornaments). Almost every privy councillor then in town was
present—exceeding above a hundred in number.

'About half-past two o'clock, Earl Moira, of his Royal
Highness' council, being also a privy councillor to the King,
brought a message from the Prince to the President of the
Council, Earl Camden, desiring his attendance on the Prince
in an adjoining room, according to the usual form, to communicate to him officially the return to the summons, &c.
The noble Earl accordingly went with Earl Moira, made the

necessary intimation to his Royal Highness, and returned to the company; who, during this time of waiting were highly gratified with seeing the Princess Charlotte on horse-back, accompanied by two grooms, make the tour of the beautiful gardens in the rear of the palace. Her Royal Highness appeared to be in excellent health and spirits.

'After Earl Camden's return, the Prince approached in grand procession, preceded by the officers of his own household, and several of his own council, among whom were Earl Moira, Lords Keith, Cassilis, Hutchinson, Mr. Sheridan, Mr. M. Angelo Taylor, Mr. Tyrwhitt, Colonel McMahon, Colonel Bloomfield, General Hulse, Mr. Bicknell, &c., &c. (His Chancellor, Mr. Adam, was, by accident not present, and there was a delay, in consequence of his Royal Highness' anxious desire of his presence.) The Prince was also accompanied by all the Royal Dukes. They passed through the room where the privy councillors were assembled, through the Circular drawing room, into the grand saloon (a beautiful room in scarlet drapery, embellished with portraits of all the most distinguished Admirals who have fought the battles that have given us the dominion of the seas); and here the Prince seated himself at the top of the table, his Royal brothers and cousins seating themselves on each hand, according to seniority, and all the officers of his household, not privy councillors, ranging themselves on each side of the entrance to the Saloon. The privy councillors then proceeded, all in full dress, according to their rank—the Archbishop of Canterbury, the Lord Chancellor, the Archbishop of York, the Lord President, the Lord Privy Seal, &c., &c., &c., and, as they severally entered, they made their reverence to the Prince, who made a graceful return to each, and they successively took their places at the table; and lastly, Mr. Fawkener and Sir Stephen Cottrell took their seats as Clerk, and Keeper, of the Records.

'The Prince then spoke to the following effect:—

'"My Lords,

'"I understand that by the Act passed by the Parliament, appointing me Regent of the United Kingdom, in the name, and on behalf of his Majesty, I am required to take certain oaths, and to make a declaration before your lordships, as prescribed by the said Act. I am now ready to take these oaths, and to make the declaration prescribed."

'The Lord Privy Seal then rose, made his reverence,

approached the Regent, and read from a Parchment the oaths
as follows. The Prince with an audible voice pronounced
after him :—

   '" I do sincerely promise and swear that I will be faithful,
and bear true allegiance to his Majesty, King George.

'" So help me, God."

   '" I do solemnly promise and swear, that I will truly and
faithfully execute the office of Regent of the United Kingdom
of Great Britain and Ireland, according to an Act of Parliament passed in the fifty-first year of the reign of his Majesty
King George the Third (entitled ' An Act ' etc.), and that I
will administer, according to law, the power and authority
vested in me by virtue of the said Act ; and that I will in all
things, to the utmost of my power and ability, consult and
maintain the safety, honour, and dignity of his Majesty, and
the welfare of his people.

'" So help me God !"

   ' And the Prince subscribed the two oaths. The Lord
President then presented to his Royal Highness, the declaration mentioned in an Act made in the 30th year of King
Charles II., entitled, " An Act for the more effectual preserving the King's person, and government, by disabling Papists
from sitting in either House of Parliament," and which
declaration his Royal Highness audibly made, repeated, and
subscribed. The Lord President signed first, and every one
of the Privy Councillors in succession signed these instruments
as witnesses, and the same was delivered into the hand of the
Keeper of the Records.

   ' The Prince then delivered to the President of the Council
a Certificate of his having received the Sacrament of the
Lord's Supper at the Chapel Royal of St. James, on Sunday
the 27th of January, which was also countersigned, and
delivered to the Keeper of the Records, who deposited all
these instruments in a box at the bottom of the table.

   ' The Lord President then approached the Regent, bent
the knee, and had the honour to kiss his hand. The Royal
Dukes followed, and afterwards, the Archbishop of Canterbury, and all the rest, according to the order in which they
sat at the long table, advancing to the chair on both sides.
During the whole of this ceremony, his Royal Highness maintained the most graceful and dignified deportment ; and it
was remarked, that there was not the slightest indication of

partiality of behaviour to one set of men more than to another.

'The Ceremony being closed, a short *levée* took place in the drawing room, where his Royal Highness addressed himself to the circle ; and, afterwards, he gave an audience to Mr. Perceval, who had the honour of again kissing his hand as First Lord of the Treasury and Chancellor of the Exchequer.'

The Regent did wisely in not changing his Ministry, and Perceval turned dutifully towards the rising sun. It was said that in a visit he and the Chancellor (Lord Eldon) paid the King on Jan. 26th, that he turned his back on the King, a monstrous piece of rudeness in Court etiquette. Probably the poor old blind, half-demented Monarch never observed it ; but others did, and there were several epigrams thereon, the following being the best—

> 'The people have heard, with delight and surprize,
> That his Minister's conduct has op'd the K——'s eyes ;
> That with just indignation his Royal breast burn'd,
> When he thought he saw Per——l's back on him turned ;
> Exclaiming, "Thank G—d ! I've recover'd my sight,
> For I now see you, Sir, in your own proper light." '

The Queen had the custody of the King's person, but had to account to a Council consisting of the Archbishops of Canterbury and York and several Noblemen of high rank, and her first Council under the Regency was held on Feb 13th.

About this time there was an improvement in the King's health ; so much so that on the 8th of February the Queen and the Princess Augusta were allowed to have an interview with him, and on the next day and for two or three others, he appeared on the Terrace and walked for a time accompanied by the Physicians in attendance upon him.

CHAPTER III.

Story of a crime—The Shanavests and the Caravats—Gluttony—
Smuggling bullion—A Tar at the theatre—Deposition of French
Colours in Whitehall Chapel—The Duke of York reinstated as
Commander-in-Chief—The Regency Fête—Account of the enter-
tainment.

AND now, for a while, we will leave Royalty alone, and note
anything particular that occurred—not that there ever was
much general news recorded—there were no country correspondents to the London Newspapers, which were but of
small size, and with very little space to spare for what we call
News.   As these little scraps of information will be scattered
throughout this book, I may at once say that they will, perforce, have no sequence one to another except that of
Chronological order.

At the beginning of February, as a dragoon was returning
from duty to his quarters, which were at a small public-house
called 'Barndean Hut,' near Petersfield, in the New Forest,
his attention was arrested by the cries of some person in distress, which induced him to ride up to the spot from whence
they proceeded, where his humanity was shocked on beholding
a woman tied to a tree, with the tears, which her situation and
suffering had produced, actually frozen to her cheeks, and,
horrid to relate, quite naked, having been stripped and robbed
of every article of dress, by two villains, who, afterwards, left
her in that deplorable condition.   The dragoon instantly cut
the cords that bound her hands and feet to the tree, and,
having in some measure restored her to the use of her limbs
by rubbing them, wrapped her up in his cloak, placed her on
his horse, and proceeded on to his quarters, where he soon
after arrived ; and, as he was conducting the shivering object
of his care into the house, she looked through a window that

commanded a view of the kitchen, and, in a faint voice, exclaimed, 'There are the two men that robbed me of my all, and used me so cruelly.' The soldier, in consequence, entered the kitchen and secured the men, who were the next day taken before a magistrate, and, after the necessary examination, fully committed to Winchester jail, for trial at the next assizes.

Ireland has always been a sweet boon to England ever since the Union ; and faction fights used to abound. Among others were those of the Caravats and Shanavests—the Capulets and Montagues of their time ; and the etymon of the names of two formidable factions, which embraced the greater part of the lower order of people in the two counties of Tipperary and Limerick, is thus given :—

It was at a trial of some of these at a Special Commission at Clonmel, and *James Slattery* was under examination.

Chief Baron. What is the cause of quarrel between these two parties—the Shanavests and the Caravats ?

A. I do not know.

Q. What's the true reason ?

A. I cannot tell.

Q. So, then, according to your account, I am to understand that each party attacks each other by way of defence.

Q. (by a juror). Were the men who were concerned in the affray in the month of August, the same that were concerned at the races of Coolmoyne ?

A. They were.

Q. Do you know a man of the name of Pauddeen Car ?

A. I do.

Q. He is your uncle ; was not he the principal ringleader and commander of the army of Shanavests ?

A. He is a poor old man, and not able to take command.

Q. (by Lord Norbury). What was the first cause of quarrel ?

A. It was the same foolish dispute made about May-poles.

Q. (by the Chief Baron). Which is the oldest party ?

A. The Caravats were going on for two years before the Shanavests stirred.

Q. Why were they called Caravats ?

A. A man of the name of Hanly was hanged ; he was prosecuted by the Shanavests, and Pauddeen Car said he would not leave the place of execution until he saw the Caravat about the fellow's neck, and from that time they were called Caravats.

Q. For what offence was Hanly hanged?

A. For burning the house of a man who had taken land over his neighbour's head.

Q. Hanly was the leader of the Caravats?

A. Before he was hanged, his party was called the Moyle Rangers. The Shanavests were called Pauddeen Car's party.

Q. Why were they called Shanavests?

A. Because they wore old waistcoats.

We occasionally hear of feats of gluttony, but, as a piece of downright lunacy, the following can scarcely be matched.

Morning Chronicle, Mar. 26th: 'A blacksmith at Strout ate on Tuesday, for a trifling wager, a pint of periwinkles with the shells, in the space of ten minutes. Being desired to repeat this disgusting feat he readily did it, but he is now so dangerously ill that he is not expected to recover.'

Bullion both Gold and Silver got scarcer and scarcer, so much was exported: and, early in 1810, large quantities of Dollars were stamped at Birmingham with the image and superscription of George III.; in fact, the dollars stamped in 1797 and down to 1810, inclusive, were about five millions— but they were smuggled out of the kingdom wholesale. On the 19th of March an official rise of 10 per cent. in their value took place, in the hopes that raising them to 5s. 6d. would be prohibitory to their exportation, but it was not: more still were needed, and on April 15th 300,000 dollars were sent to Boulton and Watts, Soho Works, Birmingham, to be stamped, 'and the same quantity are to be forwarded in a few days.' The price fell on the 25th of April to 5s. 1d. per dollar.

On the 27th of March, the Duke of Gloucester was elected Chancellor of the University of Cambridge, by a majority of 114 over his opponent, the Duke of Rutland.

We may take the following as an example of how Jack fooled away his prize-money :—'A Tar, who had just received his prize-money, lately engaged a small provincial Theatre entirely to himself: he took his seat in the centre of the pit, furnished himself with an inordinate quantity of beer, punch, and tobacco, &c., and requested the performances to commence, as no one should enter the Theatre but himself; at the close of every speech which pleased him, he presented the Actor with a glass, and when the curtain dropped, he transferred his stores to the stage, and invited the whole of the *Dram. Per.,* to partake.'

Under date of the 8th of April, we read: 'A very singular

discovery has been made at Colchester, respecting the sex of a servant who had lived thirty years in a family in that town, as housemaid and nurse. Having lately paid the debt of Nature, it was discovered that the deceased was a man.'

On the 5th of May, the Court of Common Council voted the Regent, the freedom of the City of London in *an Oak box*, but the presentation was abandoned as it was found that etiquette forbade the Regent accepting the Freedom, as he then stood in the position of Sovereign.

On March 5th the English troops under the command of General Graham, engaged and defeated a much superior French force under the command of Marshal Victor, at Barrosa in Andalusia, after a severe conflict. How thoroughly the French were then beaten, may be judged by the fact that an Eagle and twelve standards were taken from them. A sergeant of the 87th, or Prince's Own Royal Irish Volunteers, who took the Eagle, was promoted to an Ensigncy, and ordered to be removed to his own regiment, on the first Vacancy. On the 18th of May, these Colours were taken, with great military ceremony, from the Parade in St. James's Park, to Whitehall Chapel, and deposited on each side of the Altar. It was a fine sight, and three Royal Dukes, York, Cambridge, and Gloucester, were present, besides many generals, and the Spanish and Portuguese Ambassadors.

Apropos of the Duke of York, he formerly had a mistress named Mary Anne Clarke, who abused her position by selling Commissions in the Army at a cheap rate, and using her influence over the Duke to confirm them. In 1809, Mr. Wardell, M.P. for Oakhampton, brought the scandal before the House of Commons, and, although the House eventually found that there was nothing in the evidence to prove personal corruption, or criminal connivance on the part of his Royal Highness—yet public opinion against him was so strong, that he had to resign his position as Commander-in-Chief.

The Regent and the Duke of York were tied together by strong bonds of fraternal feeling, and the first important act of the Regent was to re-appoint his brother to his old position on the 25th of May. This naturally created great dissatisfaction, for his former resignation only saved the Duke from the ignominy of being cashiered, and Viscount Milton moved in the House of Commons on the 6th of June: 'That upon a deliberate consideration of the recent circumstances under which his Royal Highness the Duke of York retired from the

Command of the Army in March, 1809, it appears to this
House that it has been highly improper and indecorous in the
advisers of the Prince Regent to have recommended to his
Royal Highness the re-appointment of the Duke of York to
the Office of Commander-in-Chief.' It is astonishing how the
opinion of the House of Commons varied during two years, for
this motion, when put, was only supported by 47 members—
against 296.

But although he obtained the post, he had to run the
gauntlet of public opinion, and which way that went is shown
by the accompanying Satirical print, 'The Soldier's Welcome
Home ! ! !' where the Duke of York amid the Cheers of his
friends, Buckingham, Temple, and Grenville, is leaping into
the portals of the Horse Guards, the Regent standing just
inside to welcome him. A figure, I presume meant to be
John Walter, is pointing to *The Times* Newspaper. There were
several others, but this is best suited to this book.

The next event of public note, and next to the appointment
of the Prince of Wales to the Regency, it was the principal
topic of conversation of the year, was a grand fête given to
upwards of 2,000 of the Nobility and gentry, including the
French Royal Family, the foreign Ambassadors, &c.—at an
estimated cost of £15,000. For fully six weeks previously all
the available weavers, tailors, mantua-makers, and milliners,
were put under requisition for it, and ample work was found
for architects, upholsterers, painters, carpenters, cooks, and
confectioners, and diamonds were borrowed for the night at
11 per cent.

This wonderful fête took place on the 19th of June, and
the company began to arrive between 9 and 10 o'clock. The
whole of Carlton House, even down to the basements, which
were utilized as supper rooms, was thrown open to the guests,
but failed to afford sufficient accommodation, so a large
portion of the garden was canvassed over and used for supper.
It is impossible, in the limits of this book, to describe the
luxury with which this palace was furnished, but I must be
excused, as Carlton House has long been numbered with the
things of the past, if I revive the description of the Throne
and Ball Rooms, simply that my readers may form some idea
of the splendour in which ' the first gentleman in Europe '
lived.

The first was hung with crimson velvet, with embroidered
ornaments in pure gold, and most massive gold fringes and

Walter. (?)   Buckingham.   Temple.   Duke of York.   Grenville.   Regent.

THE SOLDIER'S WELCOME HOME!!!

(Published June 4, 1811, by W. Holland.)

laces. The Canopy, superbly carved and gilt, was surmounted by four helmets of real gold, having plumes of the finest white ostrich feathers, many of them 17 inches in height. On each side the Canopy, were magnificent antique draperies; decorated to correspond with it, and forming back-grounds to two superb candelabra, after the antique, executed in the finest manner, with lions *couchant,* and other appropriate ornaments. Under the Canopy stood a grand state chair and foot-stool. The compartments of the room were decorated with the richest gold ornaments on a crimson velvet ground, with draperies enriched with gold fringes, *en suite.* There were two superb glasses about twelve feet high, with oriental alabaster tables, on frames, carved and gilt, in the most magnificent style. On a chimney, decorated with *or-molu* foliage of the richest sculpture, was placed a large glass in a superb frame; and on the chimney-piece and tables, were fine French girandoles of *or-molu.* In this room were no other seats than stools gilt and covered with crimson velvet. Here were whole length portraits in grand gold frames, of their Majesties, the Prince Regent, and the Duke of York. Through a door at one end of this room, a temporary stair-case presented itself to view, which communicated with the Conservatory; this erection was intended as a private passage for the Prince Regent and his particular friends to pass down to the head of the tables, when supper was announced. Opposite the above door, a door leading to the Throne room being removed, and a large glass being placed in the opposite door, on the further side beyond the Throne, the whole range of Candelabra, and the throne itself were reflected in it; and a striking *coup d'œil* was thereby produced.

The Ball room was decorated with Arabesque ornament, and figures, painted in the finest style imaginable, on gold grounds, in panels, between pilasters richly carved and gilt; the ceiling was decorated in compartments. The windows and recesses have circular tops, and they were decorated with rich blue velvet draperies, with massive gold fringes, lace, tassels, and ropes—the latter were likewise of gold. In the recesses were magnificent French plates of looking-glass, in gold frames, having sofas under them, richly carved and covered with blue velvet; the chairs to suit. Before each pilaster was placed a rich gilt pedestal, on which was a superb French girandole, carrying eight waxlights, executed in *or-molu.* The two chimney-pieces of Statuary marble, were ornamented with foliage and figures in bronze and *or-molu,* and, over them, were glasses in gold frames, and French Candelabra, worthy of the *tout ensemble.*

The Prince Regent entered the State apartments about a quarter past nine, dressed in a scarlet coat, most richly and elegantly ornamented, in a very novel style, with gold lace, and a brilliant star of the Order of the Garter ; and he arrived just at the same time as the dethroned Louis XVIII. —who was present as the Comte de Lille—and his family. Dancing began about half past eleven or twelve, and at half past two supper was announced. As one account says : ' Upon no previous occasion, and at no Court in Europe, was ever the experiment made to sit down 2,000 of the principal nobility and gentry of a kingdom to a regular supper, as was the case at the Prince Regent's fête. The largest entertainment, at the most brilliant period of the French Monarchy, was that given by the Prince of Condé at Chantilli, to the King of Sweden, when 400 covers were laid. Here covers were laid for 1,600 under canvas, and 400 in the house.'

The Times gives a short, but succinct, account of this brilliant fête, and being so, I take it, as well fitted for this book, as all accounts, more or less, are by press correspondents, and relate only to the internal arrangement and decoration of Carlton House.

' It was totally impossible, capacious as the Mansion of the Prince is, to accommodate such a number of persons in the rooms of the Mansion itself. From the central apartment of the lower range, which we have mentioned, on the south, or garden front, proceeded a broad and lofty wall, towards the southern wall of the garden, adjoining St. James's Park, which was crossed by three similar walks, from east to west, lengthwise in the garden. All these walks were closed in by walls, and covered over by awnings made for the occasion. In each of these cross walks were placed long supper tables, and at the end of each walk were communications to circular marquées, in which were tables containing all the necessary refreshments for the company, with space for the numerous servants, and assistants in attendance. The Great Walk from the house southward had in it six tables, leaving those spaces quite open where other walks crossed it. The intermediate spaces between these, were lawns, which communicated to the walks by suitable openings. The interior sides of these grand walks were lined with festoons of flowers, yielding the most odoriferous perfumes, and relieved by the verdant and softer beauties that more towering plants and shrubs could bestow. The arched roofs were ornamented in the liveliest manner, and, from them, were suspended thousands of lights, in all the different forms and fashions by which illumination can be produced. The *coup d'œil* of the whole, especially from the central south entrance to the gardens, was inexpressibly delightful, and even magically impressive. The entrance was under an illuminated arch, and the southern end of the walk was filled by an immense mirror, and ornamented at the top and sides with a superb drapery, and with artificial flowers and costly candelabra : particularly the long range of supper rooms on the grand level, at the head of which the Regent sat, at the west end of the Conservatory, inspired the highest ideas of real magnificence.

'This range, beginning from the east end, comprises the new Gothic rooms, not yet entirely finished, but temporarily hung with crimson, and the Library, beautifully ornamented with marbles. In these apartments there were two rows of tables, elegantly adorned. The centre room was left open. To the west, the eating room, &c., and the Conservatory had one long table running through both. The appearance of the Conservatory was truly striking and brilliant. The architecture of it is of the most delicate Gothic. The upper end was a kind of circular buffet surmounted by a Medallion, with the initials G. P. R. lined by festoons and antique draperies of pink and silver, and partly filled by mirrors, before which, on ornamented shelves, stood a variety of vases, candlesticks, &c., of the most gorgeous gold plate. Supplied, as indeed all the tables were, with every attainable delicacy and luxury which wealth and rank could command, or ingenuity suggest, and embellished by all the art and skill of the confectioner, with emblematical devices of every conceivable appropriate description, this table displayed a still more splendid exuberance.

'In the front of the Regent's seat there was a circular basin of water, with an enriched Temple in the centre of it, from whence there was a meandering stream to the bottom of the table, bordered with green banks. Three or four fantastic bridges were thrown over it, one of them with a small tower upon it, which gave the little stream a picturesque appearance. It contained also a number of gold and silver fish. The excellence of design, and exquisiteness of work-

manship could not be exceeded ; it exhibited a grandeur
beyond description ; while the many and various purposes for
which gold and silver materials were used were equally
beautiful and superb in all their minute details.*

'The Company, who continued to arrive from nine till half-
past twelve, were ushered into the state rooms, and soon filled
the house.   The hall was crowded with Peers and Peeresses,
and was made the same use of, as the apartments of State.
Under the grand arched doorway between the halls, was a
most elegant scarlet and gold drapery, after the antique.

'The male part of the nobility and gentry, were habited in
court suits, many richly embroidered, or in naval and military
uniforms.   The waving plumes, the elegant, variegated dresses,
the sparkling diamonds, and, still more, the native beauty
and grace of the ladies, gave a sort of enchanting perfection
to the whole of this brilliant courtly exhibition.   The *Vieille
Cour de Versailles*, with all its proud pretensions, could never
have more attractively set forth the elegant fascinations of
fashionable life, and exalted rank.

'The upper servants of his Royal Highness' household wore
a rich costume of dark blue, trimmed with very broad gold
lace ; the others wore their state liveries.   A considerable
number of the Yeomen of the Guard attended in different
parts.   The assistants, out of livery, were dressed uniformly,
in black suits with white vests.   Two of the bands of the
Guards, in state uniforms, played various airs throughout the
night.   Parties of the Foot-guards protected all the immediate
avenues, and the Horse-guards were stationed in Pall Mall,
St. James's Street, St. James's Square, Piccadilly, &c.   Everything was managed, with the assistance of the Police, with
unexampled care and convenience.'

* Nearly a waggon load of the family plate of the late Sir
William Pulteney decorated the Tables at Carlton House.   It is
said that the weight of the whole of the gold and silver plate used
on this occasion, was Six Tons.

CHAPTER IV.

Ladies' dresses at the Fête—The banquet—Carlton House thrown
open to the public—The crush—Sir F. Burdett's action against
the Speaker—Relief of British Prisoners in France—Scarcity of
guineas—Lord King and his tenants—Stories respecting the
Currency.

THE ladies had been requested to dress themselves in the
productions of British industry, and some of their costumes
were truly magnificent. They are so uniformly beautiful,
that in the examples I give, I take them as they follow, and
make the extracts for the sake of their brevity.

The Marchioness of Downshire wore a petticoat of white
satin, trimmed at the bottom with a Spanish net of embossed
silver, over which was a tunic of the most beautiful silver
stuff, of Irish manufacture, on which was delicately woven the
shamrock : over the shoulders were superb epaulettes of
embossed Spanish silver. The tunic was laced with diamond
chains, and fastened in front with large diamond brooches.
Her ladyship's ear-rings were the largest diamonds at the
fête, to which there was a corresponding necklace, and a
profusion of diamond ornaments.

The Marchioness of Sligo. A dress of white satin, with a
superb border of brilliant embroidery round the train ; a robe
richly embroidered in silver shamrock, round which was an
elegant, and brilliant border, to correspond with the dress ;
diamond stomacher, armlets, necklace, and brooches. Head-
dress, diamonds and ostrich feathers.

The Marchioness of Tavistock. Splendid dress, embroidered
in white and gold.

The Marchioness of Hertford. White satin dress, embroidered in white and gold.

3

The Marchioness of Stafford. Violet satin dress, richly embroidered in gold.

The Marchioness of Exeter. White satin, embroidered in gold.

The Marchioness Cornwallis. White satin dress, richly embroidered with amethysts.

The Marchioness Waterford. White satin dress, richly embroidered with silver.

The Countess of Cavan. A dress of white and silver tissue, with a superb border of prominent silver jonquils ; body and sleeves splendidly ornamented with diamonds. Head-dress, diamonds and ostrich feathers.

Needless to say, this grand fête was made fun of—and so we see in ' Gudgeon fishing *à la* Conservatory,' the meandering stream down the centre of the Regent's table is caricatured, and the fair ladies are provided with rods and lines. The artist has taken liberties with his subject—the Prince, for instance, sat on a plain mahogany chair, and the ' stream ' was banked up with moss and flowers. The Earl of Moira, and Sheridan, are taking wine together, and on the right of the Regent sits the Duchesse d'Angoulême. A person in plain evening dress is in the extreme right, and points to a paper on the ground, ' Admission to John Bull to look at the Gold.'

This was the subject of another caricature, called ' The Regency Fête, or John Bull in the Conservatory.' This shows John Bull, his wife, three men and one woman looking at the royal table loaded with gold plate and wine, a beef-eater and a butler guarding the plate on the table and on the buffet behind the royal chair. Says John Bull (scratching his head) to his wife : ' Why, odd Zookers ! this is marvellous fine indeed. Oh, Nan ! how we should enjoy a rasher on one of they monstracious beautiful plates. Why, now I think I shan't grumble to pay three or four Bank Tokens towards this grand treat ; methinks, I should just like a nippikin or two.' Mrs. Bull : ' Oh, John ! one of our milk-white chickens roasted by myself by our wood fire would be lusciosious indeed.' The speeches of the others are not worth reprinting.

Needless to say the privilege of visiting the scene of festivity was eagerly embraced by the public, and they came in such shoals, that the Horse Guards had to keep order, and it was feared some accident would occur. And sure enough,

GUDGEON FISHING À LA CONSERVATORY.

(*Published July, 1811, by S. W. Fores.*)

3—2

on the last day, the 26th of June, there was a pretty scrim-
mage. This is *The Times* report :—

'Yesterday being the last day that the public were permitted to view the interior of Carlton House, the crowd, from
an early hour in the morning, was immense ; and, as the day
advanced, the scene excited additional interest. Every precaution had been adopted to facilitate the entrance of the
visitors. The Horse-guards paraded in front of the House,
and were stationed at both ends of Pall Mall, and the various
streets leading from it. The pressure to gain admittance was
so great, that early in the day several females fainted away ;
many lost their shoes, and endeavoured to extricate themselves from the crowd, but this was quite impossible. The
gates were only opened at certain intervals, and, when this
was the case, the torrent was so rapid, that many people were
taken off their feet, some with their backs towards the
entrance, screaming to get out. The scene, at last began to
wear a still more serious aspect ; when it was deemed
expedient that some measure should be resorted to, to
prevent farther mischief. Lord Yarmouth, and the Duke of
Gloucester appeared, and announced to the public that the
gates would not be again opened : and that, for the sake of
preventing the loss of any lives, they had to express the
strongest wish that the persons assembled would cease from
endeavouring to gain admittance. This, however, had not
the desired effect ; as many, who probably were ignorant of
what had happened, remained, in the anxious hope of being
admitted at last.

'The greatest pressure to obtain admittance took place
about half-past two o'clock. About one, the crowd in the
inside of Carlton House had accumulated so much, that it was
found necessary to shut the gates. The line of carriages now
extended the whole length of Pall Mall, up to the very top of
St. James's Street, and, as there had been a complete
stoppage for above half an hour, hundreds of ladies left their
carriages, and hastened on foot towards the gates of Carlton
House. At this time you might see ladies and gentlemen
coming out of the crowd covered with perspiration, and
unable any longer to bear the pressure. Those who thus
made their retreat in time will be able to congratulate themselves on their superior prudence.

'Hitherto all was comparatively well, and the scene rather

afforded amusement than excited alarm. But the case was most materially altered when the gate of entrance was next opened. It became exactly like some of those rushes at our Theatres, which have sometimes produced such melancholy consequences. Those behind, irresistibly pushed on those before, and of the number of delicate and helpless females who were present, some were thrown down, and, shocking to relate, literally trod upon by those behind, without the possibility of being extricated. When, at last, the crowd got inside Carlton House gates, four females were found in a lifeless state, lying on their backs on the ground, with their clothes almost completely torn off. One young lady, elegantly attired, or, rather, who had been so, presented a shocking spectacle ; she had been trodden on, until her face was quite black from strangulation, and every part of her body bruised to such a degree, as to leave little hopes of her recovery : surgical assistance was immediately had, but her life was not expected to be saved. An elderly lady had her leg broken, and was carried away in a chair ; and two others were also seriously hurt, but, on being bled, were restored to animation. One of them was able to walk home, the other was led by two men.

' The situation of almost all the ladies who were involved in this terrible rush was truly deplorable ; very few of them could leave Carlton House until furnished with a fresh supply of clothes ; they were to be seen all round the gardens, most of them without shoes or gowns ; and many almost completely undressed, and their hair hanging about their shoulders. The crowd outside, at one time, literally carried away the Horseguards for several paces, when the animals became restive to an alarming degree, rearing on their hind legs, and beating down all within their reach with their fore ones ; several women were trodden under foot, and received considerable injury ; and five or six men were so overcome, that they fainted, and were carried off.'

The Morning Chronicle of the 29th of June says : ' The number of stray shoes in the courtyard of Carlton House, on Wednesday, was so great, they filled a large tub, from which the shoeless ladies were invited to select their lost property. Many ladies, however, and also gentlemen, might be seen walking away in their stockinged feet. About a dozen females were so completely disrobed in the squeeze, they were obliged

to send home for clothes, before they could venture out in the
streets, and one lady was so completely disencumbered of all
dress, a female domestic, in kind compassion, wrapped her up
in an apron.'

On the 6th of April, 1810, Sir Francis Burdett was, by a
majority of 38 Members of the House of Commons, sentenced
to be committed to the Tower, for a breach of privilege committed by him against the house, in an address written by
him in *Cobbett's Weekly Political Register* of March 24, 1810 :
'SIR FRANCIS BURDETT TO HIS CONSTITUENTS DENYING THE
POWER OF THE HOUSE OF COMMONS TO IMPRISON THE PEOPLE
OF ENGLAND.' After some trouble, and a great deal of rodo-
montade on his part, he was safely lodged in the fortress—
after which a slight affray took place between the mob and
the troops in which one of the former was killed, and eight
wounded.*

The demagogue did not like the position in which he found
himself, and breathed fire and fury. He would bring actions
against the Speaker, the Sergeant-at-Arms, and the Earl of
Moira, who was then Governor of the Tower. He was released,
on the prorogation of Parliament, 21st of June, 1810, and on
March 8, 1811, he brought an action against the Speaker
(Abbott) for a trespass and assault in breaking open his house
on the 6th of April, 1810. The Speaker pleaded justification,
and the case was tried on the 19th of June, when the jury
found a verdict for the defendant, thereby admitting and
enforcing the right of the House of Commons to commit for
breach of privilege.

Mention has already been made of a fund started by a
number of Merchants, Bankers, and others of the City of
London, at Lloyd's, for the 'Relief of British prisoners in
France,' which, on the 29th of June, reached about £54,000.
But their practical charity did not end here, for there was also
another fund begun ' for Relief of Portuguese sufferers during
the French Invasion,' which, on the 21st of June, amounted
to nearly £52,000. The West End, evidently tried to emulate
the City, and at Willis's Rooms, under the presidency of the
Duke of York, there was a ' Fund for the Relief of the Unfortunate Sufferers in Portugal—who have been plundered
and treated by the French Armies with the most unexampled
barbarity.' By June 29th this had reached £15,000.

* See *The Dawn of the Nineteenth Century*, by John Ashton, 1 vol.
edit., pp. 166 to 176.

Silver, as we have seen, had got, to use a mercantile phrase, 'a little easier,' but the Guinea! it was almost as scarce as Russian gold coins are now, and, in spite of every effort, it was quoted at a premium, and yet was exported.   Here is a Police report, anent it: 'Mansion House, 23rd of April. James King, guard of the Yarmouth mail coach, was brought up for examination, upon a charge of purchasing eight guineas, the Coin of this realm, at a price considerably beyond their current value.   The Charge was brought by Mr. Nalder, the Under Marshal of the City of London ; who, in consequence of information received from the Treasury, that there were persons about town employed as agents to purchase guineas for exportation, made diligent enquiry, and having found out the defendant, he marked eight guineas, and went with Sayer, the Bow Street officer, who sold those guineas to the prisoner, and received for each £1 5s. 6d.   Mr. Nalder shortly afterwards took the prisoner into custody, found the marked guineas upon him, and brought him before the Lord Mayor; the transaction being against the Statute of the third of Edward III., which subjects offenders to the penalty of twelve months imprisonment, and fine at the discretion of the Court.   The defendant was admitted to bail.'   Ultimately he was fined forty shillings.

On the 6th of May the officers rummaged a smack called the *Union*, and found, in a hole between the timbers, seven canvas bags containing 4,500 guineas, making in all 11,128 guineas found in that vessel.

The greater part of May was taken up by the discussion in the House of Commons of the Report of the Bullion Committee, which recommended the resumption of specie payments by the Bank of England as speedily as possible.   This was negatived, on the ground that the Bank paper was not depreciated—but, as a matter of fact, it was.   *Vide* the following letter from Lord King to his tenants :—

'By lease, dated 1802, you have agreed to pay the annual rent of —— in good and lawful money of Great Britain.   In consequence of the late depreciation of paper money, I can no longer accept of any bank notes at their nominal value in payment of your rent in the legal coin of the realm ; at the same time, having no other object than to receive payment of the real intrinsic value of the sum stipulated by agreement, and being desirous to avoid giving you unnecessary trouble, I shall

be willing to receive payment in either of the manners following, according to your option—

'1st. By payment in guineas.
'2nd. If guineas cannot be procured, by a payment in
Portugal gold coin, equal in weight to the number of guineas
requisite to discharge the debt.
'3rd. By a payment in Bank-paper of a sum sufficient to
purchase (at the present market price) the weight of standard
gold requisite to discharge the rent. The alteration of the
value of paper money is estimated in this manner.
'The price of gold in 1802, the year of your agreement,
was £4 per oz. ; the present market price is £4 14s., owing
to the diminished value of paper—in that proportion, an
addition of £17 10s. per cent. in paper money will be required
as equivalent for the payment of rent in paper.
'(Signed)   KING.

'N.B.—A power of re-entry and ejectment is reserved by
deed in case of non-payment of rent due. No draft will be
received.'

This gave rise to a pictorial *jeu d'esprit* entitled 'Jew
King, depreciating Bank notes.' A farmer, of the then
typical John Bull type, has called on Lord King to pay his
rent, and says to him, 'I be come to pay you some money !
but I cannot get Guineas for love nor money ! so you must
take Bank Notes.—Why ! no person ever refused them before.'
To which Lord King replies, 'I tell you I will have Guineas.
If I take Bank Notes I will have 20 per cent. I like good
profit.' With one hand he points to some Guineas, and, on
the table, are the 'Laws of Landlord and Tenant,' and 'Tables
of Interest.'

Earl Stanhope, on the 27th of June, in consequence of
Lord King's action, introduced a Bill into the House of Lords
to prevent the Gold coin from being paid or received for more
than its nominal value, or the Bank paper for less. In the
course of the debate he stated that guineas were publicly
bought at Manchester, at an advance of *twenty* per cent. by
persons from Ireland, for the purpose of paying their landlords, who insisted on gold : and the Earl of Lauderdale
declared that he knew an instance, where a landlord called
upon his tenants to pay in gold ; and the latter having represented to the steward the impossibility of procuring gold,

they were each told that there were 100 guineas at a Chandler's shop in the neighbourhood, which might be purchased; and it was a fact, that with those 100 guineas, passing from one to another, a rent of £7,000 was actually paid. The Bill passed both Houses, and received the royal assent on the 24th of July.

In *The Morning Chronicle* of the 11th of July we find : 'It has been for several weeks a known and common practice, at one shop in the City, for a man to have a twenty-shilling note,

JEW —— DEPRECIATING BANK NOTES.
(*Published July,* 1811, *by S. W. Fores.*)

and a dish of fish, for a guinea.' And so it was after the passing of Earl Stanhope's Act, the guineas were still bought at an advanced price, and the first Commitment under the Act is recorded in the same paper of Monday, the 9th of September, 1811 : 'On Friday sen'night Adkins, the Bow Street Officer, arrived at Worcester, in pursuit of one Thomas Woodford, who was known to have dealt pretty largely in guineas; having found him, Adkins offered him eight guineas, and three half-guineas, for which Woodford gave him £10 18s. 6d. in

Bank of England Notes.—He was immediately apprehended, and committed to gaol.'

It was no use trying to fight the purchase of these precious coins : every plan possible was put in force.—How is this ? 'LOST—EIGHT GUINEAS—Whoever may have found the same, and will bring them to —— shall receive ten pounds reward.' It was all of no use, the guineas used to be smuggled out of the Country as much as ever, and on July 3rd, in the Court of King's Bench, in the case of De Yonge, who had been convicted of purchasing guineas for more than 21 shillings, and whose case had been reserved for the opinion of the twelve judges, it was decided that such purchase was not an offence punishable under the existing laws.

CHAPTER V.

A smuggler's victim—Illness of Gillray—A gallant highwayman—
A Witch—Bartholomew Fair—The Comet—A practical joke on
the Queen — Women's Cricket Match — Ballooning — French
prisoners of war—Luddite riots—The King and his physicians—
His health.

THE odds and ends of gossip for July may be taken briefly as
follows—Smuggling was very common, and our grandfathers
had not the faintest notion that they were doing wrong in
purchasing wares that had never paid the King his dues.   In
fact, many were proud of it.   Sometimes they got sold, as the
following story will vouch for.   It happened that in Windsor
and its neighbourhood, a woman, clad in a long red cloak,
appeared, calling about dusk at several houses with a sample
of excellent Cognac brandy.   She stated that her husband
was waiting at a little distance with several casks of the same,
which they could sell at a very low price.   Several people
agreed to take Casks, which were duly delivered, and the
money for which was properly paid.   Alas ! alas ! when the
brandy came to be tapped it was nothing but water.

Poor Gillray, the Caricaturist, from whom I have so much
borrowed, and who exemplified the manners of his times as
well as ever Hogarth did, had been ill, and had knocked off
work for some time—yet he still lived at Mrs. Humphrey's
house in St. James's Street, attempted, while in a fit of delirium,
to throw himself out of the attic storey window.   Luckily for
him there were iron bars to that window, and his head got
jammed, which, being perceived by a Chairman waiting outside
White's Club, who instantly went to render assistance, he was
extricated, and proper persons were appointed to take care of
him.   Poor Gillray etched his last picture in 1811, and it was
entitled, 'Interior of a Barber's Shop in Assize Time,' but it

was not published until May 15, 1818, nearly three years after his death, which took place on the 1st of June, 1815. It is a comfort to know that from the setting in of his mania until his death, he was well looked after by his old friend Mrs. Humphrey.

It is hard to have to chronicle the rise and fall of a most useful invention, the percussion *Cap*, which was patented by the Rev. A. J. Forsyth, of Belhevie, Aberdeenshire, on the 11th of April, 1807. Lepage, the noted gunmaker of Paris pirated it; and Napoleon, in 1811, ordered it to be generally introduced into the French Army. It has been superseded, or rather its form has been altered by the modern breech loader.

Good manners and courtesy from Robber to robbed evidently had not gone out of fashion with Claude Duval, and a ' gentle thief' was not unknown, as the Miss Somervilles could testify. They were in a carriage with their papa, who was a surgeon, when it was stopped, on Hounslow Heath, by a *foot pad*—for there were subtle distinctions in theft in those days. The Man who robbed you, and was on horseback, was at the top of his profession—he was a Highwayman ; but the poor, scurvy rogue whose financial arrangements could not compass the dignity of a horse, was a common thief, a wolf's head, a foot pad. This mean specimen of roguery, only armed with a Clasp Knife, with many oaths, declared that he would operate upon the Surgeon to his disadvantage, unless he gave him his money. Under this compulsion Mr. Somerville gave him all he had about him, two five-pound notes, and four shillings ; meanwhile the women folk, who saw what was being done to dear papa, besought the evil-doer, with tears in their eyes, and their money in their hands, to take what his strong arm had won, and depart in peace. Then the innate chivalry of that robber arose within him, and he said, in a somewhat mixed vein of politeness, and brutality, ' Nay, ladies, don't be frightened, I never did the least injury to a woman in my life, nor never will, d—n me ; as for your money, keep it yourselves : all that I ask from you is a kiss apiece ; if you grudge me that, I'm sure you are neither sensible, nor good humoured.' *Væ Victis !* The soft penalty was paid, and the wicked man turned away from his wickedness after doing a mild ' Confiteor '—that he had spent all his money very foolishly, and the sum in which he had mulcted papa would carry him to his friends, and then he should have plenty. It was the first robbery he had ever committed, and it should be the last—and then he faded into the *ewigkeit*. But how about the stout coachman and footman who drove, and sat behind the carriage ? Probably Somerville *père* had something to say to them on his return home.

Here is another case of wickedness, by a supposed Witch, the belief in Witchcraft being a cult not yet thoroughly ignored in England, copied from the *Annual Register* of August 26th : ' At the Bridgewater assizes, Betty Townsend, a very old woman, aged 77, who for many years past has been considered by the superstitious as a *Witch*, was tried for obtaining money of a child under the following circumstances : The prosecutor, Jacob Poole, was a labouring man, residing in the hamlet of Taunton, in which parish the prisoner also resided, and he had been in the habit of sending his daughter, aged about thirteen, with apples in a basket, to market. About the 24th of January last, the old woman met the little girl, stopped her, and asked to see what she had in her basket ; which, having examined, she said to her, " Hast got any money ?" The child said she had none. " Then get some for me," said the old woman, " and bring it to the Castle (a tavern in Taunton) door, or I will kill thee." The child, terrified at such a threat from a witch, procured two shillings, and carried it to her ; when the old woman said, " 'Tis a good turn thou hast got it, or else I would have made thee die by inches." This was repeated seven times within five months, when Poole, the girl's father, going to the shop of Mr. Burford, a druggist in Taunton, to pay a little bill which he owed for medicine, found no less than seven different charges against him for money lent ; and, on inquiry, found that different small sums of two shillings, half a crown, five shillings, &c., had been borrowed by the little girl in her father's name, for the purpose, as she said, of going to market, but carried as a peace-offering to the old woman. The whole was now discovered, and Poole's wife, and another woman, took the girl with them to the prisoner's house, and interrogated her as to the facts. She admitted a knowledge of the girl, but, on being reprehended for her conduct, raved and swore, that if they dared to accuse her, she would make them " die by inches." " No," said Mrs. Poole, who appears to have thought that she knew much better how to deal with a Witch than her daughter, " that thee shall not—I'll hinder that " : and, taking a pin from her clothes, she scratched the witch from her elbow to her wrist, in three places, *to draw her blood*, a process, believed to be of unfailing efficacy, as an antidote to witchcraft. The idea of this wicked woman's power has had such an effect upon the mind of the poor little girl, that she is now reduced to such a state of debility, that she is scarcely able to take any sustenance. The Jury found the prisoner guilty (*what of?*); and the Judge observed that only her extreme old age prevented him from pronouncing on her the severest sentence the law would allow. She was sentenced to pay a fine of one shilling, and to be kept to hard labour in the House of Correction for six Calendar months.'

Bartholomew Fair must be within the recollection of many of my readers, for it was not abolished until 1855. At one time it was always opened by the Lord Mayor—yet it reads with an old-world flavour that 'Yesterday Morning (Sept. 3) the Lord Mayor, attended by the City Marshals, &c., went in procession, after having partaken of a cool tankard at the house of Mr. Newman, the keeper of Newgate, to the corner of Long Lane, West Smithfield, where the fair was proclaimed, and all its usual din and bustle commenced.' The fair was not finally suppressed until 1855.

It was not till 1835 that Bull baiting was made illegal in England, and it is refreshing to read that the bull, even for a very short time, had the best of his human persecutor, who on such an occasion ever cuts a sorry figure. *Morning Chronicle*, Sept. 4th : ' A dreadful catastrophe occurred at Chapel Wake, Birmingham, on Tuesday last. A concourse of people having assembled at the Fives Court, Lawrence Street, for the purpose of baiting a bull, the enraged animal broke loose, and ran with great fury into Coleshill Street. A Scene of the greatest confusion ensued. An infant, three months old, was killed on the spot : two women and boys were dreadfully trampled and bruised, and remain in the hospital with little hopes of recovery, and many others received injury.' *Bravo Toro!*

Annus Mirabilis ! A Regent and a Comet ! According to Shakespeare, when " beggars die, there are no Comets."* These Celestial aberrations are for far greater mundane personages—they are for the great ones of the earth only; and, again, from the same authority, we learn that 'Comets importing change,'† is fairly fulfilled in the Regency.

Of course the Caricaturist got hold of it, and fixed it for all time. 'The Comet of 1811' has, as nucleus, the *facile*

---

* *Julius Cæsar*, act ii. sc. 2.   † 1 *Henry IV.*, act i. sc. i.

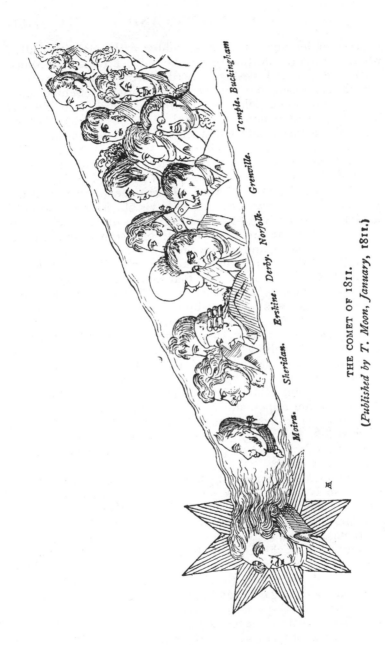

Moira. Sheridan. Erskine. Derby. Norfolk. Grenville. Temple. Buckingham

THE COMET OF 1811.

(*Published by T. Moon, January, 1811.*)

princeps of his age.   Its tail is studded with celebrities, all of whom I cannot, unfortunately, make out.   First is Earl Moira, then Sheridan and Erskine ; Lord Derby with his hydrocephalous forehead, and the Duke of Norfolk.   Behind Lord Derby is Col. Bloomfield ; behind him is Lord Grenville, and side by side with him are Temple and Buckingham, whose wig and spectacles betray him anywhere.   The last face to be recognized is that of Earl Grey.

This Comet was discovered at Viviers on the 25th of March, by M. de Flanguergues, and was again noticed by M. Pons at Marseilles on the 11th of April.   It was seen at Paris on the 20th of May, but was not generally visible in England until the latter end of August or the beginning of September.   It was nearest to the earth on the 24th of October, and then it went on its course, and in due time vanished.

In September a practical joke was played, on no less a person than the Queen.   For four consecutive days, ending Sept. 26th, Buckingham Palace, or, as it was then called, the Queen's House, was besieged by Washerwomen from morning till night.   It seems that a woman, calling herself the head of the Queen's laundry, had gone round to hundreds of Washerwomen, telling them that she had held her present situation for five years, and that she had been obliged to discharge all her staff, because they did not wash the royal linen clean, and also that they got drunk.   She was very affable with her dupes, and was not above drinking with them, or of borrowing from them, cloaks, shawls, umbrellas, and other trifles, promising some of them two guineas a week, others 4s. a day, a pot of porter, and as much rum, gin, and wine as they chose.

Early on Monday morning they began to arrive, about six o'clock, so as to set to work, and it was in vain that the porters refused them admission.   Their tale was, that the lady who had hired them, had given them the key of the laundry to let themselves in, so that they might get to work, light the fire, &c.   But, as there was no laundry at Buckingham Palace, they sent the poor women to St. James's Palace, where there was one, and, when they got there, it was only to be told that none had been engaged, nor even wanted.   One can imagine the scene, more especially as many of the poor women had come from great distances, some had left good situations to go there, and others had sent their children into the Country to nurse, in order to enable them to take the place.

1811] UNDER THE REGENCY

A more pleasing contest of women took place on the 3rd of October, 1811, in the shape of a Cricket Match between two teams, not the sort of thing as 'Actresses' Cricket, which is now played between a team each of men and women, the former being armed with broom handles, the latter with cricket bats; but a much rougher sort of thing, if we can believe the accompanying illustration, which is taken from an etching of Rowlandson's called 'RURAL SPORTS, OR A CRICKET MATCH EXTRAORDINARY. On Wednesday, Oct. 3, 1811, a Singular Cricket Match took place at Ball's Pond, Newington. The players on both sides were 22 Women, 11 Hampshire, against 11 Surrey. The Match was made between some amateur Noblemen of the respective Counties, for 500 Guineas a side. The performers in the Contest were of all ages and sizes.'

The Match really began on the 2nd of October, and lasted three days, the Hampshire team winning. The ages varied from 14 to upwards of forty.

Rowlandson sketched with a freedom approaching decided coarseness—but his sketches were natural, and in this instance valuable, as showing us Cricket as then played, although the game, with its two stump wickets, curved bats, and primitive scoring was then obsolete, at least in matches.*

But, if we can believe the same artist, Baldwin and his congeners were outdone this year by a woman descending from a balloon in a parachute. It is taken from an etching by Rowlandson, dated the 25th of October, 1811, and entitled 'Balloon Hunting.' It represents the mishaps of a party of ladies who went balloon hunting across country, in a one-horse vehicle, the shafts of which are smashed, and the horse is being reduced to docility by the driver. I know of no woman who descended by means of a parachute, in this year.

They were not novelties, for André Jacques Garnerin, the Aëronaut, came down in one in 1802, and, according to Larousse, Elisa, daughter of Jean Baptiste Olivier Garnerin, brother of the above, was the first woman who tried a 'drop from the clouds.' She made her first descent in 1815, and in 1820 had made over twenty.

Taken as a whole, the French Prisoners of War, whose numbers were ever increasing, were not a bad lot of fellows. There were many breaches of parole, and large numbers of

* The third stump was added by the Hambledon Club, 1775.

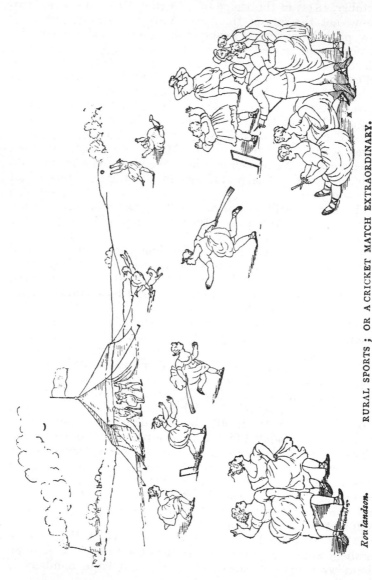

Rou landson.

RURAL SPORTS ; OR A CRICKET MATCH EXTRAORDINARY.

the rank and file, and seamen got away; for, in a Trial in the Court of King's Bench, November 14, 1811, the Attorney-General asserted that, of the French Officers, prisoners of war, on their parole, in this country, one-fourth had effected their escape: and that one condition on which smugglers from this country were permitted to land their goods in France, was the bringing over with them, a French prisoner.

RURAL SPORTS; BALLOON HUNTING.
(*By Rowlandson. Published October* 25, 1811, *by Thomas Tegg.*)

Those interned at Cupar fitted up a neat little Theatre, which was opened on the 3rd of September. A prologue composed by one of the Officers, complimentary to the inhabitants for their hospitality to the Captives, was spoken and acted. This was followed by a Comedy in verse, by Regnard, called 'Les Folies Amoureuses,' and an after piece 'Le Quaterne.' The Scene painting, interior decorations of

4—2

the theatre, Stage Apparatus, and Costumes, were all their own work : nor did they stop there, for they had an excellent band of their own.

But they could behave sternly on occasion, if there is any truth in the following story. In May, 1811, the French prisoners confined on board the *Sampson* (prison ship lying in the Medway), formed a conspiracy to forcibly take possession of the ship, and effect their escape, which was prevented by one of their number imparting secretly their projected plan to the commanding officer. Enraged at the disappointment of their hopes, they used every effort to find out the individual by whose communication their secret had transpired ; and having, as they thought, fixed upon the right man, as soon as they were locked up for the night, they formed a Court, for his trial, at which a *procès verbal* was drawn up, declaratory of their proceedings. The suspected traitor was found guilty, but there was a difference of opinion as to his punishment, and it was at last resolved and carried into effect, that he should be tattooed on his forehead and cheeks ' J'ai vendu mes frères aux Anglais abord le ponton " Le Sampson," 31 Mai, 1811.'

There is not much more to chronicle for the remainder of this year, except the Census, and we must glance at the figures to see the enormous difference in the population then, and now. In 1811, the whole population was 12,552,144, in 1881, 35,246,562, or, in other words, the population had all but trebled itself in 70 years. In the Census of 1881 the sexes were very evenly balanced, being 17,253,947 males, and 17,992,615 females, and so they were in 1811, 6,310,548 males, and 6,241,596 females.

Still the Luddite Riots must not be forgotten, for, at one time, they threatened to be somewhat serious. They began in the neighbourhood of Nottingham, the Manufacturers there, having been obliged, from the decrease of demand for their manufactures, to discharge many of their workmen, and consequently much distress was caused. Nor was this all : a certain wide frame for weaving stockings had been introduced, which saved much labour, and, consequently, fewer hands were wanted. In November, these riots became rather serious, as, not only were the obnoxious frames smashed, and manufacturers' stock destroyed, but millers, corn dealers, &c., suffered, and the military had to be called out. Their name was taken from their imaginary leader, one Captain Ludd, who never had any existence, but probably stood for the Committee of Management.

At this time, at all events, the public were free from the sickening details of illness such as they have more than once had recently—details which could do no good whatever to the outer world, and which must have been very painful to the relatives. They managed things better in George III.'s reign. If the medical men quarrelled, they did not openly wash their dirty linen, but it only was known to a few that Dr. Willis's treatment of his Royal patient, during his former illness, had been considered unnecessarily severe, and that, perhaps, they were not too well content to have him associated with them in the present crisis : still for the first year or so, the people, who really loved old Farmer George, were kept fairly acquainted with the state of his health, until it became hopeless—and then, perhaps very wisely, they only were fed with the merest details of his disorder.

In February, the King was getting so well that the Queen and one of the Princesses, on more than one occasion visited him : then he suffered from a paroxysm of mania, to which succeeded a calm, during which he took his constitutional walks on the Terrace. In March, he got better, so much so that on the 31st of March, the prayers for his recovery were discontinued in the Chapel Royal, and, at the Queen's Monthly Council, it was hoped that he would recover, so that he had the key of the Cabinet Council Despatch Boxes, and, in other ways, was treated as a responsible being. In May, his health was capricious, but still he was able to walk and ride in public. June brought a relapse, and his case was deemed hopeless, yet he still occasionally took walks. In July, he was in a very dangerous state, opiates had to be administered, and he partook of very little solid food. In August, it was said that his suite of apartments were padded to prevent his doing himself a mischief, but this was denied. September was a better month for him, but, in October, he retrograded. November and December only show him as leading a fairly healthy animal existence.

1812, OR REGENCY À LA MODE.
(*Drawn and etched by W. Heath.*)

CHAPTER VI.

1812.

The Regent's doings—The Royal Sprain—Colonel McMahon— Luddite and Factory Riots—Scarcity of Bullion—Murder of Mr. Perceval.

JUDGING by the barometer of public opinion, the satirical prints, the topic of conversation in the commencement of this year, was the Prince Regent. Occupying the exalted position that he did, he naturally was the observed of all, and his foibles and peccadilloes were made the laughing-stock, or were censured of all. And the Caricaturists did not spare him. Take this illustration as a sample; it is called ' 1812, or REGENCY à la Mode,' where we see our ' fat friend,' as Brummell called him, having his stays laced, and, during that operation, occupying himself by rouging his cheeks.

He would allow very little of his doings to be known by the public, and the movements of Royalty, as we know it in the *Court Circular,* were recorded in the baldest manner possible, except on one occasion, when the Regent sprained his ancle, and there was a very long and elaborate report thereon.

Morning Chronicle, Saturday, November 16, 1811 :—' THE PRINCE REGENT.—His Royal Highness, we are concerned to state, was not well enough to come to town yesterday. At the Party given by the Duchess of York at Oatlands, on Wednesday evening, the Duchess made arrangements for a Ball. The Prince Regent agreed to lead off the dance with his daughter, the Princess Charlotte, for his partner. Whilst his Royal Highness was leading the Princess briskly along, his right foot came in contact with the leg of a chair or sofa, which gave his leg a twist, and sprained his ancle. His Royal

Highness took but little notice of it that night, but in the morning he found it worse than he expected, &c., &c.'

Whatever was the matter with him, he did not leave Oatlands till the 9th of December, or nearly a month after the Ball. Nobody believed in the royal sprain, but the story that did gain credence, and was made the most of by the Caricaturist and the Satirist, was that the Regent, at that Ball, grossly insulted Lady Yarmouth, for which he was most heartily, and soundly, thrashed by her husband, Lord Yarmouth, and hence the royal indisposition. Walcot, as ' Peter Pindar, Esqre,' wrote one of his most scathing odes, and that is saying something, entitled ' The R——l Sprain, or A Kick from Yar——h to Wa——s, being the particulars of an expedition to Oat——nds, and the Sprained Ancle.'

There were several Caricatures, all with the same tendency. One was ' A Kick from Yarmouth to Wales, December, 1811,' which shows Lord Yarmouth holding the Regent by his coat collar and vigorously kicking him behind, the Regent yelling and trying to get away, Lady Yarmouth sitting on a sofa looking on. There is attached to this, a poetical effusion of fourteen verses, to be sung to the tune of ' The Love-sick Frog.' The first verse runs thus :

> ' A Prince he wquld a raking go.
>   Heigh ho ! said Rowly.
> Whether his people would have him or no ;
> With a rowly-powly, gammon and spinach,
>   Heigh ho ! said Anthony Rowly.'

Then there was 'The Royal Milling Match,' published December, 1811, in which depicted Lord Yarmouth, who, by a paper sticking out of his coat pocket, was ' Late a pupil of the Champion of England,' ' fibbing merrily ' on the royal countenance ; at the same time exclaiming, ' There is plenty of fair game, but no poaching on my Mannor. My action is quick, and *put in* strait forward—so !' The Regent calls out, ' Help, help, I have made a *false step*, and sprained my Ancle.' A servant coming in, says to Lord Yarmouth, ' Lord, Sir, don't be so harsh, you'll sprain the gentleman's *ancle*. By goles, this is what they call Milling indeed !' Lady Yarmouth views the scene from behind a screen.

The most amusing one I have seen, is given in the accompanying illustration, which is by Geo. Cruikshank, published January, 1812. It is called ' Princely Agility ; or, the Sprained Ancle.' The doctor at the foot of the bed (probably

G Cruikshank.

PRINCELY AGILITY ; OR, THE SPRAINED ANCLE.

(*Published, January, 1812, by J. Johnston.*)

meant for Halford) is fomenting the foot, which seems its
normal size, and says to the attendant, 'Take that *waistcoat*
away, or we shall make the town talk.'   The Princess
Charlotte is examining the foot, and exclaims, 'Bless me,
how it's swelled !'   Lady Jersey, who is administering to the
invalid prince, is inattentive to her duties ; while the Regent,
with 'two lovely black eyes,' is calling to Colonel McMahon,
' Oh ! my Ancle, Oh !—bring me my Wig—Oh ! my Ancle !
Take care of my Whiskers, Mac !   Oh, Oh, Oh, Oh, o—o—o
—oh, o !'   Sir John Douglas is feeling his pulse, saying, 'Out
a way, Mon, you are always exposing yourself.'   John Bull is
coming in at the door, but is pushed back by Adams, with
' Indeed, Bull, 'tis only a sprained ancle.'   But John Bull
says, ' John Bull is not to be fobbed off so easily, Master
Lawyer.'

George Cruikshank was not very particular as to his likenesses, as we may see by his ideal Colonel McMahon, who
was a servant worthy of his master, to whom he was most
useful.

Walcot 'Pindarised' him in an Ode, 'Mac the First,' in
which he makes him say :

> ' Once a boy, in ragged dress,
> Who would little *Mac* caress ?
> When in the streets, starv'd and sad,
> I was a *common errand lad.*'

But, be his origin whatever it might have been, he was a tool
well fitted for the use of his august master, who, it must be
owned, endeavoured to repay him ; but, also, at the public
expense.   In 1811 General Fox died, and at his death, the
office of Paymaster of the Widows' Pensions became vacant.
It was a perfect sinecure, the duties being done by others,
and the salary attached to the office was over £2,000 per
annum.   The Commissioners of 1783, and of 1808, both reported and recommended the abolition of Paymaster and
Deputy-Paymaster of Widows' Pensions, as being unnecessary,
the one having very little to do, the other, nothing at all.
The office of Paymaster had, in particular, been recommended
to be done away with, on the demise of General Fox : but it
was given to Colonel McMahon.

On January 9, 1812, on a Motion for Supply, Mr. Creevey
spoke decidedly against this appointment, and moved as an
Amendment, ' That the House would, to-morrow se'nnight,

resolve itself into a Committee of Supply, in order to give an opportunity, in the interim, for the consideration which he had suggested,' namely, that they would take into their earliest consideration, the various offices of emolument recently granted by the Crown to several of their members. This amendment was lost.

On the 22nd of February, the question of the Army Estimates being on, Mr. Bankes moved as an Amendment, ' That the amount of the sum expected to be paid to the Paymaster of Widows' Pensions, being 12d. in the pound on the said Pensions (£2,790 1s.) be deducted from the said sum.' This amendment was lost by a majority of sixteen.

But on the next night Mr. Bankes brought the matter up again, and moved the virtual abolition of the office by omitting the sum necessary to pay it—and this was carried by a majority of three.

There was consternation among the Regent's party at the temerity of the House in thus thwarting the Royal wishes, and, of course, the recalcitrant Commons must be taught a lesson, so McMahon was appointed Keeper of the Privy Purse, and Private Secretary to the Prince Regent ; and, in the caricature of ' The PRIVY PURSE and POLITICAL BEGGARS ' we find McMahon installed in his new position. *Sheridan* says, ' Dear, good, worthy Countryman, thou Pine Apple of Erin ! consider I was burnt out,* not a penny in my purse, my credit very low—do—dear Mac, for the love of St. Patrick, give me a handful.' *Buckingham :* ' I have not above a Hundred Thousand a year, these hard times. Pray remember the Poor !' *Temple :* ' With my wife's fortune, and my own, I have not above Forty Thousand a Year. Pray remember the Poor !' *Grenville :* ' I have not above Fifty Thousand a Year, a slender pittance. Pray remember the Poor !' *Mac Mahon* replies : ' Paws Off ! no Blarney will do with me ! I'm up to all your Gammon ! and so is my dear Master. I'm cosy at last, in spite of all your speeches and paragraphs, and you may all go to the Devil, your Master ! ! !'

And, doubtless, he thought he was cosy, but the Commons would not stand the job, and on the 23rd of March his appointment was brought before Parliament, and the Hon. J. W. Ward asked whether it was a fact, and, if so, what

* At Drury Lane Theatre, destroyed on the 24th of February, 1809.

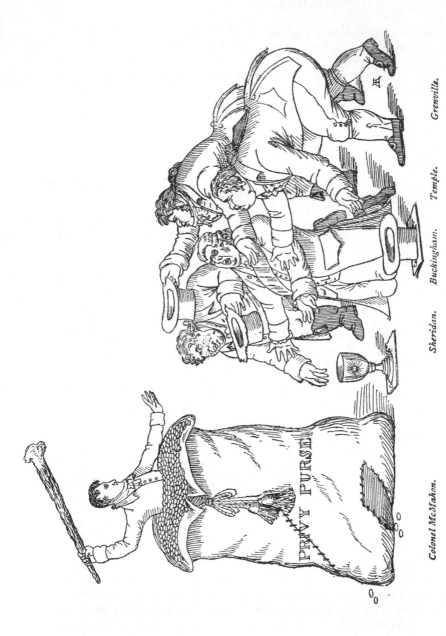

Colonel McMahon.　　　Sheridan.　　Buckingham.　　Temple.　　Grenville.

THE PRIVY PURSE AND POLITICAL BEGGARS.

(*Published April* 13, 1812, *by William Holland.*)

salary was he to have? Mr. Perceval, as Chancellor of the Exchequer, admitted the appointment, and pointed out that Colonel Taylor had occupied the same position towards the King for many years, and the same salary that was given to that gentleman had been continued to Colonel McMahon. Mr. Whitbread pointed out that Colonel Taylor's appointment was owing to the infirmities of the King, and that previously, there had been no such post.

On the 14th of April, Mr. C. W. Wynn, in the House of Commons, moved for the Production of the Appointment of Colonel McMahon to the new Office of Private Secretary to his Royal Highness the Prince Regent. A very long discussion took place, and on a division, the motion was negatived by a majority of seventy-six. But the Ministry felt that the House was decidedly against them, and the appointment was not persisted in—McMahon afterwards became a pensioner on the Privy Purse.

During the whole of January the Luddites were very violent in, and about Nottingham, doing an immense amount of mischief, in spite of all the troops could do, and they were so well organized that very few prisoners were taken. In April the agitation spread to Leeds, where machinery was broken, and cloth &c., destroyed. Then there were food riots among the Cornish miners, which lasted until the arrival of troops. More Luddite riots at Leeds. Food riots among the Colliers at Macclesfield. Then Bristol got tainted with the same lawless spirit ; then Sheffield, Stockport, Carlisle, Manchester, Bolton, and elsewhere, but these riots were principally directed against machinery. At the latter end of April, one of the chief ringleaders, a man named Walker, was arrested, and safely lodged in Chester Gaol. He was said to be General Ludd himself.

In May, there still were riots in the manufacturing district, but these principally took the form of organized burglaries. At last, on May 24th, there was a Special Commission to try those who had been captured. Some were sentenced to imprisonment, some to transportation, which, in those days really meant being sent across the seas, and sixteen were condemned to be hanged—but five, only, were left for death. In other parts of the country some were hanged, but this really served only ' *pour encourager les autres,*' for the riots still went on during June, August, and part of September ; but they were then dying out, a letter from Huddersfield, dated the 10th of September, saying, ' Several persons have been apprehended on various charges of Luddism, and are now in custody here. A number of others have, this week, abjured their illegal oath, and taken the oath of allegiance ; they see the calamities they have brought upon themselves and neighbours, by the atrocious depredations they have committed, and the delusions they have laboured under ; and it is to be hoped they will all follow the laudable example of those their associates, in discharging themselves from that unlawful and ruinous system in which they have, unfortunately, been engaged, and return to their allegiance before it is too late.' And so they did, for we do not hear much of them afterwards. They were very ignorant, the price of provisions, owing to the war, pressed heavily upon them, work was scarce, and, to their minds, looked likely to be scarcer, owing to the introduction of Machinery. Had the Home Government been a strong one, the riots might have been stifled at their birth, for there was not the false philanthropy preached then, as now, and the soldiery, both officers and men, were ready to obey orders unflinchingly, and without fear of being called to trial afterwards for their obedience.

Guineas and Bank Notes still exercised the public mind, and the former must indeed have been hoarded up when we learn, early in January, that 34,000 guineas in gold, the property of a gentleman deceased, were offered for sale on 'Change at Belfast. Bank of England notes were forged to a great extent, so much so, that the total value of the forged Notes presented at the Bank of England for payment, and refused, during eleven years, from the 1st of January, 1801, to the 31st of December, 1811, was £101,661.

> ' *Bank Notes*, it is said, once *Guineas* defied
> To swim to a point in Wade's foaming tide ;
> But 'ere they could reach the opposite brink,
> *Bank Notes* cried to *Gold*, "Help me ! Cash us ! I sink."
>
> That Paper should sink, and guineas should swim,
> May appear to some folks a ridiculous whim ;
> But before they condemn, let them hear this suggestion—
> In *pun-making*, *gravity's* out of the question.'

In September of this year Silver had risen to 6s. 8d. per oz., and Gold to £5 10s., equalling in value for a guinea £1 9s. 6d.

There is a curious story of the value of money, told in

November of this year. 'A Gentleman in the Country sent to his banker in the City, a parcel of guineas which were both light and heavy, with directions to pass the value to his credit in account. The banker, being a good and loyal subject, and unwilling to do an unlawful act, credited his correspondent, with the heavy guineas at the rate of £1 1s. each, the value by law established : but the light ones he sent to a Silver-smith, who returned for them Bank Notes, at the rate of £1 7s. each. A light guinea is thus proved to be worth 6s. more than one of standard weight.'

In April, Napoleon put out a feeler for peace with Great Britain, on the basis that the Bourbons should reign in Spain ; but, when inquiry was made whether by that, he meant Ferdinand VII. he gave no reply, and the negotiation, if ever serious, fell through.

One of the principal social events of the year was the Murder of the Right Hon. Spencer Perceval, Chancellor of the Exchequer, First Lord of the Treasury, and Prime Minister of England, who was shot by the hand of an assassin, John Bellingham, on the 11th of May, whilst passing through the lobby of the House of Commons. He was born November 1, 1762, so that, when he fell, he was in the prime of life. He was of very good family, being the second son of John, Earl of Egmont, in Ireland, and Baron Lovel and Holland in England. His family was one of the very few that really came over with the Conqueror, for Robert the second son of Eudes, sovereign Duke of Brittany, settled in Normandy, and there became possessed of the lordships of Brewehal and Ivery. As stated, he came over in the Norman filibuster's suite, and in the course of two or three generations the name of Brewehal, became changed into Perceval—and ever after-wards so remained.

Spencer Perceval, studied for, and practised at, the Bar, being made King's Counsel in 1796. In the same year, his first cousin, Lord Compton, who was member for Northampton, succeeded to his father's title of Earl of Northampton ; and Perceval, offering himself for the vacant seat, was elected without opposition. His rise was rapid, and in 1801, being then in his 39th year, he joined Lord Addington's Govern-ment as Solicitor-General. In 1802 he was made Attorney-General. When Pitt resumed the government, he retained his appointment, but resigned it at Pitt's death.

In Lord Portland's Ministry of 1807, he undertook the

duties of Chancellor and Under Treasurer of the Exchequer, and also Chancellor of the Duchy of Lancaster. In October, 1809, he was First Lord of the Treasury, and Prime Minister, and so continued until his sad end.

One may well ask why did Bellingham shoot Perceval? To this day I cannot tell. In the year 1804, a Mr. John Bellingham—who had been brought up in a Counting House in London, and, afterwards, lived three years as clerk with a Russian Merchant at Archangel, whence he had returned to England—went back to Russia on Mercantile business—was there twice imprisoned—he said falsely—and treated, according to his own account, with very great indignity. He complained to the British Ambassador at Petersburg, and also to the Secretary of Legation, but did not obtain his desired redress. He returned to England in 1809, as he said, ruined in health and fortune. But the British Ambassador, Lord Gower, declared that he used all the influence he possessed (with propriety) in Bellingham's favour; but that he was legally imprisoned for debt, upon the award of four arbitrators, two of them British Merchants chosen by himself, and the other two Russians; that his confinement was far from severe; that he was allowed to walk at large, only under the inspection of a police officer; and that he had received help in money from the Secretary of Legation.

But he was 'a man with a grievance,' and went about to different branches of the Government, detailing the *lâches* of Lord Gower, and the Secretary, for their culpable neglect in not looking properly after the interests of a British Subject. He then determined to bring his case before Parliament, and asked General Gascoyne to back his petition, and the General promised to do so, provided it had the countenance of Mr. Perceval, the Chancellor of the Exchequer, which was considered necessary in all cases which involved a pecuniary grant.

He wrote to poor Perceval *for leave to bring in a Petition*, but was answered that Mr. Perceval thought that his petition 'was not of a nature for the Consideration of Parliament.' Then he went to the Regent and the Privy Council, but to no purpose: made applications all round, but met with no good, except a reference to the Chancellor of the Exchequer: but here he had been refused help. Then he wrote a letter to the Bow Street Magistrates, stating his case—saying that he would, once more solicit his Majesty's Ministers, through them, and, failing redress from that, he continued, 'I shall then feel justified in executing justice myself; in which case, I shall be ready to argue the merits of so reluctant a measure, with his Majesty's Attorney-General, wherever, and whenever I may be called upon to do so. In the hopes of averting so abhorrent but compulsive an alternative,—I have the honour to be, &c.' The Magistrates communicated the contents of this packet to the Secretary of State, but it only resulted in a fresh disappointment.

He still kept on trying, and his idea of taking vengeance on some one, increased, until it not only became fixed, but he planned its carrying out. He had a pocket made in his coat of a peculiar size and shape, in order to carry a pistol; and on the fatal 11th of May, he hid himself behind one of the folding doors of the lobby of the House of Commons; and when, about a quarter past five, the ill-fated Chancellor made his appearance, Bellingham shot him through the heart. Poor Perceval only reeled a pace or two, faintly called out, that he was murdered, and then fell. The Illustration which I have reproduced is the best I know, and the likenesses of both murderer and victim are extremely good.

Perceval was at once raised, and carried into the Speaker's apartments, but he died in two or three minutes. His murderer made no attempt to escape, but stood holding the pistol with which he had committed the foul crime, and, when some one called out—'Where is the rascal that fired?' he coolly stepped forward, saying, 'I am the unfortunate man,' and quietly surrendered himself a prisoner. On being searched, a loaded pistol was found in his pocket—the fellow to that which he was still holding in his hand.

He was equally calm when brought before the bar of the House, acknowledging the fact, and even attempting to justify it. He was committed to Newgate, where two men were constantly with him in his cell, to prevent any attempt at self-destruction. He was brought up for trial at the Old Bailey on the 15th of May. The facts against him were concisely and clearly stated, even to that of his having pockets specially made to hold the pistols: and he conducted his own defence. He gave an account of his sufferings for the past eight years, laying the blame principally on Lord Leveson Gower, whom he regretted he had not killed in place of Mr. Perceval. 'He was obliged to the Attorney-General and the Court for setting aside the plea of insanity urged by his counsel, and could

5

assure them, whenever he should appear before the tribunal
of God, he should be adjudged innocent of the wilful murder
of Mr. Perceval.   That he perished by his hand he admitted;
but, to constitute felony, there must be *malice prepense*, the
wilful intention, which had not been proved.   In this case, he
had been robbed of his property, his family ruined, and his

MR. PERCEVAL ASSASSINATED IN THE LOBBY OF THE HOUSE OF COMMONS,
MAY 11, 1812.

mind tortured through the conduct of Government Agents;
and he was now to answer for his life, because Mr. Perceval
chose to patronize iniquity, and refuse him redress.'

Of course, this style of argument availed him nothing with
the jury, who, after a very brief consultation, brought him in

' Guilty.'   Sentence of death was passed upon him, and, as
there was very little sickly sentimentality in those days, as to
carrying out the penalty of the law, he was duly hanged on
the 18th of May : his body being given over to the surgeons
for dissection.   It is said that after his body was opened, his
heart continued its functions for four hours ; in other words,
that he was living for that time.

The day after Mr. Perceval's assassination, the Prince Regent
sent a Message to Parliament recommending a provision being
made for Mrs. Perceval and her family, and an annuity of
£2,000 was granted her, together with a sum of £30,000 to
her family.   These were voted unanimously, and two other
votes were passed by large majorities—one to provide a
monument to his memory in Westminster Abbey, the other
granting to his eldest son, Spencer Perceval, who was just
about to go to College, an annuity of £1,000, from the day of
his father's death, and an additional £1,000 yearly, on the
decease of his mother.

One would have thought that there could have been but
one feeling throughout the nation, that of horror, at this
dastardly murder, but one town was the base exception.   When
the news of his murder reached Nottingham, a numerous
crowd publicly testified their joy by shouts, huzzas, drums
beating, flags flying, bells ringing, and bonfires blazing.   The
Military being called out, and the Riot Act read, peace was
restored.

CHAPTER VII.

French Prisoners of War—Repeal of the 'Orders in Council'—
Rejoicings for the Victory of Salamanca—Saturnalia thereat.

THERE was always more or less trouble with the French
Prisoners of War during the year—as we know, many escaped,
and small blame to them—while many officers deliberately
and disgracefully broke their parole and got away.   Six
Prisoners escaped from Edinburgh Castle, made for the sea,
found a boat, and, sailing up the Firth, got as far as Hopetoun
House, where they landed, intending to go to Glasgow by
land, but the Commandant of the Linlithgow Local Militia
had information that several men had been seen skulking
about Lord Hopetoun's plantations, and, after some trouble,
they were caught, lodged in Linlithgow gaol, and then sent
back to Edinburgh.

One gained his freedom by an act of gallantry, early in
February.   'François Goyette, a French Prisoner, lately employed as a servant on board the hospital ship *Pegase*, has been
released, and sent to France by the Transport Board, as a
reward for his exertions in jumping overboard to the rescue
of the Cook and boy of the *Hydra* frigate, when upset in her
boat on Porchester Lake.'

We see, by the following, how systematic they became in
their methods of escaping :—

'Upwards of 1,000 French prisoners have escaped from this
country during the war, and so many persons have lately been
detected in assisting their escape, that those concerned have
had a vehicle made for the conveyance of Frenchmen, to
avoid suspicion or detection, exactly resembling a covered cart
used by the Calico printers, with strong doors at each end,

but with seats inside to hold a number of men.   One of them was detected about a week since, in a very extraordinary way.   Some Revenue Officers went into a public house near Canterbury, where two men were playing at cards, whom they suspected to be Frenchmen on their way to escape from this country.   They communicated this suspicion to a magistrate, who informed them that, at that hour of the night (about eight o'clock), the Constable was generally intoxicated, and it would be of no use applying to him; but advised them to procure the assistance of some of the Military in the neighbourhood, which the officers accordingly did, and surrounded the house.

'The landlord refused to open the door, saying it was too late.   The soldiers told him they were in search of deserters. A short time afterwards two men came out of the back door, and the Revenue Officers, suspecting they were two Frenchmen, secured them.   Another came out directly afterwards, whom the soldiers stopped; he, also, was a Frenchman.   They were conveyed away in Custody.   This was a mere chance detection, as the two men whom the Revenue Officers had seen at Cards early in the evening proved, not Frenchmen, but tradesmen of the neighbourhood; and, while the officers were gone to the magistrate, and after the military, a cart, such as we have described, arrived at the house with four Frenchmen.

'The fourth man, who was some time in coming out, after the others, escaped into the London road, whither he knew the cart had returned, and overtook it; but the driver would not, for a considerable time, take him up, as he had only seen him in the night-time, till he made him understand that he was connected with one Webb, the driver's employer.   It being ascertained that the three Frenchmen in custody, had been brought there in a cart, pursuit was made, and it was overtaken, and the driver and the Frenchman were taken into custody.   They were examined before a magistrate, when it appeared, from the confession of the driver, &c., that the four Frenchmen were officers, who had broken their parole from Ashby de la Zouche.   The Cart had been fitted up with a seat, to hold a number of Frenchmen.   He was employed by Mr. Webb to drive the cart.   The Frenchmen only got out of the cart at night to avoid observation.   They stopped at bye-places, and made fires under hedges.   At a place near Brentford, a woman connected with Webb made tea for them.   They stopped on Beckenham Common to rest

the horse, about ten o'clock at night, when, a horse patrol
passing at the time, suspected something to be wrong, but
could not ascertain what.   He insisted on the driver moving
off ; and when he was about putting the horse into the Cart,
an accident happened which nearly led to their discovery.
The Frenchmen all being at the back of the cart, the driver
lost the balance, when he was putting in the horse, and the
cart fell backwards, which caused the Frenchmen to scream
violently ; but it is supposed the patrol had gone too far to
hear the noise.   Webb was apprehended, and examined
before a magistrate in Kent, but he discharged him.   However, afterwards, the magistrate meeting with Webb, in Maidstone, where he was attending the assize on a similar charge,
he took him into custody.'

What was it made these French Officers so dishonour themselves by breaking their parole ?   The very fact of their being
on parole, intimates a certain amount of freedom.   It must
have been either a dull moral perception, and the utter want
of all the feelings and instincts of a gentleman, or else
ungovernable *nostalgia*, which blunted their sense of honour.
Here is a pretty list, June 30, 1812 :—

'The number of French commissioned Officers, and masters
of Privateers and Merchantmen, who have broken their
parole in the last three years ending 5 June is 692, of whom
242 have been retaken, and 450 escaped.   A considerable
number of officers have, besides, been ordered into confinement, for various other breaches of their parole engagements.'

Something had to be done to stop this emigration, so the
Government gave orders to seize all galleys of a certain
description carrying eight oars : 17 were seized at Deal, and
10 at Folkestone, Sandgate, &c.   They must have been built
for smuggling, and illicit purposes, for they were painted so
as to be perfectly invisible at night, and were so slightly
built, and swift, that in those days of no steamers, no craft
could catch them.   However, the punishment, if caught, for
aiding their escape, was severe, as three men found to their
cost.   They were sentenced to two years' imprisonment, and
two of them ' to be placed in and upon the pillory on the sea-
shore, near the town of Rye, and, as near as could be, within
sight of the French Coast, that they might be viewed, as his
lordship observed, by those enemies of their country, whom
they had, by their conduct, so much befriended.'

The French papers had accused us of ill-treating our prisoners, so that a disclaimer was necessary :—

' *French Prisoners.*—As a proof of the good treatment of the prisoners of war in this country, the following comparative statement of those sick and in health will be the best answer to the calumnies of the *Moniteur* :—

Thursday, Aug. 20, 1812.

	In health.	Sick.
On board prison ships, Hamoaze ...	6100	... 61
In Dartmoor depôt	7500	... 74

' This small percentage of sick, is not the common average of persons not confined as Prisoners of War. At Dartmoor 500 prisoners, such as labourers, carpenters, smiths, &c., are allowed to work from sun-rise to sun-set ; they are paid four-pence and sixpence per day, according to their abilities, and have each their daily rations of provisions, viz., a pound and a half of bread, half a pound of boiled beef, half a pound of cabbage, and a proportion of soup and small beer. They wear a tin plate in their Caps, with the title of the trade they are employed in, and return every evening to the depôt to be mustered.'

They had a rough sense of justice among themselves, their punishments to delinquents not quite coming up to the rigorous ' *mort aux voleurs*,' but still very severe. Here is a case : The French prisoners who were brought to the depôt at Perth, on August 13th, from Dundee, were lodged the preceding night, in the Church at Inchture, where, it is said, they contrived to draw many of the nails from the seats, and break a number of the panes of the windows ; and one of their number stole the two *mort cloths*, or palls, belonging to the Church. The beadle being sent after them to the depôt, the theft was instantly discovered, which so incensed the prisoners against the thief, that they called out to have him punished, and asked permission to do so by a Court-martial. Having held this Court, they ordered him a naval flogging of two dozen, with the end of a hard rope. The Culprit was tied to a lamp-post, and, with the first lash, the blood sprung. The punishment went on to 17 lashes, when the poor man fainted away, but he had the other 7 at another time.

They kicked over the traces sometimes, as we learn by the *Annual Register*, September 8th :—

' The French prisoners at Dartmoor depôt, on Sunday last,

had worked themselves up to the highest pitch of rage, at having a pound and a half of biscuit, and not bread, per day. The use of biscuit, it is to be observed, was to be discontinued as soon as the bakehouse had been rebuilt ; but the Frenchmen were absolutely deaf to remonstrances. A detachment of the Cheshire militia, and of the South Gloucester regiment, was drawn up on the walls surrounding the prison ; and, although they had loaded their pieces with ball, the prisoners appeared undaunted, and insulted them in the grossest terms. A sentinel on duty had the bayonet wrenched off his piece, yet nobly reserved his fire ; an officer, however, followed the Frenchman, struck him over the shoulder with his sword, and brought off the bayonet. The Frenchmen even bared their breasts to the troops, and seemed regardless of danger.

'The number of prisoners is about 7,500 ; and so menacing was their conduct, that an express was sent off to Plymouth Dock at eleven o'clock on Sunday night, soliciting immediate assistance. Three pieces of Artillery were, in consequence, sent off early on Monday morning ; and, on their arrival at the principal gate, the bars of which, of immense size, had been previously broken by stones hurled against them by the insurgents, they were placed in such directions as to command the whole of the circle which the prison describes. This had the desired effect, and order was restored. It is to be noticed that the allowance of biscuit, at which these men had so indignantly spurned, is precisely the same as that which is served out to our own sailors and marines.'

At another time (Sunday, October 11th) the *Ganges* prison ship, at Portsmouth, with 750 prisoners on board, was set on fire by one of them, and had actually a great hole burned in her, before the fire was discovered. The incendiary was soon detected, and put in irons ; he confessed his guilt, and declared it was his intention to destroy himself and companions, who were tired of confinement. To the credit of his compatriots, they all helped to extinguish the flames, and were, with difficulty, restrained from lynching the offender.

One pretty little story anent them, and I have done. A prisoner, located at Perth, was released, on account of his humanity. At the storming of Badajoz, General Walker fell at the head of his brigade, and was found by this young Frenchman lying wounded, and bleeding, in the breach. In his arms he bore the General to a French Hospital, where he was cured. General Walker gave him his address, and promised to serve him, if ever it lay in his power. The fortune of war brought the young man, a captive, to England, and, on his application to his friend the General, the latter so used his influence as to procure his release.

An act was done in this year which removed many restrictions from our trade, and promoted the manufacturing industry of the Country. It was all very well to be victorious in war, but the fact of being at war, more especially with opponents whose great efforts were to cripple the trade of the Nation, and thus wither the sinews by which war is greatly maintained, was felt throughout all classes of the Manufacturing Interest all over the Country, a power which was then beginning to make itself felt. The Act of which I speak, was the abolition of the Orders in Council which prohibited trade with any port occupied by the French, being a reprisal for Napoleon's Berlin and Milan Decrees, which interdicted commerce with England.

Petitions poured into Parliament in favour of their abrogation, and on the 24th of April Lord Liverpool laid on the table of the House of Lords, the following

' DECLARATION of the Court of Great Britain respecting the Orders in Council.

' At the Court at Carlton-house the 23rd day of April, 1812. Present his Royal Highness the Prince Regent in Council.

' Whereas his Royal Highness the Prince Regent was pleased to declare, in the name, and on the behalf of his Majesty, on the 21st day of April, 1812: " That if at any time hereafter, the Berlin and Milan Decrees shall, by some authentic act of the French Government, publicly promulgated, be absolutely and unconditionally repealed, then, and from thenceforth, the Order in Council of the 7th of January, 1807, and the Order in Council of the 26th of April, 1809, shall without any further Order be, and the same are hereby declared from thenceforth to be, wholly and absolutely revoked.'

On this being known, there were great rejoicings throughout the Country, especially at Sheffield, Leeds, and other manufacturing towns ; the beneficial effects of the alteration became immediately apparent, there being more purchases made at the Cloth Hall at Leeds, in one day, than had been known for many years. At Liverpool 1,500,000 yards of bounty goods were shipped in one week, worth £125,000, and 2,500,000 were in progress of shipment. In the same week £12,000 Convoy duty, at 4 per cent., was paid, indicating further shipments to the amount of £300,000, at the same port. The wages of Spinners, &c., advanced at once, in some cases as much as 2s. 3d. a week.

But all rejoicings were not so quiet—witness those which took place in London in honour of the Victory of Salamanca, when Wellington totally defeated the French Army under Marshal Marmont, July 22, 1812. The French left in the hands of the British 7,141 prisoners, 11 pieces of cannon, 6 stands of colours, and 2 eagles.

The Illuminations in London took place on August 17th and two following days, but they seem to have been of the usual kind. If the sightseers could not get hold of the hero of the day, they managed to lay hands on the Marquis Wellesley, his brother, who was driving about, looking at the illuminations ; and, having taken the horses out of his carriage, they dragged him about the streets ; finally, and luckily, depositing him at Apsley House. After this, they returned down Piccadilly, calling out for lights, which had a little time before been brilliant, but since had gone out. The inhabitants got from their beds and showed candles, but this did not satisfy the mob, who set to work demolishing the windows with sticks, brick-bats, stones, &c., to the great danger of life and limb.

Some glass, in Mr. Coutts's house, which cost £4 10s. a square (for plate glass was very dear then) was broken, as were also several windows at Sir Francis Burdett's, and yet both had been well lighted throughout the night. This disgraceful scene was kept up till past three A.M., and damage was done, estimated at five or six hundred pounds.

On the third and last night of their Saturnalia the outrages were, perhaps, worse than before. Not only were fire-arms freely discharged, and fireworks profusely scattered, but *balls of tow, dipped in turpentine*, were thrown among crowds and into carriages ; horses ran away in affright—carriages were overturned—and many deplorable accidents ensued in broken limbs and fractured skulls. Here are a few accidents. In Bow Street, a well-dressed young lady had her clothes set in a blaze. In the Strand, at one time, three women were on fire, and one burned through all her clothes, to her thigh. Likewise in the Strand, a hackney coach, containing two

ladies and two gentlemen, was forced open by the mob, who
threw in a number of fireworks, which, setting fire to the
straw at the bottom of the coach, burned an eye of one of the
gentlemen, his coat, and breeches ; one of the ladies had her
pelisse burned, and the other was burned across the breast.
In St. Clement's Churchyard, a woman, of respectable appearance, hearing a blunderbuss suddenly discharged near her,
instantly dropped down, and *expired*.

Apropos of Salamanca, there was a little *jeu d'esprit* worth
preserving.

'SALAMANCA LOBSTERS.

Though of Soldiers, by some in derision 'tis said,
They are Lobsters, because they are cloathed in red,
Yet the maxim our army admit to be true,
As part of their nature, as well as their hue ;
A proof more decisive, the world never saw,
For every man in the Field had " *Eclat*." '

On the 30th of September, there was a great military
function, in depositing the captured French Eagles in Whitehall Chapel.   They were five in number, two taken at Salamanca, two at Madrid, and one near Ciudad Rodrigo.

CHAPTER VIII.

Chimney-sweeps—Climbing boys—Riot at Bartholomew Fair—
Duelling—War with France—Declaration of war between
England and America—Excommunication for bearing false
witness—Early Steam Locomotives—Margate in 1812—Resurrection men—Smithfield Cattle Club.

THE Social life of a nation includes small things, as well as
great, deposition of Eagles, and Chimney-sweeps, and the
latter have been looked after, by the legislature, not before
the intervention of the law was needed. In 1789, 28 Geo. III.,
an Act was passed to regulate Chimney-sweeping. In 1834,
another Act regulated the trade, and the apprenticeship of
Children. Again, by 3 and 4 Vic. cap. 85, it was made
illegal for a master sweep to take as apprentice, any one
under sixteen years of age, and the Act further provided that
no one, after the 1st of July, 1842, should ascend a chimney
unless he were twenty-one years of age. In 1864 the law
was made more stringent, and even as late as 1875, 38 and 39
Vic. cap. 70, an Act was passed 'for further amending the
Law relating to Chimney Sweepers.' That all this legislation
was necessary is partially shown by a short paragraph of the
date 7th of August : ' Yesterday, Charles Barker was charged
at Union Hall* with kidnapping two young boys, and selling
them for *seven shillings*, to one Rose, a chimney sweep at
Kingston.' And, again, the 25th of August :—
 ' An interesting occurrence took place at Folkingham.†
A poor woman who had obtained a pass billet to remain there
all night, was sitting by the fire of the kitchen of the Grey-

---

* Union Hall was at the east end of Union Street, Borough, and
was built by subscription in 1781—for the use of the magistrates.
 † Or Falkingham, Lincolnshire.

hound Inn, with an infant child at her breast, when two chimney sweeps came in, who had been engaged to sweep some of the chimneys belonging to the inn next early morning. They were, according to custom, treated to a supper, which they had begun to eat, when the younger, a boy about seven years of age, happening to cast his eyes upon the woman, (who had been likewise viewing them with a fixed attention from their first entrance,) started up, and exclaimed in a frantic tone—"That's my mother!" and immediately flew into her arms.

'It appears that her name is Mary Davis, and that she is the wife of a private in the 2nd Regiment of Foot-guards, now serving in the Peninsula; her husband quitted her to embark for foreign service on the 20th of last January, and on the 28th of the same month she left her son in the care of a woman who occupied the front rooms of her house, while she went to wash for a family in the neighbourhood: on her return in the evening, the woman had decamped with her son, and, notwithstanding every effort was made to discover their retreat, they had not since been heard of: but having lately been informed that the woman was a native of Leeds, she had come to the resolution of going there in search of her child, and with this view had walked from London to Folkingham (106 miles) with an infant not more than six weeks old in her arms.

'The boy's master stated, that about the latter end of last January, he met a woman and boy in the vicinity of Sleaford, where he resides. She appeared very ragged, and otherwise much distressed, and was, at that time, beating the boy most severely; she then accosted him (the master) saying she was in great distress, and a long way from home; and after some further preliminary conversation, said, if he would give her two guineas to enable her to get home, she would bind her son apprentice to him; this proposal was agreed to, and the boy was regularly indentured, the woman having previously made affidavit as to being his mother. This testimony was corroborated by the boy himself, but, as no doubt remained in the mind of anyone respecting the boy's real mother, his master, without further ceremony, resigned him to her. The inhabitants interested themselves very humanely in the poor woman's behalf, by not only paying her coach fare back to London, but also collecting for her the sum of £2 5s.'

Among the home news of 1811, I mentioned Bartholomew

Fair; but for rowdyism, the fair of 1812 seems to have borne the palm :—

'The scene of riot, confusion and horror exhibited at this motley festival, on this night, has seldom, if ever, been exceeded. The influx of all classes of labourers who had received their week's wages, and had come to the spot, was immense. At ten o'clock every avenue leading through the conspicuous parts of the fair was crammed, with an impenetrable mass of human creatures. Those who were in the interior of the crowd, howsoever distressed, could not be extricated ; while those who were on the outside, were exposed to the most imminent danger of being crushed to death against the booths. The females, hundreds of whom there were, who happened to be intermixed with the mob, were treated with the greatest indignity, in defiance of the exertions of husbands, relatives, or friends. This weaker part of the crowd, in fact, seemed to be, on this occasion, the principal object of persecution, or, as the savages who attacked them, were pleased to called it, of *fun*. Some fainted, and were trodden under foot, while others, by an exertion, almost supernatural, produced by an agony of despair, forced their way to the top of the mass, and crept on the heads of the people, until they reached the booths, where they were received and treated with the greatest kindness. We lament to state that many serious accidents in consequence occurred ; legs and arms innumerable were broken, some lives were lost, and the surgeons of St. Bartholomew's Hospital were occupied the whole of the night in administering assistance to the unfortunate objects who were continually brought in to them.

'The most distressing scene that we observed arose from the suffocation of a child about a twelvemonth old, in the arms of its mother, who, with others, had been involved in the crowd. The wretched mother did not discover the state of her infant until she reached Giltspur Street, when she rent the air with her shrieks of self-reproach ; while her husband, who accompanied her, and who had the appearance of a decent tradesman, stood mute with the dead body of his child in his arms, which he regarded with a look of indescribable agony. Such are the heartrending and melancholy scenes which were exhibited, and yet this forms but a faint picture of the enormities and miseries attendant upon this disgraceful festival.'

Duelling was dying out, and if anything would help its

decline in public opinion, it would be something like the following remarks of Lord Ellenborough. They arose from an application to the Court of King's Bench, for a criminal information against two persons, for posting a Merchant at Lloyd's as a coward for refusing a Challenge. These are the learned judge's remarks on the case :—

'Really it is high time to put a stop to this spurious chivalry of the counting-house and the counter. The Court has been for these two days occupied with cases of this sort ; yesterday it was an angry linendraper of Bristol, who had been a little time in the local militia, long enough to imbibe all the worst prejudices of the army, that thought proper to post a practising surgeon for not accepting a challenge ; and, to-day, we have a mercantile man in the same predicament ; instead of posting their books, these tradesmen are posting one another. The Court desires it to be understood, that it is not necessary for the party applying for a remedy against such an outrage as this, to come perfectly unblemished before them : and that if it shall be shown to be necessary for public quiet and justice, they will interpose the remedy sought for. If the challenge in this case had been sent *eo instanti* upon the defendant's quitting the Coffee-house, the Court would have contemplated it as emanating from the venial irritation of the moment ; but it appears that he at first applied to the prosecutor for an apology, upon the refusal of which, his friend, the other defendant, was sent upon this mischievous and malignant mission to the prosecutor, in the country ; and then, because a man refuses to be hunted down when dining out at a friend's house, and challenged at six o'clock in the evening, he is to be posted for a Coward at Lloyd's Coffee-house the next morning ! *Rule Absolute.*'

Abroad we were humbling the power of Napoleon. Ciudad Rodrigos and Badajos had been captured. Marmont had had a crushing defeat at Salamanca. Madrid had been occupied, and Wellington had been made Commander-in-Chief of the Spanish Army. The Russian Campaign had proved more than disastrous to Napoleon, it was his ruin. France could scarcely get over her awful losses, which Buturlin estimates as follows :—'Slain in battle, one hundred and twenty-five thousand ; died from fatigue, hunger, and cold, one hundred and thirty-two thousand ; prisoners (comprehending forty-eight generals, three thousand officers, and upwards of one hundred and ninety thousand men), one hundred and ninety three thousand ; total, four hundred and fifty thousand, and this does not include the thousands of non-combatants who perished.'

Our relations with America had been strained for a long time ; in fact, it was evident at the end of 1811 that war was not only imminent, but all but present. The quarrel arose out of the Orders in Council, which Napoleon's decrees of Berlin and Milan had brought forth, and which the Americans asserted interfered unjustly with their trade. Of course both sides thought they were right, and the Americans, knowing we had a big war on our hands, probably imagined that here was their opportunity. They provided money, and began hostilities, almost even before declaring war, which was formally done in June. The following is the Act of Congress :—

' An Act declaring War between the United Kingdom of Great Britain and Ireland, and the Dependencies thereof, and the United States of America and their Territories.

' Be it enacted, by the Senate and House of Representatives of the United States of America, in Congress assembled, that War be, and the same is hereby declared to exist, between the United Kingdom of Great Britain and Ireland, and the Dependencies thereof, and the United States of America and their territories ; and that the President of the United States be, and is hereby authorised, to use the whole land and naval forces of the United States, to carry the same into effect ; and to issue to the private armed vessels of the United States, commissions, or letters of Marque and general reprisal, in such form as he shall think proper, and under the Seal of the United States, against the Vessels, goods, and effects of the Government of the said United Kingdom of Great Britain and Ireland, and the Subjects thereof.

' Approved.   JAS. MADDISON.

' *June* 18, 1812.'

On the 13th of October England declared war against America, all hopes of peace having been abandoned. The Americans, by every means in their power, endeavoured to seduce our Colonists from their allegiance, but without success. They suffered severely at the hands of the Canadians, and, generally speaking, they got the worst of it on land ; but, at sea, the balance was in favour of the Americans, until, on the 26th of Dec., the ports and harbours of the rivers Chesapeake and Delaware were declared to be blockaded.

The King's health did not improve, and all hopes of his restoration to reason were abandoned ; after the Meeting of the Queen's Council on the 29th of Feb., it was decided that only one bulletin should be issued monthly—which, certainly, was very regularly done, but they were so bald, as to give little or no indication of the real condition of the King.

Before closing the chronicle of this year, I will mention some miscellaneous facts, which throw light on the times.

The wife of a respectable farmer, near Liverpool, died under the following melancholy circumstances. About two years previously she discharged a maidservant, who, in revenge, spread a report that her mistress was behaving improperly with a man in the neighbourhood. This rumour came to her husband's ears, and he took it so much to heart, that he quitted his home, and did not return to it until a few weeks before his wife's death. She assured him on the word of a dying woman, that she was innocent. He believed her, and they were reconciled a few days before her death. The maidservant, being threatened with a prosecution for slander, confessed her guilt, and attested the innocence of her Mistress; the result being that she was not prosecuted, but was *excommunicated in the neighbouring Churches.*

In 1802 Trevethick and Vivian obtained a patent for a high-pressure locomotive. It seems to have been very similar to this :—' July 1. On Wednesday last, an experiment was made with a machine at Leeds, under the direction of Mr. John Blenkinsop the patentee, for the purpose of substituting the agency of steam for the use of horses, in the conveyance of Coals on the iron railway from the mines at Middleton, to Leeds. This machine is, in fact, a steam engine of four-horses power, which, with the assistance of Cranks turning a Cogwheel, and iron Cogs placed at one side of the railway, is capable of moving at the rate of ten miles an hour.'

In 1813, William Hedley, of Wylam Colliery, made ' *Puffing Billy,*' which was the first locomotive which ran on smooth rails.

Owing to the difficulties of locomotion, and the total want of Railroads, there were very few watering-places for summer resort, at which the Londoner, who really might be excused for wishing to be away from the London of that day, could go to. Brighton, or Brighthelmstone, was then the abode of

6

Royalty, and never dreamed of being as it is now, the earthly paradise of the parvenu City man, and the Israelite : Ramsgate, and all other southern places of relaxation were not in vogue, or were only confined to a very few : but Margate ! that, indeed, was a place of earthly pleasure ! Here were very few restrictions of decorum, and a contemporary account may not be uninteresting.   It is dated Sept. 3rd :—

'This sudden change of weather, from stormy gloom to welcome sunshine, has produced a corresponding effect on the visitors of this watering-place, who engage themselves in every species of amusement that ingenuity can contrive, or experience has invented. The streets, which were deserted, as being the mere channel for the rain, are now filled with sprightly misses, hurrying from library to library, in search of some favourite Novel. The News Room, instead of being attended only by dismal politicians, prognosticating disasters, are crowded with all kinds of Company : the politicians quit their Newspapers, and, rattling the dice box, anticipate the certain destruction, not only of Bonaparte, and his army in the North, but of his whole Empire : their fortune is crossed, and again they begin to doubt.

' The young females busy themselves in hunting for new Novels ; and a tender love tale, or a sprightly satire, usurps the place of horrid mysteries, or dreadful catastrophes. The more elderly ladies amuse themselves with those everlasting topics, the price of things, the fashions, and the weather. The pier and the Cliffs are crowded during the whole day ; thither, young and old, healthy and sickly, rich and poor, repair, and all inhale with rapture the fresh sea breezes, glowing with new vigour, strength, and beauty, at every respiration.

' The gardens at Dandelion were fully attended yesterday, and (such is the wonderful metamorphose) at two o'clock those sat down to breakfast, who had been usually in the habit of dining at one. The dancing soon afterwards commenced, although it was declared to be *immensely hot*, and did not conclude, until a foot race, in an adjoining field, called off the attention of the visitors.

' On Tuesday, was given the third Masquerade, at the Theatre. The characters were more numerous and better supported than at the last, with the assistance of the dresses belonging to the house. The principal were Vestals, without virtue, coquetting with frail Friars. Knights, whose only claim to the title was, that they were errant, excepting a

chosen few, who claimed the distinction of the Garter;
Yorkshiremen with the dialect of the Weald of Kent;
Farmers, whose experience was derived from Mark Lane
letters; together with a profusion of ballad singers, Flower
girls, Gipsies, and Servants wanting places. Among the latter
was an Irish woman, who, by the bye, was a *man*, in the
character of a Servant of all work; having lost her own
character, presented the following from Father Delany:

' " I, Father Delany, aver and declare,
This is Judy O'Cloggin's own true character.
She is never prophane, nor swears, by my troth—
Except, now and then, when she raps out an oath;
She is sober, indeed,—except when she's frisky,
With tasting her own Mother's Milk—*Irish Whiskey;*
She's as honest as any, with two legs to stand on—
She leaves nothing alone that she once lays her hand on:
She's Cook, Housemaid, and Scullion or I am a dunce,
For sure, in my house, she was all these at once:
Besides Lady's Maid, so nate and so clane, aye,
To my beautiful wife, sweet Mrs. Delany:
Our mansion she scour'd with a new birchen broom,
Compos'd of a pig-stye, besides a large room."

' The Assembly at the Rooms is fixed for to-night, and
to-morrow is to be given, at the same place, a grand Masqued
Ball.'

The gentleman mentioned in the following advertisement
in *The Kentish Gazette*, Sept. 11th, must have been a pleasant
and kindly country neighbour. ' GAME AND RABBITS.—*A
general invitation to qualified Gentlemen.*—Manor of Dennie,
alias Dane, in the parishes of Chilham and Molash. The
interest of agriculture on this manor, and the surrounding
country, being much injured by the great numbers of hares,
pheasants, and rabbits, the proprietor feels the necessity of
giving this GENERAL INVITATION to *Qualified Gentlemen*, to
sport at their pleasure. The manor-house is in the parish of
Chilham, very near to a place called Shottenton Thorn, and
John Packman (a servant) who resides there, has orders to
accommodate gentlemen, as well as he can, with stabling for
their horses, and with any refreshment for themselves, that
his homely mode of living can offer. The house is large,
and a limited number of gentlemen, by sending their own
bedding, may be accommodated with house room in this and
future shooting seasons ' ! !

Here is a paragraph which shows how the horrid traffic in dead bodies was on the increase. A more perfect knowledge of anatomy was necessary to medical practitioners, for medical and surgical science was rapidly advancing, and there was not the facility now afforded by having the bodies of unclaimed paupers, legally placed at their disposal. The only subjects which might, properly, be operated upon, were those of Criminals who had been hanged, and although, in those days, these were far more numerous than nowadays, they fell far short of the requirements. So recourse was had to ' body snatching,' or the removal of bodies very recently buried—which were sold to Surgeons, 'and no questions asked.' It was so lucrative that, at last, the wretches who pursued this traffic would not take the trouble, nor encounter the risk of exhuming the bodies, but they deliberately suffocated living people, a practice which actually introduced a new word into the English language, ' Burking,' from one Burke, who was executed at Edinburgh, in 1829, for this crime. Others followed in his steps, notably one villain named Bishop, who was hanged in 1831.

' The *Resurrection Men,* of London, like other combinations of Workmen, struck, it seems, the other day, and refused to supply the Edinburgh and Glasgow Schools of Surgery with dead bodies, under an advance of two guineas per subject.'

A very good thing was done this year. Hitherto parish registers had been kept very much at the sweet will of the clergyman, or of his clerk, and there was so much want of uniformity in these very valuable books that every Church and Chapelry throughout England was furnished with one— before the 1st of January, 1813, thus ensuring the similarity we now enjoy. There were 36,000 copies printed, and the paper employed, amounted to over 3,000 Reams.

The Smithfield Club Cattle Show was a very small affair to that we are accustomed to see at the Agricultural Hall at Islington. In 1812, the money value of the prizes competed for was only 210 Guineas, and the Show was held at Mr. Sadler's Yard, Goswell Street.

During this year, as last, we gave practical proof of our kindness towards our Allies, by Subscriptions being opened for ' British Assistance to the Spanish Nation,' and for ' The Relief of poor Suffering Inhabitants of the Different Governments of Russia.'

CHAPTER IX.

1813.

High price of provisions—Luddites—Smuggling—Day of Humiliation—The Cossack—Mdlle. Platoff—Discovery of body of
Charles I. at Windsor—The Queen and the mad woman—The
fasting woman of Tutbury—Fight between the *Shannon* and
the *Chesapeake*—Rejoicings for the Victory at Vittoria—Fête
at Vauxhall—*William Huntingdon, s.s.*

This Year began somewhat gloomily, for the Wars made
themselves felt.   Porter rose to 6d. a pot, Mutton 2d. per lb.,
the latter, owing, it was said, to the rot, which had carried off
whole flocks of sheep.

But, if we felt the pinch, our adversaries, or, rather, one of
them, the French, felt it as well.   There was a great deal of
illicit trading done with France, especially in our Colonial
goods ; and, to facilitate matters, and make them legal, Napoleon would issue licenses to import such a quantity of such
goods.   As is pointed out in the following quotation, the poor
French had to pay very dearly for these commodities.
' Bonaparte has lately granted 250 more licenses for the importation of Colonial produce ; and these licenses are a source
of considerable profit to himself and his favourites.   Instead
of granting to one of these a pension or a sinecure, he gives
him a few licenses, which the latter sells at exorbitant prices
—so high, for example, as 75 livres (£3 2s. 6d. sterl.), for
every hundredweight of Sugar imported ; from which sugar
Bonaparte himself, afterwards derives a high duty, as he does
from every other article so imported :—a pound of Coffee, for
instance, purchased here for *eightpence,* pays him a duty of
four shillings.   In addition to these burdens, besides exorbitant
charges for freight, there is another imposition, which renders

the Colonial produce enormously expensive to the Continental consumer, viz., that the persons importing it under those licenses are bound previously to export from France, a stated proportion, in value, of wrought silks and other articles utterly prohibited in England, which, therefore, they are obliged to throw overboard on the passage, and afterwards indemnify themselves for this loss by an additional charge on the articles imported.   Notwithstanding all these disadvantages, near twenty millions of pounds' weight of Sugar have gone from England to France during the last year.'

During the latter part of the past year the Luddites were again troublesome, and it was found necessary to make a severe example, which had the desired effect.   On the 16th of January fourteen of these rioters were hanged, at York, in two batches of seven each, and these outrages ceased.

I have already said that Smuggling was considered a very venial sin, and sometimes smuggling adventures had something amusing in them—*vide* the following :—A party of Smugglers had landed a valuable cargo near Dungeness, and, having been informed that a party of Dragoons from Hastings were to be on the look-out for them, they sent word that they would resign half their goods, if they might carry away the other half unmolested.   At the same time they gave notice that they had left 180 tubs of gin in a chalk pit, well known to the officer of the troop.   The soldiers rode off immediately to act on the smugglers' information, and the latter, of course, were equally prompt in getting their newly-run Cargo out of harm's way.   The troops duly found the tubs at the place indicated, and, with triumph, escorted them to the Custom House, where, when they came to be examined, they were found to contain nothing stronger than *water*.

On the 1st of February a proclamation was issued from Carlton House.   It is deliciously vague about 'the War,' not saying whether it was that in which we were engaged, with the French, or with the Americans.   It was probably left to the imagination and option of the taxpayers, who might ' pay their money, and take their choice.'

' GEORGE, P. R.

  ' We, taking into our most serious consideration the just and necessary war in which His Majesty is engaged, and putting our trust in Almighty God, that He will graciously bless His Majesty's arms, both by sea and land, have resolved, and do, in the name, and on the behalf of His Majesty, and by, and with the advice of His Majesty's Privy Council, hereby command, that a Public Day of Fasting and Humiliation be observed throughout those parts of the United Kingdom called England and Ireland, on Wednesday the Tenth Day of March next ensuing, so that both we, and His Majesty's people, may humble ourselves before Almighty God, in order to obtain pardon of our sins, and in the most devout and solemn manner, send up our prayers and supplications to the Divine Majesty, for averting those heavy judgments, which our manifold provocations have most justly deserved : and for imploring His Blessing, and assistance on His Majesty's Arms, for the restoration of peace and prosperity to His Majesty and His Dominions,' &c., &c.

Another Proclamation made it applicable to Scotland. On the day appointed, the Regent, his daughter, and the Dukes of York, Cumberland, and Cambridge went to the Chapel Royal, St. James's ; and the two Houses of Parliament went —the Lords, to Westminster Abbey ; the Commons, to St. Margaret's, Westminster.

About this time of the year—with the exception of the bickerings of the Prince and Princess of Wales—there was very little to interest the public ; so little, indeed, that even the advent of a Cossack, who came in the suite of a Russian Officer, created an immense sensation. Here is as early an account as any, of this important individual. *Morning Chronicle, Thursday, April 15, 1813* : ' The Cossack, and a Russian Officer, who arrived in London on Friday last, made their appearance in the City, agreeably to the notice which had been given in some of the papers. They met the Lord Mayor at the Mansion House, who accompanied them to the Royal Exchange, and Lloyd's Coffee House, where they were received with the greatest marks of approbation by the merchants, and an immense concourse of spectators. After passing through Lloyd's, they were stationed at one of the balconies looking into the Exchange, when the Lord Mayor appeared, and, after silence was obtained, gave " Success to the Emperor Alexander," with three times three, which was given with enthusiasm by all present. The Cossack's spear was ten feet long, and it was said he had killed thirty-seven Frenchmen with it.'

I give an illustration of this formidable warrior ' ZEMLANOwhin, the Brave Russian Cossack, as he appeared at the Royal Exchange, on Wednesday, April 14, 1813.'

In the evening he was taken to Freemasons' Hall, where the Grand Master, the Duke of Sussex, conversed with him through the medium of an interpreter, for some minutes. He was a great lion. Besides the etching by Heath, here given, two other artists, Heapley and Pyne, were at him, and Ackerman, the print-seller, gave him his choice of four beautiful swords, of which he chose a Turkish scimitar. He was taken to Westminster, and was allowed to play with the large sword therein preserved.

The last we hear of him is that he visited, on the 30th of April, Exhibition Rooms at Spring Gardens, where he heard a new March played on an awful instrument called the Panharmonicon. On this fiendish invention the combined noise of 200 instruments was ground out by machinery. 'The trumpets sounding victory, and the bells, with the horns and kettledrums, rejoicing for glory, gave joy to all present. The Cossack, on being introduced to the fair Albiness, seemed, by the expression of his countenance, to be much pleased ; and, on shaking hands, and giving her a salute, said, " I leave London this evening, may I take with me a lock of your hair ?" This being granted, Mr. Wigley, the Proprietor of the Rooms, presented him with an elegant locket to enclose the same.' They made a paper model of him, which was shown at Mrs. Aberdeen's Papyruseum, 19, Frith Street, Soho.

The Cossacks were wonderfully popular with the English just then. Their *Hetman*, or Commander, Count Platoff, was reported to have offered to give his daughter, and a small dowry, to any soldier who would bring him Napoleon's head. In some verses relative to Napoleon's reverses in Russia is one :—

'But, take care, Master Nap, you meet with no trap,
    To poke either leg, or your head in ;
  Loss of legs stops your flight, lose your head, why the sight
    Will be welcome at Miss Platoff's wedding.'

She figures in another Satirical print, published on November 9, 1813, called 'Cossack Sports—or, the Platoff Hunt in full cry after French Game.' Leipsig is in the background, and the Cossacks plunge into the river Elster in full chase after the 'Corsican Fox.' Count Platoff cries, 'Hark forward ! my boys, get along ! He runs in view. Yoics, Yoics. There he

ZEMLANOWHIN, THE BRAVE RUSSIAN COSSACK, AS HE APPEARED AT THE ROYAL
EXCHANGE ON WEDNESDAY, APRIL 14, 1813.

(*Drawn and etched by Heath.*)

goes. Tally ho !' His daughter is in mid-stream, thrashing her horse, and calling out, ' Hi ! Ho ! Tally ho ! for a Husband !'

There was another thing much talked about at this time, and that was the discovery of the Body of Charles I. at Windsor. This was not the first body of a Sovereign found there unexpectedly : for on March 13, 1789, the workmen employed in re-paving the Choir of St. George's Chapel, discovered the entrance into the vault where Edward IV. had been deposited ; the royal body was found enclosed in a leaden and wooden coffin, reduced to a skeleton ; on the King's Coffin lay another of wood, much decayed, which contained the skeleton of a woman, supposed to have been his Queen, Elizabeth Woodville.

The Duchess of Brunswick (mother of the Princess of Wales) died in England on March 23, 1813, and was buried with much pomp, at Windsor on the 31st of March.

The following is a newspaper account of ' THE DISCOVERY OF THE BODY OF CHARLES I. On Wednesday last, at the interment of the Dowager Duchess of Brunswick, an important discovery was made. It had been long suspected that the remains of Charles I. were deposited in a vault at Windsor. Indeed Wood, in his *Athenæ*, states the supposition. On Wednesday a search was made, a Coffin was opened, which was found to a certainty to contain the long-sought-for body. It was not at all decayed ; the severed head had been carefully adjusted by a cement to the shoulders, and the most perfect resemblance to the portraits, was remarked in the shape of the head, the pointed beard, &c., fragments of which were carefully taken off as relics, as well as to identify the body.'

Laurence Eachard (who wrote in the reign of Anne) in his ' History of England ' (vol. ii. p. 649), speaking of Charles I. being buried at Windsor, and refuting a rumour that it was not so, says, ' But to remove all imaginations, we shall here insert a memorandum, or certificate sent by Mr. John Sewell, Register at Windsor, Anno 1696, September 21. The same Vault in which King Charles the First was buried was opened to lay in a still born child of the then Princess of Denmark, now our gracious Queen. On the King's Coffin the velvet pall was strong and sound, and there was about the Coffin a leaden band, with this inscription cut through it—KING CHARLES, 1648.

' Queen Jane's* Coffin was whole and entire ; but that of

* Seymour.

I General-Count-Platoff, promise to give My Daughter in Marriage, and 2000 Rubles to any Cossack-Russian-Prusian German-Swade-Turk-John Bull-Sauny Bull-Paddy Bull-or any other Bull, who Shall bring Me the Head of Little Bony — dead or a live.

1000 Rubles

1000 Rubles

A TIT-BIT FOR A COSSACK; OR, THE PLATOFF PRIZE FOR THE
HEAD OF BUONAPARTE.

(Etched by Wm. E——s, Published January 4, 1813, by Thos. Tegg.)

King Henry the Eighth was sunk in upon the breast part, and
the lead and wood consumed by the heat of the gums he was
embalmed with.'

Sir Henry Halford published, in April, 1813, a narrative of
the examination of the royal remains, which took place in the
presence of the Prince Regent, and we see how it bears out
Eachard's account. ' On removing the pall, a plain leaden
Coffin with no appearance of ever having been enclosed in
wood, and bearing an inscription, " King Charles, 1648," in
large, legible characters, on a scroll of lead, encircling it, immediately presented itself to view. A square opening was
then made in the upper part of the lid, of such dimensions as
to admit a clear insight into its contents. These were an
internal wooden coffin, very much decayed, and the body carefully wrapped in cere cloth.'

After this was unrolled, they had a perfect view of the
King's face, and, although it had suffered from decay, 'the
pointed beard, so characteristic of the period of the reign of
King Charles, was perfect. The shape of the face was a long
oval ; many of the teeth remained, and the left ear . . . was
found entire. . . . When the head had been entirely disengaged from the attachments which confined it, it was found
to be loose, and without any difficulty was taken up, and held
to view. . . .

' The hair was thick at the back part of the head, and in
appearance nearly black. A portion of it, which has since
been cleaned and dried, is of a beautiful dark brown colour :
that of the beard was a redder brown. On the back part of
the head, it was not more than an inch in length, and had
probably been cut so short for the convenience of the executioner, or, perhaps, by the piety of friends soon after death,
in order to furnish memorials of the unhappy King.'

An examination of the muscles of the neck clearly proved
that the head had been severed from the body by a heavy
blow with a very sharp instrument, and this thoroughly confirmed the identification of the King. ' After this examination
of the head, which served every purpose in view, and without
examining the body below the neck, it was immediately
restored to its situation, the Coffin was soldered up again, and
the vault closed.

' Neither of the other coffins had any inscriptions upon them.
The larger one, supposed, on good grounds, to contain the
remains of King Henry VIII., measured six feet, ten inches

in length, and had been enclosed in an elm one, two inches in thickness; but this was decayed, and lay in small fragments near it. The leaden coffin appeared to have been beaten in by violence about the middle; and a considerable opening in that part of it, exposed a mere skeleton of the King. Some beard remained upon the chin, but there was nothing to discriminate the personage in it.'*

* In 1888-9, an exhibition of Stuart Relics was held at the New Gallery in Regent Street, and, on December 17, 1888, the following Paragraph appeared in the *Standard*:—' The Prince of Wales visited St. George's Chapel, Windsor, on Thursday last, and replaced in the vault containing the coffin of Charles I. certain relics of that Monarch, which had been removed during some investigations more than 70 years ago. These relics, having ultimately come into the possession of the Prince of Wales, his Royal Highness decided, with the sanction of the Queen, to replace them in the vault from which they had been taken, but not to disturb the coffin of the King. This task was successfully accomplished on Thursday last in the presence of the Dean of Windsor.'

There was some discussion as to what these relics were, which was set at rest by the *Globe*, January 10, 1889 :—' THE PRINCE OF WALES AND THE RELIC OF CHARLES I. Considerable curiosity, says the *Whitehall Review*, was aroused the other day as to what the relic could have been which the Prince of Wales deposited in the tomb of Charles I. at Windsor. The relic in question was, we believe, part of the vertebræ joining the head to the body of the unfortunate monarch. It appears that when the coffin of Charles I. was opened in 1813, and the king's head fell on the ground, as so graphically described in Mr. Frith's " Reminiscences," a portion of the vertebræ of the beheaded king was taken away and preserved by the eminent physician, Sir Henry Halford, from whose custody it was subsequently stolen. Luckily, full written particulars were attached to the relic, and it was, two years ago, sent anonymously to the Prince of Wales, who, fearing that it might be wanted for the Stuart Exhibition, judiciously arranged to have the relic returned. It was placed on, but not in, the coffin in the vault at Windsor Chapel.'

A further paragraph in the same Newpaper of the 14th of January, thoroughly elucidates whatever mystery there might have been about the ' relics ' :—' THE RELIC OF CHARLES I.   Sir H. St. John Halford writes to us from Wistow Hall, Leicester, with reference to the Relic of Charles I. recently placed on the coffin of that Monarch by the Prince of Wales, as follows: ' The true history of the relic is that it was given to my grandfather, Sir Henry Halford, by His Majesty George IV., at the time that the coffin of Charles I. was opened, and was given by me to His Royal Highness the Prince of Wales two years ago." '

After the publication of this report it was but a very few days before the Caricaturist had made the subject his own, and we see George Cruikshank's idea of it in the accompanying 'Meditations among the Tombs.' Sir Henry Halford is going to cut off some of Henry VIII.'s beard : the Regent saying to him, ' Aye ! There's great Harry ! great indeed ! ! ! ! ! for he got rid of many wives, whilst I, poor soul, can't get *rid* of one. Cut off his beard, Doctor, 'twill make me a prime pair of Royal Whiskers.' Lord Castlereagh (Privy Purse) behind him, says, ' How queer King Charley looks without his head, doesn't he ? ! ! ! Faith and sure, and I wonder how WE should look without our heads ! ! !'

Whilst on the subject of Royalty, I may as well chronicle a shock which poor old Queen Charlotte had—on the 2nd of May—which must have frightened her terribly, for she actually sent for the Prince Regent. A woman named Davenport was assistant Mistress of the Robes, and she was born in the Queen's palace, and had lived constantly in it, with her mother, who was housekeeper at the Lower Lodge, Windsor, having previously filled the onerous, and arduous task of rocker to the infant princesses. Miss Davenport was about thirty years of age, and, when she was young, had a fit of insanity, of which, however, she was considered cured ; and, except an occasional period of *melancolia,* was quite harmless.

However, on Sunday, the 2nd of May, she broke out, the balance of her mind having been overthrown ever since the death of the Princess Amelia. She slept in the Tower over the Queen's bedroom, and her Majesty was aroused at five in the morning by a violent noise at her door, hearing some one shrieking and screaming, and calling on the Queen of England to redress her wrongs. The bedroom had double doors, and the poor maniac, having smashed the outer door, was endeavouring to force the inner one, when Mrs. Beckendorf, the Queen's dresser, who slept in her room, opened it, and there found the poor woman clad only in her night-clothes, with a letter in her hand, which she insisted upon delivering to her Majesty. For twenty minutes Mrs. Beckendorf kept her at bay, ringing a bell all the while. A page, two footmen, and a porter, at length appeared on the scene, and over-powered the mad woman. Then Dr. Willis, who was in attendance upon the King, was sent for, and she was put into a straight jacket—which, owing to her violence, was with difficulty got on her. She was then carried into a chaise, and

MEDITATIONS AMONG THE TOMBS.

driven away to a private lunatic asylum.   The Queen's nerves must soon have recovered, for she was at a grand dinner given in her honour at Carlton House, by the Prince of Wales on the 4th of May.

On this day the fasting woman of Tutbury, Ann Moore, who professed to live without food, confessed her imposture. Her miraculous abstention from nourishment was disbelieved in, and, at her own request, a committee of gentlemen watched her.   Their vigilance proved too much for her, for nine days of such inspection reduced her to such a state of emaciation, that she put her mark to the following confession : ' I, Ann Moore, of Tutbury, humbly asking pardon of all persons whom I have attempted to deceive and impose upon, and above all, with the most unfeigned sorrow and contrition, imploring the divine mercy, and forgiveness of that God whom I have so greatly offended, do most solemnly declare that I have occasionally taken sustenance for the last six years.'   The following epigram was made on

' TUTBURY ANN.

' She kept, what none would wish to keep, her bed,
And, what few *more* would do, declin'd a dinner ;
Liv'd an eternal Lent, and shamm'd half dead,
O Lord ! forgive this *ever-lying* sinner.'

In the war with America the British fleet was not always successful.   On the contrary, and when the *Shannon* beat the *Chesapeake,* there were great rejoicings.   In Boston harbour lay the United States frigate *Chesapeake,* Capt. Laurence, 49 guns, 18 and 32 pounders, and a crew of 400 men.   Capt. Broke, commanding H.M. frigate *Shannon,* which was inferior both in weight of metal, and number of men, had long been watching it, anxiously awaiting an opportunity of an encounter. At length, on the 1st of June, he challenged a combat, by standing close in to Boston Lighthouse.   He had not to wait long, for he had the pleasure of seeing the *Chesapeake* sailing out of the harbour.   He took up a position within sight of the land, and the American frigate came proudly on, conscious of victory, so much so, as to have omitted providing accommodation for the wounded.

After two or three broadsides the *Chesapeake* closed with the *Shannon,* and they were locked together, so Captain Broke gave orders for boarding, himself setting the example.   The Americans made a desperate, but undisciplined, defence, and

the assault was so fierce, that after two minutes only, of hand-
to-hand fighting, the Americans were driven from every post.
In another minute they ceased firing from below, and cried
for quarter. The Union Jack was then run up, and the whole
was over in fifteen minutes from its commencement. The
British lost 23 killed, and 56 wounded, out of a crew of 330
men : the Americans about 70 killed and 100 wounded.
Captain Laurence, who was among the latter, subsequently
died, and was honourably buried at Halifax. One can

SHANNON *v.* CHESAPEAKE.
(*Published September* 1, 1813, *for the proprietor of* ' *Town Talk.*')

scarcely believe the astonishment and humiliation of the
spectators on shore of this combat, when they saw their fine
ship which sailed away so shortly before, in all the pride of
expected victory, taken away in bondage, instead of returning
with her captor.

George Cruikshank gives us his idea of the naval engagement in a long etching (which I have divided into two)
published in ' Town Talk,' of the 1st of September, 1813. It

is called ' BRITISH VALOUR, and YANKEE BOASTING, or SHANNON versus CHESAPEAKE,' and is full of bombast, both in drawing, and words. The Americans are evolved out of his inner consciousness, but I presume it was the current type of the time, as our delineation of a Citizen of the United States of America, is, when pourtrayed in one of our comic papers. Evidently they were considered as Puritans, and depicted as Maw-worms. Captain Broke has hold of one by the hair, and is crying out, ' Down with your Stripes, you Swabs, or D——me, we'll stripe you.' The sailor who has hold of one of the dead, by his pigtail and breeches, calls out to another, ' Stand clear, Mess-mate, whilst I heave a few of these lubberly Yankee Doodles overboard.' The sailor kicking a Yankee into the sea, says, ' Go along, d——n you, don't you see they are waiting dinner for you ?' This probably refers to a dinner which was to be given to the victors on their return. In the dinner tent one is saying, ' Friends, I think you had better come and sit down, for if we wait till the *Chesapeake* comes back, I am afraid the dinner will be cold.' Another replies, ' Why, I don't think they will want much dinner, for they seem to have got their Belly full.'

On the 21st of June, near the town of Vittoria, the Allied forces under Lord Wellington, attacked the French Army under Joseph Bonaparte, aided by Marshal Jourdain, and gained a most complete victory ; having driven them from all their positions, and taken from them 151 pieces of cannon, 415 waggons of ammunition, all their baggage, provisions, cattle, treasure, &c., and a large number of prisoners. On the 5th and 6th of July there were brilliant and general illuminations in London in celebration of this victory. Much mischief was done by fireworks being let off in the streets, but at Bow Street, fifty people were punished for so doing, and very properly too, one man at least, who for the sake of throwing his squibs with surer aim, attached to each of them a leaden weight, of weight sufficient, it was believed, to kill a man, if it had struck him on the head.

On the 20th of July there was a grand public fête at Vauxhall, in honour of the same event, which commenced with a dinner at 5 p.m., the Duke of York presiding, accompanied by all his brothers, except the Prince Regent. At this dinner was shown Marshal Jourdain's *baton*, which was picked up on the field of battle by a sergeant of the 87th Regiment. Then the gardens were illuminated on a scale of

Geo. Cruikshank.

BRITISH VALOUR AND YANKEE BOASTING.

7—2

grandeur never before attempted, bands played, the visitors promenaded, and there were three displays of fireworks, and the whole closed with dancing, the company not separating until 2 a.m. Numbers of tickets for the evening fête, not including the dinner, were sold at from three to ten guineas each.

On the 1st of July, at Tunbridge Wells, died a curious character, William Huntingdon (his proper name being Hunt), S. S., 'Sinner Saved,' as he delighted to call himself, Minister of the Gospel at Providence Chapel, Gray's Inn Lane. Born in the Weald of Kent, of very poor parents, he had a rough early life, as errand boy, labourer, and cobbler. Then he was 'saved,' and began preaching, first at Thames Ditton, then in London, at Margaret Street Chapel, and, by the power of faith and prayer, he finally built the Chapel of Providence. In his 'Bank of Faith' he tells his reader somewhat of the commencement of this Chapel :—

' I will now inform my reader of the kind providence of my God at the time of building the Chapel, which I named Providence Chapel (1788): and also mention a few free-will offerings which the people brought. They first offered about eleven pounds, and laid it on the foundation at the beginning of the building. A good gentleman, with whom I had but little acquaintance, and of whom I bought a load of timber, sent it in with a bill and receipt in full, as a present to the Chapel of Providence. Another good man came with tears in his eyes and blessed me, and desired to paint my pulpit, desk, &c., as a present to the Chapel. Another person gave me half-a-dozen chairs for the Vestry ; and my friends Mr. and Mrs. Lyons furnished me with a tea-chest well stored, and a set of china. My good friends Mr. and Mrs. Smith furnished me with a very handsome bed, bedstead, and all its furniture and necessaries, that I might not be under the necessity of walking home in the cold winter nights. A daughter of mine in the faith gave me a looking-glass for my chapel study. Another friend gave me my pulpit cushion and a bookcase for my study. Another gave me a bookcase for the vestry. And my good friend Mr. E. seemed to level all his displeasure at the devil ; for he was in hopes I should be enabled, through the gracious arm of the Lord, to cut Rahab in pieces ; therefore he furnished me with a sword of the Spirit—a new Bible, with Morocco binding and silver clasps !'

His preaching was of a decidedly ' Revivalist ' type ; but his enthusiasm doubtless reclaimed to order and decency many of the lower classes. He mingled his religion with much worldliness, and he married Lady Sanderson (the widow of Sir James Sanderson, Bart., Lord Mayor of London), who was a constant attendant at his chapel, by which he became possessed of a considerable addition to his property. After the demolition of his Chapel in Margaret Street, the wealthier portion of his congregation proposed to build him another ; and accordingly erected a Chapel in Gray's Inn Lane, at an expense of £9,000. A day was appointed for opening it ; but he refused to officiate in it at all, until it should be made his own personal freehold : and, so great was the devotion of his followers, they resigned their shares in his favour.

He had a nice house at Pentonville, and it was there that his effects were sold on the 24th of September. All his disciples wanted some personal relic of him, and the consequence was, that the goods fetched fancy prices. As an instance, an old arm-chair, intrinsically worth about fifty shillings, fetched sixty guineas, and other articles in like proportion. There were several caricatures of this auction, but they afford neither profit nor amusement to the modern reader.

CHAPTER X.

Russia was an Ally against Napoleon, worth courting, and,
consequently, the Emperor was made a Knight of the Garter.
The Mission that was sent out to invest him was splendidly
appointed. The King of Arms had a new tabard, robes, &c.,
and he, and all his suite, had new carriages especially built for
the occasion. They took out with them the Statute passed
at the last Chapter, authorizing the election of the Emperor
as a member of the Order, with the Great Seal of England in
a gold box and blue velvet case ; and also the proceedings of
the Election, similarly garnished. They took out a complete
set of habiliments, decorations, and ornaments, necessary for
his investiture, and, as my readers may not know what was
then necessary for turning out a respectable and regulation
Knight of the Garter, I transcribe them.

Shoes of white kid, ornamented with silver lace and roses.

Stockings and pantaloons of white silk, manufactured for
the purpose, in one.

The Jacket, or Doublet, and trunk, of rich white silver
tissue, ornamented with silver lace, in imitation of point lace.

A sword with gold hilt, the belt and scabbard covered with
rich crimson velvet.

A surcoat of rich Crimson Velvet.

A large silver lace rosette for the right knee.

The Installation Garter, richly embroidered, for the left knee.

A superb mantle of Garter blue Velvet, lined with white
lustring : the badge of the Order richly embroidered. The

mantle is fastened on the neck with blue and gold rope, with two long rich tassels.

A hood of Crimson Velvet, which is worn on the right shoulder.

The gloves, white kid, trimmed with very broad silver lace.

A Spanish hat of black velvet, with a beautiful large plume of Ostrich and Heron's feathers.

The splendid Gold Collar of the Order, with the medal of St. George, to hang on the breast, with large bunches of broad white ribbons and rosettes.

Two Stars of the Order richly embroidered.

Flowing ringlets of hair, with a bunch of white ribbons to tie them.

This latter item shows how minutely the Emperor's outfit was provided. It was an age of wigs—and the Emperor's close, military cut hair, was not *en régle.*

Another event, which people talked about, at the time, was the death, on the 11th of August, of Henry James Pye, Poet Laureate, aged 69. He was the son of a Country gentleman, and was educated at Magdalen College, Oxon. After his father's death he lived at Faringdon, was made J.P., held a Commission in the Militia, and, in 1784, was elected M.P. for his County. His circumstances becoming involved, he had to sell his paternal estate. In 1790 he was made Poet Laureate, and, in 1792, was appointed one of the Magistrates for Westminster. He was not very remarkable as a poet, and, probably, his best read poems were 'Faringdon Hill,' and 'The Progress of Refinement.'

There were several candidates for the honour of being his successor, including Sir Walter Scott. There is a little epigram concerning two of them, worth repeating—

'Croker and Wharton are *roasted* so dry
　　By every *impartial* Review,
That, combined, they would make but a bad kind of stew,
　　But, certainly, never a—Pye.'

The choice eventually fell on Robert Southey (Nov. 29, 1813).

During the year we hear occasionally of the French Prisoners. On the 14th of April, two of them, on board the *Samson,* prison ship, of which we have heard before, in connection with a traitor being tattooed, fought a duel, and one was killed. Having no swords, they used two sticks, on the end of each of which was fastened a pair of scissors. The duel was meant to be *à l'outrance*, for one received a mortal wound in the stomach, from which his bowels protruded, yet he still fought on as long as he could. The prisoners, at last, applied to the ship's surgeon, who sewed up the wound, but the man died very shortly afterwards.

There must have been a bad lot on board that ship *Samson*, for we read :—

'July 19. A most diabolical conspiracy has been charged to have been formed on board the *Samson* prison ship, at Gillingham Reach, by three French prisoners, to murder the master's mate, and the sergeant of marines, belonging to the ship, together with several of their own countrymen. The murders were to have been perpetrated on each victim singly, as opportunities presented : when the escape of the murderer, by mixing instantly with the great body of the prisoners, was to be facilitated by the other conspirators, and lots were drawn who should commit the first murder.

'The first lot fell to Charles Mansereaux ; but this man, being troubled by some compunctious visiting of conscience, on reflecting that the sergeant was a married man, with a family, who would be left destitute by his death, determined to despatch one of the private marines in his stead. On Tuesday se'n-night, when this wretch was watching for an opportunity to effect this purpose, Thomas King, a private marine, came on the forecastle, when Mansereaux stepped behind him, and plunged a knife into his back, which passed through the kidneys, and inflicted a dreadful wound, of which the poor fellow lingered till Saturday morning, when he expired. Mansereaux was observed by a fellow prisoner, who instantly knocked him down, and secured him, or he would, probably, have escaped without being detected. Mansereaux on being confined, made a discovery of the whole plan, and named his associates, both of whom were standing by at the time of the murder.' The three prisoners were at once secured, but I fail to trace their fate.

On the 22nd of September, three French prisoners escaped, and murdered a boatman, and the story is thus told in the *Hants Courier* :—

'Three French prisoners, François Relif, Jean Marie Dantz, and Daniel Du Verge, having effected their escape from Forton depôt, engaged the wherry of the above-named George Brothers, to take them to Ryde. When off the Block-house, (according to their own assertions), they proposed

to the boatman to take them to France, promising ample
reward, and liberty to return immediately; but he, not to be
corrupted by promises or reward, resisted their proposition,
and, in consequence, they stabbed him in sixteen places,
(three of which were mortal,) and threw him overboard.

'The Frenchmen immediately directed their course to sea,
and were promptly pursued by several wherries, in one of
which were Lieut. Sullock, and three seamen of the *Centaur*,
at anchor at Spithead. In consequence of a heavy swell, and
bad management, the Frenchmen were overtaken, after a run
of about 15 miles; one of the men belonging to the *Centaur*
leaped into the wherry among the Frenchmen alone, armed
with nothing but the stretcher, with which he knocked one
of them down : they then surrendered.

'They were taken on board the *Centaur* for the night, and,
on being searched, a large sum of money was found about
them in silver, and three knives; one of them was very
bloody; and on Thursday morning they were delivered into
the hands of the civil power, and landed at the sally-port.
They were taken to the Borough Gaol, when they were again
examined. They confessed that Brothers was killed by two
of them, but that the third was no further concerned than in
lending his knife to the other, when the waterman resisted
them. More money was here taken from them, one having,
actually, concealed in his pantaloons under his boots (*sic*)
thirty-three 5s. 6d. pieces. It appears that, by the manufacture of lace, toys, &c., the prisoners accumulated a sufficient sum of money to procure a suit of genteel clothes each,
(besides the sums taken from their persons), dressed in which
they mingled with the crowd of visitors that were walking in
the depôt, eluding by their metamorphosed appearance the
vigilance of the turnkeys and military sentinels.' What
ultimately became of them I cannot find out, but, doubtless,
two were hanged.

The period of Captivity for these Prisoners of War was
drawing to a close, for Napoleon's power was waning fast, and
the reverses which he experienced at the hands of the Allies
at Leipsic on October 16th, 17th, 18th, 19th may be considered as having determined his final overthrow. The News
was told in England in a *London Gazette extraordinary*, of
November 3rd, and, on the 5th and 6th, London was
brilliantly illuminated.

'Everywhere, except opposite Somerset House, there was

the most perfect decorum and order, the crowds, both on foot, and in carriages, passed along without the slightest annoyance ; but, in the Strand, the old disgraceful nuisance of scattering dirt and crackers, and throwing every species of combustible at females, and into carriages, was practised the whole evening.'

Looking at the list of Illuminations, they were not very grand, when judged by our standard ; but there was one transparency shown at Ackermann's Repository of Arts, which, although very grisly and grim in its conception, was of decidedly artistic merit. It was called 'The Two Kings of Terror,' and I have here reproduced a portion of it. The

PART OF TRANSPARENCY AT ACKERMANN'S.

(*November* 5-6, 1813, *in honour of the victories of the Allies at Leipsig, &c.*)

whole composition is thus contemporaneously described : ' A design representing Buonaparte sitting upon a drum, in a field of battle, his hands under his chin, his elbows on his knees ; opposite is seated Death upon a dismounted cannon, in the same position, his elbows upon his knees, "staring the tyrant in the face ;" his right foot has crushed the insolent French trophy, the *ci devant* invincible French eagle, his left rests upon a cannon ball. In the background is seen the French legions, filled with dismay, flying before the conquering Germans, Russians, Prussians, and Swedes. The whole was surmounted by an emblematic Circle, indicative of Union and Strength, which was lighted by gas, and of dazzling brightness.'

In October Bavaria joined the Allies. In November a revolution took place in Holland ; the people of Amsterdam rose in a body, and hoisted the Orange Colours, and, with the ancient cry of 'ORANGE BOVEN' (Orange in the ascendant, or victorious) proclaimed the sovereignty of that house. The example of the Capital was followed by the other principal towns of Holland ; which the French troops were compelled to evacuate.

The Prince of Orange was in England, the sure asylum of unfortunate Royalty, and on the 21st of November a deputation came to London from Holland, inviting him to return. On the 28th he embarked at Deal for Holland, on board the *Warrior*, of 74 guns, and landed at Scheveningen on the 30th. The Dutch, having thrown off the French yoke, were no longer our enemies, so that we had no further reason for keeping any of that Nation as Prisoners of War, and they, amounting to 10,000 in number, were ordered to be sent back to their own country, to assist in liberating it from the domination of France. On the 2nd of December the Prince of Orange made his solemn entry into Amsterdam, when he declared his acceptance of the sovereignty, and the title of Sovereign Prince of the United Netherlands.

The *entente cordiale*, which thus, of necessity, sprung up between the English and Dutch, among other things produced the illustration overleaf, wherein is shown an English and a Dutch Sailor fraternizing. Above them, is a label 'Fendracht maakt Magt.' (*Concord makes Power*), and 'The Sea is Open, Trade revives.'

On the 1st of December the Allied Sovereigns issued a declaration at Frankfort, in which they affirmed that they did not make war upon France, but against the preponderance exercised by the Emperor Napoleon beyond the limits of his empire ; that the first use they made of victory was to offer him peace upon conditions founded on the independence of the French Empire, as well as on that of the other States of Europe ; that they desired that France might be great, powerful, and happy, and that they confirmed to the French Empire an extent of territory which France, under her kings, never knew ; that, wishing, also, to be free, tranquil, and happy themselves, they desired a state of peace, which, by a just equilibrium of strength might preserve their people from

'THE SEA IS OPEN, TRADE REVIVES.'
(*Published December* 13, 1813, *Ackermann.*)

the calamities which had overwhelmed Europe, for the last twenty years; and that they would not lay down their arms until they had obtained this beneficial result. But, either this declaration was only meant as a political display, or else they entirely misjudged Napoleon's character, when they imagined they could put bounds to his ambition, and dictate terms to him who had had all Europe at his feet—so nothing came of it.

The American War still went on. Madison was again elected President. At the commencement of the year the Americans attacked Canada direct. General Winchester attacked and took Detroit, but the English, under Colonel Proctor, with 500 regulars and militia, and about 600 Indians, advanced against him, the result being, that half his men surrendered at discretion, and the other half were nearly all cut to pieces by the Indians.

On the other hand, the Americans captured and held possession of York, the Capital of Upper Canada, seated on Lake Ontario. Henceforth, the war was principally confined this year to the Lakes, with varying fortunes, until we hear from Sir G. Provost, on the 12th of December, that both provinces of Canada were freed from the invaders, who re- tired to winter quarters. This war was, occasionally, con- ducted on curious principles, as the following will show. It is taken from the general orders issued by the Commander of the British Forces at Montreal, dated October 27th. The facts stated are, that 23 Soldiers of the United States Infantry, being made prisoners, were sent to England, and kept in close confinement, as British subjects; that General Dearborn had been instructed to put into similar confinement 23 British soldiers as hostages for the safety of the former; that the Prince Regent had given directions to put in close confine- ment 46 American Officers, and non-commissioned Officers to answer for the safety of the last 23 soldiers; and, also, to apprize General Dearborn, that if any of them should suffer death in consequence of executing the law of Nations upon the first 23 confined as British subjects, double the number of the confined American Officers should immediately be selected for retaliation; and, moreover, that the commanders of his Majesty's armies and fleets had received orders to prosecute the war with unmitigated severity against all the cities, towns, and villages of the United States, in case their Government should persist in their intention of retaliation.

The Princess Charlotte was, naturally, a prominent subject for conversation among all ranks, for she was the only child of the Regent, and, as such, heir-presumptive to the throne. She began, too, to make herself talked about a little. She was now in her seventeenth year, on the completion of which she would become of age, and she began to kick over the traces somewhat, and to show that she had a will of her own. Her childhood had not been a happy one, and she had served as a shuttlecock with which papa and mamma had played many a game. She had a mother whom she seldom saw, and a father whose habits were the reverse of domestic; she knew, perfectly well, what her future prospects were, and occasionally she showed a little temper and wilfulness.

In January, 1813, her governess, Lady de Clifford resigned her office, and Miss immediately wrote a letter, through the Queen, to her papa, saying that now she was old enough to do without a governess, and desiring that whoever should be appointed to be about her person, in the place of Lady de Clifford, should occupy the position of a lady of the bed-chamber, and not that of *gouvernante*. The Queen, the Prince Regent, and the Lord Chancellor took sweet counsel together on the subject, and their unanimous opinion was that Mademoiselle must still continue in *statu pupillari*, at all events until she came of age. The young lady was rebellious, but the higher authorities were too strong for her, and, with many sighs, she had to give in, and accept the inevitable in the shape of the Duchess of Leeds as governess.

In January, too, her mother, the Princess Caroline, wrote a very long letter to the Prince Regent, in which she animadverted very strongly on the manner in which her daughter was being brought up, especially in her being debarred from all social intercourse with young ladies of her own age. The history of this letter is interesting, as showing the relations existing between this unhappy husband and wife. The story is thus told :—*

'It is curious to trace the manner in which this celebrated letter at last reached the hands for which it was destined.

'It was transmitted, on the 14th of January, to Lord Liverpool, and Lord Eldon, sealed, by Lady Charlotte

* 'Memoirs of her late Royal Highness, Charlotte Augusta Princess of Wales,' &c., by Robert Huish, Esq., London, 1818, p. 68.

Campbell, the lady in waiting for the Month, expressing her Royal Highness's pleasure that it should be presented to the Prince Regent, and there was an open Copy for their perusal.

'On the 15th, the Earl of Liverpool presented his Compliments to Lady Charlotte Campbell, and returned the letter unopened.

'On the 16th, it was returned by Lady Charlotte, intimating, that, as it contained matters of importance to the State, she relied on their laying it before his Royal Highness. It was again returned unopened, with the Earl of Liverpool's compliments to Lady Charlotte, saying that the Prince saw no reason to depart from his determination.

'On the 17th, it was returned in the same way by command of her Royal Highness, expressing her confidence, that the two noble lords would not take upon themselves the responsibility of not communicating the letter to his Royal Highness, and that she should not be the only subject in the empire, whose petition was not permitted to reach the throne. To this, an answer was given, that the contents of it had been made known to the Prince.

'On the 19th, her Royal Highness directed a letter to be addressed to the two noble Lords, desiring to know whether it had been made known to his Royal Highness, by being read to him, and to know his pleasure thereon.

'No answer was given to this letter; and, therefore, on the 26th, she directed a letter to be written, expressing her surprise that no answer had been given to her application for a whole week.

'To this an answer was received, addressed to the Princess; stating that in consequence of her Royal Highness's demand, the letter had been read to the Prince Regent on the 20th, but that he had not been pleased to express his pleasure thereon.

'Here the correspondence closed; and no ulterior benefit accrued from it to the afflicted mother, nor to the daughter.'

The Princess Charlotte, however, did see more of Society, for she went to the Splendid Fête given by her father, at Carlton House, on the 5th of February, in honour of her Majesty's birthday, and at the ball which followed she danced with her uncle, the Duke of Clarence, afterwards William IV. Then she went to the Opera with the Duchess of York, and she also kept her birthday with great festivities, but she was not presented at Court, as she was resolute in being presented by no one except her mother.

In February, Warwick House was allotted to her, as a residence, and all her baggage, saddle horses, &c., were removed thither. Here, however, her mother was forbidden to visit her, and the chronicles of the times dilate strongly on an accidental meeting of the mother and daughter in Hyde Park, where they drew their respective carriages close together, and embraced each other through the windows, conversing together for some ten minutes.

When her maternal grandmother, the Duchess of Brunswick died, her father hinted to her the propriety of a visit to her mother, leaving it to her whether it should be before or after the funeral. Needless to say, but very few hours elapsed before she, accompanied by the Duchess of Leeds, and Miss Knight, were at Blackheath, where the Princess of Wales then lived.

She was now a young woman, and would be of age early next year, so it was time to look about for a husband for her; and the person pitched upon was none other than the Prince of Orange, whom we have lately seen as going back to Amsterdam, to enjoy his own again. At this time he was serving in Spain as *aide-de-camp* to Lord Wellington; but it was represented to him that there were other things for him to do, and he quitted the seat of war, and came over to England, possibly rejoicing in the anticipation of the good things coming to him; and on the 14th of December, he was formally introduced at Warwick House, by the Prince Regent, to the Princess Charlotte, whom he was expected to woo and win. His suit and its success belong to 1814, and will be told in its place.

Of the condition of the poor old King, this year, we hear very little; the monthly bulletins were certainly issued, but they were of the most meagre description. Madame d'Arblay, even, although she was over here, and had the best of opportunities for hearing about him, only mentions him once, in her letters to her father, in May:—

'The beloved King is in the *best state possible* for his present melancholy situation: that is, wholly free from bodily suffering, or imaginary mental misery, for he is persuaded that he is always conversing with Angels.'*

* 'Memoirs, vol. vii. p. 6.

CHAPTER XI.

A Cat in a Conflagration—Scramble for Exchequer Bills—A Matrimonial Dispute—An old Debtor—A Volunteer Dinner—A Man and Hedgehog—Torpedoes—Slavery—Gambling on Napoleon's Life—Gas Lighting.

AND now to wind up the year with a little *de omnibus rebus,* which would not fall into any particular place, yet are worth keeping, as indicative of the times of which I write : they have no connection with each other, so are taken in chronological order.

On the 4th of April, a fire broke out at the 'Commercial Hall,' Skinner Street, Newgate Street, the Hall which, valued at £25,000, was the capital prize in the City Lottery. It was a bad fire, and two firemen were injured, but no lives lost. When at its fiercest, a Cat was seen on a part of the buildings which would soon inevitably be in flames. There was no human being to be burnt, so the sympathy of the crowd went out towards Pussy. There was no way of escape for her, except by an alarming leap, for the walls had crumbled and fallen in, and this leap Pussy could not make up her mind to take. The flames were encroaching, and gathering round her, and the mental tension of the Crowd was getting tighter and tighter every minute, when a gentleman enthusiastically offered £5 to anyone who would rescue the Cat. A fireman was induced to make the attempt, and with great difficulty got behind the Cat, and forced her to take the leap, from the fifth storey, when she fell into the midst of the spectators unhurt ! The fireman immediately received his promised reward.

The following scene, of ' hastening to be rich,' is almost on a par with what might be witnessed in the time of John Law and the South Sea Bubble, or that of King George (Hudson)

of Railway fame.   It is thus recorded in the *Annual Register* :
' April 7 : This morning, as early as five o'clock, a crowd of
brokers and others, beset the Exchequer-bill office, in order
to put down their names for funding Exchequer Bills.   Such
was the scramble to get in, that a number of the persons were
thrown down, and many of them injured ; some fainted by the
excessive pressure of the crowd, and a few had their coats
literally torn off their backs.   The first 14 names (chiefly
bankers) subscribed seven millions out of the twelve required ;
and, very early in the day, notice was given that the subscription was full. . . . That the first characters in the country,
as bankers, merchants, and others, are to be marshalled by
police officers, exhorted to be patient, cool, and passive, till
they can enter the Exchequer through a door, a third part
opened by a chain, and of which the aperture is scarcely
sufficient for a moderate sized man to get in, is disgraceful in
the extreme.'

(*Ibid.*) April 11th : ' For the first time this season nine
Mackerel were brought to the beach at Brighton, which were
immediately purchased for the London Market at 6s. 6d. each.
The following day, another boat arrived with 28 more, which
were bought with equal avidity at the same price.   On
Thursday, a third boat brought 93, which fetched after the
rate of £40 per hundred.   Not a single Mackerel has been
retailed there, but all have been sent off to the metropolis.'

At the Quarter Sessions held at Truro early in May a
certain Joseph Little was placed at the bar, charged with
having violently assaulted his wife.   When Mrs. Little
appeared to give evidence against her turbulent mate, he
addressed her in a plaintive tone, and the following dialogue
took place :—·

' My dear, I am sorry to see you here.'

' So am I.'

' I hope you will forgive me this once, and I will never lift
my hand to you again.'

' You have broke your promise so often that I cannot trust
you.'

' My dear life, don't send me back to prison again; you have
always been a good, honest, sober, and virtuous wife to me.'

' It is for the good of your soul that you should be
punished.'

' You need not fear me, I will give you all my property, and
part from you, if you wish it.'

' I know it is for my safety, and for your salvation, that you should be confined a little longer.'

And after this billing and cooing, John Little brought a counter charge of assault against his wife, and was ultimately bound over to keep the peace.

One would have thought that the great age of the under-mentioned debtor would have protected him from his ruthless creditor, who, however, was no gainer by his act.   May 13th : ' A few days since, a poor infirm man, aged 103, from York-shire, was delivered into the custody of the Marshal of the King's Bench, for a debt of *Twenty Pounds ! !* The poor man's appre-hensions were so great on entering the prison, that he was seized with a sudden and violent illness, which induced the Marshal, on a representation of the case, to have him removed to a comfortable apartment in Belvidere Place ; but, notwith-standing every alleviation which humanity could suggest, was promptly administered, he expired the same evening.'

Next ' silly season ' — London Newspapers please copy : ' July 21 : On Saturday se'nnight was pulled, in the garden of Mr. Jones, at Lodge-my-Loons, a little north from Glasgow, a strawberry, which weighed fully one ounce, and measured 6½ inches by 5.'

Our Volunteer officers grumble somewhat at the expenses contingent upon their position, but they had a harder time of it under the Regency.   August 14th : ' At Lincoln Assizes an action was tried, brought by the Landlord of the Bull Inn, at Market Deeping, against the Cornet of the Ness Volunteers for the expenses of a dinner and liquor for 54 of the corps. The party sat down to dinner about half-past four o'clock, and mostly retired before ten.   The quantity of liquor charged was as follows : *One hundred and twenty-six bottles of port, forty-eight of sherry, sixty-four half-crown bowls of punch, and twenty of negus, besides ale and porter.*   The Jury gave a verdict in favour of the innkeeper, only taking off sixpence per bottle on the port wine.'

Have we yet forgotten ' Brummy ' and the ' Man and Dog fight ' so graphically described in *The Daily Telegraph* by Mr. James Greenwood ?   Here is a variation on the brutal theme. October 25th : ' W. Moore of Loughborough, bricklayer, a few days ago, laid a wager of three shillings, that he could, with his hands tied behind him, *worry to death* a hedgehog, with his face.   He commenced his extraordinary undertaking by prostrating himself on the ground, and attacking the exterior of his prickly antagonist with his nose. In a few minutes his face was covered with blood, and he appeared to have little chance of success ; however, at length having pressed the little animal till it had protruded its head, he snatched at it, and bit it off, thereby winning the wager, to the great amusement of the brutal spectators.'

Another illustration of there being nothing new under the sun, is that Torpedoes were known early in the Century, nay, even before that. *The Morning Chronicle* of October 29th has an article upon them, part of which I transcribe :—

'AMERICAN TORPEDOES.

'Much abuse has been heaped on the American Government for endeavouring, in their present contest with this country to avail themselves, for the destruction of English vessels, of submarine machines disgraceful to humanity, and contrary to the laws of war ; and it has been said that such machines would only have been encouraged in a Jacobin State, with a Jacobin president at its head. We are far from approving the introduction into warfare of any such machinery as that in question. But, while we deliver this opinion we think it but fair to state what is not so generally known ; that, in the encouragement of this disgraceful plan, we are as much concerned as the Americans.

'In 1804 Robert Fulton, styling himself an American citizen, was invited by Lord Liverpool, then Lord Hawkesbury, to this country, to show his Majesty's ministers his plans of submarine navigation and attack ; and on the 20th of July that year, he entered into a contract with Mr. Pitt and Lord Melville, the principal conditions of which were—

'"His Majesty's Dockyards and Arsenals to make and furnish all such articles as may be required, which are applicable to this purpose.

'"If any circumstance should arise to prevent Government carrying this plan into execution, then the parties are to name two commissioners, for the purpose of examining the principles, and trying such experiments as they may think proper ; and, if it should appear to the majority of the members, that the plan is practicable, and offers a more effectual mode of destroying the enemy's fleets at Boulogne, Brest, or elsewhere, than any mode in practice, and with less risk, then Government is to pay the said Robert Fulton, forty thousand pounds, as a compensation for demonstrating the principles, and making over the entire possession of his submarine mode of attack."

'When the Administration, of which Mr. Fox, and Lords Grey and Grenville were at the head, came into office, they were a good deal surprised, on Mr. Fulton's claiming performance of this contract, to find that such an instrument actually was in existence. The plan would never have met with any encouragement from that Administration ; but, as it had already been accepted, they were under the necessity of agreeing to allow the necessary experiments to be made, or paying the forty thousand pounds. Earl Grey, then at the head of the Admiralty, gave orders, reluctantly enough, that Mr. Fulton should be supplied with whatever he required as necessary for the success of his experiment, and the execution was entrusted to one of the ablest and most enterprising officers of the Navy. Several attempts were made on the enemy's vessels at Boulogne ; but from one circumstance or other, the plan was found impracticable. On Mr. Fulton's still insisting on the payment of the forty thousand pounds, the matter was submitted to four arbitrators, who, after a full investigation, pronounced the plan not so far *novel, practical, or effective,* as to entitle Mr. Fulton to the sum in question.'

The Slave Trade Bill of 1807, it must be remembered, did not *abolish* Slavery, but only prohibited the Traffic in Slaves ; so that no vessel should clear out from any port within the British Dominions, after May 1, 1807, with Slaves on board, and that no Slave should be landed in the Colonies after March 1, 1808. So that the following advertisement in *The Morning Chronicle* of November 16th was strictly within the bounds of legality :—

'JAMAICA SLAVES to be Let or Sold, being Fifty-four in Number, all young or middle-aged, of both sexes, and well seasoned, having for some years worked together in the parish of Clarendon. Any purchaser with good security would have every reasonable indulgence for his payments.'

I am bound to say that this advertisement was a novelty in an English Newspaper ; and in the same journal of November 19th, appeared an indignant letter on the subject.

'SIR,—Nothing can be more repugnant to the feelings of Englishmen, than to read in an English Newspaper, peculiarly devoted to the cause of Freedom, the advertisement which appeared in the first page of Tuesday's *Chronicle*, relative to the offer of " Fifty-four Jamaica Slaves." Surely, Sir, this offensive advertisement must have been inserted without due consideration, and, I am sure, *without your knowledge ;* especially at the time when we are about to *Christianize* the whole world !

'For the sake of humanity, and the best feelings of every true Briton, I trust that this abominable advertisement will not make its appearance a second time in your respectable Paper, and remain, yours, &c.,

'Libertas.'

'Among the gambling policies ever open in the city, the " life of Bonaparte " has long been a favourite object for scandalous speculations, and for the last twelve months had been *done* at from 2 to 2½ per cent. per month, as the dangers to which he was exposed seemed to diminish or increase. In the beginning of this present December, policies to a *very large amount* have been negotiated, and *Twelve Guineas* given to receive One Hundred, if the Tyrant be alive on the 1st of January.'

Gas lighting in the streets of London was first introduced in August, 1807, when Golden Lane Brewery, and a portion of Beech and Whitecross Streets were illuminated by its means. The Gaslight and Coke Company got their Charter in 1810, and had lamps outside their offices in Pall Mall ; but progress in this direction was very slow, and the old oil lamps died hard. We read in *The Morning Chronicle* of December 20th : 'The Gas lights which have been exhibited in the two Palace Yards, and in some of the streets of the neighbourhood, during the sitting of Parliament, will, upon its adjournment, be discontinued ; and those places only be lighted, for which the Company has contracts.'

CHAPTER XII.

1814.

THE year 1814 was an *annus mirabilis* for England, as will be seen as it is unfolded. It began with a fog, not an ordinary fog, but one which, from its exceptional character, was enshrined as part of the history of the Country. It prevailed in London, and many miles round, during the whole of the last week of 1813 until the 4th of January, when it cleared off—the mails and other conveyances were delayed, and many accidents happened. It was no respecter of persons, for the Regent, who was going to visit the Duke of Rutland at Belvoir, in order to stand personally as Godfather to the baby Marquis of Granby, was delayed a day by this fog, so that the Christening had to be postponed, and the young Marquis had to be a day longer in an unregenerate state.

A dragoon, who left London for Windsor at 6 p.m. with particulars of the passage of the Nive by the Allied Armies, did not arrive until 4 a.m. in consequence of the fog, although he got a lanthorn and candle at Hounslow. A sergeant of the West Kent Militia, which corps was then garrisoning the Tower, stepped off the wharf into the river, and was drowned —and there were other fatalities.

Ireland was in its chronic state of bloodthirsty rebellion, as the two following paragraphs in *The Morning Chronicle* of January 1st show. 'The Barony of Lower Ormond, in the County of Tipperary, has lately manifested a spirit of wickedness unknown in that part of the country. A few nights since, the Haggards of the Rev. Edward Farmer, of Spring-mount, near Cloughjordan, of Mr. Thompson, and the Rev. Mr. Conolly, near Ballingarry, were maliciously set on fire, and totally consumed. The ruffians also posted notices that if a reward was offered, they would burn the haggards of the subscribers.'

'On the evening of the 8th instant half-past five o'clock, as George Wayland, Esqre, was going out of his house at Toureen, near Dundrum, in the County of Tipperary, accompanied by his herdsman, one of a party, who were perceived lying in wait at a short distance from the hall door, discharged a blunderbuss at him, loaded with balls and slugs, the contents of which grazed his legs and passed through his clothes. Immediately after, a servant boy of Mr. Wayland, going towards the house, was fired at by the same party, and so dreadfully wounded, that he has since died.'

The number of troops required then, as now, in Ireland, together with the fact that we had two wars on our hands, at the same time, caused stock to be taken of the available 'food for powder' remaining, and we find, according to a statistical account taken this year, that the number of men in Great Britain, capable of bearing arms, from 15 to 60 years of age, amounted to 2,744,847 ; or about four in every seventeen males.

Our Navy was a large one, on paper, for the total number of ships at the commencement of this year was 1032 (including those in ordinary, &c.) : of which there were, in commission, 116 sail of the line, 20 from 50 to 44 guns, 157 frigates, 110 sloops of war, 7 fire-ships, 199 brigs, 40 cutters, and 50 schooners, the total of ships in commission being 768.

The Regent set out on his journey to Belvoir Castle, having, of course, to do the distance in his travelling carriage. At Denton, he was met by some two or three hundred horsemen, the gentry and yeomanry of the County, who had assembled to welcome him to Belvoir. On the arrival of the Prince, the air was rent with a general burst of loyal enthusiasm. Many females, wives and daughters of the tenantry of the House of Rutland, joined in the cavalcade, and galloped like lunatics to keep up with the Regent's carriage. Arrived at Belvoir, on the descent from his carriage of the 'vir illustrissimus,' a Royal salute of 21 guns was fired from the Castle, and the Regent's *âme damnée*, the Duke of York, also was similarly honoured.

It was with great difficulty and much persuasion, that the good folk of Rutlandshire were prevented from making greater asses of themselves, and debasing themselves by removing the horses from the Royal Carriage, and transforming themselves into beasts of draught.   The honoured host, of course, was at the door to receive his guest, and the Rev. Dr. Staunton, by virtue of the tenure of a Manor of Staunton, in Nottingham-shire, did his *devoir*, suit, and service, by presenting the Regent, as representative of the King, with an exquisitely worked gold key of Staunton tower, which is an outwork, and yet the chief stronghold of the Castle, the command of which is held by the family of Staunton, and the tenure by which they held the Manor of Staunton is, that they were formerly required to appear, with soldiers, to defend this strong post, in case of danger, or at the requisition of the Lord of the Castle.

January 4th, the day of the christening of the little Marquis of Granby, was also the birthday of his father, the Duke of Rutland, so that the two events, combined with the Royal visit, made an event of unexampled rarity in the annals of Rutlandshire.   Whenever was babe received into the fold of Christ, under more illustrious mundane auspices?   His two godfathers were the Prince Regent and the Duke of York, *in person ;* his godmother was the Queen, represented by her Grace the Dowager Duchess of Rutland.   The Archbishop of Canterbury himself ' performed the baptismal ceremony with solemnity, and graceful expression,' and what more could be done for the child?

After this ceremony, the swine were fed.   Open house and lavish hospitality were the order of the day, and the ' piggies ' availed themselves of it.   The *grand seigneurs* sit down to dinner—and the οἱ πολλοί go to their troughs, to eat as much, and drink as much, as they possibly could.   ' At Belvoir Castle all partake of the festivities, for, although the doors are not immediately thrown open to admit improper persons, yet the tenantry, and persons of respectability have access thereto, and such is the affability and condescending amiable manners of her Grace the Duchess of Rutland, that her whole suite of rooms are open for the inspection of all ranks, and even the curiosity of seeing the young Marquis is acceded to.   Mr. Douglas, the Duke's butler, entertained the tenantry with an oval Cistern of strong punch, containing 50 gallons, when the tenantry drank " Long life to the young Marquis "—" Many returns of the day to the Duke "—and " God preserve our Noble Prince Regent." '

This latter was attired, in compliment to his host in ' the Belvoir uniform of scarlet and buff,' and, to the toast of his health, ' His Royal Highness replied with much eloquence, but evidently at first, labouring under the affection of fine feeling, and concluded by assuring the noble host, that, as long as he lived, he should never forget the respectful manner in which he had been received at Belvoir Castle.'

This hospitality went on for days ; and we read, ' The house contains more than two hundred individuals, who partake daily of the festivities.   The Cistern of punch, under the management of Mr. Douglas, administered in the Servants' Hall on Tuesday, to the household and tenantry, laid many a brave fellow prostrate.   The passages of the house reminded one of a Castle taken by storm, and the young Marquis, the Noble Host, and the Prince Regent, were toasted until articulation ceased.   Many were found the next day in the sub-terraneous passages of the Castle, with symptoms of recovering animation.   The punch was not out at 10 o'clock on Wednesday morning.

' This cistern, according to the history of the County, was filled with Cordial when John, Duke of Rutland, father of the present Duke, was born.   The silver Cistern is 16 feet in circumference, holds 60 gallons, and is a matchless piece of Workmanship.   Ale, at the rate of 21 strike to the hogshead, is now making, to be kept till the young Marquis comes of Age.'

This Saturnalia ceased on January 7th, when the Prince left on a visit to the Earl of Winchilsea at Burleigh ; but whilst in the country, he was keenly scanned by the eyes of critical sportsmen, and the result, as regards his horsemanship, is thus given :—

'LETTER FROM GENERAL T. TO J. MC.M., ESQ., IN LONDON.

> Dear Mac, we are passing our time here most gaily,
> Events by the dozen are happening daily :
> We left Burleigh the 2nd—you never were there ?
> The house stands in a quadrangle forty feet square ;
> 'Tis built on a terrace, with fine freestone walls,
> On a level 'tis said with the top of Saint Paul's.
> WINCHILSEA, you know,'s a mechanical man.
> For having it measured, he's forming a plan.

LONSDALE, you know, is a noble old fellow,
With a fine open heart, and a capital cellar,
We do just as we like, and have excellent cheer,
For guests, horses, and dogs, are all treated well here.
WALES would have a hunt, so we hunted on Monday,
In spite of the fog, and the hard frost of Sunday.
           And O ! some gentle Muse indite
              My bold, aspiring lay,
           While in hasty verse I write
           " The hunting of that day !"
Now I think on't, the task would be rather too hard,
And you'll hear it describ'd by our Treasury Bard :—
For I watch'd him all thro' the field, and I saw
He was scanning the picturesque look of a thaw,
He hated a *Fox* from the time of his birth,
And ran foul of a *Pit*, as Reynard took earth.
As for WALES, he soon staked a thorough bred mare,
His legs, arms, and chest, were all quite *militaire*.
A mere Bond Street rider, Tom Musters would say,
Sits damn'd well by rule, as I told him one day ;
He's abroad in all cases not taught in *ménage*,
And rides at a leap, as he would at a charge ;
In short, one might swear he ne'er hunted before,
By his heading the hounds, as he would do his corps ;
And YORK on the fences made desperate attack,
And was giving the *word of command* to the pack ;
Determined to give his Conscience relief,
And, for once, be in person, *Commander in Chief*.'

What a contrast was the keeping of the coming of age of
the Princess Charlotte, the heir to the throne ! which happened at the same time, on the 7th of January. ' In the
morning her Royal Highness's tutors and principal attendants
were introduced to her Royal Highness at Warwick House,
and paid their respects in due form. A number of nobility,
persons of distinction, and her private circle of friends, called
at the house, and left their respectful inquiries and congratulations on the return of the day.' She spent the remainder of the day quietly, and without fuss, with her mother,
at Connaught House.

The Regent returned from his tour in time for the Day of
Thanksgiving, 13th of January, and he attended Divine service
at the Chapel Royal, St. James's, in state. He wore ' a purple
top wrapping coat, ornamented in a most splendid manner with
gold lace, fringe, and frogs, with the Order of the Garter.'
Besides a great number of the nobility, the procession was
formed as follows : —

'The Gentlemen Ushers and Grooms in waiting.

'Six Heralds, with their superb and splendid Mantles, with other ornaments.

'Four Sergeants at Mace, with gold Maces, and their elegant Collars ; King at Arms, in his superb dress, with his sceptre of Office, Sir Isaac Heard.

'York Herald, and Genealogist of the Bath, Sir George Naylor, in his splendid dress, with the Order of the Bath.

'Windsor Herald, Francis Townsend, Esqre., also in his splendid dress and appropriate ornaments.

'The Duke of York.

'The Sword of State.

'The Prince Regent,

followed by his Lord in Waiting, &c.

'Eight of the Gentlemen Pensioners, with their Battle Axes, closed the procession.'

The phenomenal fog, which obtained at the end of 1813 and the commencement of 1814, was immediately followed by very heavy falls of snow, unprecedented in the memory of man. On one occasion it snowed incessantly for 48 hours. Few carriages could travel, and the land seemed deserted. In London, the water-pipes in houses were all frozen, and open plugs were running in the streets. Of course this water froze, and added to the general inconvenience, and the state of the streets may be judged by the following : 'Mr. Maxwell, of skating celebrity, agreed for a considerable wager, to skate from Long Acre to the Parade in St. James's Park in five minutes, which he performed with ease, ten seconds within the time, to the no small amusement of a numerous concourse of spectators.'

Coals went up to any price ; and no wonder. There were no railways, and the large inland beds of coal were only worked for local use, so that London was dependent upon Sunderland, and the north-eastern ports, for her coal supply ; and this, of course, came at once to an end with such a frost as this was. A remedy was proposed, but was never acted on. 'Supposing nine-tenths of the housekeepers of the metropolis to have laid in coals sufficient for their consumption— some to the month of June, but generally throughout the whole of the summer season—it would be an act of benevolence on their part without affecting their interest, to sell their overplus stock, at reduced prices, to the needy individuals in their respective neighbourhoods, who are unprovided with that fuel, or who can afford to supply themselves only from week to week. This, it is conceived, *might be done at 6s. 6d. or 7s. a sack, whereas double that sum is now asked.*'

The snow-drifts were terrible all over the country, and even near London, in many places, the snow drifted higher than the Coaches. On Finchley Common, in the course of one night, it drifted to a depth of sixteen feet ; on Bagshot Heath, and about Cobham and Esher, all traffic was stopped. The Kent and Essex roads were the only ones passable. From the country came worse news. The snow in the Midland Counties was very deep ; indeed at Dunchurch, a small village on the road to Birmingham, through Coventry, for a few miles round, the snow was twenty-three feet deep, and no tracks of travellers were seen for many days. The Cambridge Mail Coach was snowed up, and completely covered, for eight hours, when, at last it was dragged out by fourteen waggon-horses, the poor passengers, meanwhile, being almost frozen to death. These examples must suffice, for my space cannot accommodate anything like one hundredth part of the snow-stories of this time.

The Thames was frozen over, and upon it was held a ' Frost Fair,' which, as, owing to the greater width of the arches of the bridges which span it, it is hardly likely to occur again, I must be pardoned, if I somewhat dilate upon.

Sunday, Jan. 30.—Immense masses of ice that had floated from the upper part of the river, in consequence of the thaw on the two preceding days, now blocked up the Thames between Blackfriars and London Bridge ; and afforded every probability of its being frozen over in a day or two. Some venturous persons, even now, walked upon the ice.

Monday, Jan. 31.—This expectation was realized. During the whole of the afternoon, hundreds of people were assembled on Blackfriars and London Bridges, to see several adventurous men cross and re-cross the Thames on the Ice ; at one time seventy persons were counted walking from Queenhithe to the opposite shore. The frost on Sunday night so united the vast mass, as to render it immovable by the tide.

Tuesday, Feb. 1.—The floating masses of ice having been stopped by London Bridge, now assumed a solid surface over the river from Blackfriars Bridge to some distance below Three Crane Stairs, at the bottom of Queen Street, Cheapside. The watermen, taking advantage of this circumstance, placed notices at the end of all the streets leading to the City side of the river, announcing a safe footway over it, which, as might be expected, attracted immense crowds to witness so novel a scene.   Many were induced to venture on the ice, and the example thus afforded, soon led thousands to perambulate the rugged plain, where a variety of amusements were prepared for their entertainment.

Among the more curious of these was the ceremony of roasting a small sheep, which was toasted, or rather, burnt over a coal fire placed in a large iron pan.   For a view of this spectacle sixpence was demanded, and willingly paid.   The delicate meat when *done*, was sold at a shilling a slice, and termed Lapland Mutton.

Wednesday, Feb. 2.—The Thames now was a complete FROST FAIR.   The Grand Mall, or walk, was from Blackfriars Bridge to London Bridge.   This was named ' *The City Road,*' and was lined on both sides with booths and petty tradesmen of all descriptions.   Eight or ten printing presses were erected, and numerous pieces commemorative of the 'Great Frost' were printed on the Ice.   Many of these have come down to us ; among them are the following :

> ' Amidst the Arts which on the Thames appear,
> To tell the wonders of this *icy* year,
> PRINTING claims prior place, which, at one view,
> Erects a monument of THAT and YOU.'

> ' You that walk here, and do design to tell
> Your children's children what this year befell,
> Come, buy this print, and it will then be seen
> That such a year as this hath seldom been.'

' *Friends, now is your time to support the Freedom of the Press. Can the Press have greater liberty ?   Here you find it working in the middle of the Thames ; and if you encourage us by buying our impressions, we will keep it going in the true spirit of liberty, during the Frost.*'

> ' Behold, the River Thames is frozen o'er,
> Which, lately, ships of mighty burden bore ;
> Now, different arts and pastimes here you see,
> But printing claims superiority.'

Besides the above, the Lord's Prayer, and several other pieces were issued from these Presses, and they were bought, as mementos, with great avidity.

Thursday, Feb. 3.—More people than ever ventured on the

THE FROST FAIR.

ice. Swings, book-stalls, dancing in a barge, drinking and eating booths, skittles, knock-'em-downs, and all the appurtenances to a Fair on land were there on the Thames. The ice was strong and firm, and although there were fairly smooth parts, yet, in the main, it was very rough.

Friday, Feb. 4.—Every day brought more people, and additions to the petty merchants who vended their wares, at twice or thrice their value, because of the rarity. Any old goods could be passed off if only duly labelled 'Bought on the Thames,' 'From Frost Fair,' &c., and money was literally shovelled into their pockets, as everyone wanted some lasting reminiscence of this great Frost. The watermen mulcted all who visited the Fair, of 2d. or 3d., and you were expected to repeat the compliment on your return. They were said to have taken as much as £6 each, in the course of the day.

An ugly accident was nearly happening this day, for three persons—an old man, and two lads—having ventured on a piece of ice above London Bridge, it suddenly detached itself from the main body, and was carried by the tide through one of the arches. They threw themselves flat upon the ice for safety, and, luckily, were observed by the boatmen at Billingsgate, who, with laudable activity, put off to their assistance, and rescued them from their impending danger. One of them was able to walk, but the other two were carried, in a state of insensibility, to a public-house, where they received every attention their situation required.

Saturday, Feb. 5th.—The morning of this day augured rather unfavourably for the continuance of FROST FAIR. The wind had shifted to the south, and a light fall of snow took place. The visitors to the Thames, however, were not to be deterred by trifles. Thousands again ventured, and there was still much life and bustle on the ice.

The footpath in the centre, or '*City Road,*' was hard and secure, and thousands promenaded thereon. Gaming had now its votaries ; there were E. O. Tables, Rouge-et-Noir, Teetotums, Wheels of Fortune, Prick the Garter, &c., and a brisk business they plied in emptying the pockets of their dupes. Skittles were being played in many places, drinking tents were filled with females, and their companions, dancing reels to the sound of fiddles, while others sat round large fires, drinking rum, grog, and other spirits. There were for the more temperate, tea and coffee, and people were earnestly requested to eat, in order that in after years they might be able to say that they had indulged in a good meal in mid Thames.

The Morning Chronicle of February 4th says:—'Notwithstanding the heavy thaw of Tuesday night, an immense multitude continues to assemble between London and Blackfriars Bridges. Booths, hoisting the flags of all nations, and painted with *Cherokee* taste, everywhere gladdened the sight, while bands of Pandean minstrels, relieved by the dulcet strains of the *tin* trumpet from all sides, delighted the ear.

' In the centre of the river, a narrow stream defied the power of the frozen region, and marked the path "where once the current ran." This interruption, however, so far from impeding the gambols of the day, increased the sport, and added to the profit of the stewards of the scene. A few small planks in some cases, and an old boat or two in others, with the addition of *Charon's fare*, kept the communication entire, and enlivened the pastime.

' In some parts of the stream where the width of the unfrozen water admitted of it, boats completely bent for sail, with their full equipments, attracted the heedless throng. In these were placed food for the hungry, and for the thirsty, relief; *gin* and *gingerbread*, with *other cordials*, were here on sale, at moderate prices—" *Ubi mel—ibi apes.*" The Crowd poured toward this magnetic point with extraordinary avidity. Men, women, and children were often seen in one promiscuous heap. Although it is impossible not to feel anxious to afford every opportunity of cheering, by playful pastime, the nipping severity of the season, yet we cannot disengage our mind from the hazardous consequences of such an exhibition as we are now noticing.

' Between the bridges the river is entirely covered, not with a regular, even frozen surface, but with an incongruous accumulation of icy fragments, and congealed piled snow, which, during the partial thaws, was disengaged up the river, and wafted downwards ; this having been intercepted by the intervention of the bridges, and partially united by the frosts of the last two or three days, has completely covered the surface of the water. It is yet extremely dangerous, and was, in many places, last night, set in motion by the influx of the tide, and carried, with extreme velocity, against the piers of the bridges. Some watermen, more foolhardy than others, ventured to cross opposite Temple Gardens, and one of them nearly lost his life by the experiment. The public ought carefully to prevent the young men and thoughtless part of the community from indulging in experiments of this description, which may terminate fatally.'

Towards the evening of the 5th of February rain fell in some quantity, the ice gave some loud cracks, and large pieces were detached, and floated off with booths, printing-presses, and people on them. No lives, however, were lost. Perhaps the last thing printed on the ice was a letter:—

'To Madam Tabitha Thaw.

'Dear dissolving dame,

'FATHER FROST, and SISTER SNOW, have *boneyd* my borders, formed an *idol of ice* upon my bosom, and all the LADS OF LONDON come to make merry: now, as you love mischief, treat the multitude with a few CRACKS by a sudden visit, and obtain the prayers of the poor upon both banks. *Given at my own press*, the 5th Feby., 1814.

'THOMAS THAMES.'

The thaw had now fairly set in, the ice, broken up, swept everything in the shape of light craft, barges, &c., irresistibly before it, and damage was done to the extent of many thousands of pounds. There was some loss of life, but it was small, and altogether every one was very well rid of 'The Great Frost of 1814.' Before I finish with the subject, I must quote some verses (which, although doggerel, are very original) attached to 'A View of FROST FAIR, as it appeared on the ICE on the RIVER THAMES, February 3, 1814.'

'All you that are curious downright,
And fond of seeing every sight,
If to the Thames you had repair'd,
You might have seen a famous fair.
Diversions of every kind you'd see,
With parties drinking of coffee and tea,
And dancing too I do declare,
Upon the *Thames*, they call FROST FAIR.

It was really curious for to see
Both old and young, so full of glee,
The drinking booths they enter'd in
And call'd away for purl and gin,
Some play'd at Threadle my Needle, Nan,
The lasses slipt down as they ran,
Which made the men quite full of glee,
The young girls legs' all for to see.

The Watermen, so neat and trim,
With bottle fill'd with Old Tom Gin,
And others bawl'd among the throng,
" Who's for a Glass of Sampson strong ?"
" Here's Nuts, and Gingerbread, who buys ?"
" Come, boys, and win my Mutton Pies.
Come, ladies, they're both hot and nice,
Fear not to eat them on the Ice."

Boys and women, not a few,
Upon the Ice, they ventured too,
And swings there were, I do declare,
To take a ride up in the air.
And booths, wherein you might regale,
And have a pint of beer, or ale.
And skittle playing, I do declare,
Upon the Thames, they call Frost Fair.

Now to conclude my Icy song,
I'm glad to see the Frost is gone,
And ships, and barges, all afloat,
And watermen rowing of their boats,
Black diamond barges to appear,
That coals, they may not be so dear.
So, toss a bumper off with cheer,
And bid adieu to Frosty Fair.'

With regard to this frost, for once, Justice was rendered to
Ireland, and she shared its pleasures, with ' the bloody Saxon '
(*Gentleman's Magazine,* vol. 84, part i. p. 189) : ' So completely
suspended has been the internal intercourse between *Dublin*
and the interior, that on 17th January, no fewer than fifteen
hundred country mails were due in the Irish Capital ; and, in
consequence of the obstruction to the regular mails, arising
from the severity of the weather, the accumulated newspapers, at the Post Office, amounted to no less than *ten tons* in
weight.'

On the same page it is recorded that ' Fifty Gentlemen
dined in a tent fixed on the ice on the river *Tweed*. One of
the company was present at a similar fête held on the *Tweed*
in 1740.'

The Lords Lieutenant of the different counties had a
circular sent them from Lord Sidmouth, conveying the
Regent's wishes for their guidance in this juncture, part of
which is as follows :—

' It will be obvious to your Lordship, that the first and
immediate duty to which your attention should be directed, is

that of providing all practical means for removing from the highways and principal roads of communication lying within your Lordship's County, the obstructions which have taken place from the late heavy falls of snow, so that his Majesty's subjects may be able to traverse the same, without danger or impediment, as occasion shall require.

' The discharge of this duty is, fortunately, most compatible with the further object which his Royal Highness has anxiously in view, inasmuch as it will enable your Lordship to ensure employment for various classes of individuals, who, for the present, are deprived of their usual earnings by the inclemency of the season.

' Your Lordship will be aware of the necessity of giving immediate attention to the Prince Regent's commands on this important subject; and you will accordingly communicate, without delay, with the magistracy, and through them with the trustees of turnpike roads, the overseers of the poor, the surveyors of the highways, and other subordinate officers within the districts and parishes of the County, in such manner, as to insure the most speedy and effectual means of carrying his Royal Highness's pleasure into effect.'

After the melting of this snow, came very heavy floods in almost every part of the country.

CHAPTER XIII.

Burning of the Custom House—De Berenger's fraud on the Stock Exchange—Lord Cochrane inculpated—Price of provisions—Arrival of the Duchess of Oldenburgh—The Capitulation of Paris, and fall of Napoleon—Papa Violette—Elba.

ON the morning of Saturday, February 12th, the Custom House in London was burnt down. The first Custom House stood on the same site as the present one, and was *rebuilt* in 1385. In Queen Elizabeth's time a larger House was built on the same spot, which was burnt in the Great Fire. Wren was the architect to a new one, which was destroyed by fire in 1715. Its successor was doomed to the same fate ; its ruin was complete, and for a time it paralyzed the Commerce of the Port of London.

' The actual loss to Government by the sudden destruction of the Custom House cannot be calculated ; books, bonds, debentures, pearls, coral, valuable property of every description, and securities of all kinds have been consumed. Business is, and must be, quite at a standstill for some time ; numerous vessels ready to sail cannot clear out, and, consequently, the injury to the mercantile world will be most severe and distressing. The private property lost within the building is very considerable. We have heard of several Gentlemen who had left large sums of money in their desks, ready to make payments on the following day. One has lost upwards of £6,000 in bank notes, which will be irrecoverable, as the memorandum of the numbers was in the desk with the notes, and met the same fate.

' A very fine collection of pictures which the Commissioners had permitted a gentleman to leave in deposit, till it would be convenient for him to pay the duties, amounting to £1,500, were destroyed. A very genteel young man, in appearance, was stopped by some police officers in Thames Street, and, on searching him, his pockets and breeches were found to be stuffed with coral beads, silk handkerchiefs, and other valuables of small bulk. It appeared that his boldness in venturing nearer the gunpowder than even the firemen dared to do, had enabled him to obtain this booty.'

This month is remarkable for one of the most daring attempted frauds on the Stock Exchange ever perpetrated. It was executed by one Charles Random de Berenger, a French refugee, and an officer in one of the foreign regiments. It was alleged that with him were associated Lord Cochrane, the Hon. Andrew Cochrane Johnstone, and several others. It appears from the evidence on the trial, that early on the morning of the 21st of February, a gentleman, dressed in a grey great-coat over a scarlet uniform, on which was a star, knocked at the door of the Ship Inn at Dover, and said that he was the bearer of very important despatches from France. This gentleman, all the Witnesses swore, was Berenger.

He sent a letter signed R. Du Bourg, Lieut.-Colonel, and Aide-de-Camp to Lord Cathcart, to Admiral Foley, the Port Admiral at Dover, advising him that he had just arrived from Calais with the news of a great victory obtained by the Allies over Bonaparte, who was slain in his flight by the Cossacks, and that the Allied Sovereigns were in Paris.   Berenger posted up to London, which he entered, having his horses decked with laurels, in order to make a stir.   It was felt on the Stock Exchange.   *Omnium*, which opened at 27½, rose to 33 ; but as the day wore on, and no confirmation came of the news, they receded to 28½.   Business in that Stock was done that day to the tune of half a million of money.   Lord Cochrane and others had previously given instructions to several Stockbrokers to sell Omniums for them on the 21st of February to an enormous amount.   One deposed that on that date he sold—

> For Lord Cochrane,   £139,000 Omnium.
> „ Cochrane Johnstone, £120,000   do.
>   Do.   £100,000 Consols.
> „ Mr. Butt,   £124,000 Omnium.
>   Do.   £168,000 Consols.

And he further deposed that he always considered that any business he did for Mr. Butt was to be placed to Lord Cochrane's account.

Another Stockbroker sold for the same three gentlemen, about £565,000 Omnium. Another had sold £80,000 on their account; and yet another had had instructions to sell a very large sum for the same parties, but had refused.

In the end Lord Cochrane and Mr. Butt were condemned to pay to the King a fine of a thousand pounds each, and J. P. Holloway five hundred; and these three, together with De Berenger, Sandon, and Lyte, were sentenced to imprisonment in the Marshalsea for twelve Calendar Months. Further, Lord Cochrane, De Berenger, and Butt, were to stand on the pillory for one hour before the Royal Exchange once during their imprisonment. This latter part of their punishment was afterwards remitted. Lord Cochrane's name was struck off the Navy list, he was expelled from the House of Commons, his arms were taken down from his stall as Knight of the Bath, his banner torn down, and kicked ignominiously out of Henry VII.'s Chapel in Westminster Abbey.

By very many he was believed innocent, and, on his seat for Westminster being declared vacant, he was enthusiastically re-elected. He escaped from Custody, was captured, and had to serve his time. On June 20, 1815, he was told that his imprisonment was at an end if he would pay the fine imposed upon him; and on July 3rd he reluctantly did so with a £1,000 bank note, on the back of which he wrote :—' My health having suffered by long and close confinement, and my oppressors being resolved to deprive me of property or life, I submit to robbery, to protect myself from murder, in the hope that I shall live to bring the delinquents to justice.'

On the very day he was released, he took his seat again in the House of Commons. It is not my province to follow his life, but in 1832 he received a ' free pardon '; he was restored to the Navy List, gazetted a rear-admiral, and presented at a levée !

There is a little bit of domestic news chronicled on March 9th, which is interesting when we contrast the prices at which we are now supplied with the same commodities. ' Covent Garden Market.—The extreme severity of the weather has rendered all the fruits and vegetables of the season dear beyond all precedent. The following are the prices of some of the articles :—Asparagus, £1 4s. per hundred; Cucumbers, £1 1s. per brace; best Pines, £2 12s. each; Grapes, £3 3s. per pound; Endive, 8s. per dozen; best Broccoli, 16s. per bundle; second ditto, 7s. per ditto; French Beans, 8s. per

100 ; Mushrooms, 5s. 6d. per pottle ; best Kale, 12s. per basket ; Nonpareil Apples, 8s. per dozen ; Colmar Pears, £1 10s. per dozen ; Cos Lettuce, 4s. per dozen ; Mint, 1s. 6d. per bunch ; Greens, 16s. per dozen ; Spanish Onions, 12s. per dozen.'

This scale of prices would never have done for the Clergyman mentioned in the next day's paper. ' A Clergyman, of the name of Matheson, was minister of Patterdale, in Westmoreland, for sixty years, and died lately, at the age of ninety.   During the early part of his life his benefice brought him only twelve pounds a year ; it was afterwards increased (perhaps by Queen Anne's bounty) to eighteen, which it never exceeded.   On this income he married, brought up four children, and lived comfortably with his neighbours, educated a son at the University, and left upwards of one thousand pounds behind him.   With that singular simplicity, and inattention to forms which characterize a country life, he himself read the burial service over his mother, he married his father to a second wife, and afterwards buried him also.   He published his own banns of marriage in the church, with a woman whom he had formerly christened, and he himself married all his four children.'

On March 31st an illustrious lady, the Duchess of Olden burgh, sister to the Emperor of Russia, entered London in great state, having been met at Sheerness by the Duke of Clarence on behalf of the Regent, who sent one of his Carriages for her accommodation and use.   Ostensibly she only came to pay a complimentary visit to the Regent, but every one surmised that such was merely a blind to cover a political mission, for which she was well adapted.

To show what importance was attached to her visit, I give an official account of her reception.

'The procession entered London, by Parliament Street, at a quarter before four o'clock, in the following order :—

Two Light Horsemen.

The Duke of Clarence's travelling Chariot and four, in which were his Royal Highness and Colonel Bloomfield.

Two Light Horsemen.

Two footmen and an outrider in the Royal liveries.

' The Prince Regent's Carriage, drawn by four bays, in which was her Imperial Highness the Grand Duchess,

Duchess of Oldenburgh, accompanied by the Princess Volo-
chowsky, Madame Aladensky, and the Countess Lieven.

'At each door of the Carriage one of the Prince Regent's
footmen rode. The Carriage was followed by a party of
Light Horse.

'The third carriage was another of the Prince Regent's, in
which were the Prince Gargarine, General Turner, &c.

'The Russian Ambassador's Carriage, with his Excellency
in it, finished the procession.

'They proceeded through the Horse Guards, out at the
Stable Yard, St. James's, up St. James' Street to the
Pulteney Grand Hotel, where her Imperial Highness was
received by sentinels placed at the door for that purpose.
She was handed out of the carriage by the Duke of Clarence
and Colonel Bloomfield, who conducted her to the apartments
prepared for her.

'The Duke of Clarence took his leave, and proceeded to
Carlton House, and had an interview with his Royal brother,
the Prince Regent. He afterwards returned to her Imperial
Highness, to express the Prince Regent's congratulations on
her safe arrival in England.

'A grand dinner was given in the evening in her honour at
Carlton House. The table was laid for twenty-five covers,
and the Queen, the Princesses, the Duke and Duchess of
York, &c., were all assembled to receive her Highness.'

And now we come to the great event of the year, beside
which all other news, however important, pales, and is a
thing of nought. The fall of Napoleon, and manner of it,
hardly belongs, in a strict sense, to Social England of the
time, and yet it is so indissolubly bound up with it, that a
succinct account of it is necessary for the perfection of this
book, and, as the shortest and best contemporary narrative of
these events, that I know of, is contained in the *Annual
Register*, I use it. The French occupied the heights before
Paris—the Allies were about to storm them ; in fact, the
heights of Romainville had been carried.

'A redoubt and battery in the enemy's centre kept d' Yorck
in check for some part of the day ; but their flank being
exposed by the loss of the heights of Romainville, and their
losses in every part of the field, reduced them to the
necessity of sending a flag of truce to propose a cessation of
hostilities, on the condition of their yielding all the ground

without the barrier of Paris, till further arrangements could be made. The heights of Montmartre were at this time about to be stormed, and the village of La Villette had been carried by Woronzow's division, which was pushing on to the barrier; the Sovereigns of Russia and Prussia, and Prince Schwartzenberg, however, being desirous of saving the Capital from being sacked, most humanely agreed to the proposal: two aides-de-camp were sent to put the terms in execution; the battle ceased; and, at four in the afternoon, Count Nesselrode, the Russian Minister, went into Paris. Thus terminated this important day (March 30th), which was not without considerable loss to the Allies; but it was final.

'The Metropolis of France being thus laid prostrate at the feet of hostile armies, no determination ever occurred of greater moment, in a moral and political view, than the treatment it was to receive. Besides the lust of rapine and pillage which prevails in the mass of all military bodies, feelings of resentment for the long and atrocious injuries inflicted upon the countries of Europe, by the relentless ambition of the French ruler, must have inspired a strong feeling of retaliation: and the flames of Moscow, in particular, must have kindled in the Russian troops an impatient ardour for spreading the same destruction through the streets of Paris. So fiercely did this passion rage, that the Emperor Alexander is said almost to have descended to supplications, with the more indisciplined of his bands, to induce them to forego their vindictive purposes. But this benevolent sovereign, with his illustrious confederates, must have shuddered at the idea of involving the innocent, as well as the guilty, inhabitants of a vast city in the direst calamities. Moreover, the declarations of the Allied Powers had been filled with sentiments of goodwill towards the French Nation, the happiness, and, even, prosperity of which, they professed to have in view, as far as was compatible with the welfare of its neighbours. Mere retaliatory mischief is always ignoble, and generally unjust, since its effects cannot be limited to suitable objects. From these considerations, though we may justly praise, we cannot wonder at the pacific and conciliatory measures that were immediately adopted by the victors on this great event.

'The first important act was the capitulation which resulted from the armistice granted by the Allied Powers. Its most material articles were the evacuation of Paris, by the troops of Marmont and Mortier, at seven in the morning of the 31st, taking with them all their military appurtenances; the entire separation of the National Guard and Municipal Gendarmerie from the troops of the Line, leaving their future condition to the determination of the Allied Powers; and the relinquishment of the Arsenals, Magazines, &c., in the same state as when the Capitulation was proposed. On the same day, the entrance of the Sovereigns into Paris took place, the ceremonial of which is thus described by Sir C. Stewart: "The Cavalry, under the Grand Arch-Duke Constantine, and the guards of all the different allied forces, were formed in columns early in the morning on the road from Bondi to Paris. The Emperor of Russia with all his Staff, his Generals, and their suites present, proceeded to Pantin, where the King of Prussia joined him with a similar Cortége. These Sovereigns, surrounded by all the Princes in the Army, together with the Prince Field Marshal, and the Austrian Etat-Major, passed through the Faubourg St. Martin, and entered the barrier of Paris about eleven o'clock, the Cossacks of the Guard forming the advance of the March. Already was the crowd so enormous, as well as the acclamations so great, that it was difficult to move forward; but, before the monarchs reached the Porte St. Martin to turn on the Boulevards, there was a moral impossibility of proceeding. All Paris seemed to be assembled and concentrated in one spot; one spring evidently directed all their movements: they thronged in such masses round the Emperor and King, that, with all their condescending and gracious familiarity, extending their hands on all sides, it was in vain to attempt to satisfy the populace." In the French account it is added that, before the Chiefs of the three armies entered any house, they made their troops file off before them, to preserve discipline, and prevent disorders. They then alighted at the house of the Prince of Benevento (Talleyrand), and the Emperor of Russia issued a declaration expressing the intentions of himself and Colleagues. It affirmed that the Allied Sovereigns would no more treat with Napoleon Bonaparte, nor with any of his family; that they respected the integrity of Ancient France, as it existed under its legitimate kings, and would, perhaps, do more for it; and that they would recognize and guarantee the Constitution which France should adopt.

'On April 1st, the members of the Senate assembled in

consequence of an Extraordinary Convocation, the Prince of Benevento being President. They passed a Decree, " that there shall be established a Provisional Government, charged to provide for the wants of the Administration, and to present to the Senate the plan of a Constitution which may suit the French People." This Government was to consist of five members, who were then nominated, Talleyrand's name standing first. On the proposal of a Senator, the following Articles were voted. That the Senate and Legislative Body are integral parts of the intended Constitution: that the Army, as well as the retired officers and soldiers, shall retain the ranks, honours, and pensions they at present enjoy : that the Public Debts shall be inviolable : that the sale of the National Domains shall be irrevocable : that no Frenchman shall be responsible for the public opinions he may have expressed : that liberty of worship and conscience shall be maintained, as well as liberty of the Press, subject to legal penalties for its abuse.

'At a sitting of the Senate on the following day, a Decree passed, which, after a preamble asserting "that in a Constitutional Monarchy the Monarch exists only in virtue of the Constitution or Social Compact," proceeded to show, in a number of Articles, in what manner Napoleon Buonaparte had violated his compact with the French people ; and, as the consequence declared :

'1. That Napoleon Bonaparte had forfeited the throne, and the hereditary right established in his family is abolished.

'2. That the French people and the Army are released from their oath of fidelity towards Napoleon Bonaparte.

'3. That the present Decree shall be transmitted by a message to the Provisional Government of France, conveyed forthwith to all the Departments and the Armies, and immediately proclaimed in all the Quarters of the Capital. A similar resolution was, on the same day, adopted by the Legislative body.

'During these transactions in the Capital, Napoleon moved his army from Troyes by Sens towards Fontainbleau. He arrived at Fromont on the 30th, and would have been in Paris had it not been in the possession of the Allies. On learning what had passed, he retired to Corbeil, and thence to Fontainbleau, whence, on April 4th he sent Marshals Ney and Macdonald, and General Caulaincourt, to carry to the Senate his proposal of submitting to the decision of that body,

and of the French people, and to abdicate in favour of his
son.

' This proposition being rejected, he announced an un-
conditional abdication in the following terms : " The Allied
Powers having proclaimed that the Emperor Napoleon was
the only obstacle to the re-establishment of the peace of Europe,
the Emperor Napoleon, faithful to his oath, declares that he
renounces, for himself, and heirs, the thrones of France and
Italy ; and that there is no personal sacrifice, even that of
life, which he is not ready to make for the interests of
France." '

So fell Napoleon, deserted by all ; his valet, Constant, ran
away and robbed him of 100,000 francs ; his Mameluke,
Rustan, left him, and reaching Paris, would not accompany
his master to Elba.   Madame Junot says :

' Few persons are aware that Napoleon was doomed to death
during the few days which preceded his abdication, by a band
of Conspirators composed of the most distinguished chiefs of
the Army.

' " But," said one of them in the council in which these
demons discussed their atrocious project, " what are we to do
with him ?   There are two or three among us, who, like
Antony,* would exhibit their blood-stained robes to the
people, and make us play the part of Cassius and Brutus.   I
have no wish to see my house burned, and to be sent into
Exile."   " Well," said another, " we must leave no trace of
him.   He must be sent to heaven like Romulus."   The
others applauded, and then a most horrible discussion commenced.   It is not in my power to relate the details.   Suffice
it to say, that the Emperor's death was proposed and discussed
for the space of an hour, with a degree of coolness which might
be expected among Indian savages, armed with tomahawks.
" But," said he who had spoken first, " we must come to
some determination.   The Emperor of Russia is impatient.
The month of April is advancing, and nothing has been done.
Now, for the last time, we will speak to him of his abdication.
He must sign it definitely, or——"   A horrible gesture followed the last word.'

Baron Fain, in ' The Manuscript of 1814,' says that on the
night of the 12th of April, Napoleon attempted to kill himself by poison : all weapons of destruction having been re-

* They alluded to the Duc de Bassano, Caulaincourt, Bertrand,
and some others.

moved out of his reach, but he had kept the poison by him too long, and it had lost its virtue. It simply gave him great pain.

A treaty between the Allied Powers and Napoleon was signed on the 11th of April. By its articles, after his solemn renunciation for himself and his descendants, of the Sovereignty of France and Italy, it was stipulated that Napoleon, and Maria Louisa, should retain their rank and titles for life, and that all the branches of his family should also possess the title of Princes : that the Island of Elba should form a separate principality, to be held by him in full sovereignty and property for life ; that there should be granted to him an annual revenue of six million of francs,* with reversion of one million to the Empress, and that, to the members of his family, a revenue of two and a half millions of francs should be assigned. That the Duchies of Parma, Guastalla, and Placentia should be granted in full sovereignty to the Empress, with succession to her son and descendants. That the property possessed by Napoleon in France, as Domain, should form a capital not exceeding two millions of francs, to be expended in gratifications to persons according to a list given in by him ; that free passage should be given to all of the family, and their suites, who chose to establish themselves out of France, and an escort of 1,200 or 1,500 of the Imperial Guard to Napoleon himself, to the place of embarkation ; and that he should be allowed to take with him, and retain, 400 men, as his guard.

There were a few other Articles to the treaty which was signed by the Ministers of the Allied Powers—England dissenting and refusing signature to the assignment of Elba to Napoleon, and that of the Italian Duchies to Maria Louisa.

And so for a time he fades away, but many, very many Frenchmen thought, and spoke, lovingly of Papa Violette, and Caporal Violette, and hugged themselves with the idea ' En printemps il reviendra :' a prophecy which we know was fulfilled. Bunches of violets similar to the illustration on the opposite page were freely sold in France, and my reader

---

* There was an epigram made on this allowance—

  ' Celui qui devora de nombreux bataillons,
  Qui nagea dans le sang, qui vécut dans la crime,
    N'a de rente que six millions—
    Ce n'est pas un sou par victime.'

will find that it contains portraits of the Emperor, Maria
Louisa, and the King of Rome.

But he was supposed to be safely caged at Elba, and the
Caricaturists held high revel over his downfall. I should have
liked to have reproduced some of them, but I have already

VIOLETTES.

done so in another book.* Monsieur, the French King's
brother, afterwards Charles X., made his public entry into
Paris, and was received with every demonstration of joy by
the inhabitants.

* 'English Caricature and Satire on Napoleon I.' London:
Chatto and Windus.

CHAPTER XIV.

EASTER MONDAY fell on the 11th of April, and on that day London was brilliantly illuminated, very much better than usual; but then lights and transparencies had only been, hitherto, used for Victories—this was for PEACE, which was welcomed by all with heartfelt thankfulness. The Duchess of Oldenburgh, at the Pulteney Hotel, had 'THANKS BE TO GOD' in variegated lamps. The Duke of Northumberland wreathed the head of his immortal lion with laurels; the statue of King Charles I. close by, was covered with laurels. Carlton House had its pillars entwined with lamps, the entablature marked out with them. On the parapet were six large stars; in the centre were the Arms of France supported by the figure of Fame, with laurels, under which was LOUIS XVIII. A pedestal of fire supported two large stars: on the left, were Russia and Austria; on the right, Prussia and England; whilst in the centre was a bit of deliciously bad French—'*Vive* LES BOURBONS,' all done in silver lamps.

I have but space to mention one more, and that is Ackermann's in the Strand, which was, if possible, more emblematical than usual. It is thus described: 'A Transparency: The Tyrant Corsican is attacked by Death under the walls of Paris; the grisly Monarch has placed his foot upon his breast, and holds in one hand an hour-glass, which, almost expended, leaves him just time enough to reflect upon the murders and other atrocities which have attended his wicked Career. The other hand grasps a massive iron spear, with which he is sup-

posed to have been dealing out destruction among the armies
of Bonaparte. The fallen Tyrant, in an attitude of terror,
supplicates Death to arrest his fatal purpose. Beneath him
are broken eagles, torn National Flags, &c., and in his hand
he grasps the shattered bloody remains of a sword. On the
Walls of Paris are seen Cossacks, and other Russians, Prussians,
Austrians, &c., who are raising the standard of the Bourbons.
This transparency was surmounted by a brilliant circle of gas-
lights, indicative of the union of the world in the Holy Cause ;
over this circle was a large white flag spotted with *fleurs de lys*,
hung out in triumphant display over the tattered, debased,
tricoloured banner of the Revolution. On each side of the
principal transparency was a smaller one ; the first representing
Bonaparte blowing bubbles, which burst as fast as created ; in
the other, he was seen amusing himself with building houses
and Castles of Cards, which, tumbling down as fast as they are
put up, are truly emblematic of the vast achievements of his
reign ; a bottle under the table indicative that all his designs
have ended in smoke, and a lanthorn to be useful to him
should he be inclined to look after his vanished Crown.'

The Illuminations were general throughout the Country,
and one transparency at Aberdeen (April 14th) deserves
notice. It was in the window of a Stocking Manufacturer,
and represented a Dutch woman fitting herself with a
comfortable worsted stocking, exclaiming, 'Thank God !
Aberdeen hose again.'

Louis *le désiré* was laid up with gout at Hartwell in Buckinghamshire, and did not hurry himself to enter into his
kingdom. It had to be done, however, and, moreover, he
had to face a public reception in London on the 20th of
April. The Prince Regent, and many of the Nobility, met
him at the Abercorn Arms at Stanmore : his postilions being
clad in white, with white hats, and white cockades. This
fancy for exhibiting white, in honour of the colour of the
Bourbon flag, took odd expression, for some people exhibited
sheets, and even pillow-cases were requisitioned. All the
nobility and gentry of that part of Middlesex, and, indeed,
almost all who could muster a horse, went a mile or so from
Stanmore to meet the King, and accompany him ; nay, there
were even the regulation fools, who took the horses out of his
Carriage, and drew him in what they called *triumph* to the
Abercorn Arms, where the poor old gouty King was lifted
out, and tottered to the Inn, where the Regent awaited him.

10

No longer the Comte de Lisle, he was now Louis the Eighteenth, the *désiré* of his people, and a very important person.

They waited at the Inn until the procession was formed, and then they set out in the following order, at twenty minutes past three :—

One hundred Gentlemen on horseback.

Horse Trumpeters in their splendid gold lace dresses.

A numerous party of the Royal Horse Guards.

Six Royal Carriages, beautiful bays to each, the servants with white Cockades.

An outrider to each Carriage.

A party of the Royal Horse Guards.

1st Carriage. The great Officers of the French Crown ; the Dukes d'Havre and de Grammont, Captains of his Majesty's Guards ; Count de Blacas, Grand Master of the Wardrobe ; and Chevalier de Riviere, his Majesty's first Equerry.

2nd Carriage. The King of France, the Prince Regent, the Duchesse d'Angoulême, the Prince de Condé.

3rd Carriage. The Duc de Bourbon.

4th Carriage. The Duchess d'Angoulême's Ladies of Honour.

5th Carriage. Equerries of his Majesty.

6th Carriage. Other Officers of the Royal Household.

An Officer of the Royal Horse Guards rode at each window, and a numerous party of Horse closed the procession.

They proceeded at a slow trot till they came to Kilburn, when they commenced a walking pace, and a groom to the head of each horse was added.

The greatest respect was shown by the people on the route, who displayed laurels, white ribbons, &c., and hailed the Royal party with general acclamation. They passed through Hyde Park, and down Piccadilly, to Albemarle Street ; down which they turned, receiving the compliments of all the Royal Princesses, who had been invited by the Duchess of Oldenburgh to see the Procession from the Pulteney Hotel, and stopped at Grillon's Hotel, where the King was to lodge. Here the King, leaning on the arm of the Prince of Wales, hobbled into a drawing - room, and sank, exhausted, into an arm-chair; but as soon as he had recovered somewhat, he thanked the Prince Regent in no measured terms. He expressed his gratitude for the favours conferred upon him, stating that he had been indebted to his Royal Highness for the preservation of his life, and even for his daily subsistence, and he had now to express his obligations to his Royal Highness for the restoration of the House of Bourbon. It was impossible for him to find language to convey in adequate terms the sense of gratitude he felt, or the delight he now experienced.

The Prince Regent replied briefly, deprecating any gratitude towards himself, and then the King took off the Cordon and Star of the Order of the Holy Ghost, which he wore, and with them decorated the Prince Regent, who then retired.

The next day, at Carlton House, he was made a Knight of the Garter, then held a *levée* at Grillon's Hotel, and received an address from the Corporation of the City of London. He left London early on the morning of the 23rd of April, escorted part of the way by the Duke of Sussex; and as soon as he entered the County of Kent he was met by Lord Camden, who was Lord-Lieutenant, and, accompanied by him, reached Dover. On the way, refreshments were ordered, and in readiness, for the King at every inn where he changed horses, so that he might not experience any delay or inconvenience. 'On the King stopping at Dartford to change horses, when the animals were taken from the Carriage, the populace proceeded to draw it without horses, and even ascended the very steep hill out of the town; but the numbers who exerted their strength to it enabled them to proceed at a very quick pace. At Rochester, the populace drew his Majesty's Carriage above a Mile.'*

On this day, 23rd of April, hostilities were suspended between Great Britain and France, both by sea and land. On the morning of the 24th the Prince Regent, and the Duke of Clarence took leave of the French King, who set sail for France, and arrived at Calais without accident. Napoleon

---

* This insensate folly still obtains occasionally; but I never met with but one instance of women sinking to the same depth of degradation. It is in the *Morning Chronicle* of the 5th of May, 1814, on p. 2, under heading *St. Sebastian Mail.*—'Don Antonio entered Valencia in the Coach of the President of the Regency. His Majesty would not permit the Arragonese Ladies to draw his Coach.'

left Fontainbleau, where he took an affectionate farewell of
his Old Guard, on the 21st of April, and embarked at Frejus,
in Provence, for Elba, on the 28th of April, where he landed
on the 4th of May.

On the 1st of May the Marquis of Wellington was created
a Duke, and on the 10th of the same month the House of
Commons granted him an annuity of £10,000, in addition to
the grants already bestowed upon him—which might be
redeemed for a sum of £400,000 to be spent in an estate.

At last we had got Peace, so long desired, which was to be
the panacea for all evils.   The war had been so long, that its
taxation almost ceased to be burdensome.   The farmers had
had a fine time of it, and had coined money, and, somehow or
other, our trade with the world had not come to a standstill,
in spite of Napoleon's fulminations, and our own Orders in
Council.   Still the return of Peace brought with it a drop
in the prices of most things.   Pepper fell from 21d. to 14d.
per lb.   Sugar from 120s. to 90s. per cwt.   Brandy could be
bought at 4s. 6d. to 4s. 10d. per gallon, and a general drop of
about 20 per cent. took place on all manufactured goods.
Here is a picture of ' Peace and Plenty, or, Good News for
John Bull ! ! ! '

Louis XVIII. proposes ' Here's the Prince Regent, and his
Allies !' to which John Bull replies, ' Huzza ! with all my
heart, and may we never want better friends.'   There is a
board ladder, down which come provisions lowered in price,
as Porter 3d. a pot.   Bread 9d. a quartern.   On the table,
Beef is 4d. a pound.   Claret 1s. 6d. a bottle ; whilst Burgundy
in the wine-cooler is priced at 2s. a bottle.   On the left, the
land is being tilled, and goods are being landed, whilst
Napoleon is seen in the distance sitting disconsolately on the
island of Elba.

We were now to have an influx of visitors to England.   The
Duchess of Oldenburgh was still here, being fêted and
lionized, having dinner at Carlton House, or a steak done
on a shovel, and washed down with stout, at Whitbread's
Brewery.   The Prince of Orange landed at Harwich on the
29th of April, and, after seeing the Prince Regent, ' would
a-wooing go,' and accompanied the Regent on a visit to his
daughter as her acknowledged suitor.   Marshal Blücher (Old
General Vorwärts) came over here very early in May, and
took up his residence at the Foreign Hotel in Leicester
Square.   But all arrivals paled before the expected visit of

'PEACE AND PLENTY, OR, GOOD NEWS FOR JOHN BULL !!!'

the Emperors of Russia and Austria, and the King of Prussia. The kitchen in St. James's Palace was repaired, and newly fitted up for the establishment of the two first-named potentates. And 'A pair of massy golden Eagles, nearly as large as life, were made a few days since by Messrs. Rundell and Bridge, for the Prince Regent's table. This beautiful ornament is to be placed, as we understand, at the head of the dinner-table near the Royal Guests, as a respectful compliment to the Emperor of Russia, and the King of Prussia, whose standards bear this imperial bird. The eagle is placed with his talons on the verge of a nest, which is most admirably formed after Nature. The beak is turned to a horizontal position, and his eye fixed on the object below ; the wings are gracefully extended, and raised above the head. In the back of the bird is concealed a lamp to contain burning spirits, over which any plate may be applied with ease, and made warm.'

At length the promised day arrived, and on the 7th of June, the Emperor of Russia, and the King of Prussia, came into London, quite unannounced and quietly.

Morning Chronicle, June 8, 1814 : 'His Imperial Majesty, Alexander of Russia, his Prussian Majesty, and the illustrious Princes and Princesses in their respective suites, arrived yesterday in London, at different hours, and by different routes, to avoid the *éclat* of a public entry, and, consequently, to avoid the pressure of the multitudes who had assembled to welcome their approach. The Crowds which had gathered from all parts of the Metropolis, in the direction which they were expected to take, was immense. In fact, from Charing Cross to Blackheath the way was almost impassable ; and it was well that the Royal Visitors were advised to come *incog.,* for it would have been with infinite difficulty that the escort could have penetrated through the compact body of the people assembled, without the interference of military force, by which mischief might have ensued.

'We are informed, indeed, that the route which was taken, arose from an arrangement previously made, in consequence of certain recent events, which made the appearance of an illustrious Personage in a Procession, inconvenient ; and that as he could not go forth to meet and receive his high guests, it was determined that they should be advised to enter the Metropolis privately. We do not believe this sarcastic method of accounting for the disappointment which was so generally felt; as we cannot suppose that, because his Royal Highness could not himself partake of the magnificent display which was prepared for the occasion, he would prevent it from taking place altogether. We believe, on the contrary, that the Emperor of Russia and King of Prussia have uniformly expressed their earnest desire of avoiding all ceremony, and of being allowed to do in London as they did in Paris, to go about and see everything worthy of notice without ostentation.

'The Emperor of Russia arrived at half-past two o'clock, at the Pulteney Hotel, in so private a manner that the post-boys did not know who they were driving. He travelled in Count Lieven's Carriage, without a single attendant; he passed all the attendants in the lower part of the Hotel without his being known, and had run up to the first flight of stairs, when Prince Gargarine announced that it was the Emperor. At the same instant his sister, the Grand Duchess, met him on the stairs, and they saluted each other in the most affectionate manner. The Emperor afterwards embraced the interesting child, Prince Alexander.*

'The joyful tidings of the arrival of the Emperor resounded not only throughout the house, but in the street, where there was an immense concourse of people, who expressed their joy by repeated huzzas and 'Long live the Emperor,' &c., &c. He, in consequence, appeared, a short time afterwards, at the balcony, and bowed in the most condescending manner, and which he continued to do, at intervals, till eleven o'clock at night, the people rending the air with shouts of applause. The Earl of Morton, the Queen's Chamberlain, waited upon the Emperor in the name of the Queen, to express her congratulations on his arrival in England.

'At half-past four the Emperor went in Count Lieven's Carriage, accompanied by his Excellency, to pay his respects to the Prince Regent at Carlton House; but he went in so private a manner that the escort of Horse who were appointed to attend him, missed him, but they escorted him back to the Pulteney Hotel. His Imperial Majesty was most kindly received by the Prince Regent. The Emperor declined seeing any visitors yesterday at the Pulteney Hotel, but the inquiries of the Royal Family, the Foreign Princes in

* The son of the Duchess of Oldenburgh, then about three years old.

that country, and personages of distinction were innumerable. Pulteney Hotel, for the reception of the Emperor, has been fitted up in the most magnificent and princely style ; at least, the principal apartments which were occupied by the Grand Duchess, who has given them up to her brother, the Emperor. No pains, nor expense, has been spared by Mr. Escudier on the occasion ; he has had a new state bed put up by Mr. Oakley for the Emperor. The Grand Duchess and the Emperor dined together, without any other person being present.

'The Prince Regent, for the purpose of showing all due attention to the Emperor, prepared a Royal residence for him in St. James's Palace, in the Duke of Cumberland's apartments, which, although small, are extremely splendid, which has been newly fitted up for the occasion, a new state bed of Crimson Velvet, with gold lace and fringe, a crown at the top, and appropriate ornaments. Yesterday, the Lord Chamberlain, the Lord Steward, the Duke of Montrose, and Col. Thornton, were in attendance the whole of the day, till seven o'clock, full dressed, in expectation of the Emperor coming there to take up his residence. A guard of honour, with two bands, in their state uniforms, attended in the Court-yard, opposite the house, during the day.

'The King of Prussia, his sons, and their numerous suites, came also in a very private manner, and arrived at Clarence House, St. James's, about three o'clock. A party of the Yeomen of the Guard, Royal Servants, and attendants, as at Cumberland House, were in readiness to receive him. His Majesty appeared highly delighted at his residence, and after viewing it, partook of some refreshment. A few minutes before four o'clock, his Majesty, attended by his Aide de Camp, went to Carlton House to pay his respects in a very private manner to the Prince Regent. His Highness received him in a similar gracious manner as he did the Emperor of Russia. His Majesty remained with the Prince about half an hour. His Majesty received visits from the Prince of Orange, the Duchess of Oldenburgh, and a number of others. His Majesty visited the Duke and Duchess of York, whose house is opposite to Clarence House.

'At a quarter past eight o'clock, her Majesty, and the Princesses Augusta and Mary, arrived at the Palace from Windsor. At nine o'clock her Majesty held a Private Court, for the purpose of receiving one of the principal gentlemen of the Emperor of Russia's Court, to formally announce to the

Queen the arrival of the Emperor of Russia in her Capital. He was introduced to the presence of her Majesty by Earl Morton, her Chamberlain, and was most graciously received, and her Majesty expressed her pleasure to receive the Emperor.

'At six o'clock, the Marshal General Blücher arrived in St. James's Park, by the Horse Guards, in the Prince Regent's open Carriage, escorted by a party of light horse. He was recognised by an eager public, who paid their respects to such a gallant man, by whose persevering skill the Allies proved victorious. The Carriage was surrounded and followed by an incalculable number of horsemen and pedestrians, all vieing with each other who should give him the most marked attention, and the greatest applause. The Drivers, as directed, made first for Carlton House, to pay his first respects to the Prince Regent, and that his Royal Highness might have the first pleasure of receiving him. The drivers made for the gates in the Park near the Stables, and, no sooner were the gates opened to receive the carriages, than there was a general rush in of horsemen and the public at large. Such was the zeal of the populace to follow the gallant and venerable General, who has so justly acquired so much military fame, that all restraint upon them was obliged to give way : the two sentinels at the gates, with their muskets, were laid on the ground, the porter was completely overpowered, and it was with the greatest difficulty, with the assistance of several persons, that he could get the gates shut. The multitude proceeded up the yard of Carlton House, with the General's Carriage, shouting the praise of Blücher.

'The Carriage stopped at the side door, but he was not allowed to enter Carlton House that way. On its being known who had arrived, Cols. Bloomfield and Congreve came out, dressed in full regimentals, and received the General uncovered, and in that state conducted him, arm in arm, to the front and principal entrance of Carlton House, that all possible respect might be shown him, followed by the populace. The cause of rejoicing being known to the crowd assembled in Pall Mall, they lost all respect for the regularity of the place ; they instantly scaled the walls, and lodges, in great numbers, and their impetuous zeal upon this occasion was indulged, and the great doors of the hall were thrown open to them, some of the gentlemen on horseback nearly entering the hall.

'After the first interview of the General with the Prince,

as interesting a scene took place, probably, as ever was beheld.
A British Sovereign, in the person of the Prince Regent, conferring an honour on a foreign General, for his meritorious
services, in the midst of the acclamations of his people ; and
the Prince Regent returned from his private apartments hand
in hand with the gallant Blücher, and in the centre of the
grand Hall, surrounded publicly by his people, placed on his
shoulder, and fastened with his own hand, a blue ribbon, to
which was hung a beautiful medallion, with a likeness of the
Prince, richly set with diamonds.   Marshal Blücher knelt
whilst the Prince was conferring the honour, and, on his
rising, had the honour to kiss the Prince's hand.   The Prince
and the General bowed to the public, and their ecstasy and
acclamations in return exceeds all description.

' The General, afterwards, had an interview with the Prince
for about half an hour, and then proceeded in his Carriage to
the house of Mr. Gordon, in St. James's Palace, adjoining the
Duke of Cumberland's, followed by an immense multitude ;
some got into the Carriage with him.   The Crowd remained
in the Court-yard till dark, huzzaing, and the gallant General
frequently showing himself at the window to gratify them.
The public were indulged with remaining in the Court-yard
at Carlton House during the evening, and they testified their
loud applause to all who arrived to partake of a grand dinner
given by the Prince to the King of Prussia, and his sons, the
Princes, the Prince of Mecklenburg, the Prince of Orange,
several other Foreigners of distinction, the most of the Foreign
Ambassadors, and Ministers, Count Munster, the Duke and
Duchess of York, the Duke of Cambridge, the Cabinet
Ministers and their Ladies, the Officers of the State and
Household, and their Ladies.

' The Princes, sons of the King of Prussia, had the horses
taken out of their Carriage, and were drawn by the people to
their Hotel in Jermyn Street.   The Prince de Metternich,
General Platow ' (our old friend the Cossack Hetman), ' and
General Barclay de Tolly, drove to the respective hotels taken
for them.   The only triumphal entry was that of the venerable
and gallant Blücher.   He was met four miles beyond Dartford, by a detachment of horse, and he approached town
amidst the enthusiastic shouts of surrounding myriads.   They
avoided Shooter's Hill, and crossed Bexley Heath to Eltham.
Indeed, the whole way from Dover was one continued
Jubilee.'

Here I end the account given by ' our own correspondent '
of that day.   Its grammar and construction may be found
fault with, but though doubtless written in a great hurry, its
facts are correct.

Rough old Blücher was, undoubtedly, of all the brilliant
throng, the favourite of the Mob.   He shared with Schwart-
zenburg, Barclay de Tolly, and Platoff in Swords of honour,
value 200 guineas each, given by the City of London.   His
popularity must have had its inconveniences.   When he went

BLÜCHER GREETED BY HIS NUMEROUS FRIENDS IN THE PARK, 1814.

to Ascot races on the 10th of June, he was cheered more
than the Allied Sovereigns ; it was as much as he could get
to the Royal Stand, hundreds of men and women insisting on
shaking hands with him the moment he alighted.   When,
after a race, he rode down the Course in company with the
Duke of York, he could hardly get along, so great was the
throng.   It was only by shaking thousands of hands, that he
could make any progress.   Nothing was heard but shouts of

'Blücher! Blücher!' the ladies in the Stands waved their handkerchiefs, and the gallant old Bear saluted them in turn.

There was a poem entitled—

'PRINCE BLÜCHER AND THE BRITISH LADIES.

A Free Paraphrase of Horace.   Book I, Ode 8.

" Lydia, dic, per omnes
Te deos oro," &c.

Say, Ladies, by the Gods above,
Why, with such fond officious love,
Ye haste to spoil that Man of Glory,
Old BLÜCHER, doomed to live in Story?
Why should he dread the peaceful plain,
Whom War and dust assailed in vain ?
Why should the Veteran fear to ride
On horseback at his Monarch's side ;
Or, if he chance to take a drive,
Take chances to return alive ?
Cleaves he the Thames ? 'tis said for him
The Ladies all will learn to swim !
Though, cat-like, ev'ry mother's daughter
Feels strong aversion to the water.
In vain he shuns the soap or razor,
Each maid becomes mustachio-praiser.
Though vile before, in him to smoke
Is only deemed a pleasant joke ;
While, strange to say, the British Fair,
For his sake, doat upon grey hair !
Why does he hide ?   Nay rather let him
A petticoat and mantle get him ;—
In this will BLÜCHER do no more
Than what ACHILLES did before ;
Whom, though in other things outdone,
He might well imitate in one.
Thus may he safely pass along,
Unheeded, through the female throng ;
For scarce, I ween, their rapture reaches
To any worth—but worth in Breeches.'

Whenever he stirred out he was mobbed, he had to undergo as much handshaking as any President of the United States of America; and really, the Caricature of ' Blücher greeted by his numerous Friends in the Park,' is not very much exaggerated (*see p.* 155).   Poor old ' Vorwärts' is being prodded and tickled, by his fair friends.   Take another instance.   On

the 24th of June, he visited Portsmouth, in company with
the Allied Sovereigns ; but his friends (?) pursued him there.
Here is a contemporaneous account of how his friends treated
him.   'After the amusements of the day had closed, with the
setting sun, an event occurred, which gave fresh life to the
town.   A Coach, drawn by eight horses, drew up at the
Crown Inn, or Clarence Hotel, and, who should alight but
the gallant Blücher.   He was identified on alighting from the
Carriage, and on no occasion in London, were the populace
more numerous ; the eagerness to grasp his hand, by both
sexes, was unparalleled.   " Blücher ! Blücher !" filled the air.
" Shew me the Conqueror of the Tyrant :" " Come forward,
Blücher !" was exclaimed on all sides.   The gallant veteran
appeared at the window with his accustomed cheerfulness,
and the air was rent with applause ; and it was several minutes
before the disputants could agree whether immediate silence
was respectful.   Lungs carried the day, and, when the roar
was out, the General, in English, with a bumper in his hand,
drank to the health of the Company.   It may easily be
imagined in what manner this toast was returned.

'The populace became appeased, and soon after a Carriage
drew up, and was immediately surrounded.   Blücher got into
it in haste.   A party of sailors shoved in, and swore they
would be true to a good Commander.   Up mounted half a
dozen ; but, at this time, an escort of dragoons, previously
stopped by the crowd, and, consequently kept back, appeared.
Some got off by accident, but two kept their stations.   The
Government House was a few hundred yards distant, and the
two sailors, elated as Men of War's men by victory, danced
on the top of Blücher's Carriage.'

> 'When BLÜCHER was told that, to add to his store,
>   The REGENT an Order design'd,
> He said, ' I'm with Orders so cover'd, *before*,
>   I only can hang it *behind*.'
>
> Sir Charles,* ever ready, due homage to pay,
>   Thus answer'd the vet'ran, " If so,
> Then all who have heard of thy actions will say
>   It ne'er can be hit by the foe." '

He was an inveterate gambler, but, on the principle that
'dog does not eat dog,' whenever he played with the officers
of his own staff, he always returned them the money he won

* Stewart.

from them : but he gave one of them, a Prussian Count, a lesson. Having won some £3,000 from him, he sent for him next morning, and read him a lecture on the folly of play, instancing himself as an example, ingrained, through the practice of a lifetime, and he ended his jobation by telling his sub. that he would return him his money, on condition that he would promise never to lose more than a, comparatively speaking, nominal sum a night. This the young man promised, and Blücher handed him half his losses, keeping the other half sealed up for a twelvemonth, when it might be had on application, if the promise had been kept.

Captain Gronow, does not give a pleasant picture of Blücher. ' Marshal Blücher, though a very fine fellow, was a very rough diamond, with the manners of a Common Soldier. On his arrival in Paris, he went every day to the *Salon*, and played the highest stakes at *rouge et noir*. The *Salon*, during the time that the Marshal remained in Paris, was crowded by persons who came to see him play. His manner of playing was anything but gentlemanlike, and when he lost, he used to swear in German at everything that was French, looking daggers at the Croupiers. He generally managed to lose all he had about him, also the money his servant, who was waiting in the ante-chamber, carried. I recollect looking attentively at the manner in which he played ; he would put his right hand into his pocket, and bring out several rouleaus of Napoleons, throwing them on the red or the black. If he won the first *coup*, he would allow it to remain ; but when the Croupier stated that the table was not responsible for more than ten thousand francs, then Blücher would roar like a lion, and rap out oaths in his native language, which would doubtless have met with great success at Billingsgate, if duly translated ; fortunately, they were not heeded, as they were not understood by the lookers-on.'

The Hon. Grantley F. Berkeley* says : 'So madly in love with old Blücher were the English populace, that, during a review, while one mob was following the heels of the late Lord Londonderry, and another the heels of Blücher, so that it was impossible for either hero even to sneeze in private, both chanced to do the same thing. Blücher was vociferously cheered for it, and Lord Londonderry hissed and hooted—so much for the worth of popular worship. . . . Nothing could be more remarkable than the perfect understanding that

* 'My Life and Reminiscences,' 1866, vol. iii., pp. 3 and 4.

existed between him and his admirers, considering that he knew not a word of what was said to him, and they found his German quite as unintelligible as their English. It was not then the fashion to bore remarkable people for their autographs or photographs. His new friends, too, were not aware that his signature was even more difficult to make out than his remarks ; they, therefore, rested content with the honour of a grip from the old soldier, and talked of it ever after, in the family circle, as the greatest honour that could have befallen them. . . . The favour with which the Emperor was regarded was extended to his uncouth Cossacks, which not even their filching and swallowing the oil from the street lamps—gas then not having come into use—affected in any material degree.'

CHAPTER XV.

Royal festivities—The Emperor of Russia, the King of Prussia, and General Blücher at Oxford—Banquet at Guildhall—Departure of the Allied Sovereigns—Signature of Treaty of Peace—Proclamation of Peace—State Thanksgiving at St. Paul's Cathedral.

But I have been doing precisely as they did in 1814, almost neglecting the august potentates of Russia and Prussia, in the all-absorbing Field Marshal. Let us see how they spent their time.

We know all about their first day in London. On the next (June 8th) the Emperor of Russia had breakfasted by eight, and afterwards walked in Kensington Gardens with his sister; then went to see Westminster Hall and Abbey, and the British Museum. At one he held a *levée* at Cumberland House, which he used as his state apartments, and was visited by the Prince Regent, who, afterwards, attended the *levée* of the King of Prussia, at Clarence House. Between five and six both sovereigns attended the Queen's Court, to be introduced to her Majesty, and they all dined together with the Prince of Wales at Carlton House.

There was one thing the English people could scarcely understand. We have seen that both Kaiser and King had splendid state beds provided for them. With singular unanimity they both did away with them at once; both were accustomed to the hardships of war. The Czar would sleep on nothing but a straw palliasse, and the King ordered all the fine satin wood furniture to be removed out of his bedroom, and a plain table and glass, with one common chair to be substituted. When the bed was removed, his Majesty's camp equipage was brought in, whence were taken a leathern mattress and bolster, which were placed upon an ordinary Couch.

On the 9th the Czar, accompanied by Lord Yarmouth and Col. Bloomfield, rode in Hyde Park, between seven and eight. Thence they rode to Westminster, through Southwark to the City, past the Royal Exchange, through Finsbury Square, the City, and New, Roads, down Edgware Road, and Hyde Park to the Pulteney Hotel. After breakfast, he and his sister quietly went through the Strand and City, and visited the London Docks. In the afternoon the King of Prussia was made a Knight of the Garter, and so was the Emperor of Austria, in his absence. Afterwards, the Prince of Wales was invested with the Order of the Golden Fleece by the Austrian Minister, and that of the Golden Eagle by the Prussian monarch.

On the 10th the two foreign monarchs breakfasted together, and then went to Ascot races ; dining, afterwards, with the Queen at Frogmore.

June 11th. The Emperor of Russia, Duchess of Oldenburgh, &c., visited the Bank of England. Afterwards the two monarchs held court, at their respective palaces, for the reception of addresses from the City of London. They, and the Prince Regent, dined with Lord Liverpool, who was the Prime Minister, and, afterwards, everybody went in state to the Opera. When I say everybody, I mean it, for, judge of the astonishment of all, when, just as the Second Act of the Opera was about to commence, a voice exclaimed, ' The Princess of Wales !' and, surely, there she was, entering a box, accompanied by Lady Charlotte Campbell. There was a universal shout of applause from the whole house, whereupon the two sovereigns and the Prince Regent rose and *bowed*, to her, a courtesy which she returned with a deep reverence. This was her revenge. The Queen, at the instance of the Regent, had refused her permission to attend a drawing-room, where she might meet the sovereigns, and she chose this method of securing their notice.

Next day (12th) was Sunday, and the King of Prussia went to service at Westminster. In the afternoon, the Czar and King, accompanied by their suites, rode in Hyde Park, and the description of this *promenade à Cheval* is as follows : ' It would seem as if every horse in the Metropolis had resorted thither. The pressure was intolerable : the horses were so jammed together, that many Noblemen and Gentlemen had

11

their knees crushed, and their boots torn off. We did not hear of any fatal Accident. The interesting BLÜCHER was so cruelly persecuted, that he dismounted, and took refuge in Kensington Gardens ; but here, being afoot he was more annoyed. He set his back against a tree,* and seemed at length quite exhausted. The coarse kindness of our mob is more formidable to him than all the enemies he ever encountered.' At night they dined again at Carlton House.

On the 13th at nine a.m. the illustrious visitors embarked at Whitehall Stairs, for a trip by water to Woolwich. It must have been a very pretty sight to have seen the carved and gilded barges, not only of the Admiralty, the Navy, and the Ordnance Board, but of all the City Companies, as brave as bunting and silken flags could make them, all rowed by watermen, in uniform, with huge silver badges on their arms. Add to this beautiful scene, the launches of the *Enterprise*, and of the Men-of-War at Deptford, and Woolwich, several boats with bands of Music, and the *coup d'œil* must have been charming. There is always plenty to see at Woolwich Arsenal (it then had a Dockyard), and they saw it, for they did not return till late in the evening, just in time for a dinner at the Marquis of Stafford's, and a ball at the Earl of Cholmondeley's.

This gadding about must have been tiring work, for the Emperor of Russia did not get to his hotel, from the ball, till three o'clock a.m., and he was off for Oxford, by half-past six. The Prince Regent started at a quarter to six. No time, however, was wasted on the journey, for nine relays of horses, for each carriage, were provided to do the 58 miles. The Regent who was accompanied by the Prince of Orange, arrived about half-past ten, the time appointed, but they were not quite ready for him. They scrambled together some kind of a procession, and the Chancellor laid the Maces of the University Bedels, at his Royal Highness's feet. Of course, he graciously returned them, and, by this time, the Mayor and the Civic portion of the procession had arrived, and they all proceeded to the Divinity Schools. Here, of course, was presented the inevitable address, after which, the Regent was conducted to *Christ Church*, where apartments had been prepared for him.

A few minutes after one o'clock, the Czar arrived, accompanied by his sister, who was attired in 'a plain travelling

* See page 155.

dress, with a large straw bonnet, shaded by a broad pendant feather.' This bonnet was the latest thing from Paris, which the Duchess brought over with her, and which speedily became the fashion. It went by the very undignified name of 'the Oldenburgh Poke,' and my reader will meet with it in the coming illustrations. They drove to Merton College.

Very shortly after, the King of Prussia and his sons, drove up, and went to Corpus Christi. Both sovereigns barely gave themselves time for refreshment, but went directly to call upon the Regent, who received them in his cap and gown. They then visited all the objects of interest in the most interesting city in England. About four o'clock old Blücher (who was to be made a D.C.L.) arrived, and received the ovation which his presence always produced. Of course, the people wanted to drag his carriage, but good sense prevailed, and they were not allowed to make fools of themselves. In the evening, at half-past seven, a grand banquet was served to about two hundred guests, of whom the Regent's party comprised fifty. This took place in the Radcliffe Library, the upper gallery of which was thrown open to people to walk round, and view the dinner. The stone staircases were small, and the pushing and crowding were great. Hats, caps, and shoes were flying in all directions, and many, at last, extricated themselves, with their gowns and coats torn in pieces. The military were called in, and order was restored. The banquet lasted till eleven, when the guests went through the City to see the illuminations, which, however, were extinguished by a tremendous thunderstorm between twelve and one.

Next morning the degrees were conferred, in the Theatre, on the Emperor of Russia, the King of Prussia, the Duke of Wellington (*in absentia*), Prince Metternich, Count Lieven, and Blücher. Of course fun was made of this grizzled old warrior being made a D.C.L., and Cruikshank drew a picture of him looking at himself in a glass in utter astonishment (see next page).

Another picture also by G. Cruikshank, shows Oxford, as it was supposed to have been during the visit of the sovereigns, Alexander, the Duchess of Oldenburgh (who has mounted a cap and wig on the crown of her 'Poke'), and Blücher, being excessively amiable to the Dons. Cossacks vested in Gowns, and Caps, are the order of the day, and fraternize right

11—2

jovially.   A dinner in Christ Church Hall, and a Ball ended the day.

We hear more about poor Blücher's unfortunate popularity. ' The gallant Blücher seems to have been the peculiar favourite

BLÜCHER SURVEYING HIMSELF AS A D.C.L.

of the people.   He could not stir without a crowd, and the vehemence of their salutations has been almost painful to him.   His rooms at Christ Church were generally surrounded

Cruikshank.

DOCTOR BLÜCHER.

(*Satirist, July 1, 1814.*)

by a crowd of people. On the morning of Wednesday, he was sitting at the end of his bed, the window being quite open, smoking his long pipe, in a white vest with a ribbon over it, with complete military *sang froid*. He frequently advanced to the window, and bowed. The excessive joy of the people almost overpowered him in the Theatre on Thursday. Two of the newly-created doctors were obliged to rescue him from the hands of the people by force, or he must have sunk under their pressure.'

After receiving their degrees, the two sovereigns returned to town, of course, immediately to resume dining, and Balls. On the 16th the Czar went to see the Charity Children, numbering seven thousand, at St. Paul's. In the evening, both sovereigns dined with Lord Castlereagh, and then went to Drury Lane Theatre, after which there was a ball at the Marchioness of Hertford's.

On the 17th they visited Chelsea Hospital; spent a fairly quiet day, and dined at Merchant Taylor's Hall. The King of Prussia seems to have had tastes identical with those of the Shah of Persia, at his visit here in June 1873, for, at eleven in the morning, he, accompanied by the Prince Royal, Princes William and Frederick of Prussia, Prince Mecklenburgh, General d'York, Platoff, and several other of our illustrious visitors had a dejeuner at Lord Lowther's. The most celebrated pugilists were in waiting to exhibit their skill. Jackson, Cribb, Tom Belcher, Richmond, Cropley, Oliver, Painter, and some others. After breakfast they set to, and there was some excellent sparring, as might be expected.

A Banquet was given on the 18th at the Guildhall, by the City, on a scale of magnificence never since equalled. The Regent and his Royal guests went in the utmost state with one hundred Yeomen of the Guard—the Kings at Arms. Six heralds and all Herald's College. The Lord Mayor, Sheriffs, Aldermen, and Civic Officers all on horseback, met them at Temple Bar, and accompanied them to the Guildhall, which was most superbly fitted up, principally with crimson velvet, gold fringe, lace, lines, and tassels.

At the eastern, or upper, end of the Hall, on a platform elevated above the level of the floor, covered with Turkey carpeting, was placed a very large table, at which stood three massive carved and gilt chairs covered with crimson velvet, decorated with gold fringes, under a lofty Canopy of rich crimson velvet, lined with crimson sarsnet, and rich velvet draperies reaching to the floor, tied back with gold ropes. In front of the dome of the Canopy were placed the Sword and Sceptre; and, on the top, the Royal Crown of the United Kingdom, boldly carved on a large scale, and gilt; over which hovered a Dove, with the olive branch, in proper colours, as in the act of alighting, in allusion to the establishment of Peace, and in compliment to the three great Personages sitting under the Canopy. In the centre sat

THE PRINCE REGENT.

On his right.	*On his left.*
The Emperor of Russia.	The King of Prussia.
Duke of York.	Duchess of Oldenburgh.
Prince Henry of Prussia.	The Hereditary Prince of Wirtemberg.
Duke of Cambridge.	Countess Lieven.
Duke of Orleans.	Duke of Kent.
Duke of Saxe Weimar.	Prince of Bavaria.
Prince Augustus of Prussia.	Prince Metternich.
The Duke of Oldenburgh.	The Prince of Cobourg.
Count de Merveldt.	Duke of Gloucester.
Prince of Hardenberg.	Prince William of Prussia.
Count Fernan Nunez, Duke of Montellano.	The Prince of Orange.
	Princess Volkonské.

There were besides, the Archbishop of Canterbury, the Ministers, the Speaker of the House of Commons, all the Officers of State, including the Prince Regent's Household, the flower of the Nobility, Foreign Ambassadors, &c., &c.

Never was such a banquet seen. The very waiters were not hired, but were Citizens, and other gentlemen of respectability, dressed alike, in black, with white waistcoats, who gratuitously offered their services upon the occasion, and not only acted as waiters, but superintended and took care of the great quantity of Plate that was used, the value of which was estimated to exceed Two Hundred Thousand Pounds. The Lord Mayor, the Right Hon. William Domville, was made a Baronet.

The Royal guests must have been thankful that the next day (the 19th) was a Sunday. The Emperor went to the Chapel of his Embassy in Welbeck Street, after which, he and his sister went to a Quakers' Meeting in Peter's Court, St. Martin's Lane. On their return to their hotel the Emperor gave audience to many people, on business; then called on the Princess Charlotte, stopped with her half an hour, and then drove to Chiswick to visit the Duke of Devonshire, returning to the Pulteney Hotel at seven, and to a party at the Regent's to meet the Queen in the evening.

The King of Prussia went to Church at St. George's, Hanover Square. After luncheon he drove to Sion House, Isleworth, to visit Earl Percy, and thence to Oatlands, where he dined with the Duchess of York.

On the 20th there was what was called a Grand Review in Hyde Park, but the few soldiers there mustered must have been a poor show to those monarchs, who had only just been face to face with grim War on a very large scale. Both sovereigns went, without state, to take leave of the Queen, and both dined at their hotels; both afterwards going, in the evening, to the Fête given by White's Club at Burlington House.

The 21st was principally taken up with receiving visits, &c., and a State Concert of Sacred Music at Carlton House.

On the 22nd, early in the morning, both Czar and King left London for Portsmouth, where there was to be a grand Naval Review in their honour, on the 25th of June. Fifteen sail of the line, and fifteen frigates, performed various Manœuvres, and the day concluded with a grand entertainment at Government House, where the Royal party was joined by the Duke of Wellington, who had just arrived home.

This finished their visit, and they sailed from Dover on the 27th. Almost the last we hear of them is: 'HASTINGS, June 27th.—The Emperor of Russia, the King of Prussia, and the Grand Duchess of Oldenburgh passed through this neighbourhood yesterday on their way to Dover. The Emperor and Duchess of Oldenburgh stopped their carriage for some time at Fairlight, near the town, and, in the most condescending manner, shook hands with the peasantry, and distributed cakes, &c., among the children.' Cruikshank draws this incident in 'Russian Condescension, or the Blessings of Universal PEACE.'

On May 30th a definitive treaty of Peace was signed at Paris between Great Britain and France, by which the Islands of Malta, the Mauritius, Tobago, St. Lucia, and the Cape of Good Hope were ceded to Great Britain, and illuminations in joy therefor, took place on June 9, 10, 11. But the Proclamation of Peace was not made until the 20th of June. I

RUSSIAN CONDESCENSION, OR THE BLESSINGS OF UNIVERSAL PEACE.

(*July 11, 1814.*)

have witnessed one in my lifetime, that of 1856, and a very shabby ceremonial it was, the heralds looking especially comical, in a hybrid costume consisting of a cheese-cutter Court hat, a gorgeous mediæval Tabard, modern black trousers with a broad gold lace stripe, and patent leather boots.

On the 20th of June, 1814, a party of Horse Guards was drawn up about the gate of St. James's Palace, where the Beadles and Constables, and all the officers of the City of Westminster, attended.

The Officers of Arms, Sergeants at Arms, with their Maces and Collars; the Sergeant Trumpeter, with his Mace and Collar, the trumpets; Drum Major and drums; and the Knight Marshal and his men, assembled in the Stable-yard, St. James's; and the Officers of Arms, being habited in their respective tabards, and mounted, a Procession was made thence to the Palace gate in the following order:—

Knight Marshal's Men, two and two.

Knight Marshal.

Drums.

Drum Major.

Trumpets.

Sergeant Trumpeter.

Pursuivants.

Sergeants { Heralds. } Sergeants
at Arms. { Kings of Arms. } at Arms.

Being come before the gate, the senior Officer of Arms present (attended on his left hand by the next in rank) read the Proclamation aloud; whereupon the Procession moved on to Charing Cross in the following order:—

Horse Guards to clear the way.

Beadles of Westminster, two and two, bareheaded, with Staves.

Constables of Westminster in like manner.

High Constable, with his Staff, on horseback.

Officers of the High Bailiff of Westminster, with white wands, on horseback.

Clerk of the High Bailiff.

High Bailiff and Deputy Steward.

Horse Guards.

Horse Guards to flank the Procession.

Knight Marshal's men, two and two.

Knight Marshal.

Drums.

Drum Major.

Trumpets.

Sergeant Trumpeter.

Pursuivants.

Horse Guards to flank the Procession.

Sergeants at Arms. { Heralds. Kings of Arms. } Sergeants at Arms.

Horse Guards.

At Charing Cross the Officer of Arms next in rank read the Proclamation, looking towards Whitehall; after which the Procession moved on to Temple Bar, the gates of which were shut; and the Junior Officer of Arms, coming out of the rank between two trumpeters, preceded by two Horse Guards to clear the way, rode up to the gate, and, after the trumpets had sounded thrice, knocked with a cane. Being asked by the City Marshal from within, 'Who comes there?' he replied, 'The Officers of Arms, who demand entrance into the City to publish his Majesty's Proclamation of Peace.' The Gates being opened, he was admitted alone, and the gates were shut again. The City Marshal, preceded by his Officers, conducted him to the Lord Mayor, to whom he showed his Majesty's warrant, which, his Lordship having read, returned, and gave directions to the City Marshal to open the gates, who, attending the Officer of Arms on his return to them, said on leaving him, 'Sir, the gates are opened.' The trumpets and guards being in waiting, conducted him to his place in the procession, which then moved on into the City (the Officers of Westminster filing off, and retiring as they came to Temple Bar); and, at Chancery Lane End, the Proclamation was read a third time. Then the Lord Mayor, Aldermen and Sheriffs, joining the procession immediately after the Officers of Arms, moved on to the end of Wood Street, where the Cross formerly stood in Cheapside. And the Proclamation having been there read, the procession continued to the Royal Exchange, where the Proclamation was read for the last time, and the procession returned by the way of Gracechurch Street through Lombard Street.

The Trumpets sounded thrice, previous to, and immediately after, each reading.

On the 7th of July the Prince Regent went in State, accompanied by the Members of the House of Lords and the House of Commons, the Foreign Ambassadors, &c., to St. Paul's Cathedral, to render thanks to God for the re-establishment of Peace. The line of route was mainly kept by Volunteers and Yeomanry, there being so very few regular troops available. The Procession was alternately Horse Guards and State Coaches, the last, of course, being that of the Prince Regent, who was gorgeous in his robes, and hat with a plume of ostrich feathers. The Duke of Wellington, who, now that the Allied Sovereigns had gone, was the lion of the day, accompanied the Prince in his carriage, clad in his new Ducal Robes, and when they alighted at St. Paul's, walked by the Prince's right hand, carrying the Sword of State. The Service was not a long one, and the sermon was preached by the Bishop of Chester.

It must have been a beautiful sight, the Cathedral holding nearly 10,000 persons, the male portion being gay in uniform, official robes, or Court dress, and the ladies dressed as they should be on so joyful an occasion. All the Royal Dukes, except the Duke of York, were present, and as old Blücher had not yet left England, he had to take part in the ceremony. The Prince Regent was much hissed both going and returning.

CHAPTER XVI.

City banquet to the Duke of Wellington—Costly vegetables—The Princess Charlotte—Squabbles about her presentation at Court —The Regent hooted—The Princess Charlotte and the Prince of Orange—Her future husband, Prince Leopold—Her flight from Warwick House, and return.

I STILL must chronicle feasting and rejoicing. This time it is the City of London who honoured the national Hero, the Duke of Wellington, with a banquet. Some may grumble at this way of doing honour to merit, but, after all, it is but one mode of public recognition. The Government cannot spend the public money on such matters. Private acknowledgment would be worthless, so the City of London always throws itself, so to speak, into the breach, and bridges over a chasm most gracefully. Their hospitality hurts no one, as it comes from their own funds, and it supplies a national want, and as such, is recognized as an honour done by the nation. So a feast was made, on the 9th of July, to welcome home the Conqueror of Napoleon. Nationally, the Duke was well rewarded, both with titles and money, but the graceful act of a public reception was wanting as a crown.

The preparations were as magnificent as if for the Allied Sovereigns, but the feast had this difference—the Lord Mayor was the real Host. In the former he was subsidiary, the Regent, of course, being the central star. This was a National welcome, and, if there were not so many High Mightinesses present, it was none the less hearty. It is of no use wearying my readers with details of the festivity, but I wish to point out what was typical of the age in dining. It is not so long ago that ' nous avons changé tout cela.' I, and very many of my readers, recollect the time when ' the board ' literally ' groaned ' under the provisions laid upon it, and which *heu mihi !* we were expected to carve, if placed before us.   It was profusion, meant to honour your guests, but still unnecessary, and now, would be repulsive.   But why ? oh ! why ? was there, at this feast, placed on a side table ' a large Baron of Beef, and near it a beautiful blue and white China jug, which will hold twenty-three gallons of stout, on the top of which (?) will be displayed the Union Flag ?'   One thing may be said in its defence, and it is a fact not generally known, that, after a Civic banquet, all the food that is left, is given to deserving poor families, who thus benefit by the festivities of their richer brethren.   I believe this also obtains with the banquets of some of the City Companies.

Prior to the dinner, the Duke was presented with the Freedom of the City (an honour which any one under the rank of a monarch does not despise) in a gold box, and a splendid sword.   Most of the Royal Dukes, and all the Cabinet Ministers, together with large numbers of the Nobility, were present.   There was a gruesome long list of toasts, among which was ' the Ladies,' proposed by the Duke of Wellington.   Poor man ! he little thought what his gallantry would cost him, or perhaps, even he, the dauntless, might have quailed before what he had to undergo, with the exception of the last sentence, which probably served as the gilt to the pill.   ' Towards the close of the evening, a temporary staircase was opened from the galleries, into the body of the Hall, by which the Ladies descended, and passed round the hustings, and every one had the honour of shaking hands with the Immortal Hero, and the Royal Dukes, *and some of the younger ones were saluted by his Grace.'*   We afterwards learn that ' nearly Seven Hundred Ladies were in the Galleries.'

Apropos of what I wrote about dining, at this period, hear Captain Gronow, when writing on the same theme : ' Even in the best houses, when I was a young man, the dinners were wonderfully solid, hot, and stimulating.   The *menu* of a grand dinner was thus composed :—Mulligatawny and Turtle Soups were the first dishes placed before you ; a little lower, the eye met with the familiar salmon at one end of the table, and the turbot, surrounded by smelts, at the other.   The first course was sure to be followed by a saddle of mutton, or a piece of roast beef ; and then you could take your oath that fowls, tongue and ham, would as assuredly succeed, as darkness after day.

'Whilst these never-ending *pièces de résistance* were occupying the table, what were called French dishes were, for custom's sake, added to the solid abundance. The French, or side dishes, consisted of very mild, but very abortive, attempts at Continental cooking, and I have always observed that they met with the neglect and contempt they merited. The universally adored, and ever popular potato, produced at the very earliest period of the dinner, and eaten with everything, up to the moment when sweets appeared. Our Vegetables, the best in the world, were never honoured by an accompanying sauce, and, generally, came to the table cold. A prime difficulty to overcome, was the placing on your fork, and, finally in your mouth, some half dozen different eatables which occupied your plate at the same time. For example, your plate would contain, say, a slice of Turkey, a piece of stuffing, a sausage, pickles, a slice of tongue, cauliflower and potatoes. According to habit and custom, a judicious and careful selection from this little bazaar of good things was to be made, with an endeavour to place a portion of each in your mouth at the same moment. In fact, it appeared to me that we used to do all our compound Cookery between our jaws.

'The dessert—generally ordered at Messrs. Grange's, or at Owen's, in Bond Street—if for a dozen people, would cost, at least as many pounds. The wines were chiefly port, sherry, and hock ; claret, and even Burgundy, being then designated as " poor, thin, washy stuff." A perpetual thirst seemed to come over people, both men and women, as soon as they had tasted their soup ; as from that moment everybody was taking wine with everybody else, till the close of the dinner ; and such wine as produced that class of Cordiality which frequently wanders into stupefaction. How all this sort of eating and drinking ended was obvious, from the prevalence of gout, and the necessity of every one making the pill-box their constant bedroom companion.'

It must have been costly, too, to have then acted as Lucullus ; for those were not the days when steam annihilated distance, and brought tropical fruits to our doors, and when any vegetable could be grown, at any time, by means of electric light, and never allowing the plants any rest or sleep. Then, at all events, rarities in vegetables fetched a price, such as we should not now dream of paying. *Vide* the following : 'It is a standing order in the wealthy Company of Grocers to have plenty of green pease at their dinner, when they do not exceed the price of *four guineas a quart ;* this year, from the unfavourableness of the season, they were not to be obtained under the price of six guineas; and, in consequence, the members were obliged so far to *narrow* their indulgence, as to put up with turtle, turbot, venison, house lamb, turkey poults, asparagus, and French beans.'

This year of 1814 must, I am afraid, be given up to the high and mighty ones of this portion of the world, for it was, as I have said, an *annus mirabilis,* and ordinary people were, so to speak, nowhere.

Now it is the Regent's daughter. She came of age—she wanted a household of her own ; she wanted unrestricted intercourse with her mother—and she wanted a husband.

She had no love for her father ; what child could have any filial affection for a father who cared nothing for his daughter? She was forbidden to see her mother, and consequently longed for her. She was legally of age, and still was treated as a child.

The episode in her life, I am about to relate, is curious, and I have endeavoured to take the most temperate authorities on the subject, so that, whilst being contemporaneous, they are, as far as one can judge, historically unbiassed. She could have had no love for her father, for his failings were of public notoriety, and he never lavished any of his affection upon her. Her mother, too—badly brought up in a petty German Court, where licence was familiar—had, certainly, been indiscreet. Her Peers absolved her from anything worse than indiscretion, and I, who have studied her life, and written it (not as it appears in the ' Dictionary of National Biography,' for, there, it has been maimed, editorially), thoroughly endorse their verdict.

Of course, her public life began on her attaining her 18th year, when she legally became of age, Her mother wished, very naturally, to present her to the Queen, as launching her in life ; but the Queen had a son, the father of Mademoiselle, who was not on good terms with his wife ; and, although mother and son were not the best possible friends, still the probability is, that grandmamma thought that papa was best judge of his daughter's welfare, and therefore backed up the stern parent. *Ergo,* Mamma was nowhere, and went abroad, having an increased allowance, which she would not touch.

The *imprimatur* of a young lady's life, in Court circles, is, naturally, her presentation at Court ; with men, it differs. I recollect a tailor, in Fenchurch Street, being presented—the Lord knows why, probably because he made the clothes for the Lord Mayor's footmen. But this case was different—this was the heiress to the throne—a *personnage*, of whom there could be no doubt. Her mother was not a *persona gratissima* at Court ; and although she used to spend somewhat dreary days with Grandmamma Charlotte, and her Aunts at Windsor, she had not yet been presented legally, nor had she yet achieved the other grand step in her young life, and natural ambition of her sex, that of obtaining a husband.

She got a godmother, for her presentation, in the shape of the good fairy, the Duchess of Oldenburgh. I have not been able to unravel what this lady's mission was, but I know that both she and her brother backed up the suit of the Prince of Orange as husband to the coming Queen of England.

This Drawing Room took place on June 2nd, and the Princess started for the first time as 'the Daughter of England,' and went, in more than Cinderella state, in an elegant State Carriage—all her own—with splendid hammer Cloth of Scarlet and Gold, with the Royal Arms, and Union Wreath richly embroidered in the centre on White Satin. New harness of black leather and raised brass ; three footmen, and a brand new coachman, all in brand new liveries. For the first time in her life she was somebody ; for, let alone all this magnificence, she was assisted into her carriage by her would-be *fiancé*, the Prince of Orange.

According to the 'Court Circular' of the time, the Duchess of Oldenburgh must have been exceeding magnifical, and more than rivalled the famous creature, 'the *Prox*,' two of whom came over in three ships ; for I read, 'The Duchess of Oldenburgh went in State in three of the Prince Regent's Carriages.'*

It was, specially, on this occasion the Prince Regent was hissed, as politely hinted at in the account of the Allied Sovereigns' Reception (see p. 150). I do not say that His Royal Highness did not care to face the Populace on this latter occasion ; it was thought so generally, and the Satirical prints, so often misnamed *Caricatures*, were *de bon accord*. These prints filled the part of our so-called Comic papers. There was no *Punch*, or the innumerable host of its followers now existing ; and, what is more universally taken as good-

* At the moment of her entrance into what is now Buckingham Palace—then the *Queen's House*—the first gun was fired, announcing the signature of the Definitive Treaty of Peace.

humoured *badinage,* was just the same then, only the sense of humour was different. It is, perhaps, a little coarse to our taste, but then our grandfathers had not the advantage of the artistic education of a School Board, and they acted on such lights as were vouchsafed to them.

His conduct to his wife, at this time, rendered him very unpopular, and, in those days, people were accustomed to express their satisfaction, or the reverse, with either a Prince or an Actor. Nowadays, goodness only knows what might happen were popular opinion so expressed. Luckily, our Princes are too good men to have a shadow of unpopularity ; and, as to Actors—well—it might end in an action for libel, or, slugs in a saw-pit.

I give a plain, and unadorned, version of the reception of the Regent, on this occasion, as reported in a paper, certainly not unfriendly to him. ' Pall Mall and St. James's Street were kept perfectly clear for carriages to enter the Park, by the Stable Yard. The Prince Regent, with his superb retinue, passed along Pall Mall without interruption ; but his carriage no sooner entered the Park, than the multitudes assembled there recognized his Royal Highness, and he was annoyed by the most dismal yells, groans and hisses, which continued the whole way from the Stable Yard to the Queen's House. The horses were put to their full speed to carry his Royal Highness through this ungracious scene. A very different welcome was given to the Military Heroes on their way to the Palace. It was with extreme difficulty that Lord Hill, Lord Combermere, and Lord Beresford were permitted to pass on in their Carriages, as the people wanted to take out the horses, and yoke themselves to the harness.'

Launched into life, she became more independent. Papa had provided a husband for her, but we all know the old proverb, that ' You may take a horse to the water, but you can't make him drink.' She did not like the Prince of Orange, and, as any excuse is better than none, she made use of the fact that her husband *in posse* wanted to take her to Holland, if only for a fortnight, in order to show her the Country, and present her to his people. This she refused utterly to do, and the breach between them, which had been widening gradually, became complete. He had been treated with but scant courtesy, during the visit of the Allied Sovereigns, so much so, that it was commented upon. One exemplar will suffice.

'The Hereditary Prince of Orange, who was announced as the intended husband of our Princess Charlotte, and, consequently as the Consort of our future Queen, has not been treated with much ceremony; while the other Illustrious Foreigners had State Carriages and Royal liveries, the Prince was suffered to shift for himself, and to find a lodging at the house of his *Tailor.*'

In fact, she would not have him, and Papa did not like it. Naturally, the Satirists of the time got hold of their estrangement, and improved the occasion. I reproduce one print, 'Miss endeavouring to excite a Glow with her DUTCH Plaything.' The Princess says to her father, 'There! I have kept it up a long while; you may send it away now, I am tired of it. Mother has got some better play-things for me.' The Regent replies, 'What! are you tired already? Take another spell at it, or give me the whip.' To which the Princess answers, 'No, no! You may take the Top, but I'll keep the whip.'

There was another, 'The Dutch Toy.' The Princess is represented as whipping a Top, with the letters P. O. painted on it, saying, 'Take this for Ma! and this for Pa! and this! and this! for myself, you ugly thing, you.' Through an open door the Regent's arm is seen, carrying a portentous birch rod; and he warns her that if she does not find pleasure in whipping the Top, he will exercise his paternal authority with the instrument which he bears. There are others, but they are hardly worth repeating.

She had met with her fate. We all know that there is in a woman's life but one 'Prince Charming.' Sometimes he never comes, but, as a rule, he does. Well! here was a case. That fairy Godmother, the Duchess of Oldenburgh, living at her Pulteney Hotel, could, of course, entertain any guests she liked; and one morning, Prince Leopold of Saxe-Coburg, whilst paying a visit to the Duchess, met with the Princess Charlotte. People have given up thinking of how marriages are made, and put the onus on a Higher Power, and say they are made in Heaven. She met her *kismet*, and, as far as is publicly known, her brief life was spent happily. England, as a nation, ought to be very thankful for this union, for it gave our most gracious Queen Victoria one of the wisest and kindest Counsellors possible—King Leopold of Belgium. There must be many, besides myself, who read these pages, who recollect the kindly old gentleman who used to come

MISS ENDEAVOURING TO EXCITE A GLOW WITH HER DUTCH PLAYTHING.

(*Published July 1, 1814, by Fores.*)

over here, just as if he was going to pay a call in the next
street, without any fuss, and to whom one would regret the
not paying the ordinary courteous form of recognition,
because he was so unostentatious.   The History of Europe
knows the effect of his quiet counsel.

But who would recognize him in the accompanying illustration? *Ay de mi!*   He and the Princess Charlotte danced that

THE DEVONSHIRE MINUET.
(Published May 29, 1813, by William Holland.)

Minuet, and are no more ; but, for the time being, they were
a handsome, graceful couple.

The Orange affair fell through ; and, as far as I am concerned, who only have to deal with what people talked about
in England at that time, there is an end of it.   But something, or somebody, irritated Papa, and he resolved that
Mademoiselle's independence must be curtailed, and that in
future she must live—well, not exactly with him, but under

his roof, at Carlton House.   I have read all I know that there
is to be read on the subject, and I prefer letting one of the
parties tell the tale.   It, and much more, can be found in
'The Autobiography of Miss Cornelia Knight, Lady Companion
to the Princess Charlotte of Wales' (2 vols.   London, 1861).

'About this time the Bishop,* who often saw the Chancellor, and Lord Liverpool, and was, also, I believe, employed
by the Regent, who, formerly, disliked and despised him,
hinted to Princess Charlotte, in a private conversation, and to
me, *on paper*—as I wrote to him on the subject—that, unless
Princess Charlotte would write a submissive letter to her
father, and hold out a hope that in a few months she might
be induced to give her hand to the Prince of Orange, arrangements would be made, by no means agreeable to her inclina-
tions.   Her Royal Highness wrote to the Regent a most
submissive and affectionate letter, but held out no hope of
renewing the treaty of marriage.

'This letter was sent on Saturday, the 9th of July.   We
heard various reports of the intentions of the Regent : it was
said that I, and the servants, were to be dismissed, and that
an apartment was being fitted up for the Princess Charlotte at
Carlton House.   Prince Leopold of Saxe-Coburg, a handsome
young man, a General in the Russian Service, brother-in-law
to the Grand Duke Constantine, and a great favourite with
the Emperor of Russia, told Miss Mercer Elphinstone many of
these particulars.   He had been once at Warwick House, the
Duchess of Leeds and myself being present.   Miss Mercer
Elphinstone, who was intimately acquainted with him, came
in while he was there.   He paid many compliments to
Princess Charlotte, who was by no means partial to him, and
only received him with civility.   However, Miss Mercer
evidently wished to recommend him ; and when we drove in
the Park, he would ride near the carriage, and endeavour to
be noticed.   There were reasons why this matter was by no
means agreeable to Princess Charlotte.   However, he certainly
made proposals to the Regent, and, though rejected, found
means to get into his favour.

'In the mean while, it was reported that he was frequently
at Warwick House, and had even taken tea with us, which
not one of the princes had done, except Prince Radzivil,
whom we invited to sing, and accompany himself on the
guitar.   We heard that Lady Ilchester and Lady Rosslyn

* Of Salisbury.

were talked of as being about Princess Charlotte, and I had hints from some of my friends, particularly from Lady Rolle, that a change was about to take place.

' However, the letter of the 9th remained unanswered till the 11th, on which day the Bishop was detained almost the whole morning at Carlton House, and, at five, Princess Charlotte and I were ordered to go over. Her Royal Highness was too ill to obey ; but I went, and found the Regent very cold, very bitter, and very silent. I, however, took the opportunity of contradicting any false reports he might have heard relative to the Prince of Saxe-Coburg, and he answered that this Prince was a most honourable young man, and had written him a letter which perfectly justified himself, and said that he was invited by Princess Charlotte ; but that it was Prince Augustus of Prussia, and not he, who was in the habit of going to Warwick House. I justified Prince Augustus, as he well deserved ; and apologized for Princess Charlotte's not coming over to Carlton House. The Prince said she must either come the next day, or Baillie must come to say she was not capable of walking over.

' Next day, Baillie said she was quite capable of going over, and advised her so to do ; but she was really so ill, and so much affected, that it was impossible. Her Royal Highness, therefore, wrote to the Regent, entreating he would come to her. The Duchess of Leeds, who, unfortunately, had been ordered to send in her resignation some time before, but still came as usual to Warwick House, called that morning, but I could not persuade her to stay till the Prince's arrival, as she said he might think it improper her being there.

' About six, he came, attended by the Bishop, only (as I supposed) ; but he came up alone, and desired I would leave him with the Princess Charlotte. He was shut up with her three quarters of an hour, and, afterwards, a quarter more with the Bishop, and her Royal Highness. The door then opened, and she came out in the greatest agony, saying she had but one instant to speak to me, for that the Prince asked for me. I followed her into her dressing-room, where she told me the new ladies were in possession of the house ; that I, and all the servants, were to be dismissed ; that she was to be confined at Carlton House for five days, after which she was to be taken to Cranbourne Lodge, in the midst of Windsor Forest, where she was to see no one but the Queen, once a week ; and that if she did not go immediately, the

Prince would sleep at Warwick House that night, as well as all the ladies. I begged her to be calm, and advised her to go over, as soon as possible, assuring her that her friends would not forget her. She fell upon her knees in the greatest agitation, exclaiming, "God Almighty, grant me patience!" I wished to stay and comfort her, but she urged me to go to the Prince, for fear of greater displeasure.

'I went to him, and he shut the door; the Bishop was with him. He told me he was sorry to put a lady to inconvenience, but that he wanted my room that evening for the ladies, repeating what Princess Charlotte had already told me. I asked in what I had offended, but he said he made no complaint, and would make none; that he had a right to make any changes he pleased, and that he was blamed for having let things go on as they had done. He repeated his apology for putting a lady to the inconvenience of leaving the house at so short a notice; and I replied that, my father having served His Majesty for fifty years, and sacrificed his health and fortune to that service, it would be very strange if I could not put myself to the temporary inconvenience of a few hours. He then said that in the arrangements at Carlton House there was a room which I might have for a night or two, if I had nowhere to go. This I declined, thanking him, but saying I had lodgings, which, fortunately, were now vacant; and that Lord and Lady Rolle, who seemed to know much more of the business than I did, had, to my surprise, offered me their house, for the last fortnight. I then made a low courtesy to him, and left the room.'

This, and what occurred afterwards, formed the topic of conversation for the time; and, of the Comic Prints, which naturally followed, the accompanying one, by George Cruikshank, is the most amusing. It is called, ' The R——t kicking up a Row; or, Warwick House in an Uproar!!!' The Regent, addressing Miss Knight and the Princess's ladies, says, ' Get out! get out! you faggots! Get out of the House, I say. Zounds! I've burst my stays. What! what! you'll let her see her mother, will you?!!! Oh! you Jades! But I'll soon put a stop to that—I'll lock the young baggage up, that's what I will; and I'll kick you to the Devil, and that's what I will. So turn out! turn out! out! out! and be d——d to you all.'

The Princess is seen running away to her mother, crying out, ' Oh, mamma! mamma! Pappe's going to whip me.

Oh ! oh ! oh ! !' The Bishop of Salisbury is in the background looking on. The Bishop is aghast, and says, ' Dash my wig, here's a pretty kick up ! ! !' John Bull is looking in at a window, wondering ' What the Devil is he about, now ?'

THE R——T KICKING UP A ROW; OR, WARWICK HOUSE IN AN UPROAR !!!

(*G. Cruikshank fec.*)

Directly after the interview with the Princess, described by Miss Knight, the former left Warwick House, and hailing a hackney coach in Cockspur Street, ordered the coachman to drive to Connaught House, at the corner of the Bayswater and Edgware Roads, her mother's residence. We get a graphic view of this in an illustration called ' PLEBEIAN SPIRIT ; or Coachee and the Heir Presumptive.' The Princess, who, to judge by the size of the coin she is tendering, is paying lavishly,* says, *les larmes aux yeux*, ' Coachman, will you protect me ?' to which the gallant Jehu, hand on heart, replies, ' Yes, your Highness, to the last drop of my blood.' I have not given the background, for it is too painful. Britannia and the British Lion appear, and *both* are weeping, the Lion very copiously.

Mamma was not at home, but was sent for, and met on the road from Blackheath. The news somewhat upset her, but she adopted the very sensible plan of seeking advice from her friends, Mr. Whitbread and Earl Grey ; but, neither being at home, she drove to Connaught House, and Mr. Brougham was sent for. Meantime Papa did not know what to do, so he sent for his Ministers, and consulted with them ; and, so grave was the occasion, that a Council was held at the Foreign Office, and also at Carlton House. In fact, to judge properly of the unprecedented gravity of the situation, I need only mention that when the Queen heard of it, *she immediately left a Card party she was holding.* A National Revolution could hardly have had a greater effect.

Then remonstrance was tried with this wicked, rebellious girl, and first was sent my lord the Bishop of Salisbury, followed by the Duke of York, who seems to have had *carte blanche* to promise anything ; there was the Lord Chancellor, Lord Ellenborough, Adam, the Chancellor of the Duchy of Cornwall, and yet more, all come to see what they could do with this awful young lady, who had given her papa's nerves such a rude shaking. Her kind uncle, the Duke of Sussex, she would see, because he came independently, and, afterwards, asked pertinent questions in her behalf in the House of Lords.

Let Lord Brougham, who had so much to do with this interview, describe it : ' After dinner I first begged the Princess Charlotte to give me a full account of what had caused her flight. She said she could not bear any longer the treatment she met with in changing her ladies without her consent, and of interrupting her intercourse with her

* According to *The Morning Chronicle* of July 15th she gave him three guineas.

mother and Margaret (meaning Miss Mercer),* her most
intimate friend; and that it was her fixed resolution, after
throwing herself on her mother's protection, to reside with
her entirely.   But she dwelt much upon the match; and,

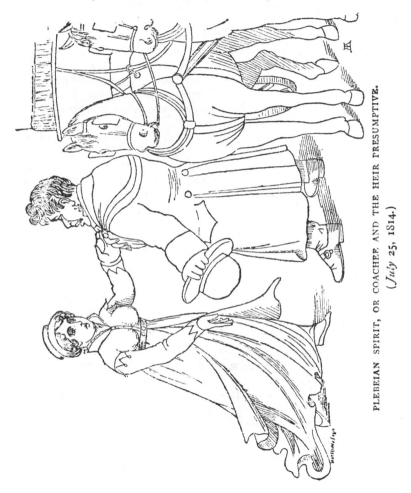

PLEBEIAN SPIRIT, OR COACHEE AND THE HEIR PRESUMPTIVE.

(*July* 25, 1814.)

although I repeated what I had often assured her of, that
without her consent freely given, it never could take place,

* Afterwards Lady Keith, and wife of Count Flahault.

she said, " They may wear me out by ill-treatment, and may represent that I have changed my mind and consented."

' We then conversed upon the subject with the others, and, after a long discussion on that and her lesser grievances, she took me aside, and asked me what, upon the whole, I advised her to do. I said at once, " Return to Warwick House, or Carlton House, and on no account to pass a night out of her own house." She was extremely affected, and cried, asking if I too refused to stand by her. I said, quite the contrary ; and that as to the marriage, I gave no opinion, except that she must follow her own inclination entirely, but that her returning home was absolutely necessary ; and in this all the rest fully agreed—her mother, the Duke of Sussex, Miss Mercer, and Lady Charlotte Lindsay, for whom she had a great respect and regard. I said that, however painful it was for me, the necessity was so clear and so strong that I had not the least hesitation in advising it. She again and again begged me to consider her situation, and to think whether, looking to that, it was absolutely necessary she should return.

' The day now began to dawn, and I took her to the window. The election of Cochrane (after his expulsion owing to the sentence of the Court, which both insured his re-election and abolished the pillory) was to take place that day. I said, " Look there, Madam ; in a few hours all the streets and the park, now empty, will be crowded with tens of thousands. I have only to take you to the window, show you to the crowd, and tell them your grievances, and they will all rise in your behalf." " And why should they not ?" I think she said, or some such words. " The commotion," I answered, " will be excessive ; Carlton House will be attacked —perhaps pulled down ; the soldiers will be ordered out ; blood will be shed ; and if your Royal Highness were to live a hundred years, it never would be forgotten that your running away from your father's house was the cause of the mischief ; and you may depend upon it, such is the English people's horror of bloodshed, you never would get over it." She, at once, felt the truth of my assertion, and consented to see her uncle Frederic (the Duke of York) below stairs, and return with him. But she required one of the royal carriages should be sent for, which came with her governess, and they, with the Duke of York, went home about five o'clock.

' Before she went, however, she desired me to make a

minute of her declaration that she was resolved not to marry
the Prince of Orange, and that, if ever there should be an
announcement of such a match, it must be understood to be
without her consent, and against her will.   She added, " I
desire Augustus [Duke of Sussex] and Mr. Brougham would
particularly take notice of this."   When I had made the note,
it was read distinctly, and signed by all present, she signing
first, and six Copies were made and signed, and one given to
each person present.'*

And so this little episode was ended.   Who, think you,
scored ?   I must say, I think that victory was on the side of
Mademoiselle.

* 'The Life and Times of Henry, Lord Brougham,' written by
himself, 1871, vol. ii. p. 229.

CHAPTER XVII.

State of Ireland—The Regent *fêtes* the Duke of Wellington—The Jubilee in the Parks—Public opinion thereon—The Celebration.

AMONG other Home topics, just at this time, was one so familiar to us—the disturbed state of Ireland. Take this one month of July. Mr. Long, of Ardmayle, was shot almost on his threshold. Two men with blackened faces entered a cottage at Woodhouse, Co. Waterford, and shot (gallant fellows!) a girl of twenty years of age. Here is the account of a riot arising out of an Orange demonstration, taken from *The Belfast Commercial Herald* :—

'A dreadful riot, attended with very melancholy circumstances, took place at the Race Course of Downpatrick. It appears that a very great and unusual assembling of country people, all armed with sticks, and some with pistols, was observed on the Race Course on Friday (July 15th), and it was understood that a preconcerted disturbance was to be the consequence, as, for several days before, it was said without hesitation that "the Orangemen had their day on the 12th of July, and they (the Threshers, or whatever name they go by) should have theirs on the Friday of the Races." About four o'clock on that day, a quarrel (many present say a sham fight) took place between two men, which, in an instant, attracted a great crowd, apparently on the watch, and a disturbance ensued, and continued for a considerable time, till it became so alarming, that the magistrates found it necessary to send to Down for a detachment of the Middlesex Militia quartered there.

'When the military were drawn up, the rage of the assembled crowd was directed almost wholly against them, and they were assailed with volleys of stones from behind the tents, and many opprobrious names. The Militia, all this time, kept their ground with the greatest coolness ; the great mass (some thousands, it is said), emboldened by the quiet manner in which the soldiers acted, advanced so near as to bid them defiance, pelting them with stones, by which some of them were injured and knocked down.   The soldiers were then ordered to fire with blank cartridge ; but this only made the mob more riotous.   They were then ordered to fire with ball ; two men instantly fell, and a great many were wounded ; four or five are in the Infirmary.   A number of the rioters were taken prisoners, and lodged in jail; one of them, we have heard, had four pistols in his possession, another had two.'

On July 21st the Prince of Wales gave a *fête* in honour of the Duke of Wellington, which, in magnificence, rivalled that famous one with which he celebrated his becoming Regent. Two thousand five hundred persons were invited, and the Queen, the Princesses, and all the available Royal Family were present.

About this time the English prisoners of war were returning from France ; but, although they, naturally, had sad tales to tell of their sufferings in the French prisons and hulks, yet many came back materially benefited by their incarceration ; for the British Government arranged that those with good education should teach those who were ignorant, for which they received a small recompense, and, consequently, many came home able not only to read and write, but instructed in mathematics sufficiently to be of great assistance to them in their future life as sailors.

Truly I said this was an *Annus mirabilis*, for now, on the 1st of August, was to be the public Celebration of Peace, and the date was fixed because it was the Centenary of the Accession of George I., founder of the present dynasty in England : and this public rejoicing was christened 'The Jubilee.'   The following is, substantially, a correct programme, but it was published in a newspaper a fortnight before, and, afterwards there were some slight modifications ; but I think it is the best contemporaneous short account, of the amusement provided for the people.

'THE GRAND JUBILEE.

' OFFICIAL PROGRAMME.

'These amusements will begin with the ascent of a magnificent balloon of sufficiently large dimensions to take up two persons in the car affixed to it.   It will ascend about five o'clock; later in the day, a smaller balloon, of 20 feet in diameter, will also ascend, and a copious display of fireworks from it will be exhibited in the higher regions of the air: it will then be made to descend; and, upon its second ascension, another display of brilliant fireworks will also take place at a great elevation from the ground.   Still later in the evening, several other balloons, upon a smaller scale, will be dispatched towards the clouds, charged with various fire-works, which will be seen with effect at a lofty height, and, after these are expended, the hydrogen contained in these balloons will be inflamed, and will produce a brilliant appearance, resembling in splendour the most striking meteoric phenomenon.

'Over the Canal* has been thrown a beautiful Chinese bridge, upon the centre of which has been constructed an elegant and lofty pagoda, consisting of seven pyramidal stories.   The pagoda will be illuminated with the gas† lights, and brilliant fireworks, both fixed and missile, will be displayed from every division of this lofty Chinese structure.   Copious and splendid girandoles of rockets will also be occasionally displayed from the summit, and from other parts of the towering edifice, which will, at times, be so covered with jerbs, Roman candles, and pots de brin, as to become in appearance one column of brilliant fire.   Various smaller temples and columns constructed upon the bridge, will, also, be vividly illuminated; and fixed fire-works of different devices, on the balustrade of the bridge, will contribute to heighten the general effect.

'The Canal will also be well provided with handsomely decorated boats, at the disposal of those who wish to add this amusement to the numerous pleasures.

'The whole margin of the lawn will be surrounded with booths for refreshment, which will be illuminated in the evening, interspersed with open marquees provided with seats for the accommodation of the company.

'The Malls of the Park will be illuminated with Chinese lanterns, ornamented with picturesque and grotesque devices, and every tree will have variegated lights intermingled with its foliage.   Bands of music will be stationed at various distances, and spaces will be provided at different parts of

* The Ornamental Water in St. James's Park.

† Our ordinary Gas (Carburetted Hydrogen) was always then, and long after, called ' the Gas.'

the lawn, for those who delight in the pleasures of the dance ; the whole forming a Vauxhall on the most magnificent scale.

' In addition to the foregoing list of amusements, the Public will have a full view of the Royal Booth, and of the grand fire-works in the Green Park, which will be displayed from a fortress or Castle, the ramparts of which are 100 feet square, surmounted by a round tower in the centre, about 60 feet in diameter, and rising to the height of over 50 feet above the ramparts.   Four grand changes of fire-works will be exhibited from this stupendous Castle, the whole elevation of which exceeds 90 feet.

' To secure to every one a complete view of this edifice and its decorations, notwithstanding its great height and dimensions, it is so constructed as to revolve on its centre, so that each side will be successively presented to the assemblage of the Company.   The Castle, thus exhibiting the appearance of a grand military fortification, is intended, allegorically, to represent War, and the discharges of artillery, small arms, maroons, &c., may be regarded as descriptive of the terrors of a siege.   On a sudden, this will cease : in the midst of flames, clouds of smoke, and the thunder of artillery, the lofty fortress, the emblem of destructive war, is transformed into a beautiful temple, the type of glorious peace. The lower and quadrangular compartment is embellished with Doric columns of porphyry ; the circular edifice which surmounts it is decorated with the lighter Ionic columns of Sienna marble.   The whole will be brilliantly illuminated, and adorned with allegorical transparencies, executed by the masterly pencils of artists of the first eminence.'

What fun was made of this childish Exhibition ! These were the *panem et circenses* to reward the people for their having lavishly given of their blood and gold ; and its conception was pretty universally put down to the Prince Regent ; the Chinese Bridge and Pagoda were so highly suggestive of Brighton.   Many were the verses on this Jubilee and its putative author.

'THE FATHER OF HIS COUNTRY.

Princes of old, if wise and good,
Were *Fathers* called—and so they should—
And give the little girls and boys
Plenty of gingerbread and toys.

13

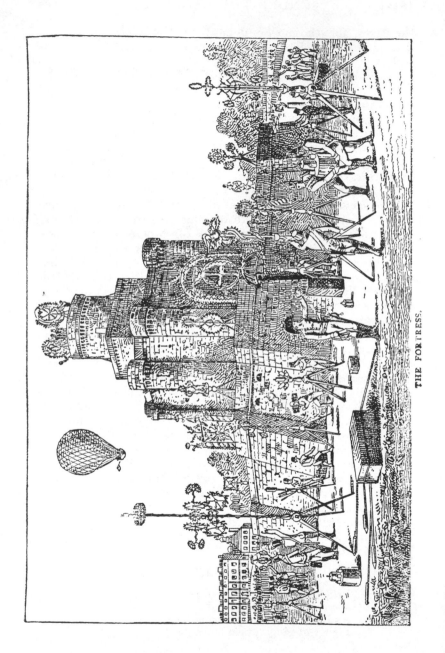

THE FORTRESS.

" *Our* Pa," says Biddy to her brother,
" Is quite as good as a *Grandmother !*"
" Grandmother! hush! 'tis treason stark !"
Cries Jacky, " Say a *Grand-Monarque !*" '

One of the greatest sources of ridicule connected with this
Jubilee was ' the Naumachia,' a mimic combat on the Serpentine, between an English and French fleet. Of course the
Three Deckers and Frigates must necessarily be small, so they
were manufactured at Woolwich, out of ship's-boats : and the
following lines give a very fair idea of popular opinion on the
fête :—

' JOHN BULL, the other day, in pensive mood
Near to the Serpentine Flotilla stood ;
His hands were thrust into his emptied pockets,
And much of ships he muttered, and of rockets,
Of silly Fêtes—and Jubilees unthrifty—
And Babies overgrown, of *two-and-fifty ;*
I guess'd the train of thought which then possess'd him,
And deem'd th' occasion fit, and thus addressed him :

Be generous to a fallen foe,
    With gratulations meet,
On Elba's *Emperor* bestow
    Thy Lilliputian fleet ;

For with his Island's narrow bounds
    That navy might agree,
Which, laugh'd at daily here—redounds
    In ridicule to thee.

Says JOHN, " Right readily I'll part
    With these, and all the gay things,
But it would break the R——'s heart
    To take away his playthings." '

The chaff was great about these ships—see under :—

' A simple Angler, throwing flies for trout,
Hauled the main mast, and lugg'd a First Rate out.'

' A crow in his *fright*, flying over the Fleet,
Dropped something, that covered it all, like a sheet.'

The Chinese Bridge, and even the Fireworks were made
fun of.

' I overheard a silly Cambridge Clerk,
Thus mutter, as he passed St. James's Park :
" What's this ? A Bridge ? How hard to be got over !
Oh ! 'tis the Ass's BRIDGE, I do discover." '

'The R—— thinks to make us stare,
        By raising rockets in the air ;—
    His scheme to please will fail, he'll find,
        Since we for it must *raise the wind.*'

The pseudo Peter Pindar (*C. F. Lawler ?*) has a great deal
to do with the Jubilee, and published divers satirical poems
thereon. 'Liliputian Navy !!! The R——t's Fleet, or, John
Bull at the Serpentine.' 'The P——'s Jubilee.' 'The
R——l Showman.' 'The R——l Fair, or Grande Galante
Show,' and one on the sale of the Temple of Concord—'The
Temple knock'd down ; or R——l Auction. The last lay of
the Jubilee.'

The following short account of the Jubilee is taken from a
contemporary morning journal.

'Yesterday being the Centenary of the Accession of the
House of Brunswick, and the Anniversary of the glorious
Victory of the Nile, was selected as the day for a Jubilee in
celebration of the Peace. The plan of the arrangements for
the Show in the Parks, has already been given, together with
a description of the preparations. Considerable uncertainty
hung over the public mind as to the actual day of exhibition,
in consequence of the notice advertised and posted up, stating
that it would depend upon the state of the weather ; an uncertainty not a little heightened by the unpromising appearance of the morning. Numbers, however, regardless of notification, or weather, and determined to have a day of it,
particularly those who lived at a distance from the scene of
operations, set out from home, and were seen flocking, at an
early hour, to the Parks. At length, the firing of cannon
announced that the day was considered favourable, and that
the Jubilee would commence. The population of the Metropolis then poured forth in a continued stream, or, rather flood,
to witness the exhibition. Shops were shut, business was suspended, houses were left to take care of themselves, and the
Strand, Oxford Street, and Piccadilly, were nearly blocked
up by masses of people of all descriptions, including many
women with infants in their arms, all hurrying on to see the
Show.

'It had been previously understood, and the public notices
posted up certainly led to that impression, that all the
entrances to St. James's Park, save those leading into the
space allotted to the holders of tickets, would have been
open to the public. It turned out, however, that counter

orders had, in the meantime, been given, and the passages by the Horse Guards, and the Spring Garden-gate were alone opened for persons without tickets to enter the Park. The gate at New Street, although a notice was posted up at its side, intimating that it had been deemed expedient to open it to the public, remained shut. This, of course, greatly increased the pressure; numbers flocked to the Stable-yard; but there all admittance to the Park, without tickets, was refused. Some relief, however, was afforded by allowing an egress by this gate to the persons in the Park.

'Hyde Park, and the Green Park, except the space in the latter railed off, were opened *ad libitum* to the public, and the view of the numerous and varied groups in these two Parks formed an enlivening *coup d'œil*. Booths and flying barracks (as they were called) and open stands of a more humble description, appeared in every direction, with all sorts of refreshments; liquors and liquids, to satisfy the hunger, cheer the spirits, and allay the thirst of the almost innumerable crowd that pressed upon all points where anything was to be seen. A number of marquees, as has already been stated, were pitched upon the lawn on both sides of the canal in St. James's Park,* for the use of the holders of tickets, that being the principal part of the space allotted to them, and these were interspersed with several booths and flying barracks for furnishing refreshments. A number of benches were also placed in this space, besides those in the marquees.

'For the public at large, who had the range of the Parks, there was little accommodation in the shape of seats. Those who were tired of promenading were glad to lean against a tree, or find seats upon the ground; many brought their provisions with them, and partook of a family or a picnic collation, the earth alike their table and their seat. In this manner the time was passed till the hour arrived. On the commencement of the grand shew the first object of attraction was the ascent of a Balloon.

'The Balloon was placed in the ground in front of the

---

* Pepys speaks of this on more than one occasion, notably '1660, Sept. 16. To the Park, where I saw how far they had proceeded in the Pall Mall, and in making a river through the Park, which I had never seen before since it was begun.' Evelyn also mentions it: '1662, Dec. 1. Having seen the strange and wonderful dexterity of the sliders on the New Canal in St. James's Park,' &c.

Queen's Palace.   The operation of filling it commenced as early as nine o'clock in the morning, but it was not sufficiently inflated till a few minutes before six in the evening.   About four o'clock the immense body of spectators assembled in St. James's Park, and in the Green Park, being in the more immediate vicinity of the spot whence the balloon was to ascend, were surprised and gratified by the appearance of a balloon of small dimensions coming, as it were, from Hyde Park, or Kensington Gardens.   This contributed for some time, to suspend any feeling of impatience which might have shewn itself in consequence of the large balloon not being ready to ascend at the stated hour (five o'clock).

'Some time before six o'clock, a report of the firing of guns, as of the promised naval engagement on the Serpentine River, reached the ears of the same persons, many of whom seemed to be actuated by a momentary desire to change the scene of action, and to share in the fight, the report of which they had heard from afar.   The manifestation of this spirit, however, was merely momentary ; they quickly became more peaceably inclined ; and, whether apprehensive that they might only come in to witness the *conclusion* of the sea fight, or resolved, on more mature deliberation, to be satisfied spectators of an aerial flight, and of the destruction of ' a Fortified Castle,' which (strange to tell) was, through the aid of fire, to be transformed into the ' *Temple of Peace* '—they, with a few exceptions, took the advice given them in the printed recommendations, and remained on the ground they had originally occupied.

'About twenty minute ' efore six, the Balloon, being then sufficiently inflated, was elevated from the situation it had hitherto occupied, and the car, which was extremely splendid and brilliant, being affixed to it, Mr. Sadler, junior, mounted into the car, which was decorated with four flags.   Being supplied with the necessary quantity of ballast, of cards for signals, &c., the youthful and intrepid Aeronaut, being liberated from the chains by which his chariot was confined to the ground, began to ascend in a most solemn and majestic manner, so far as the observers were concerned, yet with a degree of rapidity which must have unstrung the nerves of any one entirely unused to such lofty excursions.

'The Balloon took a direction inclining towards the south-east, and was in sight for about half an hour.   It was generally reported that Mrs. Henry Johnston was to have accompanied Mr. Sadler, but we could not perceive that either she, or any other lady mounted the car.

' Between eight and nine o'clock, the Grand Sea Fight took place on the Serpentine River, where ships of the line, in miniature, manœuvred and engaged, and the Battle of the Nile, was represented in little. Of this mock naval engagement on the great Serpentine Ocean, it would be extremely difficult to give any adequate description. It is, perhaps, sufficient to observe, that it was about on a par with spectacles of a similar nature, which have been frequently exhibited at the Theatres.

' After the ascent of the Balloon, one part of the company in the sacred enclosure, sauntered about the brown banks of the Canal, while the rest disturbed the green surface of the water in wherries. No attempt at amusement presented itself for a long time, except a species of boat race between two watermen, but this did not attract, nor was it deserving of much attention. While the crowd within the enclosure were thus languishing for want of amusement, the people in the Mall, although they had been kindly forewarned that the best amusements would take place in Hyde Park, thought it desirable, on the principle by which sin first began, to attempt an incursion on the space within. Several lads jumped over the enclosure, but they were immediately pursued by the Artillerymen who guarded the rails, at small distances from each other, and ejected from this supposed seat of bliss, after some rough treatment from their pursuers. The mob, without, endeavoured to vent their anger against the envied occupiers of the enclosure, and, especially, against the soldiers, by a very liberal and ingenious application of all the slang at their command. As it grew dark, these incursions were effectually prevented by an increased number of guards.

' At the same time the lamps and the Chinese lanterns were lighted ; the former were dispersed over the lawn in crescents and moons, elevated to a small distance from the ground. The Chinese lanterns hung in the walks midway between the trees, and were decorated with a great variety of objects, though not with much taste ; some represented Mr. Sadler's balloon, others the Ark of Noah ; on one was painted the Tower of Babel, on another the Pagoda ; on some, Mr. Kean as *Richard*, on others the Great Mogul.

' The Bridge, with the Pagoda, was soon entirely lighted ; and the reflection of the lights gave to the whole Canal the

THE TEMPLE OF CONCORD.

appearance of a lake of fire. Notwithstanding the beautiful object, yawning was very prevalent for an hour or two, and great strife arose concerning the possession of the benches, but the attention of the Combatants was soon diverted to the loud cannonade which commenced in the Green Park. The firing continued for a long time, and, immediately it ceased, an immense flight of rockets arose from the top of the Pagoda, on the Canal, and traced a thousand brilliant paths through the sky, which the smoke of the cannonade had rendered brown and opake.

' From this time a contest in brilliancy arose between the Fortress in the Green Park, and the Pagoda on the Canal. An incessant variety of wheels and stars appeared at intervals on both these structures, and, at other times, immense flights of rockets rapidly succeeded each other, and, now spent themselves in the air, now fell slowly as showers of fire. Large numbers of Roman candles threw forth to a vast distance blue stars in rapid succession, and balls of fire, shot to an immense height, burst into innumerable sparks.

' In the intervals of the fire-works, the Pagoda, which was entirely covered with lamps, shewed a calm mass of uniform light. Large masses of fire, we understand, fell in George Street, and other adjacent streets, but they extinguished themselves as they touched the ground, and, we believe, no mischief was done.

' We were as heartily glad when the cockle-shell fight was over, as we had been tired of waiting for it. We were afraid, at one time, that it would have neither beginning nor end. Indeed, there had been a wretched skirmish between four and five in the afternoon, between an American and an English frigate, at the conclusion of which, the English colours were triumphantly hoisted on the rebel Yankee. After this, followed a dreary interval of some hours, in which no one seemed to know what was to come, or what had gone before, and in which we at last sought refuge among our old friends, the booths of Bartholomew Fair.

' While here we had nearly missed the battle of the Nile altogether, something like the old woman who went to see a ship launched, and, while she was stooping down to buckle her shoe, the ship went off! After the Naumachia, the moon rose, and the Chinese lanterns were lighted. At a signal given, the fire-works in the Green Park were let off, and four of the little fleet in the Serpentine were set on fire. The

swans screamed, and fluttered round the affrighted lake.   But
it is in vain to deny the beauty of the scene that followed, nor
have we room to do justice to it.

' After the conclusion of the Fire-works, the Grand Meta-
morphosis took place of the Fortress into the Temple of
Concord, by the removal of all the Canvas fortifications, thus
displaying the Temple brilliantly illuminated, moving upon an
axis, and exhibiting the transparencies of which a description
has already been given.   The lateness of the hour at which
the Show concluded, renders it utterly impossible for us to
give the particulars more in detail.   The Parks continued
crowded long after midnight.

' The Pagoda, at about twelve o'clock, took fire, and after
continuing burning for about a quarter of an hour, fell in with
a great crash, in a slanting direction towards the Mall.   The
Catastrophe surprised no one but the Contrivers of the
erection.'

CHAPTER XVIII.

The celebration of the Jubilee continued—Sale of the Properties—
Continuation of the Fair—Departure of Queen Caroline for the
Continent—Scarcity of Gold—French prisoners of war—State
of the streets—Red tape in the Navy—English visit France—
The War with America—Treaty of peace with America.

THE allegorical paintings on the Temple were by Howard,
Stothard, Smirke, Woodforde, Dawe, Hilton, &c.

Sadler had a really perilous voyage, for the network of his
balloon got out of order and the balloon nearly collapsed ; in
fact, it was only saved by his hanging on to the pipe of the
balloon : then, wanting to descend, the valve would not work
because it was frozen, and, when it did work, did not let out
the gas fast enough, and would have carried him into the river,
at Sea Reach, had he not cut a gash in the balloon, and landed
in Mucking Marshes, on the Essex Coast, sixteen miles below
Gravesend.

There was a metrical account of this fête, which shows the
popular feeling on the subject, which was called

‘THE REGENT'S REMONSTRANCE TO JOHN BULL.

> Oh, JOHNNY, most ungrateful JOHNNY !
> But just escap'd from fangs of BONEY,
>   You still must growl and grumble ;
> The peace just made, and all things right,
> The bread quite cheap, and taxes light,
>   And I, your servant humble.
>
> What would you have ? You growling elf,
> You think of nothing but yourself ;
>   Nay, show your teeth,—you cannot bite,
> What could be done for love or money,
> All that is comical or funny,
>   Has been my study and delight.

Your peevish humours to destroy all,
Did I not ask the Allies Royal
  To come to London here to see you ?
And did you not, for days and nights,
Stare yourself almost blind with sights ?
  I'd fain, I vow, twice *double d* ye.

Then to add further to your glee,
I give you a grand Jubilee,
  'Cause we have reigned a hundred years ;
I put my hands in both your pockets,
And, in return, you've Congreve's rockets,
  And booths for all your pretty dears.

Besides, if you were not a lout,
You'd smile to see the roundabout,*
  And all the pretty pictures in it ;
With all the fireworks blazing forth !
Some east, some west, some south, some north,
  And pop-guns bursting every minute.

Why, surely, JOHN, you 'gin to dote,
Come, take a ride in this cock boat !
  See how it *floats* on *real* water !
A race ! A race ! I vow there is !
I see a smile upon your phiz,
  I'll go and call my *vife* and *darter !*

Nay, patience, JOHNNY, do not fidget,
You have not seen our little bridge yet,
  And *top on* it the grand *Pagoda ;*
Then, whilst you're walking on the lawn,
You'll bless the day when you were born,
  To see such sights, and call for soda.

Come, take another walk with me,
To view the ships upon the sea,
  I mean the Carlton—Hyde Park ocean ;
Full twenty vessels *of the line*
Now sail upon the Serpentine,
  To give of *Nile* a brilliant notion !

But see ! they're close engaged in battle,
Hark ! how the thund'ring cannons rattle !
  A broadside now from *Victory !*
Behold the shade of Nelson rise !
Would he were here to *feast* his eyes,
  And grace the days of *Regency !*

---

* The revolving Temple of Concord.

Then independent of my fleets,
I've planned some palaces and streets,
    Th' expense is small—some paltry millions ;
But lo ! the pyrotechnicalities,
And gin and gingerbread hilarities,
    With all the hornpipes and *cowtillions.*

If, after this, I hear complaints,
I swear, by all the priests and saints,
    New taxes must your spirit humble,
If Vansittart* can find *one* out,
(Which once I heard the rascal doubt),
    Unless you're tax'd whene'er you grumble.'

On the 11th of October, the *Temple of Concord* was sold, and the following is a contemporary account of its sale :

'The *Temple of Concord* was, on Tuesday, *knocked down* in ninety-one lots by Mr. Creaton.

'The sale commenced with the *flag-staff* on the top of the *Upper Temple.* The brokers viewed it as a common piece of *fir,* which might be converted into excellent *firewood,* and it was knocked down at 14s.

'Four *rainbows,* in spite of the scriptural allusions which they drew forth, produced only £4 3s.

'Eight *Vestals* were sold for £14 8s.

'Eight pair of *Ionic Columns* coloured to imitate Sienna marble, produced £21 8s. 6d.

'The *Doric columns,* of which there were sixteen pairs, painted in imitation of porphyry, averaged £1 12s. 6d. per pair.

'The four *pyramidal pillars* (shaped like Cannon) ornamenting the corners of the first platform, were purchased by an individual, with all their appurtenances, for £16 9s.

'The *Cornices,* doorways, &c., with the inscriptions, on which Mr. Creaton sported many patriotic remarks, went off as follows :—

	£	s.	d.
The Regency (*proh pudor*)	0	7	0
Peace Returning	0	7	0
Europe rescued	0	8	0
Strife descending	0	8	0
The Triumph of Britannia	2	10	0
The Golden Age restored	3	10	0
The Sceptre of the Bourbons restored ...	3	3	0

---

* Then Chancellor of the Exchequer.

	£	s.	d.
War desolating the earth	3	3	0
Frederick and Blücher	2	12	6
Francis and Schwartzenberg	2	12	6
The Regent and Wellington	3	0	0
Alexander and Kutusoff	2	15	0
The Arms of England and France ...	2	2	0
„ Austria and Holland	2	0	0
„ Russia and Prussia	2	0	0
„ Spain and Portugal	2	0	0

'The mechanical fountains, which are eight in number, sold for £10 16s.

'The sale of the exterior of the Temple of Concord concluded at five o'clock. It produced the gross sum of £200 2s. 6d. We should be glad to know what was the prime cost of the materials used in this structure, as well as the sum expended in preparing and setting them up.'

There were, unfortunately, many accidents during the Celebration of this Jubilee. At the burning of the Pagoda one man was killed on the spot, six others injured, and one of them died shortly afterwards. The cause of the burning of this ill-fated building was that there was not room for a rocket wheel to revolve; the consequence was that the fierce fire played on one part of the woodwork and ignited the whole building. In Hyde Park, lads and men climbed the trees, whose branches would not bear their weight, but broke, and not only did the climbers injure themselves, but those on whom they fell.

At Kensington Gardens, just at the close of the fire-works, two rockets, instead of behaving properly, and rising skywards, took a horizontal direction, one striking a gentleman in the calf of his leg, the other, another gentleman in the body—and he was borne, apparently much injured, by four men, into a neighbouring marquee. The rocket sticks falling caused minor accidents, which is not to be wondered at, when we consider that they were from six to eight feet long, an inch broad, and half an inch thick.*   However, people sheltered themselves under the trees, some in the numerous Marquees, where the safest were those under the tables—and some put their umbrellas up, as a protection.

After this fête, the booths were not removed, and a regular

* In a *jeu d'esprit* on the Jubilee, the Serpentine was called 'The River Styx.'

fair sprung up, with its usual accompaniments of swings, roundabouts, wild-beast shows, fat women, and dramatic entertainments, to which were added the attractions of *E.O. tables—Black and White Cocks—Dice Tables*—and a game with dice, called *Under and over Seven*. This gambling the police did not even make a show of stopping. There were donkey racing, jumping in sacks, running for smocks, &c.—and there were printing presses, where, on payment, people had the privilege of themselves pulling off a typographical souvenir of the fair. Nay, it was even contemplated to print a *Jubilee Fair Journal*.

It was anticipated that this fair would last until the 12th, and so it possibly might have done, had it been conducted with anything like decency and order ; but as these were conspicuously absent, Lord Sidmouth, Secretary of State for the Home Department, ordered it to be closed on the night of Saturday the 6th. This order, the booth-keepers petitioned against, on the plea that, on the strength of its being open for a longer time, they had laid in a large stock of provisions, liquor, toys, &c., which would be thrown upon their hands. Lord Sidmouth's order not being enforced, they kept on, so that it was found necessary to issue another—which was acted on—and the fair ceased with the night of August 11th.

A contemporary newspaper speaking of it, says, 'Never, within the memory of man, has there been witnessed such scenes of drunkenness and dissipation as these fooleries have given rise to, and the misery they have brought upon thousands is extreme. A report from the pawnbrokers would be an awful lesson to governments how they encourage such riot. Since the delirium, from the example of the highest quarter, began, the pawnbrokers have more than trebled their business ; clothes, furniture, and, worst of all, *tools*, have been sacrificed for the sake of momentary enjoyment ; industry of every kind has been interrupted, and many hundreds of starving families will long have to remember the *æra* of the Park Fêtes.'

I wind up this account of the Jubilee with the following 'Epigram on the P—— R——'s expressing a wish for the continuance of the Fair in Hyde Park :

'The R —— we have oft been told,
    Prefers the *Fair* when *stout* and *old* ;
Now, here we've cause to think him wrong
    For liking *any Fair too long*.'

And now, having exhausted the chief events of this memorable year, I must fill up my account of the remainder of its existence with notices of passing events, as they occur, a course which must naturally be discursive.

First of all, the Princess of Wales left England for the Continent on the 9th of August, in the *Jason* Frigate, landing at Hamburg on the 16th. She was weary of the petty persecutions and slights she had perpetually to undergo ; and, refusing to use the extra allowance granted her by Parliament, went into voluntary exile, against the advice of her sincere friends, who, however, could not feel as she did ; for, in her position, she could not help feeling the social indignities that were heaped upon her. From these, at least, she could be free when away from England. She left its shores in a very modest and unassuming manner, being driven to the sea shore in a pony-cart—(the Chronicler giving, as a saving clause, ' by her own coachman '). Her dress might, at the present time, perhaps, be thought rather *prononcée*, but it was only fashionable then. She wore a dark cloth pelisse, with large gold clasps, and a cap of violet and green satin, of the Prussian Hussar Costume, with a green feather, which we should think rather a fetching costume for a lady of forty-six.

We have heard of the scarcity of gold coin, and how, during the War-time it used to be smuggled out of the Country ; it must have gladdened some hearts to have read, under date of August 19th, ' *Guineas* may shortly be expected to reappear. Seven-shilling pieces, which should be considered as their *avant-couriers*, already peep out !' Anent this lack of gold coin there was an amusing skit published thereon in this year, which I reproduce, partly for the illustration which represents a beadle in all his glory,—a being that is fast fading away. The Cocked hat has already gone, and I know not now where to find what would be termed, heraldically, ' a beadle in his pride.'

The following is entitled ' A Whole Family Lost.'

' O Yes ! If any of the relatives or next of kin of one Mr. Guinea, who about the year 1800 was much seen in England, and is supposed to be an Englishman, will give information where he can be met with, they will be handsomely rewarded, on application to Mr. John Bull, *Growling Lane* opposite *Threadneedle Street*. A proportionate reward will be given for information relative to his son Mr. Half-Guinea ; or his Grandson, young Seven Shilling piece. Papers innumerable

C. W

A WHOLE FAMILY LOST.—*November* 24, 1814.

14

have been issued in consequence of their disappearance, but all in vain ; and they are believed by many persons to have left the kingdom ; though others shrewdly suspect they lie hid somewhere in the Country waiting for more favourable times before they dare make their appearance, as they have reason to suppose they would be instantly *taken up*, and put in *close Confinement.* Their sudden disappearance is particularly to be regretted, as they were in great favour with the people, and enjoyed the *King's Countenance* to such a degree that they actually bore the *Royal Arms.* Notwithstanding they are people of real worth, yet it must be confessed that, by getting occasionally into bad Company, they have lost some of their weight in society, yet, if they will return, all faults will be forgiven ; no questions will be asked, but they may depend upon being received with open arms by their disconsolate friends, who, by this temporary separation have learnt to appreciate their sterling worth. They resemble each other very closely, and may very easily be known by their *round faces*, and by their complexion, which is of *bright yellow ;* for though they, it is true, were born, and acquired their polish in London, yet it is well ascertained that the family originally came, and derived their name, from the Coast of *Guinea*, a place too well known in *Liverpool* to require any description.

GOD SAVE THE KING.'

'LINES SUGGESTED BY HEARING IT SAID THAT THE R—G—T WAS IN THE ARMS OF MORPHEUS.

> In Morpheus's arms as the R—g—t once lay,
> " Ecod !" said the God, " this old boy is no feather ;
> If he slept but as soundly by night as by day,
> I should envy e'en ATLAS himself this hot weather." '

Under date of August 31st, we find that 'the number of French prisoners who have been sent to France since the conclusion of the peace, exceeds sixty-seven thousand men. It is said that only nineteen continental prisoners of war (who are Poles) now remain in this country. The American prisoners in England already amount to three thousand eight hundred. They are chiefly seamen.'

A newspaper cutting of September 3rd, shows us the state of the Streets of London in 1814 : 'The shameful manner in which the Contractors for lighting the streets perform the duty, has long been the subject of complaint. After the shops are shut, and consequently the lamps in their windows extinguished, the streets are almost in a state of utter darkness. An attempt is to be made, we observe, to light Fleet Street with *gas.* We hope the experiment will succeed.

'The same complaint may be made against the paving,— for the defects of the paving are more owing to the way in which the paviours do their work, than to the water companies. The stones sent from Aberdeen, are no longer square, but conical. They have a broad top, and narrow to the bottom— so that these inverted cones have no bond—and the streets being improperly laid too convex, so as to make every waggon incline to one side, the stones are constantly disturbed; and, a hole once made, every wheel increases it. The Commissioners ought to reform the system altogether.'

Here is a little anecdote of red tape in the Navy : 'According to an established form in the Navy, when a ship is paid off, no officer must quit the port, or consider himself discharged, until the pennant is struck, which can be done only by the cook, as the last officer, at sunset; and, should he be absent, no other person can perform the office, however desirous the Officers may be of taking their departure, and although there may not be a single seaman or marine on board. A curious instance of this took place last week, at Plymouth, on the *Caledonia's* being paid off. When the time arrived for hauling down the pennant, no Cook could be found, from which cause the officers were under the necessity of waiting a day or two, until he made his appearance.'

Immediately on the Restoration of the Bourbons it was the proper thing for every English man and woman who could afford it, to pay a visit to Paris, and a motley group, I fancy they were, a jumble of the Aristocracy, and the Cheap Tourist. Captain Gronow thus describes this 'irruption of the Goths and Vandals' : 'Thousands of oddly dressed English flocked to Paris immediately after the war : I remember that the burden of one of the popular songs of the day was, " All the world's in Paris ;" and our countrymen and women having been so long excluded from French Modes, had adopted fashions of their own, quite as remarkable, and eccentric as those of the Parisians, and much less graceful. British beauties were dressed in long strait pelisses of various colours ; the body of the dress was never of the same colour as the skirt ; and the bonnet was of beehive shape, and very small. The characteristic of the dress of the gentleman was a coat of

14—2

light blue, or snuff colour, with brass buttons, the tail reaching nearly to the heels; a gigantic bunch of seals dangled from his fob, whilst his pantaloons were short, and tight at the knees; and a spacious waistcoat, with a voluminous muslin cravat and a frilled shirt completed the toilette.'

The end of this year leaves the Congress of Vienna, which met to settle all International matters arising out of the war, still sitting, and I cannot refrain from quoting the following epigram upon it :

'SISTÈME DU CONGRÉS.

L'Espagne est cause de tout,
L'Allemagne prétend tout,
La France assiste tout,
L'Angleterre embrouille tout,
La Hollande souffre tout,
Venise consulte tout,
Le Portugal écoute tout,
La Suède a perdu tout,
Le Danemarc craint tout,
La Sardaigne trompe tout,
Les Jésuites sont partout,
Le Pape bénit tout ;
Si Dieu ne pourvoit à tout,
Le Diable emporte tout.'

When treating of the American War we left the Americans at the end of 1813 retiring into winter quarters. This year the fortunes of this silly war were somewhat unequal. The absurd system of reprisals was abolished, and the hostages exchanged, as other prisoners of war — altogether, things looked like coming to a close. The great feature of this year's campaign, was the Capture and burning of Washington, on 24th of August, which, virtually, ended the War. The Capitol, the Arsenal, the Dockyard, with a frigate ready to be launched, Treasury, War Office, President's Palace, the Rope Walk, and the great bridge across the Potomac were all destroyed.

There seems to have been a great joke about President Madison losing his supper on this occasion, as, for instance, in the *Morning Chronicle* of October 15th, is the following: 'Although MADISON was deprived of his *supper* in consequence of the British troops entering his mansion at Washington, yet it must be some consolation to him that he did not lose his *desert.*' The same occurs in the dialogue accompanying this

THE FALL OF WASHINGTON; OR, MADDY IN FULL FLIGHT.

(Published October 4, 1814, by Fores.)

illustration which is entitled 'The Fall of Washington, or Maddy in full flight.'

The three bystanders say, respectively, 'Jonathan, where thinkest thou our President will run now?'—'Why, verily, to Elba, to his Bosom friend!'—'The great Washington fought for Liberty, but we are fighting for shadows, which, if obtained, could do us no Earthly good, but this is the blessed effect of it.' Madison, who carries under his arm 'A plan for laying England under Contribution,' 'Project for the Conquest of Canada,' 'Correspondence with Boney,' &c.,—says, 'Who would have thought of this, Man? To oblige us to run from the best Cabinet Supper I ever order'd—I hope you have taken care of Boney's promissory notes—The people won't stand anything after this.' His companion says, 'D—n his Notes! what are they good for, now? We should get nothing but iron, he hasn't any of his stock of Brass left, or some of that would have helped us through!'

Two bystanders say, 'I suppose this is what Maddis calls benefiting his Country!'—'Why it will throw such a light on affairs that we shall find it necessary to change both *men* and *measures*.'

Two English Men-of-War's men standing by, say to each other, 'I say, Jack! what is that there man of war that was to nihilate us, as Master Boney used to say?'—'Aye, Messmate, he is a famous fighter over a bottle of Shampain; why he'd have played Hell with us if we had let him sit down to supper.'

Proposals of peace were made, and a treaty signed at Ghent, on the 24th of December, thus making out the Christmas 'Peace on earth and good will towards men,' and a happy ending to this year.

CHAPTER XIX.

1815.

Health of the King—Extension of the Order of the Bath—Wife selling—A Sailor's frolic—'Nelson's Lady Hamilton'—'The Pig-faced Lady'—The advantage of being able to play the violin —Napoleon's escape from Elba.

NEITHER this, nor any of the succeeding years of the Regency, can produce any string of events to vie with 1814. After that stirring year, all others fall flat. Still, with the exception of Napoleon's hundred days, we shall probably find more social chit-chat in them, than those which have preceded them in this Chronicle. Unfortunately for me there is no *sequence* of events, and my narrative must, necessarily, be made up of disjointed fragments culled from various sources, but which, nevertheless, illustrate the idea of this book—the Social life of the period.

First of all, let us look at the health of the poor old King, now nearly half forgotten   One bulletin will suffice, as it exactly expresses his state for the year. 'WINDSOR CASTLE, *February* 4.—The King continues in good health; but since the last Report his Majesty has been less uniformly tranquil than he was during some preceding months.' His bodily health was good, and mentally he was generally composed, and tranquil, with occasional outbursts of furious mania, and, in any case, his mental alienation was continuous: he never recovered his reason.

One of the first public acts of the Regent, in this year, was to enlarge the Order of the Bath. The long and arduous duties of our troops merited some reward when peace was obtained; and, although they only did their duty, as our troops do now, they were not thanked, as now, by the Sovereign after every little skirmish, nor were medals so lavishly given as now. Every one knows the length of time before the Waterloo medal was issued to all who were worthy of its receipt. The orders of Chivalry were few, and it was then an honour to receive a decoration. Going on at the present rate, knighthood will soon be about on a par with the Order of SS. Maurice and Lazarus.

At all events, the extension of the Order of the Bath was fixed upon, and a good choice it was, because it was not of mushroom creation, as it was instituted in 1399. After Charles II., it fell into abeyance, until George I. revived it in 1725. The *London Gazette* of 3rd of January, gives the ordinance enlarging this Order of Chivalry, which, henceforth, was to consist of Knights Grand Cross, Knights Commander, and Companions. The number of Knights Grand Cross was limited to 72 ; 60 Military and 12 Civil. This number might be exceeded by the addition of Princes of the Blood Royal holding high Commissions in the Army and Navy. The rank required for this dignity is that of Major-General in the Army, and Rear-Admiral in the Navy. The Civilians should have rendered eminent services to the State, either in civil, or diplomatic employment. The Second Grade was not to exceed 180 in number, exclusive of foreign officers holding English Commissions, but these were, for the present, limited to 10, but might be increased. This honour was only bestowed on Lieutenant-Colonels, and Post-Captains. The Companions embraced a wide field, their number was much larger, and anyone was eligible for the decoration who had received a medal, or other badge of honour, or had been mentioned by name in the *London Gazette* as having been distinguished by valour in action. The members now, according to Debrett for 1888, are Knights Grand Cross—50 Military, 25 Civil ; Knight Commanders—123 Military, 80 Civil ; Companions— 690 Military, and 250 Civil.

Things matrimonial must have been very bad, for I find the record of no less than three sales of wives during this year. The first is in January : ' MATRIMONIAL SALE.—Tuesday s'en night, a man named John Osborne, who lived at Gondhurst, came to Maidstone, for the purpose of disposing of his wife by sale ; but, it not being market day, the auction was re- moved to the sign of ' The Coal-barge,' in Earl Street, where she was actually sold to a man named William Serjeant, with her child, for the sum of one pound. The business was con_ ducted in a very regular manner, a deed and covenant being given by the seller, of which the following is a literal copy :

'I, John Osborne, doth agree to part with my wife, Mary Osborne and child, to William Serjeant, for the sum of one pound, in consideration of giving up all claim whatever, whereunto I have made my mark as an acknowledgement.

'MAIDSTONE, *January 3*, 1815.   × '

The next case is in July : 'SMITHFIELD BARGAIN.—One of those scenes which occasionally disgrace even Smithfield, took place there about five o'clock on Friday evening (July 14th), namely—a man exposing his wife for sale.   Hitherto we have only seen those moving in the lowest classes of society thus degrading themselves, but the present exhibition was attended with some novel circumstances.   The parties, buyer and seller, were persons of property ; the lady (the object of sale), young, beautiful, and elegantly dressed, was brought to the market in a coach, and exposed to the view of her purchaser, with a silk halter round her shoulders, which were covered with a rich white lace veil.   The price demanded for her, in the first instance, was eighty guineas, but that finally agreed on was fifty guineas, and a valuable horse upon which the purchaser was mounted.   The sale and delivery being complete, the lady, with her new lord and master, mounted a handsome curricle which was in waiting for them, and drove off, seemingly nothing loath to go.   The purchaser in the present case is a celebrated horsedealer in town, and the seller, a grazier of cattle, residing about six miles from London.   The intention of these disgusting bargains is, to deprive the husband of any right of prosecution for damages.'

The third example is as follows : 'On Friday last (September 15th) the common bell-man gave notice in Staines Market, that the wife of —— Issey was then at the King's Head Inn, to be *sold*, with the consent of her husband, to any person inclined to buy her.   There was a very numerous attendance to witness this singular sale, notwithstanding which only *three shillings and four pence* were offered for the lot, no one choosing to contend with the bidder, for the fair object, whose merits could only be appreciated by those who knew them. This the purchaser could boast, from a long and intimate acquaintance.   This degrading custom seems to be generally received by the lower classes, as of equal obligation with the most serious legal forms.'

'A SAILOR'S FROLIC. — Yesterday (February 9th) morning
early, a sailor who had been lately paid off, and who had been
riding in a coach, about the streets, with a fiddler playing,
the preceding night, strolled into Covent Garden Market,
when he was asked by one of the basket women whether
he wanted anything carried for him? He replied that he
wished to be carried himself, to a place where he could get
some breakfast. The woman, who wanted to go home to her
lodging in St. Giles's, agreed to take him in her basket, to a
coffee shop at the corner of High Street; the sailor got in,
first getting his pipe lighted, and sat cross-legged, smoking his
pipe, in the woman's basket, which was set upon her head
by others of her own fraternity. She went off, followed
by a great concourse of spectators of every description, and,
without once resting, took her load to its destination,
when the sailor rewarded her with a pint of rum, and a pound
note.'

On the 17th of January died 'Nelson's Lady Hamilton,'
whose career was a remarkable one. Born of poor parents, at
a little village in Cheshire, Amy Lyons early went into domestic
service. Being very beautiful, she soon attracted notice, with
the usual result. After being the mistress of more than one,
Mr. Greville took her under his protection, and, when he
deserted her, she associated herself with that arch quack
Doctor Graham, of 'Celestial bed,' and 'earth bathing' notoriety. While with him she posed as *Hebe Vestina*, a part for
which her beautiful face and figure eminently fitted her.
She ultimately married the celebrated virtuoso Sir William
Hamilton, who was the English Ambassador at Naples. At
that Court her vivacity was much appreciated, and she was the
constant companion of the Queen. Of her connection with
Nelson everybody knows.

During the War the farmers had coined money, in spite of
their wretchedly bad farming; but the introduction of foreign
wheat, and a not too plentiful harvest, brought about a state
of things, of which we are now experiencing a parallel. Under
date of February 13th we read : ' In many counties of England,
the farmers are giving up their leases in great numbers. A
farm belonging to Bethlehem Hospital, which let a few years
since for £1,100 per annum, and was afterwards risen to
£6,000 per annum, is now offering for £4,000 per annum, but
with little prospect of its being taken at that rent.' Does not
this read like a chapter of to-day? The rents raised until

the farmers could not farm profitably, and then the land un-occupied.

' The Pig-faced lady ' is to be heard of in several European countries; but, perhaps the earliest one noticed in England, although not a country woman, was Frau Tanakin Skinker. Of her, however, we only hear through the medium of a very rare book published in London in 1641 entitled, ' A certain relation of the Hog-faced Gentlewoman,' but of her, together with an old black-letter ballad on another damsel equally afflicted, I have already written in my book on ' Humour, Wit and Satire of the Seventeenth Century.'

In February, 1815, there was a widespread belief in the existence, in London, of such a monstrosity, and she is depicted in the illustration overleaf, called ' Waltzing a Courtship.' There is also another engraving of her, showing her seated playing the piano, but very thinly veiled, so that her porcine countenance is plainly visible. I believe there is also another, but this I have not seen, where she is seen standing by a table, on which is her silver feeding-trough.

The Times, which was not quite so matter of fact then as now, gives the following account of ' her sowship.' In its issue of February 16th is the following : ' There is, at present, a report in London, of a woman, with a strangely deformed face, resembling that of a pig, who is possessed of a large fortune, and, we suppose, wants all the comforts and conveni-ences incident to her sex and station. We, ourselves, un-wittingly put in an advertisement from a young woman offering to be her companion, and, yesterday morning, a fellow trans-mitted to us another advertisement, attended by a one-pound note, offering himself to be her husband. We have put his offer in the fire, and shall send his money to some charity. Our rural friends hardly know what idiots London contains. The pig's face is as firmly believed in by many, as Joanna Southcott's pregnancy, to which folly it has succeeded. Though no Parson Tozer has yet mounted the rostrum to preach in support of the face, there is hardly a company in which this swinish female is not talked of; and thousands believe in her existence. The story, however, is an old one. About fifty-three years ago, it is well remembered by several elderly people, there was exactly the same rumour. It was revived, with but slight effect, about thirty years since ; and now comes forth again in its pristine vigour. On the original invention of the pig-faced woman about the year

WALTZING A COURTSHIP.

1764, a man offered to make her an ivory trough to feed out of. . . .'

The following is the advertisement referred to: it appeared in *The Times* of Feb. 9th. 'FOR THE ATTENTION OF GENTLE-MEN AND LADIES. A young gentlewoman having heard of an advertisement for a person to undertake the care of a lady, who is heavily afflicted in the face, whose friends have offered a handsome income yearly, and a premium for residing with her for seven years, would do all in her power to render her life most comfortable; an undeniable character can be obtained from a respectable circle of friends; an answer to this advertisement is requested, as the advertiser will keep herself disengaged. Address, post paid, to X Y, at Mr. Ford's, Baker, 12, Judd Street, Brunswick Square.'

The advertisement which follows is probably that rejected by *The Times*, but inserted in *The Morning Herald* of Feb. 16th. 'SECRECY. A single gentleman, aged thirty-one, of a respectable family, and in whom the utmost confidence may be reposed, is desirous of explaining his mind to the friends of a person who has a misfortune in her face, but is prevented for want of an introduction. Being perfectly aware of the principal particulars, and understanding that a final settlement would be preferred to a temporary one, presumes he would be found to answer the full extent of their wishes. His intentions are sincere, honourable, and firmly resolved. References of great respectability can be given. Address to M. D., at Mr. Spencer's, 22, Great Ormond Street, Queen's Square.'

Captain Gronow refers to this lady.* 'Among the many absurd reports, and ridiculous stories current, in former days, I know of none more absurd, or more ridiculous, than the general belief of everybody in London, during the winter of 1814, in the existence of a lady with a pig's face. This interesting specimen of porcine physiognomy was said to be the daughter of a great lady residing in Grosvenor Square.

'It was rumoured that during the illuminations which took place to celebrate the Peace, when a great crowd had assembled in Piccadilly and St. James's Street, and when carriages could not move on very rapidly, "horresco referens!" an enormous pig's snout had been seen protruding from a fashionable-looking bonnet in one of the landaus which were passing. The mob cried out, "The pig-faced lady!—the pig-faced lady! Stop the Carriage—stop the Carriage!" The coachman, wishing

* 'Recollections and Anecdotes,' 1863, p. 111.

to save his bacon, whipped his horses, and drove through the crowd at a tremendous pace; but it was said that the coach had been seen to set down its monstrous load in Grosvenor Square.

'Another report was also current. Sir William Elliot, a youthful baronet, calling one day to pay his respects to the great lady in Grosvenor Square, was ushered into a drawing-room, where he found a person fashionably dressed, who, on turning towards him, displayed a hideous pig's face. Sir William, a timid young gentleman, could not refrain from uttering a shout of horror, and rushed to the door in a manner, the reverse of polite; when the infuriated lady, or animal, uttering a series of grunts, rushed at the unfortunate baronet as he was retreating, and inflicted a severe wound on the back of his neck. This highly probable story concluded by stating that Sir William's wound was a severe one, and had been dressed by Hawkins, the surgeon, in South Audley Street.

'I am really almost ashamed to repeat this absurd story; but many persons now alive can remember the strong belief in the existence of the pig-faced lady, which prevailed in the public mind at the time of which I speak. The shops were full of Caricatures of the pig-faced lady, in a poke bonnet and large veil, with "A pig in a poke" written underneath the print. Another sketch represented Sir William Elliot's mis-adventure, and was entitled, "Beware the pig-stye."'

The *Annual Register*, which is supposed to contain nothing but facts, is responsible for the following, under date Feb. 25th: 'A foreign journal contains the following laughable anecdote of a French fiddler of the name of Boucher, who, lately, came to push his fortune in London. On his arrival at Dover, across the Channel, he had the mortification to see his fiddles seized by the officers of the Customs. It was in vain he protested that they were not articles of Commerce, but instruments for his own use; and that, if he meant to make money by them, it was, at least, not by their sale. The fiscal agents were deaf; the fiddles must pay duty. To fix the amount, their value must be estimated: and Mr. Boucher was desired to set his own value on the fiddles; he fell into the snare, and fixed a very moderate price.

'Then, in virtue of Custom-house regulations unknown to our travelling musician, they offered him 15 per cent. more than the valuation, and declared they would keep the instruments. Our artist was in despair; he complained, he prayed,

he threatened, but all in vain ; there was only one resource,—
that of going to London to claim the interference of the
French Ambassador ; but, to do this, he must part from his
dear fiddles, the instruments of his glory, and his fortune.
He wished, at least, to bid them a last adieu, and, taking up
one of them, he brought from it such melodious, but doleful
sounds, as corresponded with his feelings. The Custom-house
officers, attracted by the notes, formed a group round him,
which gradually increased, so that the office could no longer
contain the collected auditors. They begged the musician to
pass into a large lobby, to which he, unwillingly, assented.
There, on the top of the staircase, he performed several
pieces which charmed even fiscal ears. Animated by his
success, the artist surpassed even himself, and the enthusiasm
of his audience was at its height, when they heard *God save
the King* executed, with the most brilliant variations. How
repay so much talent and complaisance ? Everything was
forgotten ; even the regulations of the Custom House. " Sir,"
said the Chief of the Customs to the French Virtuoso, " take
back your fiddles ; you may boast of a finer, because a more
difficult triumph than that of Orpheus. He melted only the
infernal deities, but you have made the douaniers of Dover
relent." '

Here is a curious superstition which comes from a Bath
paper : ' A young woman, who had been married only three
months, and lived at *Widcomb*, being summoned to answer a
charge of a breach of the peace, at the instance of her
mother-in-law, threw herself into the river, at *Widcomb*, and
was drowned. Every means to discover the body have,
hitherto, been ineffectual, on account of the great height of
the river, through the late rains. It is curious, however, to
observe some of the methods which fancy, or superstition, has
suggested in order to find the body :—among others, a large
drum, carried in a boat, has been beaten down the river,
under the idea that its sound would alter when approaching
the drowned person ; and a small loaf, laden with quicksilver,
has been set afloat, which, it is presumed, would be stopped
in its progress, by attraction, when approaching the immersed
object.'

In this month of February an event occurred, which stirred
Europe to its very foundation. The lion, so fondly believed
to be caged at Elba, got unchained, and, leaving his petty
island kingdom, on the 26th of Feb., he landed at Cannes on

the 1st of March. There was consternation, to use the mildest term, all over Europe. The French king believed that he would soon be driven back ; but in his advance, his army increased like a vast snowball, and poor Louis had once more to retire. The Congress at Vienna was broken up, unregretted by any one, and the Allies entered into a compact, engaging themselves not to quit the field until Napoleon was subdued. The news was not received here until the 10th of March, and the *Times* of next day, fairly foams over it. 'Early yesterday morning, we received by express from Dover, the important, but lamentable intelligence, of a civil war having been again kindled in France, by that wretch Buonaparte, whose life was so impolitically spared by the Allied Sovereigns. It now appears that the hypocritical villain, who, at the time of his cowardly abdication, affected an aversion to the shedding of blood in a civil warfare, has been employed during the whole time of his residence at Elba, in carrying out secret and treasonable intrigues with the tools of his former crimes in France,' &c.

The Newsboys in London must have reaped a rare harvest.

'Twang went the horn ! " Confound that noise !"
I cried, in pet—"these plaguy boys
Are at some tricks to sell their papers,
Their *blasts* have given me the *vapours !*"
But all my senses soon were stranded,
At hearing, " Buonaparte's landed !"
" Landed in France !" so ran the strain,
And " with eleven hundred men."
" Ho, post !"   " Who calls ?"   " This way."   " I'm coming !"
" The public, surely, he is humming,"
Said I.   " A paper—what's the price ?"
" A shilling."   " Why, that's payment twice !"
" As *cheap as dirt*, your honour, quite ;
They've sold for half-a-crown to-night."
" But is the news authentic, friend ?"
" *Ofishul*, sir, you may depend.—
The *Currier* third edition."   " So !
Well, take your money boy, and go."
Now, for the news—by what blunder
Has he escaped his bounds, I wonder.'

Rothschilds had the first news, one of their clerks coming express from Paris to tell them. Doubtless they took advantage of their information.

CHAPTER XX.

Anti-Corn Bill riots—Riots in the north—Ratification of the Treaty of Peace with America—Attempt to steal the Crown—Epithets applied to Napoleon—The Prince of Wales' debts.

At home our domestic peace was seriously interrupted at this time. Doubtless, with a view to assuage the agricultural distress, a measure was proposed, prohibiting the importation of corn, except when it had reached a price considered by the great body of the consumers as exorbitant. This, having once tasted comparatively cheap bread (the quartern loaf was then about 1s.), his Majesty's lieges did not like, and meetings against it were held all over the place, and Resolutions passed, the first of which is as follows, the others all hingeing upon it :—

' 1. *Resolved.* That it is the opinion of the Committee, that any sort of Foreign Corn, Meal, or Flour, which may, by law, be imported into the United Kingdom, shall, at all times, be allowed to be brought to the United Kingdom, and to be warehoused there, without payment of any duty whatever.'

The Mob, in those days, were even more unthinking than they are now, and, whilst the respectable portion of the community were agitating in a legitimate manner, they *acted*, according to their lights.

On the 6th of March many groups assembled near the Houses of Parliament, about the usual time of meeting, and the Lobby and avenues of the House were so crowded, that it was necessary to increase the force of constables, who ultimately cleared them. Those ejected stood on the steps, and cheered, or groaned, at the Members as they passed in ; then they took to stopping Members' carriages, making them walk through a hissing and hooting crowd, and gradually went from bad to worse.

15

There were no police, as we know them, in those days—that is, there was no large body of stalwart, well-drilled men—consequently, whenever there was a riot, the Military had the task assigned to them of putting it down. They drove the people away from the House, but only to go elsewhere, and, no longer having the fear of the soldiery before their eyes, they gave unlimited scope to their powers of destruction.

They began at Lord Eldon's in Bedford Square ; tore down his railings, with which they forced an entrance into his house, smashed the windows, and all the furniture they could get at. At Mr. Robinson's, who introduced the Corn Regulations, they tore up his railings, got into his house, smashed some of his furniture, throwing the rest into the street, and destroyed many valuable pictures. At Lord Darnley's, Mr. Yorke's, and Mr. Wellesley Pole's, all the windows were smashed. Lord Hardwicke's house was attacked, but little mischief was done, owing to the arrival of the Military. They went to Lord Ellenborough's, but he behaved bravely ; he opened the door, and, standing before them, inquired into the meaning of it all. They yelled at him that it was ' No Corn Bill ! No Corn Bill !' upon which he spoke a few words to them, and they cheered, and left him. There were the Horse Guards and three regiments of Foot Guards under orders ; but they were scarcely made use of, and that only in the most pacific manner.

Next day (the 7th) they met, in the same manner, near the Houses of Parliament, and, when driven thence, went forth to seek what they could devour, but the Military were abroad, parading the streets, and guarding each house that had been wrecked. The rioters paid another visit to Mr. Robinson's, and seeing no signs of soldiers, thought they could throw stones at the shutters with impunity. They reckoned, however, without their host, for the soldiers were inside the house, from which seven shots were fired, one of the Mob falling dead, shot through the head. He was not identified, but was believed to have been a naval officer.

This was too warm to be pleasant, so they went to Baker Street, where the brave fellows smashed the doors and windows, and tore up the iron railings, at the house of Sam Stephens, Esq., late M.P. for St. Ives, the said house being then under the solitary care of an elderly female. Then these heroes, animated by their last exploit, tried to wreck No. 38, Harley Street, the house of an inoffensive lady, named Sampson, broke the windows of two houses in Wimpole Street, and three in Mansfield Street, Portland Place. The excitement spread to the City, and a Mob collected in Finsbury, whence they valiantly marched to Chiswell Street, where they broke a few windows at Whitbread's Brewery.

The next night, the 8th, the riots were continued, but were rather worse. The Mob was charged once by the Military, and dispersed, only to form again in another place. It was time that something should be done, and *le Roi fainéant* at Carlton House woke up, and on the 9th issued a long proclamation all about the wickedness of rioting, and offering £100 reward on conviction of any of the rioters. But the thing was wearing itself out, and on this day nothing worthy the name of a riot took place, except when they broke the windows at the house of Mr. Davies Giddy, M.P. for Bodmin, who retaliated by firing on the Mob, whereby a boy was wounded in the neck. But there were more Military about this day, which may account for its comparative quiet, and Lord Sidmouth, as Home Secretary, had issued a Circular to every parish in the Metropolis, urging them to take individual action in suppressing the riots, each in its own locality. There was an attempt to get up a riot in Canterbury, but no mischief was done, except a few broken windows, and it was promptly quelled.

About the same time in March there were more serious riots occurring at the seaports at Durham and Northumberland, among the sailors employed in the Colliery trade. They wanted an increase of wages, and they did not like the introduction of machinery, fearing that it would interfere with their livelihood. Take one instance, as an example.

'March 20. A serious riot took place at Bishop Wearmouth, near Durham. It appears that Messrs. Neshams, the extensive coal-dealers of that place, have been for several years busily employed in erecting railways, and other conveniences, to save the labour of men and horses in conveying coals from the pit. The keel men, who are employed to convey the coals in boats or barges, had, it seems, taken offence at these improvements; and this afternoon, having first moored their barges opposite Messrs. Nesham's premises, they proceeded, in a riotous manner, to demolish their works. After completing the destruction of the most expensive and valuable part of the waggon road, which was the object of their animosity, they set fire to an immense pile of coals,

15—2

which burned with great fury during the whole night, presenting a grand and awful spectacle for many miles round. The rioters previously overpowered all the proprietors, and their friends, who had assembled to repress the tumult. Mr. Robinson, the collector of the Customs, Mr. Biss, and several other gentlemen of respectability, were repeatedly knocked down and bruised. It was three o'clock the next morning before the rioters were dispersed by the arrival of the military.'*

On the Tyne, the sailors and keel men took possession of the river, making a chain of boats right across it, and they would not allow a vessel to pass without a regular permit. The efforts of the local magistrates, and conciliatory propositions from the merchants, proving insufficient to restore obedience, whilst the sailors in other ports were also manifesting a disposition to combine for similar purposes, Government determined to interpose with effect, in order to quell this dangerous spirit. A strong force, both Naval and Military, was collected at the disturbed ports, which was so judiciously applied, that no resistance was attempted on the part of the sailors, and their coercive system was immediately broken up. Reasonable offers were then made to them, and tranquillity was restored. Not a life was lost, and only a few of the ringleaders were apprehended.

The ratification of the Treaty of Peace with America arrived in London on the 13th of March, and created no comment. The main points in this treaty are contained in Article 1, of which the following is a portion : — '. . . All hostilities, both on sea and land, shall cease as soon as this Treaty shall have been ratified by both parties hereinafter mentioned. All territory, places, and possessions whatsoever, taken by either party from the other during the war, or which may be taken after the signing of this Treaty, excepting only the Islands hereinafter mentioned, shall be restored without delay, and without causing any destruction, or carrying away any of the artillery or other public property, originally captured in the said forts or places, and which shall remain therein upon the exchange of the ratification of this Treaty, or any slaves or other private property. And all archives, records, deeds, and papers, either of a public nature, or belonging to private persons, which, in the course of the war,

* The Corn Bill passed the Commons on the 10th of March, and the Lords on the 20th.

may have fallen into the hands of the officers of either party, shall be, as far as practicable, forthwith restored, and delivered to the proper authorities and persons to whom they respectively belong.'

Article 2 provides for cessation of hostilities.

Article 3 for the exchange of prisoners.

Article 4 deals with the Islands and boundaries in dispute, and appoints two Commissioners, one on each side, to settle them.

Articles 5, 6, 7, and 8 relate to the boundaries and powers of the Commissioners.

Article 9 relates to making peace between the Indians on both sides.

Article 10 provides for the joint abolition of the slave trade.

Why the American prisoners were not released, on receipt of the Ratification of the Treaty, I cannot say, but that they were not is evidenced by the fact that, on the 6th of April, those confined at Dartmoor attempted to escape ; having armed themselves with knives, they attacked their guards, who in self-defence fired on them, killing seven of the prisoners, and wounding thirty-five. A coroner's jury brought in a verdict of ' justifiable homicide.'

The following story is best told by the Police Report :—

'ATTEMPT TO STEAL THE CROWN FROM THE TOWER.

' LAMBETH POLICE OFFICE.* — Yesterday (*5th April*) MARGARET MOORE was brought before Sir Daniel Williams, and underwent a second examination, charged with an attempt to steal the King's Crown from the Tower, on Friday, the 31st March last.

' Elizabeth Eloisa Stackling, Deputy Keeper of the regalia in the Tower, deposed, that about one o'clock in the afternoon mentioned, the prisoner came and asked to see the regalia—the usual charge for such exhibition is eighteenpence, but the prisoner having offered her a shilling, and she, supposing her, from her appearance, to be a soldier's wife, consented to take it. She proceeded to show her the regalia in the usual way, until she came to the last article, the Crown.

* Lambeth Street, Whitechapel, removed to Arbour Square, Stepney, and now called the Thames Police Office.

This is contained in a case, and is never taken out; she opened the case, and held it with both hands, on the ledge of a table, except when she was obliged to disengage one hand and point out particular jewels. She had just been describing the *aqua-marine*, a jewel of great value, when the prisoner stared, and in an instant thrust her hand through the centre bar of the railings, or grating placed there, and seizing hold of the centre bow of the Crown, pulled, with great violence, to draw it forth.

'Witness put her hand at the top of the bow, and bottom of the Crown, to preserve it, while the prisoner kept struggling, with still greater violence, to get it away. The struggling continued for about five minutes, and she at length got the Crown from her grasp. She, then, put the Crown at a distance behind her, and instantly slipped the bolt of the entrance, secured the prisoner and called for assistance. When help was obtained she sent for the Governor, but the Ward-keeper having come in, a Constable was also sent for, who soon arrived and took the prisoner into Custody. She was searched, and about £5 in money was found upon her; there were also some papers. In the struggle between the witness and the prisoner there were two bows of the Crown broken from the socket; a string of pearls was also broken, which rolled upon the floor, some inside the railing, and some outside, where the prisoner was. They were subsequently picked up by the witness, assisted by the Governor.

'The prisoner being called upon for her defence, said that she was a single woman, residing at No. 3, Union Street, Apollo Gardens; she was a milk woman, and had a girl of about thirteen years of age, her daughter, residing with her; she was a widow, her husband, who was a labouring man, had been dead about eleven years; is not acquainted with a soldier, nor was she ever in company with one, nor had she been to the Tower in her life before the day in question. Being asked by the magistrate why she came so far from home, she replied she very often went to Thames Street to buy salt herrings.

'Then, said the Magistrate, what induced you to go to the Tower?

'*A.* I went on Friday, purposely to see the lions; no one was with me—I then went to see the Crown.

'*Q.* How came you to snatch that article from the keeper?

'*A.* I thought it a pity that so valuable a thing should

remain there, while half the nation was starving for want of
bread !   I wished, also, at the time, to take the whole of what
was there, and give it to the public !

' Q. Who told you to do this, or who was it put that good
thought into your head ?

' A. I had no adviser whatever.

' Jeremiah Brett, one of the Chief Constables, deposed to
having taken the prisoner into custody.   When he was conveying her away in the Coach, he asked her why she had
made an attempt to seize, or lay hands on the Crown, and
why she might not as well have laid hold of one of the
lions ?   She replied—she was not such a fool, for she knew
better than that.

' Upon being asked by the Magistrate to state a little more
particularly who she was, she said she was a Welshwoman, from
the county of Carmarthen, and had been brought up in the
principles of the Church of England.   About ten years ago
she purchased some ground from Mr. Henry Hooper, of
Apollo Gardens ; and, about five years ago, built a small
house, in which she lives, and which has already cost her
£110.   She was to have paid £150.   Her other houses and
property were stolen from her by ejectments, executions, &c.,
and her losses amounted, at least, to £500.   She never had
any idea of stealing the Crown, until she saw it, and was only
impelled by the motive already stated.   Does not recollect
that she ever thought of providing for the poor until then.

' Mr. Swift, the Keeper of the Jewels in the Tower, was
then called, but it was stated that he was out of town, and
would not return before Saturday, or Monday.

' The evidence of this witness, however, being deemed
necessary, the Prisoner was remanded for a final examination.'

On Tuesday, April 11th, she was again examined, but a
number of persons attended, who had known her for many
years, and, as their unvarying testimony was that she was
mentally deranged, she was discharged.

Whilst on the subject of the Regalia, I may mention the following, which is taken from *The Gentleman's Magazine*, May 19,
1814 : ' An interesting discovery has lately been made by the
Keeper of the Regalia in the Tower.   In cleaning out some
secret places in the Jewel Office, a Royal Sceptre was found,
equalling in splendour and in value the others which are there
exhibited.   It is imagined, from the decayed state of its case,
and the dust wherewith it was enveloped, that the Sceptre

must have been thrown into that neglected corner, in the confusion of Blood's well-known attempt on the Crown Jewels, nearly a century and a half ago.'

The war on the Continent was going on, but though it does not come within my province to narrate its progress, I may mention some *bon mots,* which being produced here, belong to the social life of the period.

On Louis le Désiré.

' The Paris folks, when I inquired
If Louis really was " desired,"
" We had (said they), but one desire,
That Master Louis should—*retire*." '

A Conversation between Two Gensdarmes, modelled on *THE TIMES.*

' *First Gensdarme.*   What is the news ?
Second Gensdarme.   *Ma foi !* the news is short.
The *Tiger* has broken out of his den.
The *Monster* was three days at sea.
The *Wretch* has landed at Frejus.
The *Brigand* has arrived at Grenoble.
The *Invader* has entered Lyons.
Napoleon slept last night at Fontainbleau.
The *Emperor* enters the Thuilleries this day.'

Here are some of the names by which he was assailed by *The Times :*

The Tyrant.
The impious tyrant.
The flagitious tyrant.
The wretched tyrant.
The Corsican tyrant.
The wretch.
The impious wretch.
The Corsican.
The impious Corsican.
The rebellious Corsican.
The usurper.
The Corsican usurper.
The homicide.
The impious homicide.
The Outlaw.
The Corsican outlaw.
The infamous outlaw.
The perjured outlaw.
The impious outlaw.

The rebel.
The perjured rebel.
The traitor.
The perjured traitor.
The Brigand.
The Thief.
The Robber.
The Murderer.
The Tiger.
The Monster.
The Villain.
The Criminal.
The notorious Criminal.
The Prisoner.
The Assassin.
The Incendiary.
The Impostor.
The bloody and perjured chief, &c.

This man of many names gave us much trouble just at this time.   Lulled in false security, everything was being put on a peace footing, only to be brought again to its old dimensions, and Sergeant Kite was once more abroad, and active.

A few disjointed *ana* must fill up the time until we come to the next halting stage of history—the Battle of Waterloo.

RECRUITING.

Of course London has vastly increased in population since 1815, and Visitors come by rail, or steamboat, from all parts of the earth, but the difference in the number of visitors to the British Museum in one year, is very marked.   In the year ending March 25, 1815, they amounted to 33,074 ; in that ending Dec. 31, 1889, to 504,537, and this does not include the visitors to the Natural History Department, at South

Kensington, which, although removed from the parent building, is part of the Institution, and is governed by the same trustees.

The Prince of Wales was utterly reckless in his expenditure; he put no kind of curb to his extravagance, and left no whim ungratified. The consequence was he was again fearfully in debt.

'THE CIVIL LIST.

' " John Bull," exclaims old Nick, " pray mind,
The Civil List is now behind :"
"Good Lord !" cried John, " why, what a bore,
It was *behind*, you know, *before*." '

Here is a list of the Prince of Wales's debts :

Debts 1787	...	...	...	...	£161,020
Debts 1795	...	...	...	...	640,080
					801,100
Debts paid in three years to Feb., 1815, from Extraordinary Allowances to the Prince					150,000
Sum granted for outfit Feb., 1812, and applied to debts	...	...	...	...	100,000
Paid from Droits of Admiralty, 1813			...		39,000
Paid from Feb., 1815, to May, 1815, one q^r of £50,000	...	...	...	...	12,500
Paid in three years from Duchy of Cornwall to Feb., 1815	...	...	...	...	39,000
Known to be remaining unpaid May, 1815	...				339,000
Total of debts contracted by the Prince	...				£1,480,600

The Newspaper from which this is taken goes on to say :
' The public will see, by this statement, how unavailing all engagements, and all Acts of Parliament hitherto passed, have been to prevent the system of incurring debts; but the distresses of the country now demand some effective prohibitory checks, and we trust Parliament will not separate without supplying them; although from the vote for the payment of the Russian debts, for the reduction of Guadaloupe, and the aids to Holland, there is too much reason to fear that the Senate, and the public, entertain different views as to the necessity of economy, and that the public must encounter the awful trial of a protracted system of profusion and prodigality.

' The statement of the debts was extracted from the

Journals of Parliament, and when £339,000 was described
as the *known* excess still due, the term *known* was certainly
used to signify *avowal*, but not to embrace the *total*, for there
is great reason to believe that treble £339,000 would not
release the Prince Regent from his pecuniary embarrass-
ments.'

Needless to say, the satirical artists seized upon the occasion,
and I reproduce one picture, called 'Answer to John Bull's

'ANSWER TO JOHN BULL'S COMPLAINT.'

Complaint.' As may be perceived from his dress, poor John
is reduced to a pitiable plight, and he has laid his case before
the Regent. To him 'the first Gentleman in Europe' replies, 'Why! you unnatural Grumbler! after I have done all
I could to get rid of your Money, you still grumble? Did I
not give you a *Fête*? Did I not build you a *Bridge*? Did I

not treat you to a smell of all the nice things at my *Feast*?
Did I not sign the *Corn Bill*?   Did I not refuse your *Address*?
Have I not drunk whole Pipes of Wine, for fear it should be
wasted?   Have I not spent all your Money, because you
should not spend it yourself?   Have you not got the Income
Tax to keep you sober? and, as for your Dress, the thinner
the better for the summer season.   So, Johnny, go home to
work, 'tis all for the good of your Country.'

CHAPTER XXI.

News of the Battle of Waterloo—Rejoicings—After career of Napoleon — His abdication and flight — Goes on board the *Bellerophon*—Arrives at Torbay—His habits on board—Ordered to Plymouth—Crowds try to get a glimpse of him—His protest against being sent to St. Helena—Transferred to the *Northumberland*—Opinion as to the Prince Regent's conduct towards him—Sails for St. Helena.

At a quarter past eleven on the night of the 21st of June, the Hon. Major Percy arrived at the office of Earl Bathurst, Secretary of State for War—bearing despatches from the Duke of Wellington dated the 19th, giving an account of the actions which had taken place since the 15th, and including the Battle of Waterloo. Earl Bathurst opened the despatches, and he and their bearer immediately waited, with them, upon the Prince Regent. The Lord Mayor had notification of the great Victory early in the morning of the 22nd, and the guns of the Tower, and St. James's Park thundered forth their salute of gratulation. The funds went up with a bound, *Omnium* vibrated between a rise of 8 to 10 per cent. and left off 8⅛ per cent. higher.

The following placard was posted up :—

'Mansion House, *Thursday, June 22, 1815.*
' Notice having been given that the Public Offices will be illuminated Friday and Saturday evening next, in consequence of the late glorious Victory,
'The Lord Mayor recommends to the inhabitants of this City to defer illuminating their houses till that time.'

And, accordingly, on the 23rd, all the Government, and City public offices lit up ; but it does not seem to have been a very grand illumination, probably because the time for preparation was somewhat short.

After the battle of Waterloo,* Napoleon hastened to Paris ; and, tired, and covered with dust as he was, he immediately met his Ministers, and told them the extent of his disasters. They laid the intelligence before the Houses of Legislature, and, on the morning of June 22nd, Napoleon received a deputation from the Chamber, who submitted to him, that 'the state of war in which France was involved, concerned much less the nation than himself, and that the Assembly had the means at command, if he would act so disinterested a part, as to restore to it freedom of action, according as circumstances might dictate.'

This was a pretty broad hint to Napoleon to abdicate, and he took it as such, and sent the following reply :—

'Frenchmen ! When I began the war to uphold National Independence, I relied on the union of all efforts, all wills, and on the co-operation of all national authorities. I was justified in anticipating success, and I braved all the declarations of the Powers against my person. Circumstances seem to be changed. I offer myself as a sacrifice to the hatred against France. May your enemies prove sincere, and may it appear that they wage war against me alone ! My political life is terminated. I proclaim my son, under the title of Napoleon II.,† Emperor of the French. The present Ministers will form the Council of the Provisional Government. The interest which I take in my son induces me to invite the Chambers to organize a Regency without delay, by a special law. Unite for the general safety, and to secure national independence.

'NAPOLEON.

'At the Palace of the Elysée, June 22, 1815.'

But the Ministry did not see it in the same light, the building was rapidly crumbling, and it was *sauve qui peut* with

---

* From this time until Napoleon sailed for St. Helena, I quote, sometimes at length, from my book, 'English Caricature and Satire on Napoleon I.,' because I then wrote, thoroughly imbued with the subject, and with every authority at hand—I can do no more now, than to add a little to it.—J. A.

† This title was never recognized by the French *Nation* until the assumption of Imperial dignity by Louis—under the title of Napoleon III.

the rats.   Napoleon was politically dead, and even *The Times* must needs kick him.

'June 30, 1815. . . . The wretch, with the blood of so many thousands on his head, seemed to carry about with him all the coolness of that apathy which is part of his physical constitution ; and, so degraded and demoralized are the Parisian populace, that they could see the butcher of their race without the least emotion.   He is, however, spoken of in the journals, and in the debates, without any share of that respect which was but lately attached to his name.   After his former abdication he was invariably termed the " Emperor," but now he is called nothing but " Napoleon." '

Abdication is a game that cannot be played more than twice, the result, then, being considered final, so Napoleon retired to Malmaison, virtually a prisoner, for he had not been there long ere General Becker came to him, and informed him that he was appointed by the Provisional Government to command the troops detailed for his protection.   Napoleon knew the meaning of this message, but even being made a prisoner by his own soldiery did not quell his spirit.

The presence of Napoleon at Malmaison embarrassed the Government, and Becker had orders to convey Napoleon, with all speed, to the Isle of Aix.   Accordingly, they set out, and reached Rochefort on the 3rd of July, where he remained until the 8th, when he embarked on board the *Saale* frigate, but without any hope of getting to sea, because of the blockade of the port by the *Bellerophon* and other English men-of-war.   He occasionally landed on the Isle of Aix ; but all hopes of reaching America seems to have been abandoned, as Las Cases and Savary were sent on board the *Bellerophon* to inquire of Captain Maitland whether he knew anything of the passports which Napoleon expected from the British Government, and whether any opposition would be offered to his sailing to the United States.   Captain Maitland replied that he knew nothing of the intentions of his Government, but he, certainly, could not allow any ship of war to leave the port, and, in the course of conversation asked, ' Why not seek an asylum in England ?'

The hint, thus dropped, fructified ; for, after another visit of Las Cases and General Lallemand on board the *Bellerophon*, on July 14th, avowedly to repeat their various questions, the

matter was openly discussed, and, on mentioning the result of
their interview to the Emperor, he agreed to this course, and
desired Las Cases to tell Captain Maitland to prepare to
receive him, and his suite, the next day.   At the same time,
he entrusted General Gourgaud with an autograph letter to
the Prince Regent, directing him to take it to England, and
deliver it into the Prince's hands.

From the date of this letter, which was the 13th, it would
seem that Napoleon had, on the previous day, made up his
mind what course to pursue.   The following is the text of the
letter :—

' YOUR ROYAL HIGHNESS,—Exposed to the factions which
divide my Country, and to the enmity of the greatest Powers
of Europe, I have terminated my political career ; and I come,
like Themistocles, to throw myself upon the hospitality of the
British People.   I place myself under the protection of their
laws, which I claim from your Royal Highness, as the most
powerful, the most constant, and the most generous of my
enemies.   NAPOLEON.

' ROCHEFORT, *July* 13, 1815.'

On the 15th, then, Napoleon and suite went on board the
Bellerophon, where they were received by Captain Maitland
and his officers ; the Emperor saying, ' I have come to throw
myself on the protection of your Prince and Laws.'   He was
treated on board the *Bellerophon* with every consideration by
Captain Maitland.   He was still looked upon as Emperor, and
dined off his own gold plate, the dinner being ordered by his
own *maitre d'hôtel ;* and, when he visited the *Superb,* he was
received with all the honours accorded to royalty, with the
exception of a salute being fired.   On the 16th of July they
set sail for England, and at daybreak on the 24th they were
close to Dartmouth.   Napoleon rose at six, and went on the
poop, surveying the coast, which he much admired, exclaiming, ' What a beautiful country ! it very much resembles Porto
Ferrajo at Elba.'

About 8 a.m. they anchored at Torbay, and no sooner was
it known that Napoleon was on board the *Bellerophon,* than
the bay was covered with vessels and boats full of people.   A
neighbouring gentleman sent the Emperor a present of fruit.
What a different reception from the language of *The Times !*
(July 25, 1815):

' Our paper of this day will satisfy the sceptics, for such there were beginning to be, as to the capture of that bloody miscreant, who has so long tortured Europe, NAPOLEON BUONAPARTE. Savages are always found to unite the greatest degree of cunning to the ferocious part of their nature. The cruelty of this person is written in characters of blood in almost every country in Europe, and in the contiguous angles of Africa and Asia which he visited ; and nothing can more strongly evince the universal conviction of his low, perfidious craft, than the opinion, which was beginning to get abroad, that, even after his capture had been officially announced, both in France and England, he might yet have found means to escape.

' However, all doubts upon this point are at an end, by his arrival off the British Coast, and, if he be not now placed beyond the possibility of again outraging the peace of Europe, England will certainly never again deserve to have heroes such as those who have fought, and bled, at Waterloo, for this, his present overthrow. The lives of the brave men who fell on that memorable day will have been absolutely thrown away by a thoughtless country, the grand object obtained by their valour will have been frustrated, and we shall do little less than insult over their remains, almost before they have ceased to bleed. But Fortune, seconding their undaunted efforts, has put it in our power to do far otherwise.

' Captain Sartorius, of the *Slaney* frigate, arrived yesterday with despatches from Captain Maitland of the *Bellerophon*, confirming all the antecedent accounts of Buonaparte's surrender, with various other details, and closing them by their natural catastrophe—his safe conveyance to England. He is, therefore, what we may call, here. Captain Sartorius delivered his despatches to Lord Melville, at Wimbledon, by whom their contents were communicated to Lord Liverpool, at his seat at Coombe Wood ; summonses were immediately issued for a Cabinet Council to meet at 12 o'clock ; what passed there was, of course, not suffered to transpire ; our narrative must therefore revert to the *Slaney* frigate, and the accounts brought by her. She had been sent forward, by Captain Maitland, to Plymouth, with the despatches announcing that Buonaparte was on board the *Bellerophon*, with a numerous suite. But it was the intention of Captain Maitland himself, to proceed to Torbay, and not land his prisoners until he had received orders from Government.

16

'Buonaparte's suite, as it is called, consists of upwards of forty persons, among whom are Bertrand, Savary, Lallemand, Grogau,* and several women.   He has been allowed to take on board carriages and horses, but admission was denied to about fifty cavalry, for whom he had the impudence to require accommodation.   This wretch has really lived in the commission of every crime, so long, that he had lost all sight and knowledge of the difference that exists between good and evil, and hardly knows when he is doing wrong, except he be taught by proper chastisement.   A creature—who ought to be greeted with a gallows as soon as he lands—to think of an attendance of fifty horsemen! He had, at first, wanted to make conditions with Captain Maitland, as to his treatment, but the British officer very properly declared that he must refer him, upon this subject, to his Government.

'When he had been some time on board, he asked the Captain what chance two large frigates, well manned, would have with a seventy-four.   The answer, we understand, which he received to this inquiry, did not give him any cause to regret that he had not risked his fortune in a naval combat, with the relative forces in question.   By the way, we should not have been surprised if he had come into an action with the two frigates, and then endeavoured to escape in his own, and leave the other to her fate.   It has been the constant trick of this villain, whenever he has got his companions into a scrape, to leave them in it, and seek his own safety by flight. In Egypt, in the Moscow expedition, and at Waterloo, such was his conduct.

'He likewise had the assurance to address a letter to the Prince Regent, and M. Grogau, one of his party, was put on board the *Slaney* as the bearer of it ; but, when the vessel reached Plymouth, the officer on duty there, with a decision that does him credit, refused Grogau permission to land : the letter is said to have been conveyed by Captain Sartorius, and its purport was understood, on board, to be a request for passports for America.   We should have supposed that he had received too many checks before, for his presumption in addressing letters to the British Government, ever to have hazarded the experiment again ; but all reproofs are thrown away upon his callous heart ;—not that we should object to his humbly addressing the British throne for mercy, if he has anything to urge in extenuation of his crimes ; but the time

* General Gourgaud.

has not yet come ; a momentary gleam of resolution on the part of his own government, indicated by the imprisonment of Labédoyère, and others, led us to hope that his trial might have been safely entrusted to those to whom it primarily, and of natural right, belongs ; but, though this hope may have proved transitory, he is not, therefore, above the criminal justice of other countries, where established law, and a regular execution of it, prevails.

' The first procedure, we trust, will be a special Commission, or the appointment of a Court Martial to try him for the murder of Captain Wright. It is nonsense to say, as some have, that Courts Martial are instituted only to try offences committed by soldiers of the country to which they belong : it was an American Court Martial that tried and shot Major André as a spy ; and Buonaparte himself appointed commissions of all kinds, and in all countries, to try offences committed against himself.'

In a letter from on board the *Bellerophon*, Napoleon's *personnel* is thus described :

' I observed his person particularly, and can describe him thus :—He is about 5 feet 7 inches in height, very strongly made, and well proportioned ; very broad and deep chest ; legs and thighs proportioned with great symmetry and strength, a small, round, and handsome foot. His countenance is sallow, and, as it were, deeply tinged by hot climates ; but the most commanding air I ever saw. His eyes grey, and the most piercing you can imagine. His glance, you fancy, searches into your inmost thoughts. His hair dark brown, and no appearance of grey. His features are handsome now, and when younger, he must have been a very handsome man. He is rather fat, and his belly protuberant, but he appears active, notwithstanding. His step, and demeanour altogether commanding. He looks about 45 or 46 years of age. In fact, he is very like the picture exhibited of him in the Adelphi, and also several of the prints.

' He is extremely curious, and never passes anything remarkable in the ship, without immediately demanding its use, and inquiring minutely into the manner thereof. He also stops and asks the officers divers questions relative to the time they have been in the service, what actions, &c. ; and he caused all of us to be introduced to him, the first day he came on board. He also asked several questions about the marines, particularly those who appeared to have been some time in the service,

and about the warrant officers, midshipmen, seamen, &c. He
was but a very short time on board when he asked that the
boatswain might be sent for, in order that he might look at
him, and was very inquisitive as to the nature of his duty. He

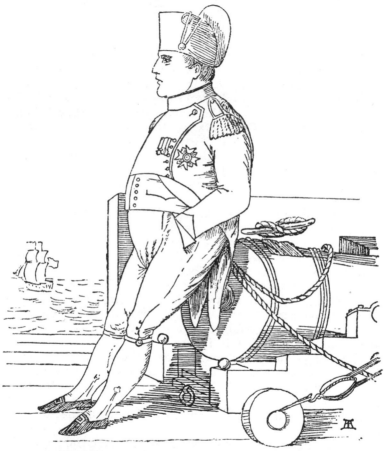

BONAPARTE ON THE QUARTER-DECK OF H.M.S. *NORTHUMBERLAND.*
(Drawn during his passage to St. Helena. Published, January 1, 1816,
by Thomas Palser, Westminster Bridge Road.)

dresses in green uniform, with red facings and edged with red,
two plain gold epaulettes, the lapels of the coat cut round and
turned back, white waistcoat and breeches, and military boots
and spurs, the Grand Cross of the Legion of Honour on his

left breast. He professes his intention (if he is allowed to reside in England) to adopt the English customs and manners, and declares that he will never meddle with politics more. The Army, which left Paris, and united with others on the Loire, wanted him to rejoin them and resume his title, which he refused to do. He declares that not another "*goutte de sang*" shall be shed on his account. Fortunate, indeed, it would have been if he had really been of this opinion some years back.

'His followers still treat him with the greatest respect, not one of them, not even the Duke of Rovigo himself, ever speaking to him, without being uncovered the whole time. He does not appear out until about half-past ten, though he rises about seven. He breakfasts in the French fashion at eleven, and dines at six. He spends most of the day alone in the after-cabin, and reads a great deal. He retires to bed about eight. He has not latterly been much upon the quarter-deck. His suite is composed of fifty people.'

I give an illustration of 'Bonaparte on the Quarter-deck of H.M.S. *Northumberland*, drawn during his passage to St. Helena,' which fully bears out the above description.

On July 26th orders came for the *Bellerophon* to go to Plymouth, which being reached, two frigates, the *Liffey*, and *Eurotas*, were anchored, one on either side of her, and kept strict guard over her. No boat from the shore was allowed to come within a cable's length* of her, and ships' boats continually rowing round her, kept that space clear.

Visitors from London, and all parts of England, came to get a glimpse of him, and the sea was literally alive with boats of every description. The following is by an eye witness† :—

'There is nothing so dull as mere fact, you'll admit,
While you read my detail, unenlivened by wit.
My friends will believe, though they're told it in rhyme,
That I thought to return in a far shorter time.
When at one we're resolv'd, by half past on the move,
And by two, but a trio, we reach Mutton Cove ;
When approaching the quay, such a rabble and rout,
That we ask, "My good friend, what is all this about ?"

---

* A measure of about one hundred fathoms. In all marine charts a Cable is deemed 607·56 feet, or one-tenth of a Sea Mile.

† 'A Visit to Bonaparte in Plymouth Sound," by a Lady. Plymouth, 1815.

" They are rowing a race, and some boats are come in,
While these people are waiting till t'others begin."
Well aware of our folly, with risible lip,
The boatman we told to make haste to *the* ship ;
On the colours of fish,* here by hampers-full landing,
We gaze for amuzement, while still we're kept standing ;
At length to the Admiral's stairs we have got,
See his party on board, and hear tunes from his yacht.
The day is delightful, the gale just enough
For the sea to look lively, without being rough.
With those first at the ship, our sight costs the dearer,
As we've longer to wait, and not, in the end, nearer ;
For by land, and by water, so different the case is,
'Twas long before we were jam'd into our places ;
But on further advice, we'll at present be dumb,
For half the spectators, you know, are now come.
In one boat, a bevy, all sarcenet and veil,
In the next some good fellows are toping their ale.
" Avast ! here's the gun boat."   " Aye, here it come smack."
And the ladies cry, " Captain, they'll drive us all back."
Then some bully our men " Skull out there, skull out."
And others check these with, " Mind what you're about."
Here's a crazy old boat, laded dry with a shoe,
There, a gay painted barge is forced on our view ;
In this, while Don Solus is jeered by the mob,
" See that empty boat, turn it out."   " Here's a fine job."
Cries one, of some dozens squeezed into the next,
" I've left the pork pie, Oh dear, I'm so vex'd."
In the long boat, that shows a profusion of oar,
From the Captain bursts forth a most terrible roar
At his men ; but the anger about whom, or what,
Though they may remember, we soon had forgot.
Here, infants were crying, mothers scolding outright,
While the next party laughs at some comical sight.
Now, watches and spy-glasses make their appearance,
And Impatience, that vixen, begins interference ;
To beguile her, through portholes we eagerly stare,
For the nobles on deck are all taking the air.
" Hey-dey, what a bustle !" then " All safe, all safe."
The crowd is return'd to its chatter and laugh.
" Pray, what was the matter ?"   " From the boat, near the ship,
A woman fell over, and so got a dip."
But a hum of applause, yes, his triumph is full,
Yet this hum of applause has betrayed our John Bull,
" What hum of applause ? come, I prithee, be brief."
Why, John was delighted to see them *ship beef.*

---

* Mackerel.

With a smile 'tis observed by the Briton polite,
How the glee of the crowd was improv'd, by the sight,
For the rough, honest tar, had declared from his heart,
That he thought this a sight that would beat Bonaparte.
Some, again, with composure, predict peace and war,
Others look at the great folks, and fancy a star ;
But we, much fatigued, six o'clock now approaching,
And on our good nature we thought them encroaching,
When boats are made bridges, nay, tempted to think
That through some of these freedoms, not strange we should
    sink.
But here I must mention, when all was most merry,
As here is each size, from the long-boat to wherry,
When the crowd should disperse, I was fearful, I own,
Lest your small boats, by barges, should then be run down.
But a truce with our hopes, our predictions and fears,
For now, yes, at last, our grand object appears ;
And now, every eye to the ship is directed,
Though to see Bonaparte, I no longer expected ;
For between us what number of men ! and aghast
We stood, as still thicker and thicker the mast. [? mass]
But now see Napoleon, who seems in his figure,
What we call mediocre, nor smaller, nor bigger ;
For, in spite of our fears, how it was, I can't tell,
What our distance allowed of, we saw very well.
But, in this we're full right, for now, hurry scurry,
Boat rows against boat, with the madness of fury ;
The show was all over, but time was out staid
By some, and by others, attempts were still made
To get round the ship, in hopes Bonaparte might
At some place yet be seen, thus to perfect their sight.'

This doggerel helps us to realize the intense desire of the
British public to get, at least, a glimpse at Boney, that great
bugbear, who for so many years had been so great a terror to
them, and whose existence, every one, from the highest to the
lowest, had acutely felt in that tenderest place of our social
economy—the breeches pocket. They all but carried out the
threat made twelve years previously, of putting him in *Pid-
cock's Menagerie, vide* the following extracts from a contemporary pamphlet :*—

'The desire of all ranks to see him was excessive ; the
guard boats were unable to prevent them from closing the
ship, and it was amusement on board to look at the boats con-
tending for places. Napoleon generally walked the quarter-

* 'Interesting Particulars of Napoleon's Deportation for Life to
St. Helena,' &c. London, 1816. Printed for W. Hone.

deck about eleven in the forenoon, and half-past six in the afternoon. He ate but two meals in the day, both alike, meat of every description, different wines, coffee, fruit, &c. Immediately after each meal, he rose first and the others followed ; he then either went on the quarter-deck or in the after-cabin, to study. The comedy of *The Poor Gentleman** was performed before him. He was much pleased at it ; it went off very well. The scenery was good, but somewhat better dresses were wanted for the *female midshipmen.*†

'The immense number of persons who daily flock from all parts of the country, to take a view of the person of Napoleon, is incalculable. He generally gratified the public curiosity by making his appearance every afternoon for two hours.

'Upwards of one thousand boats were from morning to night round the *Bellerophon*. The seamen of the *Bellerophon* adopted a curious mode to give an account to the curious spectators in the boats of the movements of Napoleon. They wrote in chalk on a board, which they exhibited, a short account of his different occupations. "At breakfast."—"In the cabin with Captain Maitland."—"Writing with his officers." —"Going to dinner."—"Coming upon deck," &c.'

Las Cases says :—' It was known that he always appeared on deck towards five o'clock. A short time before this hour all the boats collected alongside of each other ; there were thousands ; and so closely were they connected, that the water could no longer be seen between them. They looked more like a multitude assembled in a public square than anything else. When the Emperor came out, the noise and gestures of so many people presented a most striking spectacle ; it was, at the same time, very easy to perceive that nothing hostile was meant, and that, if curiosity had brought them, they felt interested on going away. We could even see that the latter sentiment continued to increase ; at first, people merely looked toward the ship, they ended by saluting ; some remained uncovered, and, occasionally, went so far as to cheer. Even our symbols began to appear amongst them. Several individuals of both sexes came decorated with red carnations.'

Napoleon knew that St. Helena had been fixed upon as the place of his future residence, and did not at all relish the idea ; but it was not officially announced to him until

---

* By George Colman the Younger.
† *i.e.*, the midshipmen who took female parts.

July 30th or 31st, when Lord Keith went on board the
Bellerophon, and presented him with the following despatch :

*' Communication made by Lord Keith in the name of the
English Ministers.*

' As it may, perhaps, be convenient for General Buonaparte
to learn, without further delay, the intentions of the British
Government with regard to him, your Lordship will communicate the following information.

' It would be inconsistent with our duty towards our country,
and the Allies of his Majesty, if General Buonaparte possessed the means of again disturbing the repose of Europe.
It is on this account that it becomes absolutely necessary he
should be restrained in his personal liberty, so far as this is
required by the foregoing important object.

' The island of St. Helena has been chosen as his future
residence ; its climate is healthy, and its local position will
allow of his being treated with more indulgence than could
be admitted in any other spot, owing to the indispensable
precautions which it would be necessary to employ for the
security of his person.

' General Buonaparte is allowed to select amongst those
persons who accompanied him to England (with the exception of Generals Savary and Tallemand) three officers, who,
together with his surgeon, will have permission to accompany
him to St. Helena ; these individuals will not be allowed to
quit the island without the sanction of the British Government.

' Rear-Admiral Sir George Cockburn, who is named Commander-in-Chief at the Cape of Good Hope and seas adjacent,
will convey General Buonaparte and his suite to St. Helena ;
and he will receive detailed instructions relative to the
execution of this service.

' Sir G. Cockburn will, most probably, be ready to sail in
a few days ; for which reason it is desirable that General
Buonaparte should make choice of the persons who are to
accompany him, without delay.'

Of this interview Las Cases says : ' I was not called before
the Emperor. The bearers of his sentence spoke, and understood French ; they were admitted alone. I have since heard
that he objected, and protested, with no less energy than logic,
against the violence exercised on his person. " He was the

guest of England," said Napoleon, "and not its prisoner; he came of his own accord to place himself under the protection of its laws; the most sacred rights of hospitality were violated in his person; he would never submit voluntarily to the outrage they were preparing for him; violence, alone, should oblige him to do so," &c.'

That the Government was in earnest as to his departure was soon shown, for orders came on August 4th for the *Bellerophon* to weigh and join the *Northumberland*, which was the ship in which Napoleon was to take his passage to St. Helena. He issued a formal protest:—

'I hereby solemnly protest in the face of heaven and mankind against the violence that is done me; and the violation of my most sacred rights, in forcibly disposing of my person and liberty. I voluntarily came on board the *Bellerophon*—I am not the prisoner, I am the guest of England. I came at the instigation of the Captain himself, who said he had orders from the Government to receive, and convey me to England, together with my suite, if agreeable to me. I came forward, with confidence, to place myself under the protection of the laws of England. When once on board the *Bellerophon*, I was entitled to the hospitality of the British people. If the Government, in giving the Captain of the *Bellerophon* orders to receive me and my followers, only wished to lay a snare, it has forfeited its honour, and disgraced its flag.

'If this act be consummated, it will be in vain for the English henceforth to talk of their sincerity, their laws, and liberties. British faith will have been lost in the hospitality of the *Bellerophon*.

'I appeal to history; it will say that an enemy who made war for twenty years against the English people, came spontaneously, in the hour of misfortune, to seek an asylum under their laws. What more striking proof could he give of his esteem and confidence? But how did England reply to such an act of magnanimity? It pretended to hold out a hospitable hand to this enemy; and, on giving himself up with confidence, he was immolated!

'NAPOLEON.

'*Bellerophon*, at Sea, *Friday, Aug.* 4, 1815.'

This might have been good logic had it not been for the

little episode of Elba, which showed that neither honour, nor treaties, could bind him, and the contiguity of England to France was far too near.   His residence here would be a fruitful source of intrigue and danger to both countries. Every reason of sound policy was for his complete isolation ; but, whether that sentence was carried out either humanely,

BOXIANA, OR THE FANCY.
(*Published by Mr. Jones, 5, Newgate Street, October* 1, 1815.)

or with even a show of deference to Napoleon's feelings, is another question, which needs no discussion here.

On the 6th they anchored off Start Point, and were soon joined by the *Northumberland* and two frigates, full of soldiers, who were to form the garrison of St. Helena.   By order, the arms of Napoleon's suite were taken from them, but the ex-Emperor was allowed to retain his sword.   All their money, diamonds, and saleable effects were put under seal, but

Napoleon kept his plate, baggage, wines, and provisions. The search of his personal effects greatly exasperated him.

Between one and two o'clock p.m. of the 7th of August the transfer from the *Bellerophon* to the *Northumberland* was made, and then, as there was nothing else to wait for, ' Cæsar and his fortunes' sailed for St. Helena.

There were but a very few satirical prints anent him published after his departure, and, I think, not one after the news of his safe arrival at St. Helena. There was a sense of relief that now he was powerless for mischief, and a revulsion of feeling set in. It was then the heyday of Boxing, and it was felt repugnant to all feelings of English manliness, to ' hit a man when he was down.' The Prince of Wales was severely remarked on for his conduct to his illustrious Captive, and the following poetry was exceedingly popular.

The illustration on p. 251, which is separate from, but goes well with the song, is called ' BOXIANA, or the FANCY,' and the poem is an ' Epistle from TOM CRIBB to BIG BEN, containing some Foul Play in a Pugilistic Encounter,' August, 1815 :—

> ' What, Ben ! my big hero, is this thy renown ?
> Is *this* the *new Go*—kick a man when he's down ?
> When the foe has *knockt under*, to tread on him then ?
> By the fist of my father, I blush for thee, Ben !
> Foul ! Foul ! all the *Lads of the Fancy* exclaim—
> *Charley Shock* is electrified—*Belcher* spits flame—
> And *Molyneux*—aye, even Blackey, cries Shame !
>
> Time was, when *John Bull* little difference spied,
> 'Twixt the foe at his feet, and the friend at his side ;
> When he found (such his humour in fighting and eating),
> His foe, like his beefsteak, the better for beating !
> But this comes, Master *Ben*, of your curst foreign notions,
> Your trinkets, wigs, thingambobs, gold lace, and lotions ;
> Your Noyeau's Curacoa's, and the Devil knows what—
> (One swig of *Blue Ruin* is worth the whole lot)—
> Your great and small *crosses* (my eyes ! what a brood !)
> A cross buttock from *me* would do some of 'em good—
> Which have spoil'd you, till hardly a drop, my old porpus,
> Of pure English *claret* is left in your *corpus*.
> And (as *Jim* says) the only one trick, good or bad,
> Of the *Fancy*, you're up to, is *fibbing*, my lad !
> Hence it comes, *Boxiana*, disgrace to thy page !—
> Having *floor'd*, by good luck, the first *Swell* of the Age,
> Having conquer'd the *prime one* that *mill'd* us all round,
> You kick'd him, old *Ben*, as he gasp'd on the ground !—

Aye—just at the time to show spunk, if you'd any,
Kick'd him and jaw'd, and *lag'd** him to Botany!

Oh, shade of the Cheesemonger !† you who, alas !
Doubled up, by the dozen, those Mounseers in brass,
On that great day of *milling*,‡ when blood lay in lakes,
When Kings held the bottle, and Europe the Stakes,
Look down upon *Ben*, see him *Dunghill* all o'er,
Moult the fall'n foe that can harm him no more ;
Out, cowardly *Spooney !* again and again.
By the fist of my father, I blush for thee, *Ben !*
To show the *white feather*§ is many men's doom,
But what of *one* feather ! *Ben* boasts a whole *Plume ! !'*

And so Napoleon fades away.

* Transported.   † Shaw the Lifeguardsman.
‡ Battle of Waterloo.   § Cowardice.

CHAPTER XXII.

Effects of Napoleon's capture—The Navy in 1815—Margate and Ramsgate—French Prisoners of war—Treaty of Peace with France—Napoleon's house—A soldier's letter—A zealous Lord Mayor—Hotels and clubs in 1815.

THE effect of the capture and banishment of Napoleon was felt immediately, a great strain was taken off Europe, and it was known to all, that the peace, after so long a conflict, would be enduring. On the 17th of August we read, 'The impressment of seamen is directed to be discontinued at all the seaports, as also the receiving of volunteers, except for the peace establishment. Orders have been issued at the different ports to pay off the Navy ; and the seamen are to be sent to their respective homes, in small vessels, to be in readiness for that purpose.'

The Navy was a rough school then, and the officers mainly came from a very different class to that from which they are now recruited. What a Midshipman's berth was like then, we may learn from the following extract from a letter :

'The Midshipman, whose *Friends were not born before him,* as the phrase goes, is easily distinguished amongst his more fortunate companions in arms ; you generally see him attired more like the prodigal son returning from his occupation of a swine-herd, than a British officer. His perforated worsted hose, shoes which have a very great resemblance to *sandals,* thread-bare pantaloons which were once blue, a tattered " *uniform !*" coat, and a slouched hat, show that " poverty, and not his will, consents."

'A Midshipman's berth (in a dark cockpit under water) has long been proverbial for the convenience, and elegance of its comforts ; a large deal table, abundantly ornamented with hieroglyphicks, a form, and some broken chairs, two beautiful

brass candlesticks, well charged with grease, lights which
seem to render darkness more visible, about ten plates and
dishes, seven knives and forks, five pewter spoons, with cups
and saucers in proportion, two old decanters without necks,
and a very large stock of empty bottles, usually form the earthly
stock of its utensils.   To describe the valet, or attendant,
would, indeed, be a difficult task ; perhaps the reader can call
to mind Le Sage's description of Domingo, whose vigilance
prevented Gil Blas' escape from the Cavern ?   If so, I need
not trouble you with anything further on the subject, except
that the one is, generally, the counterpart of the other.'

In the following, under date of October 3rd, we see the
germ of our present steam navy : 'We understand that a
distinguished British Officer, who had an opportunity of viewing the steam frigate at New York, pronounced it to be the
most formidable battery of defence ever invented (they are
to be stationed at all their different seaports) : and the Officer
alluded to, has, we hear, strongly recommended their adoption,
particularly for the Bay of Gibraltar.'

Steam had already been introduced into our Mercantile
marine, and we find (September), 'A *Margate* hoy of large
dimensions, propelled by steam, goes constantly to and fro
from London to Margate.   From its novelty, and the certainty of its arrival within a given time (about twelve hours),
it is much thronged with passengers.'

It was the fashionable month for those popular watering-
places, Margate and Ramsgate, and how our grandparents
took their holidays is thus described : ' How very different is
a watering-place from the rest of the world !   In a commercial town every face you meet, carries the word " business," everyone seems so absorbed in his own cares, as not
even to be conscious of the existence of his fellow men.   Life
seems to have an object, you involuntarily quicken your pace,
cast your eyes straight forward, and enumerate to yourself
the several matters you have to transact.   There is nothing
of all this at a Watering-Place, there you find the inhabitants
divided into two classes, *gapers*, and *smilers*.   By the gapers
must be understood, those who are here to spend their money,
and be amused ; and, by the smilers, those who are here to
gain their money, and be maintained.

' Now the employment of the gapers is to lie in bed all the
fore part of the day, " the dewy hour of prime," to wear a
great coat, brown hat, brown shoes, bathe, and ride half a

mile on a donkey, with a boy behind to whip it, read the
newspapers during the middle of the day, and in the evening
to dine, to go to a promenade in a ball-room, where during
nine-tenths of the time everyone sits still ; or, to the theatre,
where the pure air, and pure light of heaven are shut out, to
make room for otto of roses and Argand lamps.   Thus the
amusements of the citizen are scarcely varied by his journey,
or, rather, his voyage, for the packets bring the mass of
visitors to Margate.   The first effort the worthy Cit makes to
get rid of the foul air of London, is to stow himself and family
on board the hoy ; here he finds eighty or a hundred amateurs
of fresh air.   Then if the wind be fair, and not too strong,
they proceed tolerably well, but should the wind be foul,
which Heaven in its great mercy forefend, such a scene opens,
such qualms, and faintings,

> "Such revisitings,
> As make day hideous, and us poor fools of nature
> Most horribly to shake our dispositions." '

Although there was virtually peace throughout Europe, the
Definitive Treaty of Peace, between the Allied Powers and
France, was not signed until the 20th of November, at Paris :
consequently the prisoners of war were not released.   We
can well understand the irritation of the poor fellows, who
knew that it was only red tape that was preventing their
return to their country and homes, and are, therefore, not
surprised to hear (September 13th), that ' the prisoners in
confinement on board the prison ships at Cowes, meditated
escape on the night of the 1st instant, but their plans were
fortunately detected, through the perseverance and exertions
of Lieutenant Whaley, 18th Regiment of Foot, Commanding
Officer on board the ships.   To show the length they intended
to go, if necessary, to effect their purpose, they had actually
sworn themselves to secrecy, by drinking their own blood
mixed with cold water.'

They were rather expensive acquaintances, for I find that
the cost of them, during the greater part of the war, for provisions, clothing, and superintendence, was calculated, in
detail, to amount to £1,000 per diem—and this was exclusive
of building materials used for their prisons.

The text of the Treaty arrived here on the 27th of November.   London was illuminated, Peace was proclaimed, as was
also a Day of Thanksgiving.

Napoleon's House and furniture were manufactured here, and were ready for shipment by the end of October. I have but space to describe the house ; suffice it to say, that the furniture was fitted for the use of an opulent gentleman, rather than for the quondam ruler of Europe. ' The framework for the house is nearly completed at Woolwich. The front is in the Grecian style. It is about 120 feet in length, containing fourteen windows, and a fine open corridor. The depth of the building is about 100 feet, with a back corridor, almost making the whole structure square.—It is two stories high, and will have an elegant cottage appearance. The ground-floor of the right division of the house, contains Bonaparte's apartments. In the centre of this wing is his drawing-room, which, as well as the other apartments for his accommodation, is about 30 feet in length, by a breadth of 20. This proportion runs through the whole. Next, is his dining-room, with an adjoining library, behind which, is a capacious billiard-room. His bedroom, dressing-room, and bath, are of course connected. The left division of the edifice contains apartments for the officers of his suite. The rear comprises the servants' and store rooms. The kitchen is detached from the regular building, and yet perfectly convenient to the dining-room, without communicating any offensive fumes to the principal range of rooms. This is of no small value in a sultry climate. The Hall is plain, and merely furnished with seats. The corridors will furnish a cool and shaded promenade.'

China, stationery, and two fowling-pieces, one with percussion locks, and every necessary appertaining to them were sent out, as well as artisans to fit up the house ; and the whole of this consignment, weighed nearly five hundred tons.

The following letter, which seems genuine, tells a tale of what our soldiers went through in the early part of this century :—

' Paris in France 5th *Sept.* 1815.

' Dear Mother and Sister,—I have taken the oppertunity of writing these lines to you hoping it will find you in good health, as it now leaves me at this present thank be to God for it. I am very sorry I did not anser your Letters as I had not opportunity for we was very busy fighting the french a long time every day in the Mountains in Spain and I always had good luck til one day I received two balls one hitt me

17

right on my brest plate and knocked me downe and as soon
as I got my wind agen I fired about ten rounds more and
then another hitt me through my hip which was bad along
time and one came through my Haversack and another throw
my trowsers and shirt and that same night was very wet and
no fires could be lighted and it was very cold on the Mountains
but the Dockter was very good to me and after that we drove
the french into their own Country and made them beg for
peace and then we went into Ammerica into upper Kanndy
where we had all the fighting with the Yankeys till we got a
piece of them seven hundred miles up the Contrey nigh to the
falls of Naygaray which you know is 1 of the 7 wonders of the
world and there my Captain was so kind as to give me a pass
without date and I workd for a large farmer all winter and had
plenty of vittles and a good bed fit for any Gentleman and
the Ridgment was then ling in Barns and when the men had
to get up their hare was frose to their heads and they could not
pull the Blankets from the floore and I thote myself well
off and this farmer bid 100 Dollars for my discharge and we
returned to Spithead and was 6 weeks on the Water which is
4 thousand 5 hundred miles and is colled a good passage* and
wee could not get a shore after all this for we was ordered to
french flanders and at last we have got to Paris and is in the
Buss de bulling near to it which is a very fine place like a
grove for a gateway and the french is very civil funny fellows
to us now cause they know we can defend ourselves and they
do not care for nothing but to get our Monney which theare
is plenty way to spend and theare is shows and Montybanks
every night and sundays and all and there is no Justesses or
Methodys to stop them and there is all sorts of sights and
Bartlemy fair is nothing to it and we are now agen commanded by brave Duke Wellington that always conqurs—
and there is soldiers of all sorts here past all telling Rooshons
Prooshons and Austrions and Jarmans of all kind and the
Rooshons are verry good naturd creatures and will do anything for an Englishman and says their prayrs every Morning
and night and will fight their ennemis for ever for the
Emperor and the Virgin Marey the same as we do for king

* Of course, now-a-days we can hardly understand this; but the
old tubs used to take their time then.—It is recorded in the 'Annual
Register' of 1815, as follows : '16 December.—A vessel is arrived
in the Thames from New South Wales after an extraordinarily
short passage of less than five months.'

George and old England, and the Prushons is very quiet men and smokes all day long and the Austrions is fine tall fellows and the foot is drest as handsome as our Horse Officers and all our Officers is very good Gentlemen and we think to stay in france two Years and I am very contented—dear mother I wish it was not so far off or you and Bet coud come for I have savd some Monney and I larnt a littel french in Kannday but it is not the same sort it is here give my kind love to all inquiring friends and pray God bless you all from your loving son til death,'——&c. &c.

What would the modern *Patres Conscripti* of the City say if a Lord Mayor were to appear like unto this? 'We are happy to state that the Lord Mayor has commenced his Office with the most commendable alacrity. His lordship visited Billingsgate market at five o'clock on Tuesday morning; and, yesterday morning, about the same hour, perambulated the streets, and visited the different watch-houses in the City. From a continuation of this conduct, at uncertain periods, we anticipate the most beneficial results.' I have seen no more records of these visits, and thence judge that some judicious friend had whispered in his ear, the advice of Talleyrand to a young diplomat—'Sur tout, mon ami, pas trop de zèle.'

A very few more odds and ends, and I must close the Chronicle of 1815. On the 5th of December, was hanged, at Newgate, John Binstead, convicted of forgery, and at his execution a peculiar superstition is recorded: 'While on the scaffold, Binstead, in conversation with the Rev. Mr. Cotton (the ordinary of Newgate), requested that his hands might not be applied to persons who came to be rubbed for the wen.'

Of the Hotels and Clubs of this time Captain Gronow writes thus: 'There was a class of men, of very high rank, such as Lords Wellington, Nelson, and Collingwood, Sir John Moore, and some few others, who never frequented the Clubs. The persons to whom I refer, and amongst whom were many members of the sporting world, used to congregate at a few hotels. The Clarendon, Limmer's, Ibbetson's, Fladong's, Stephens', and Grillon's, were the fashionable hotels. The Clarendon was then kept by a French cook, Jacquiers, who contrived to amass a large sum of money in the service of Louis the Eighteenth, in England, and, subsequently, with Lord Darnley. This was the only public hotel where you could get a genuine French dinner, and, for which, you seldom paid less than three or four pounds ; your bottle of champagne, or of claret, in the year 1814, costing you a guinea.

'Limmer's was the evening resort for the sporting world ; in fact, it was a midnight Tattersall's, where you heard nothing but the language of the turf, and where men, with not very clean hands, used to make up their books. Limmer's was the most dirty hotel in London ; but, in the gloomy, comfortless coffee-room, might be seen many members of the rich squirearchy, who visited London during the sporting season. This hotel was frequently so crowded that a bed could not be obtained for any amount of money ; but you could always get a very good plain English dinner, an excellent bottle of port, and some famous gin-punch.

'Ibbetson's Hotel was chiefly patronized by the clergy and young men from the universities. The Charges there were more economical than at similar establishments. Fladong's, in Oxford Street, was chiefly frequented by naval men ; for, in those days, there was no club for sailors. Stephens', in Bond Street, was a fashionable hotel, supported by officers of the army, and men about town. If a stranger asked to dine there, he was stared at by the waiters, and very solemnly assured that there was no table vacant. It was not an uncommon thing to see thirty or forty saddle horses, and tilburys, waiting outside this hotel. I recollect two of my old Welsh friends, who used, each of them, to dispose of five bottles of wine, daily, residing here in 1815, when the familiar joints, boiled fish, and fried soles, were the only eatables you could order.

'The members of the clubs of London, many years since, were persons, almost without exception, belonging exclusively to the aristocratic world. "My tradesmen," as King Allen used to call the bankers and the merchants, had not then invaded White's, Boodle's, Brookes', or Wattiers' in Bolton Street, Piccadilly ; which, with the Guards, Arthur's, and Graham's, were the only clubs at the west end of the town. White's was decidedly the most difficult of entry ; its list of members comprised nearly all the noble names of Great Britain.

'The politics of White's Club were, then, decidedly Tory. It was here that play was carried on to an extent which made many ravages in large fortunes, the traces of which have not disappeared at the present day. General Scott, the father-in-law of George Canning, and the Duke of Portland, was known to have won at White's, £200,000, thanks to his notorious sobriety, and knowledge of the game of whist. The General possessed a great advantage over his companions by avoiding those indulgences at the table which used to muddle other men's brains. He confined himself to dining off something like a boiled chicken, with toast and water ; by such a regimen he came to the whist table with a clear head, and, possessing, as he did, a remarkable memory, with great coolness and judgment, he was able honestly to win the enormous sum of £200,000.

'At Brookes', for nearly half a century, the play was of a more gambling character than at White's. Faro and Macao were indulged in to an extent which enabled a man to win, or to lose a considerable fortune in one night. It was here that Charles James Fox, Selwyn, Lord Carlisle, and other great Whigs, won and lost hundreds of thousands ; frequently remaining at the table for many hours without rising.

'On one occasion, Lord Robert Spencer contrived to lose the last shilling of his considerable fortune, given him by his brother, the Duke of Marlborough ; General Fitzpatrick being much in the same condition, they agreed to raise a sum of money, in order that they might keep a faro bank. The members of the club made no objection, and ere long, they carried out their design. As is generally the case, the bank was a winner, and Lord Robert bagged, as his share of the proceeds, £100,000. He retired, strange to say, from the fœtid atmosphere of play, with the money in his pockets, and never again gambled. George Harley Drummond, of the famous banking house, Charing Cross, only played once in his whole life at White's Club, at whist, on which occasion he lost £200,00 to Brummell. This event caused him to retire from the banking house of which he was a partner.

'Lord Carlisle was one of the most remarkable victims amongst the players at Brookes', and Charles Fox, his friend, was not more fortunate, being, subsequently, always in pecuniary difficulties. Many a time, after a long night of hard play, the loser found himself at the Israelitish estab-lishment of Howard and Gibbs, then the fashionable, and patronized, money-lenders. These gentlemen never failed to make hard terms with the borrower, although ample security was invariably demanded.

'The Guards' Club was established for the three regiments

of Foot Guards, and was conducted upon a military system. Billiards and low whist were the only games indulged in. The dinner was, perhaps, better than at most clubs, and considerably cheaper. I had the honour of being a member for several years, during which time I have nothing to remember, but the most agreeable incidents. Arthur's and Graham's were less aristocratic than those I have mentioned ; it was at the latter, thirty years ago, that a most painful circumstance took place. A nobleman of the highest position, and influence in society, was detected in cheating at cards, and, after a trial, which did not terminate in his favour, he died of a broken heart.

'Upon one occasion, some gentlemen of both White's and Brookes' had the honour to dine with the Prince Regent, and during the conversation, the Prince inquired what sort of dinners they got at their clubs ; upon which, Sir Thomas Stepney, one of the guests, observed that their dinners were always the same, " the eternal joints, or beefsteaks, the boiled fowl with oyster sauce, and an apple tart—this is what we have, sir, at our clubs, and very monotonous fare it is.' The Prince, without further remark, rang the bell for his cook, Wattier, and, in the presence of those who dined at the Royal table, asked him whether he would take a house, and organize a dinner club. Wattier assented, and named Madeson, the Prince's page, manager, and Labourie, the cook, from the Royal kitchen. The Club flourished only a few years, owing to high play that was carried on there. The Duke of York patronized it, and was a member. I was a member in 1816, and frequently saw his Royal Highness there. The dinners were exquisite ; the best Parisian cooks could not beat Labourie. The favourite game played was Macao.'

CHAPTER XXIII.

1816.

Day of Thanksgiving—'Battle for the Standard'—Return of the troops—Frozen game brought over by Esquimaux—The Regent's practical joke—Rejection of the Prince of Orange by the Princess Charlotte, and acceptance of Prince Leopold as her husband— Her marriage—' The R——l Whiskers '—The Regent's yacht.

THIS new year began well. The 18th of January was chosen as a solemn day of Thanksgiving to the Almighty for the blessings of Peace—a form, which one would have thought, would, out of the commonest sentiment of gratitude, have taken place six months previously, after Waterloo, and the submission of Napoleon ; but, of course, gratitude to God must needs be subservient to diplomatic Red Tape ; and HE had to wait for the expression of the nation's thankfulness. This day was also the Queen's birthday, and the guns were fired, and the coloured lamps were lit at night, in token of the country's joy at having so gracious a person so long spared to them, so ' Serve God and honour the Queen' was thoroughly, and properly, carried out at an economical rate. There was also, out of pure generosity, something thrown in. The French Colours, taken at Waterloo, two in number, were deposited in the Chapel at Whitehall.   Country newspapers please copy the following : ' The ceremony was conducted with perfect order ; and, associated, as it was, with the duties of religious worship ; the memory of the Contest in which the trophies were won, and the sight of the brave veterans who had survived its carnage, the influence it produced was not of an ordinary nature, but rather approached to a sentiment of sublimity ' (*Times*).   Perhaps a portion of the ' sublimity ' was owing to the fact that the Guards ' were dressed in new clothing, with Caps on a new principle, and, as we are informed, far superior in comfort to the wearers.'

This Military tailoring is a craze which seizes great minds at times. It has needed the colossal brains of the Duke of York, the Prince Regent (who, when he took to yachting, the Service prayed to be delivered from, in case he should alter their already too expensive uniform), of Albert the Good, whose hat is enshrined in the pages of *Punch*, and the Duke of Cambridge, whose attention to buttons, and facings, has won him world-wide renown—and everybody is so much better, and more efficient, from the outcome of their laborious study.

One of these Eagles was won after a stubborn fight, which would have entitled its Captor to the Victoria Cross, now-a-days. It was the metaphorical captive of the spear and bow of Sergeant Ewart, whose exploit, on his being gazetted Ensign in the 3rd Royal Veteran battalion, is thus contem poraneously chronicled. It was on the 18th of June, and on 'the afternoon of that eventful day, the 92nd Regiment, reduced to two hundred, charged a column of the Enemy, from two thousand to three thousand strong ; they broke into the centre of the column, and the moment they pierced it, the Scotch Greys dashed in to their support, when both these gallant Corps cheered, and huzzaed "Scotland for ever !" The Enemy, to a man, were put to the sword, or made prisoners. The Greys, afterwards, charged the second line, which amounted to five thousand men ; it was in the first that Sergeant Ewart captured the French eagle ; the affair is thus modestly detailed by himself : "I had a hard contest for it ; the officer who carried it thrust for my groin ; I parried it off, and cut him through the head ; after which I was attacked by one of the lancers, who threw his lance at me, but missed the mark, by my throwing it off with my sword by my right side, then I cut him from the chin upwards, and went through his teeth. Next, I was attacked by a foot soldier, who, after firing, charged me with his bayonet, but I parried it off, and cut him through the head—so that finished the contest for the eagle." ' An incident which is well commemorated by Ansdell, in his picture (1848), the ' Battle for the Standard.'

The Medals for Waterloo and bars for the Campaign were now being distributed, but it took about forty years to thoroughly give them to their rightful owners ;* their dis-

* It took longer, *vide* this extract from *The Globe*, March 18, 1889 :—' A TARDY HONOUR.—Captain Gammell is 92. It is only

tribution being about as slow as is naval prize money, or the
Banda and Kirwee booty.

The troops were not too quick in coming back from Paris,
which they had occupied, and the Foot Guards only returned
late in the year of 1815.   In fact, in January of this year, they
took up their old quarters at Windsor, in presence of the
Queen, princesses, and the most puissant Duke of York.
They wore laurels in their Caps on this occasion.   I do not
think they have worn them since.

Judging from our standpoint, one can hardly realize the
first importation of frozen meat ; and it was duly chronicled
as a curiosity : ' To such a pitch is mercantile speculation for
the luxurious now arrived, that we understand three poor
Laplanders have come over in the last packet from Gottenburg,
and are on their way to London with five sledges, laden with
Lapland Game, consisting of Tjadear (Cock of the Wood),
Cappercally Orrar (black cock), Suö Ripor (Ptarmigan),
Hjarpar (hazel hen), except the black cock all species of the
grouse, but now extinct in this country.   Those birds are
considered the greatest delicacies of the North, and are, we
are told, in the highest state of preservation.'

This was written at the end of January, and, at the beginning of February, we find that our unfortunate Northern
guests had landed on a somewhat inhospitable shore, for they
had to pay over £50 duty for imported game, and £10 freight
from Harwich to London.   But this frozen game was quite
novel, and it deserves a contemporary account of what they
thought of it at the time.   ' The state of preservation in which
these birds are, is really surprising, after travelling upwards
of one thousand miles.   They are preserved by being hung
up to freeze as soon as killed, and, afterwards, being packed
in cases, lined with skin to keep out the air.   This process so

---

within the last ten days that he has received an honour which he
won nearly three-quarters of a century ago. As Ensign James
Gammell he was present at the sortie of Bayonne, and leaving the
army shortly afterwards never applied for the medal. At last
Captain Gammell has found himself decorated with two—one the
Jubilee medal, accompanied by a letter from Sir Henry Ponsonby
on behalf of the Queen ; the other the Peninsular medal, with the
clasp for the Nive, forwarded by the Duke of Cambridge. It is
never too late to decorate a gallant man, and Colonel Balguy, who
has been active in this matter, is to be congratulated upon the
success which his efforts have attained.'

effectually preserves them, that when the packages are opened, the birds are frozen quite hard ; and those packages which are not opened, will continue in this state for some weeks. The mode in which the small birds are dressed in Sweden, is by stewing them in cream, with a little butter in it, after being larded, which, it is said, gives them an exquisite flavour : the large ones are roasted and basted with cream, which is, afterwards, served up with sauce.   These Laplanders wear a kind of great coat, made of reindeer skin, with caps and gloves of the same, which gives them a very grotesque appearance : they are very shy of appearing in the streets in this attire, on account of their attracting so many people round them.'

This absurdity of charging an import duty on game was enforced, not only in the case of these poor Laplanders, but, at other times : for instance, under date of 24th of February we read : 'A greengrocer of Brighton imported twenty partridges and two hares from France, and paid the importation duty on them ; he was, notwithstanding, convicted of exposing the said game for sale by the Magistrates at Uckfield, and fined £110, which, being unable to pay, he was committed for three months to Lewes House of Correction.'

The Esquimaux stopped all the summer and autumn in England, and were a popular exhibition.   They travelled all over the country, and we hear of one of them in the *Caledonian Mercury*, September same year : ' His canoe is esteemed a very great curiosity, weighing only 16lbs., he rows it by one oar or paddle, and is so very dexterous in managing it, that he far outsails any boat with six oars.   He is very expert in diving, and also in throwing his darts ; he is so fastened to his seat, that he cannot fall out—as a drawer, like the mouth of a purse, girds him about the loins, so that, in an instant, he may be seen to dive under the water, head down, and keel uppermost ; again, in the twinkling of an eye, he raises himself erect out of the water, and scuds along as if nothing had happened.'

On February 8th the *Alceste*, sailed from Portsmouth for China, having on board Lord Amherst, appointed Ambassador to that Country, and a numerous suite, the ships also conveying numerous presents for the Emperor.   Of this expedition we shall hear more in next year's Chronicle.

The Regent was always being satirized by the publication of some of his own puerilities, or those of his suite, who, of course, took their tone from him. The *Brighton Herald* is answerable for the following : ' A gallant Admiral, residing at the Pavilion, was, a few days since, presented by a certain Great Personage, with a beautiful milk-white mare, which it was stated, had just arrived from Hanover. Nothing was talked of but this fine creature ; and everyone seemed anxious to have her merits put to the test. The Admiral mounted, tried her in all her paces, and though he could but approve, yet he pronounced her to be greatly inferior to a favourite black mare of his own. The present, however, coming from so high a quarter, was, of course, received with every expression of duty and thankfulness. The long switching tail of the animal, not exactly suiting the Admiral's taste, he sent her to a farrier to have it cropped,—when, lo ! he speedily received intelligence that it was a *false* tail, and that, beneath it, appeared a short black one. This curious fact led to a minuter inspection, when it was at length discovered that this *beautiful white Hanoverian horse* was no other than the good-humoured Admiral's own *black mare*, which had been painted in a manner to elude his detection.' Thus it was that ' *le Roi s'amuse.*'

But the Regent was fit for better things. On the very same date that the above was recorded, we find that he ordered, at his own expense, a splendid monument to be erected at Rome, in memory of Cardinal York, the last legitimate descendant of the Stuarts.

Another serious event was preparing for him, the marriage of his daughter. We have seen that she would have none of the Prince of Orange—it is not quite certain whether, at this time, she was dotingly fond of him who was to be her partner in life for the brief portion of time allotted her. At all events, he came over here, in February, as the suitor for her hand— arriving on the 21st, and dutifully waited upon ' papa ' on the 23rd. That his suit would be a prosperous one, there could hardly be a doubt, for he was received by the Duke of Clarence, Sir R. Bloomfield (the Regent's Chamberlain), Count Hardenberg, and the Nobility then residing at the Pavilion.

' Happy's the wooing, that's not long a-doing,' says the old rhyme, and this was speedily brought to a conclusion. The Prince paid his devoirs to his future bride, and her ' stern parent,' and then gracefully retired from the scene. In those days of no Telegraphs, the news of people's happiness, or misfortunes, was longer in reaching them than now, for a

King's Messenger had to go to Paris, only to find Prince Leopold gone to Berlin, and to follow him there, in order to tell him that the English Princess Royal had been graciously pleased to accept him for her husband. On the Messenger's return, the consent of the Prince Regent was officially given, and the Lord Chancellor affixed the great Seal to the Marriage Contract.

On Thursday, the 14th of March, Lord Castlereagh appeared at the bar of the House of Commons with the following message from the Prince Regent :

'The Prince Regent, acting in the name, and on the behalf of his Majesty, having given the royal consent to a marriage between his daughter, her Royal Highness the Princess Charlotte Augusta, and his Serene Highness Leopold George Frederick, Prince of Cobourg of Saalfield, has thought fit to communicate the same to this House.

'His Royal Highness is fully persuaded that this alliance cannot but be acceptable to all his Majesty's faithful subjects ; and the many proofs which his Highness has received of the affectionate attachment of this House to his Majesty's person and family, leave him no room to doubt of the concurrence and assistance of this House, in enabling him to make such a provision, with a view to the said marriage, as may be suitable to the honour and dignity of the Country.

'G. P. R.'

The reply to this piece of blarney was a dutiful, or, more properly speaking, 'an humble,' address, to the Regent 'to return to his Royal Highness the thanks of this House for his most gracious communication of the intended marriage between,' &c., &c., 'and to express our entire satisfaction at the prospect of an alliance with a Protestant prince of so illustrious a family,' &c., &c.—and, as a matter of course, next day the House of Commons did what was expected of them, and voted a grant of £60,000 a year for the young couple, with the addition of a year's income for outfits—£40,000 for furniture, plate, &c. ; £10,000 for articles of dress for the princess ; and £10,000 to increase her Highness's jewels.

A Bill for his naturalization was brought into the House of Lords on the 26th of March, and was speedily made law. For some reason or other, perhaps because she was the daughter of her mother, the Prince Regent did not like his daughter, and, at this time, his dislike was publicly spoken of. Among other things, she was not allowed to use the Royal livery (scarlet), a petty piece of spite, and the public feeling at this time is very well reflected by the following extract from the *Morning Chronicle* of the 13th of April:

'When the Prince of Coburg came up from Brighton to the Stud-house in Hampton Park, on Saturday last, he visited both Clermont and Bottleys. The first cannot be let, but may be sold; the second cannot be sold, but may be let. Clermont is a noble house, with a park of about 350 acres, well wooded. The value, including the timber, may be about £50,000. It is seventeen miles from town, and about the same distance from Windsor. But, again, we ask, why purchase such a place when there are so many palaces unoccupied?

'One reason, rather improbable indeed, is given in answer to this question; viz., that the Prince Regent may yet have a son; and that, to set up the Princess Charlotte in royal state as *heir apparent* to the throne, when, by such an event she might be disappointed of that elevation, would be highly improper. And this reason is given for all the proposed regulations—the revolting title of *Kendal*—the green livery—the private houses—the restriction of drawing rooms, &c., &c., &c. Is there lurking under this specious pretext of future probabilities any design of a measure* (which recent circumstances, we are told, have made practicable) by which they might be realized? But, granting even the event to happen, that, by a second marriage, the Prince Regent should have a son, surely it would then be the proper season to make the arrangements for the Princess Charlotte which are now establishing, and the Prince, her august Consort, might safely rely on the generosity and justice of the Nation for an adequate provision, in any change of circumstances that might affect his fortune, in the proposed union. The subject is too delicate to enlarge upon in a journal, but it is freely discussed in the upper circles, as if it were a matter actually contemplated at Court.'

The Royal Marriage Act, which was rendered necessary by the social escapades of the sons of George III. left and still leaves a limited choice of husbands to the female scions of Royalty, and, as they must be Protestants, they are confined

* The Regent was then meditating taking proceedings for a divorce from his wife.

mainly to the petty princelets of Germany.   Time does not
change John Bull's feelings with regard to such marriages,
and the satirist from that time to our own, has always ridiculed
the comparative poverty of the husbands of our Royal woman-
hood.   It was so with Prince Albert, with the Duke of Teck,
and the other German princes who have married into our
Royal family.   John Bull, doubtless from his insular prejudices,
does not consider these marriages as equal, and, although he
spends the money, he has the grumble thereon to which he
considers himself to be entitled.

Hence the satirical print given herewith called 'THE
CONTRAST ! or the *Ci-devant* GERMAN CAPTAIN in good
Quarters !' May, 1816.   One sketch is entitled, ' A single life
on the Continent, starving on Sour Krout ! !'   On the ground
is a paper 'Thoughts on a journey to *Wales* to seek my
fortune, and better my condition.'   A mouse is nibbling at a
' Map of the Principality of Coburg eight hundred square
feet.'   The other is ' Comes to England, is made a General,*
and marries a lady of £60,000 per annum.'   On the wall is a
picture of Camelford House, where the young couple spent
their honeymoon ; and, as a change from his former meagre
fare, is shown a huge piece of roast beef, and Hock, Champagne,
and Burgundy in abundance.

Tradesmen were as eager then, as now, to catch hold of
anything new—and consequently we find the Kendal scarf
being sold, and the Coburg hat and Kendal bonnet, which
seem to have been ordinary straw work, but ' for superior
quality, and pearl-like colour, must, on inspection, have certain
claim to universal patronage.'

On the 2nd of the 'merry month of May' they were
married.   The bridegroom's costume seems to have been
somewhat scanty, but yet he appears to have been rather
proud of it, for ' Prince Leopold very frequently appeared at
the balcony to gratify their curiosity, dressed in a blue coat
and a star.'   ' At two o'clock his Serene Highness went in a
curricle to Carlton House, and paid a morning visit to his
intended bride.   He also rode round the exterior of Carlton
House to view his new travelling carriage.   His Serene
Highness afterwards returned to Clarence House a little
before half-past three, when the crowd was so numerous, and
the anxiety to see him so great, that the footmen, in letting

* In May, 1816. he was made a General in the British army, and
afterwards Field Marshal.

him out of the carriage had nearly been pushed under it. A number of women and children were forced into Clarence House against their will, by the extreme pressure. In a few minutes after, his Serene Highness walked across to York House, when the crowd behaved extremely orderly, and, at the request of a few attendants, formed a clear passage for them to pass through. . . . The Princess Charlotte of Wales,

A SINGLE LIFE ON THE CONTINENT.

at four o'clock, went in a carriage to the Queen's Palace, and had the windows down to gratify the curiosity of the crowd in Pall Mall, but they were found to be so extremely numerous, that the coachman could not, with safety, drive through them, and went through the Park. On his coming out to get into his carriage he was assailed by a number of females patting him on the back, and giving him good wishes.

This delay gave a number of men an opportunity to take off
the traces of the horses, in order to draw the carriage. They
were prevailed upon to desist, but they did so (*sic*) a second
time, and the Prince, it is supposed, would have indulged
them in their desire, had not accidents been feared, and by
exertions of the sentinels the traces were put to the carriage

THE PRINCE IS MADE A GENERAL.

again, and the carriage proceeded to Carlton House amidst
the loud huzzas of the populace.'

After all this mobbing they got properly married, and set
off for Oatlands—the Duke of York's mansion.

The bride was dressed in white llama and silver, and,
perhaps, some of my lady readers will be pleased to hear that
her frock was 'finished with a very brilliant rollio of lama,'

which must have been very comforting to her. The Queen of Sheba would (to use an Americanism) have to have taken a 'back seat' compared to the dear old Queen Charlotte, who

R——L WHISKERS, 1816.

must have been 'exceeding magnifical.' She wore 'a beautiful gold tissue, trimmed with a mixture of gold and silver, having two flounces of brilliant silver net-work, richly embossed with

18

stripes of gold lamé, and a superb head to the flounces of silver lamé border.   The whole had a most grand, novel, and magnificent appearance.'

The satirical prints may, generally, be taken as a reflex of popular opinion, be it right or wrong, and the Princess was soon credited with having the upper hand in the domestic arrangements of her new household.   She is depicted as wearing her husband's breeches, and taking the reins when driving—but this was meant for good-humoured badinage— not like the satires on the Regent, who was lampooned without mercy.   His clothes, his personal appearance, even his whiskers were not allowed to pass unscathed—as the following will show :

'1816.

R——L WHISKERS.

L'Adieu.

From a puissant Prince to his cast-off whiskers, on leaving London to make an Excursion.

Adieu, my dear Whiskers ! dear Whiskers, adieu !
I ne'er shall love Whiskers, as I have lov'd you.
So becoming your form, and so brilliant your hue,
I ne'er admir'd Whiskers, as I've admir'd you.
Your curve was so lovely, so like a horse shoe,
Not a whisker at Court was so lovely as you.
The Baron Geramb's* were immense it is true,
But they didn't sweep round half so tasty as you.
        Y————'s† Whiskers comprise hair enough for a head,
But odious the shape, and the colour is red.
Of beauty, 'tis known, that the line is a curve,
Then the prize of all beauty you surely deserve ;
For in curve so enchanting you lay on my chin,
You completely eclipsed all the *blubber* within.
Not Ganymede's self, when he waited on Jove,
Looked the model so like of the young God of Love ;
Not Apollo the bright, nor Adonis the fair,
Were like, my dear whiskers—adorn'd *to a hair !*
Not drooping Narcissus, reclin'd o'er the stream,
Himself the dear object, himself the dear theme,
Was more charm'd with *his* face, thus presented to view,
Than I've been with *mine*, when encircl'd with you.'

---

* This gentleman will be noticed in matters theatrical.
† Lord Yarmouth.

A life of indolence, and sensual gratification, brought with it its concomitant punishment, and he suffered much from gout.   There is a peep at his inner life, from a Newspaper paragraph of the 26th of March, dated Brighton : 'It is true that the Prince has been on horseback, and has rode for some time about the Pavilion lawn.   An inclined plane was constructed, rising to about the height of two feet and a half, at the upper end of which was a platform.   His Royal Highness was placed in a chair on rollers, and so moved up the ascent, and placed on the platform, which was then raised by screws, high enough to pass the horse under ; and, finally, his Royal Highness was let gently down into the saddle.   By these means the Regent was, undoubtedly, enabled to enjoy in some degree the benefit of air and exercise ; but the exercise implied little of spontaneous muscular power, and cannot, certainly, be considered as a criterion of renovated strength.'

A short trip to sea was suggested as likely to be of benefit to his health, and a Royal Yacht of some three hundred or four hundred tons burden was hauled up and put on the slips at Deptford Dockyard to be entirely new coppered and re-fitted throughout.   The estimated cost of doing this was over sixty thousand pounds ! of which the *gilding* alone is supposed to have absorbed nearly thirteen thousand five hundred pounds ! ! Why ! the very blocks to the shrouds and rigging were fully gilt, and the whole of the internal fittings were of the most gorgeous description.   The *Royal Sovereign* was re-launched at Deptford on the 8th of August, 1816, and when the workmen had done with her, she was ordered round to Brighton, to be at the Regent's disposal.

CHAPTER XXIV.

Riots and agrarian outrages—Colliers, &c., coming to London—
'England in 1816'—Riots in Newgate—Marriage of the Duke of
Gloucester—A chimney sweep's wedding—Cruelty to a 'climbing
boy'—The Mortar at St. James's Park—Lighting by means of
Gas—The Coinage.

And what was the general state of the Country at this time?
During the very celebration of the Princess's Wedding—
the people, owing to high price of provisions, and the stag-
nations of trade, were in very evil case. In those days an
empty stomach, and rioting, generally went together, and,
consequently, about this time the newspapers had to chronicle
riots of a more or less serious description. On the 6th of May,
we hear of one at Bridport where the windows of the principal
millers and bakers were smashed, and a few hogsheads of beer
stolen from a local brewer. It was soon put down by the law-
abiding inhabitants of the place, and was nothing like so serious
as that which took place at Bury St. Edmunds a few days afterwards, which sent the Sheriff of Suffolk packing off at once to
London, in order to consult with the Home Secretary, and to
request his assistance in overcoming the rioters.

For some time there had been various agrarian outrages in
the Eastern Counties, such as breaking thrashing machines,
and firing barns and ricks, and these were supposed to have
arisen because an increase of wages had not immediately followed on the rise in the price of bread. Impunity begat
audacity, and they demanded that wheat should be sold at
half a crown a bushel, and prime joints of meat at fourpence a
pound. Some of the principal inhabitants, especially at one
place, Brandon, near Bury, temporized with the Mob, and
promised them that their demands should be complied with
for a fortnight, which would give time for their grievances to
be discussed.

This satisfied them for the moment, and they dispersed giving three cheers.   But they again broke out, and, this time, destroyed some houses—and, moreover, demonstrated with bludgeons studded with short iron spikes, and, to shew their organization, they paraded a flag, having the legend, ' Bread or Blood !'   They threw fire balls about, smashed the street lamps, made an attack on some mills, and stole therefrom a quantity of flour, some of which, in their unreason, they threw into the river, and some they carried away.   Some of the West Norfolk Militia, and a party of the 1st Royal Dragoons, having arrived, they were supported by the respectable inhabitants, and for a time some kind of order was restored.

But the demon was abroad, and men began to be riotous in other places.   In Norwich the mob smashed lamps, windows, &c., and threw fire balls about, besides stoning and wounding the Military, Yeomanry, and Militia, who were there to keep the peace.   At Bury, a Mob wanted a manufacturer to deliver over to their sweet will a spinning jenny, swearing they would destroy his premises if he refused.   This he had courage enough to do, and some two hundred special Constables being enrolled —peace was once more restored.

At Cambridge they feared an irruption of the rioters from the Fen districts, swore in three hundred special Constables, and the Vice Chancellor, and heads of Colleges, resolved to arm the students, if considered necessary.   But the Fen Men were busy in their own district.   They rendezvoused at Littleport, attacked the house of the Rev. Mr. Vachel, a magistrate resident there, and wrecked it, doing about £2,000 worth of damage.   They extorted money from the inhabitants, they nearly emptied the publican's cellars, and they loaded a waggon with every gun they could find.

The decent people in those parts thought this was carrying a joke a little too far, and we read, ' These riots have at length terminated by the exertions of the magistrates, aided by a number of the gentlemen, and inhabitants of Ely, and the Royston troop of Volunteer Cavalry, together with a small detachment of the 1st Royal Dragoons, consisting of eighteen, who had, in the first instance, been sent for from Bury.   These proceeded in a body, on the 25th of May, to Littleport, and a very severe struggle ensued between them and the rioters, who had secreted themselves in different houses, and were armed with guns, with which they fired many shots at the military and civil power, and severely wounded one of the soldiers, but not dangerously. The military then received orders to fire, and the man who had wounded the soldier was instantly shot dead, and another fell, who, having lost the lower part of his face, and part of his tongue, is since dead. When this took place, the rioters were completely disconcerted, and fled in every direction ; but, by the perseverance and activity of the military and civil power, no less than seventy-three of the rioters were taken, and are now lodged in Ely Gaol. Many more were also taken, who, appearing to have been forced to join the mob, have been liberated. Amongst those taken, and now under confinement, are several persons of some property, and apparent respectability of life ; and it is very evident that rapine (not want) was the principal instigation of this unprecedented disturbance, as the parish of Littleport, on Wednesday and Thursday nights, resembled, in every respect, a town sacked by a besieging army, the principal inhabitants having been compelled to abandon their homes for the protection of their lives, and leave their properties to the mercy of this daring banditti of robbers.

'At least fifty guns and nine or ten large fowling pieces, such as are used by gunners for the destruction of wild fowl, each carrying at least four or five pipes* of powder, and as many of shot, were taken from the rioters, and plate and other articles to the value of £300 or £400 have been recovered.'

In those days the *Isle of Ely* had a Chief Justice of its own, an office which was only abolished by the Act 6–7 William IV. cap. 87, and to him the King sent two Justices to hold a Commission on these rioters, which terminated with the Capital Conviction of thirty-four persons on charges of burglary and robbery : five of them were left for death without hope of mercy, and, on the 28th of June, they were duly executed.

But these riots were not merely local—say in the Eastern Counties, they were in many parts of England.

At Bideford—there was a small riot which was soon suppressed, at Newcastle, and upon the Wear, disturbance among the 'Geordies' about the high price of food, which wanted cavalry to suppress. More riots in Essex—another at Honiton, where they burnt a farm house, at Liverpool (but that was purely political). In very fact trade was very bad, and, to

* A rough-and-ready way of loading guns, before Cartridges and Breech loaders were introduced, was by measuring out so many bowls of a Tobacco pipe full of powder and shot.

give one example, I take four consecutive paragraphs from *The Morning Chronicle* of July 3, 1816.

' As a proof of the unprecedented stagnation of trade, one day last week there was not a single entry for export or import at the Custom-house of London, a circumstance without parallel in the annals of that extensive establishment.'

' In the neighbourhood of Bilston-moor, where there are many Collieries, and a number of iron works, the workmen, consisting of some thousands, have been thrown out of employ. They have solicited in vain for work in Warwickshire, Staffordshire, and the neighbourhood. With a view of drawing particular attention to their case, they have resorted to the experiment of presenting a petition to the Prince Regent in person, to be accompanied by a present of three waggon loads of Coals. About fifty men are yoked to each waggon to drag it to town. One of the waggons proceeds by the route of Worcester; another by Coventry and Birmingham; the route of the third is by Stourbridge. The men proceed at the rate of about twelve miles a day, and receive voluntary gifts of money, &c., on the road as they pass along, declining of themselves to ask alms : their motto, as placarded on the carts, being—" Rather work than beg." '

' Upwards of *ten thousand* livery servants are said to be now out of place in different parts of England, owing to the *prosperous* state of the times, and the numerous emigrations to foreign parts.'

' The state of the times has had a very singular effect upon livings—the threat now of taking the *tithes in kind*, no longer alarms the farmer, as it is what he wishes the Clergyman to do ; and, on a Calculation, the value of Church preferment has diminished one half.'

I may as well tell the sequel of the Bilston expedition, and cannot tell it better than in the words of the same newspaper.

' One body of the Colliers, with the waggon of coals from Staffordshire, had reached Nettlebed, near Henley. Report had mentioned two, nay, three such bodies, each with a waggon. One of them proceeded by the road that leads to London through St. Alban's. They reached that place, we understand, on Tuesday evening. The Home Department had sent down Magistrates to each of the three roads, by which the Colliers might approach the Capital. Sir Nathaniel Conant* was dispatched to the St. Alban's road. The men

* From Bow Street.

were found reposing on and about their waggon. The Magistrate stated to them the impropriety of the step they had either taken of their own accord, or by the advice of others—that this was not the mode to obtain relief—that it rather tended to prevent the accomplishment of their object, because it might lead to a breach of the peace. The Colliers listened with much interest and attention to the remonstrances of the Magistrate. It had not struck them, they said, in the light in which he had placed it. They confessed they had been ill-advised, and evinced a readiness to return immediately to their homes. In consequence of this declaration, the Magistrate purchased the coals of them, which were left to be distributed to the poor, and gave each man as much money as would carry him back to his home.

' Another waggon with a party of Colliers, the one which had come by way of Henley, was met by the Magistrate at Maidenhead. The same representations were made to the men, and with the same success as at St. Alban's. The coals were bought, and, the men agreeing to return home, received sufficient to carry them thither.'

A few days later on, is a paragraph which shews that this method of ' stumping the Country ' was coming into fashion. ' The example set by the Bilston Moor Colliers in dragging their waggons and petitions through the Country, is likely to have many imitators. Besides those that entered Birmingham on Wednesday and Thursday last, soliciting relief, and who, on Friday week, passed through Wolverhampton on their way to Liverpool, on Saturday week, a waggon load of coals, drawn by eighty men, with ropes, arrived in Leicester. A strong sensation of compunction for their sufferings was excited, and they collected a considerable sum of money. A second load arrived on Monday, but the Collection was, of course, for a smaller amount. The men behaved remarkably well. They had a certificate of their necessities, signed by the minister of their parish. Another team of Colliers passed through Leicester on Tuesday last, begging their way northwards.

A little piece of poetry very well sums up

'ENGLAND IN 1816.

In eighteen hundred ten and six
Old England's glory some would fix :
Peace throughout Europe ; Royal Marriages,
New Streets, new Palaces, and Carriages.

New Stars, new Ribbons, and new Crosses,
A Coinage new, whate'er the loss is—
Splendid new Bridges, splendid Lights,
And Columns destined for our Knights!
Sounds not this well?　Then who would think
We stood on ruin's very brink?
For, now the Picture but capsize
And view it with your proper eyes.
　In London, flashy shops behold,
And new Bazaars, but nothing sold;
In every street, a carpet out,
That shews my Lady on her route,
To spend her poor remains in France,
And teach her children how to dance.
　Then for the Country—Farmers breaking,
Clothiers half ruin'd, Landlords quaking,
A solemn gloom, no sun, no hay day
Between this very hour and Lady.
The Corn, too, laid, and some say rotting,
The Luddites up in arms, or plotting—
The panic general, and the Stocks
As flat, almost, as the New Docks—
Then a Subscription by the Great,
Lest all our poor should emigrate,
A boon that seems too sure a test
Of apprehension for the *rest*.
But last, and worst, a Ministry in doubt,
Too weak to stand, too strong to be turned out.'

In August we had riots in Glasgow and Preston, and this
in spite of the ' Association for the Relief of the Manufacturing
and Labouring Poor.'　Nay, even the prisoners in Newgate
caught the infection, and organized a riot of their own, which
had a somewhat frivolous beginning.　On the 25th of August
a visitor to the prison had his watch stolen, and naturally
complained of the matter to the Keeper, who ordered all the
convicts and their visitors to be searched, and no more visitors
allowed until the watch was found.　The Convicts considered
this as a breach of their privileges, and not only refused to be
searched, but took possession of the Common Yard, and turned
out, by force, all the officers, and turnkeys.　Of course, this
conduct could not be allowed, and the Convicts were ultimately
driven into the upper wards—where, being armed with the
iron railings of the staircase, they barricaded themselves as
well as they could, and awaited results.
The Keeper, on his side, did not like the look of things;

he did not want any of his force injured, as they probably
would be, if they attempted to force the wards, held by these
desperadoes—and he disposed his men, so as to watch them
well, to see they did not escape, and then sent for instructions
to the Lord Mayor and Sheriffs, but all three were out of
town.   However, the Lord Mayor arrived on the Scene about
two in the morning, and waited till six to see if the mal-
contents would yield—but, as there seemed no chance of this,
they were informed, when the usual time of calling them to
breakfast, arrived, that unless they surrendered, they would
have no food that day.   This was an *argumentum ad hominem*
not to be denied.   One soon gave in, and, within an hour, they
were all secured.

Yet another Royal Marriage : which took place on the 22nd
of July, between William Frederick, Duke of Gloucester,
grandson of Frederick, Prince of Wales, to his cousin, the
Princess Mary, fourth daughter of George III., and, consequently, his cousin.   It was a suitable marriage, for they were
born in the same year (1776), and had long been attached to
each other.   There was nothing particular about the ceremony
except that it was solemnized in the grand saloon in the
Queen's palace, where an altar was erected—and transformed,
according to the fashion of Royal Marriages, into an unmean-
ing buffet of plate.   'The gold Communion plate was the
most massive and costly that ever was displayed upon one
occasion.   It consisted of the Altar plate belonging to King
William ; from Whitehall Chapel, two uncommonly large
dishes, richly chased with appropriate devices of our Lord's
last supper with His disciples ; the compartments round the
dishes having also appropriate designs.   Two immensely large
flagons, from the Chapel Royal, beautifully chased ; also a
large number of ewers ; several chalices, or cups of solid gold.
Each corner had most superbly gilt tripods for six candles.'

By way of contrast, and also to illustrate the manners of
the times, let us read the following account of a ' SINGULAR
WEDDING.   Tuesday evening the neighbourhood of Drury
Lane was thrown into the utmost confusion, in consequence
of an extraordinary phenomenon very seldom witnessed.
Some *sweeps*, residing in Charles Street, having been married,
they resolved to celebrate the day, and, about eight o'clock
in the evening, the bride and bridegroom, attended by eleven
couples more, all mounted on asses, and followed by several
hundreds of spectators, with tin pots, horns, dust bells, watchmen's rattles, flambeaux, etc., proceeded through Drury Lane,

and made their grand entrance into Holborn up Newton
Street to the Bank public-house, where they stopped to get
some refreshment ; but in forming the procession again, the
bride's Arabian was unfortunately thrown down by the pressure
of the mob, and the lady precipitated in the mud. This
enraged the bridegroom, who immediately dismounted, and
began by dealing several blows among his neighbours, with
extreme fury. The consequence was, that a general battle
ensued, and several heads were broken. Gardner, the beadle
of that district, came up, backed by about a dozen Knights of
the lanthorn, who succeeded in securing several of the sable
warriors, which finally dispersed the merry group.'

Apropos of chimney sweeps, we know that there was much
legislation in behalf of the climbing boys, who were still
much used, as a great deal of senseless prejudice and opposition prevailed against the use of Machines : and that these
poor boys needed some protection from their brutal masters
the following case, on the 10th of July, at the Middlesex
Sessions, will show.

'At ten o'clock yesterday morning, the trial of William
Molys took place at Hick's Hall. Our readers will recollect
that the prisoner was a master sweep, and lately stood his trial
at the Old Bailey, on a charge of murder, for having by brutal
treatment, caused the death of John Hewlings, a child of
five or six years of age, his apprentice. He was, however,
acquitted of this charge, but retained on an indictment for
an assault on the same child.

'To this charge the prisoner pleaded Not Guilty.

'Mr. Walford, for the prosecution, stated the case. He
related several cases of atrocious violence on the part of the
prisoner towards the deceased John Hewlings, who was little
more than five years old, and had been for a few months his
apprentice. The learned gentleman's statement was fully
confirmed in evidence.

'Elizabeth Ware proved that she saw the prisoner striking
at the child's legs with a brush, to force him up a chimney,
which he was unable to ascend, and then dragging him
down, and dashing him with violence against the floor. The
child screamed bitterly.

'Sarah Reeves corroborated the last Witness's testimony,
and added, that the Prisoner declared he would "serve the
boy out" when he got him home. The boy complained bitterly that his knees were hurt.

'Anne Chandler proved that the prisoner came to her

house in Whitechapel on the 23rd of April, with the deceased boy and another, to sweep a chimney, into which he put up the former, who stuck in the flue for nearly an hour. The prisoner was at length prevailed upon to get to the top of the chimney, and extricate the child, which he did, with loud imprecations upon him. The moment he got him down, he knocked him against a chest of drawers in the room ; and when the child, almost senseless from the blow, was endeavouring to recover himself, he kicked him across the chamber, and in this case, as in the former, repeated his asseveration that he would *serve him out* when he got him home.

' Mary Craig, who lived next door to the prisoner, proved, that on helping the wife of the latter, who was drunk, into her own house, she saw the child on the ground near the prisoner, who desired him to get up, which he was unable to do without the assistance of a stick. Witness looked at the boy's leg, which she found greatly swollen. At her suggestion, the prisoner rubbed the wounded part with ointment, and when he found the boy still unable to walk, he dashed him on the ground.

' George Rose, and Esther Jacobs, proved their having, on the 23rd of April, while accidentally passing near the prisoner's house, been alarmed with screams and cries of Murder, and Mercy. Rose kicked in the door, and upbraided the prisoner and his wife with their unnatural conduct. The latter held a strap in her hand, with which she avowed she had been beating the child, and repeated that she would do so again.

' The prisoner, on being called upon for his defence, put in a written paper, containing a general denial of the charge, and stating that he was a victim of persecution. He did not call any witnesses.

' The Court then summed up the evidence, and the Jury instantaneously returned a verdict of Guilty. The Court, after severely animadverting on the atrocity of the prisoner's guilt, sentenced him to two years' imprisonment.'

All Londoners know the Mortar on the Parade of the Horse Guards, which was taken from the French at the siege of Cadiz in 1812, and presented by the Cortes to the Prince of Wales. Its elaborate allegorical carriage makes it a notable feature. It was uncovered on the Prince Regent's birthday, August 12, 1816, and from that moment it was assailed with a storm of ridicule principally addressed *at* the Regent. Pictorially the satires would scarcely suit this fastidious age, but some rather smart things were written anent it both in prose and rhyme. Of the latter, the following caustic epigram is a good example :—

'On a Recent Embellishment of the Metropolis.

Useless, and hollow, and unsound,
    And silly splendour all the plan,
With venom'd reptiles guarded round,
    How like the Mortar to the Man !'

As the noble game of Cricket is now played, the stumps are drawn about sunset. In order to decide a match, would it not be practicable to take example by the following ? 'Cricket by Candle Light.—A match was played a few days ago, by night, on Sedley-green, near Bexhill, between Mr. S. Beaching, and Mr. J. Thomas, to be decided in one innings, which was won by the former. On this occasion, lanthorns were placed in different parts of the ground, and upwards of one hundred persons witnessed this nocturnal contest.'

This use of lanthorns shows that gas had not reached country neighbourhoods, nor has it yet in too many cases. Yet it was making its way in the large towns. In August the town of Preston, in Lancashire, was partially lit by gas, and this daring feat is thus recorded : 'The length of the main pipes already laid is one thousand yards ; and in this space it is estimated that more than nine hundred lights, emitting flame equal to four thousand mould candles of six to the pound, will be attached to the main pipes in the ensuing winter. The plan of lighting a considerable space by means of a single burner, placed at an elevated situation, has been carried into effect at Preston. In the centre of the Market-place, which is of considerable area, there happens to be a handsome Gothic Column 36 feet in height : on the top of this is placed a vase, in which is the burner ; and it thus becomes the substitute of twenty-five common oil lamps, but with an effect which could not be equalled by double the number, placed in the most advantageous positions.' The Chronicler's figures appear to be rather hazy, for with one flame of four and a half candle gas it is difficult to imagine a light given equal to fifty oil lamps.

The Silver Coinage was getting into a dreadfully worn condition (by the way, ours is nothing to boast of), and it had been settled that a new coinage of shillings and sixpences, to the extent of £2,500,000 should be minted ; but, 'as the period for the issue of the new coin approached, the fears of the retail dealers became general, lest the plain English shillings and sixpences should be confounded with the French ones, and the whole refused. It was at Hull, early in September, where the tradespeople first refused to receive at their normal value, all plain shillings, or, in other words, all not appearing to be clearly of our own legal currency. In the Metropolis, it was at Billingsgate market, on the 20th of September, where plain shillings and sixpences were first indiscriminately refused ; from thence, the refusal of them spread through the Borough, and, in the evening, became general throughout the Metropolis. A great stagnation in all retail trades suddenly, and naturally, ensued, and the lower orders were disposed to commit disturbances in almost every market. This embarrassing and dangerous state of things being made known to the Lord Mayor, his lordship took immediate measures to preserve the peace of the City, not by means of force, but by promptly communicating to the public, from the Mansion House, a notice, of which the following is a Copy :

' Silver Coin.—*Take Notice.*—The Bank of England do not refuse any shillings or sixpences on account of their being plain, provided they are English.

' By order of the Lord Mayor,

' Francis Hobler.

' *Saturday Morning*, Sept. 21, 1816.

' In consequence of the above notice, people assembled in crowds to take their silver to the Bank, for which they received Bank of England Notes and tokens.'

This somewhat palliated the small panic, but it was more allayed by another proclamation from ' Wood, Mayor,' that the Secretary of State for the Home Department gave notice, that ' all shillings and sixpences that can be considered as of the Established Standard in fineness, will be exchanged for new silver coin when it is issued ;' and a further notice, ' that all kind of shillings, now, or lately in circulation, are taken at the Bank of England, with the exception of French, or base metal ; they therefore recommend to all shopkeepers, dealers, and others, in order to prevent any breach of the peace, to take such silver above named, as usual,' perfectly tranquillized the public mind.

We shall, next year, hear more about the new Coinage, which was being coined at the rate of nearly 300,000 coins per diem.

CHAPTER XXV.

Smuggling—'Resurrection Men'—More riots—Orator Hunt—
Meetings at Spa Fields—Riots arising therefrom—Execution of
one of the rioters—The King's health.

SMUGGLING, and illicit distilling, were reckoned among venial
crimes, but both were practised to an extent unknown at the
present time. Let us take a few examples in chronological
order.

January 31st. 'A band of twenty-eight smugglers were
met with lately, loaded with bladders full of smuggled
whiskey, supposed to amount to 140 gallons, on their way
from the Highlands to Glasgow. The Excise Officers, who
met them, being only two in number, dared not attack them
and they all got off.'

The next reminds us somewhat forcibly of some late smuggling from one of Her Majesty's yachts: 'February 23rd. The
following singular occurrence, has, it is reported, taken place,
very recently, at Woolwich. A transport, laden with Ordnance
Stores unfit for further service, arrived from the French Coasts
for the purpose of returning them, and remained some days
before the unloading began : it at length took place, when, it
is added, some inquisitive officers of the Customs requested
to examine the Contents of the articles, and discovered that
what was considered, and marked on the packages, as shot,
shell, rockets, and other combustibles, consisted of Claret,
Champagne, silks, lace, &c. The whole, it is said, were
immediately seized, amounting to a considerable sum.'

This plan seems to have been tried on again, for in the
Annual Register, 30th March, is a similar case, in which it is
said that there were goods to the value of £7,000, for one
man, packed up as ' Return Congreve Rockets.'

The same Magazine, copying from a Glasgow paper, gives under date August 30th, the following : ' How muchsoever the regular commerce of the Country is impaired by the present pressure, there is no question that the smuggling trade continues in extreme vivacity. This extraordinary traffic appears to be conducted with a publicity that could scarcely be credited but on the testimony of one's own sight. The Smugglers, or as they are styled from the manner of Conveying the Whiskey, *Flaskers,* go in large bands on the highroads in open day, and laugh at the traveller, who, by his looks, expresses wonder at contravention of the law so undisguised, and yet so undetected. On Monday night, for instance, a gang of twenty-four, with the order of so many soldiers, and under the directions of a leader who frequently called on those lagging behind " to keep up," marched through Springbank, and the neighbouring hamlets to Cowcaddens (in the suburbs of Glasgow), where, in the face of numbers of persons, some of whom bawled out " Success to Smuggling," they entered a house, and deposited their laden flasks, until the shades of night would enable them to penetrate in safety to their re-setters in Glasgow. We are informed that the places of distillation are nearly as notorious to the inhabitants of their vinicity, as the methods of conveyance ; and whoever of the neighbours choose to make a visit to the popular distillers are regaled with undiluted spirit, wherewith to drink confusion to the Excise. Smuggled whiskey has, it is said, fallen recently 4s. or 5s. a gallon.'

' November 28th. One night last week, some smugglers displaced the layer of a tomb in the Churchyard at Fareham, and deposited therein several large kegs of contraband Spirits ; but certain officers being on the watch they had an early resurrection.'

This rifling the tomb was infinitely better than that of those ghouls, the body-snatchers, or resurrection men. In *The Morning Chronicle* of the 23rd of November is reported a ' Riot and Combination amongst the Resurrection men. Tuesday evening (18th November) the inhabitants of Canterbury Square were extremely alarmed, in consequence of a riot, which assumed the most alarming aspect, having taken place at the house of Mr. Millard, beadle to the dissecting room of Guy's Hospital, whose family were attacked by a desperate gang of resurrection men, namely, Benjamin Crouch (Captain of the gang), James Hollis, William Naples, Patrick Garneth,

Peter Hannagan, Israel Chapman, and several others, who were proceeding to acts of violence, and threatening destruction to the family of Mr. Millard, in consequence of his infringing on their profession, by employing men ignorant of their art in procuring subjects for the numerous students at the Hospital.

' Their vengeance, it appears, arose from the circumstance of two or three persons having been employed by the surgeons to procure subjects on one occasion, which came to their knowledge, and they were determined to be revenged on the beadle, who was not at all concerned. The inhabitants having collected, the rioters announced that their allowance must be raised from four guineas to six; that they would allow fourteen days for an answer, and, unless their demand was complied with, they would pay the beadle a more severe visit : at the same time wishing it to be made known that they could command trade, bad as the times were ; and in the Country, their payment was no less than £20, on some occasions. The mob became exasperated, and, but for the interference of Mr. Millard, would have torn them to pieces. They, however, got clear off, and Mr. Millard applied to the Magistrates at Union Hall, where he procured a warrant for their apprehension. Some of the party were held to bail, a few weeks ago, at the complaint of Mr. Ashley Cooper, for a similar offence.'

' October 21st. MARLBOROUGH STREET.—It was stated, yesterday, that a most extraordinary affair happened at Mr. Brookes', The Theatre of Anatomy, Blenheim Street. On Sunday evening, a man having been delivered there as a *subject* (a technical name for a dead man for dissection), in a sack— who, when in the act of being rolled down the steps, to the vaults, turned out to be alive, and was conveyed, in a state of nudity to St. James's Watch-house.

' Curiosity had led many hundreds of persons to the watch-house, and it was with difficulty the *subject* could be conveyed to this Office, where there was also a great assemblage. The *Subject* at length arrived. He stated his name to be Robert Morgan, by trade a smith. John Bottomley, a hackney Coachman, was charged also with having delivered Morgan tied up in the Sack. The *Subject* appeared in the sack, in the same way in which he was taken, with this difference, that holes had been made to let his arms through.

' The evidence of Mr. Brookes afforded much merriment. He stated that on Sunday evening, soon after seven o'clock, his servant informed him, through the medium of a pupil, that a coachman had called to inquire if he wanted a *subject*, from Chapman, a notorious resurrection man.   Mr. B. agreed to have it, and in about five minutes afterwards, a Coach was driven up to the door, and a man, answering to the description of Bottomley, brought Morgan in a sack, as a dead body, laid him in the passage, at the top of the kitchen stairs, and walked away without taking any further notice.   On Harris, witness's servant, taking hold of the subject's feet, which protruded through the bottom of the sack, he felt them warm, and that the subject was alive.

' Here the prisoner Morgan, who seems to have enjoyed the narrative, with others, burst out into a fit of laughter.

' Mr. Burrowes—the Magistrate : Is it usual, Mr. Brookes, when you receive a subject, to have any conversation with the parties who deliver it ?

' Mr. Brookes : Sometimes ; but dead bodies are frequently left, and I recompense the procurers at my leisure.

' Mr. Brookes resumed his evidence, and stated that he put his foot upon the sack, upon being called by his servant, and kicked it down two steps, when the subject called out " I'm alive," and, forcing half his naked body out of the sack, threw the whole house into alarm.   (Here the *subject* again laughed heartily.)   Conceiving that the prisoner's intent was concealment, for the purpose of inducing others to commit felony, witness armed himself with the bar of a shutter, one of his pupils brought a poker, and gave his weapon to another man in the house, whilst he flew upstairs for his pistols, which were unloaded ; but the prisoner seemed inclined to resist, and witness said to him, " Resign, or else I'll shoot you like a bug, and then dissect you in five minutes."   A Constable was sent for, and the *subject* was taken to the watch-house.   He denied any knowledge of how he came there, and said he had been made very drunk.

' After Mr. Brookes had returned from the watch-house to enter the charge against Morgan, he saw Bottomley loitering about the street, and, on scrutinizing his dress, it answered that of the person who had left Morgan there.   There was another hackney Coachman with Bottomley.

' Mr. Brookes' testimony was corroborated by Mr. Salmon, one of his pupils, and by Henry Harris his servant.   The latter was confronted with Bottomley, and he believed him to be the man who had left Morgan.

'In defence, Morgan said, that he had returned from Teddington, Middlesex, on Sunday, where he had been three days at work; that he had drunk freely on the road to London. He came through Westminster and the Park ; and, in Oxford Street, a man picked him up, and made him so drunk, that he entirely lost his senses, and had no recollection until he awoke from his stupor at Mr. Brookes's. He had no wrong intention, and he had lost 5s. and some apparel.

'Mr. Brookes stated, and he was confirmed in it, that the man was not drunk, when at his house, and the manner of his extricating himself from the sack clearly demonstrated it.'

Bottomley, in his defence, denied all knowledge of Morgan, and the Magistrate remanded them; but the Newspaper does not tell the sequel.

Undoubtedly, there was great distress throughout the nation, and there were riots all over the country. On October 18th there was a Corn riot at Sunderland, where, at market, owing to an advance in price, the Mob took away the Corn from the farmers by force and openly divided the spoil among themselves : but some of the ringleaders were arrested.

There were riots, and somewhat serious ones, too, in the iron districts of Wales, owing to a reduction of wages occurring simultaneously with a rise in provisions, and the Military had to be called out. A riot took place at Calder Ironworks, near Glasgow, and there the Military had to back up the Civil power. A Corn Riot about the same time at Walsall, where the windows of several bakers were smashed, and a New Mill gutted ; here, too, the soldiers were called out—and, a little later in the year, food riots at Dundee.

It was scarcely to be expected that London would escape scot free, and we find that she came in for her share. There was at this time a violent Mob orator named Henry Hunt, who, after the manner of his kind, was very fond of hearing himself speak. He was born on the 6th of November, 1773, in Wiltshire, and was a farmer, but, having imbibed violent Radical ideas, farming was too unexciting an occupation for him, and, embarking on the troubled sea of politics, he became the darling of the Mob. It is not in the scope of this work to speak of him except in connection with the 'Spa Fields Riots,' but I may mention that in 1819 he was sentenced to two and a half years' imprisonment, to pay a fine of £1,000, and to find security for his future good behaviour. He died in 1835.

HENRY HUNT, ESQ.

There was, unfortunately, a great deal of distress, but this was in the way of being met by giving employment on works for the general good, in the Country, and in London by very munificent donations, such as £5,000 from the Prince Regent. But public distress always has been the demagogue's opportunity; he has very little chance of being heard when working men are well employed and contented, and Henry Hunt was equal to the occasion.

On Friday, the 15th of November, about twenty thousand persons assembled in Spa Fields in consequence of a Requisition from a Committee in Shoreditch (which Requisition had been placarded all over the East End of London some days previously) addressed to distressed tradesmen, manufacturers, and mariners, calling upon them to meet for the purpose of adopting some measures with a view to their relief. The people began to assemble, and by half-past twelve many thousands were in the fields. But as no one came to address them, many were going away, when a Coach drove up, and from its window, an announcement was made that Mr. Hunt, of Bristol, was coming.

When the Coach stopped, a Rev. Mr. Parkes scrambled on to its top, whence he delivered a sensible introductory speech in which he said : ' The occasion was important and critical, and it behoved the people to conduct themselves with dignity and firmness. If they acted with due moderation—if they adhered to the Constitution—their present suffering, even severe as it was, might serve to approximate their complete salvation. But intemperance and riot must injure their cause. (*Applause.*)'

He kept on speaking until the arrival of Hunt, who, not satisfied with his predecessor's platform, retired to a public-house, 'The Merlin's Cave' (still the same sign, 131, Rosoman Street, Clerkenwell), where he addressed the assembly, from a window. During his speech he frequently waved a tricolor flag, green, white, and red, which bore these inscriptions : 'Bread to feed the Hungry'—'Truth to crush the Oppressors' —'Justice to punish Crimes.'

He certainly began his speech with references to the general distress, but he soon drifted on to the subject of Reform, and tried to excite his audience by drawing attention to the Royal, and other Incomes. Here is a specimen of his oratory: 'You have all heard of George Canning, that impudent dog, that vile, unprincipled, unmanly calumniator of the people—that miscreant, whose language failed him in applying disgraceful epithets to you: but you do not know his family; nay, I do not believe he knows his own grand-father.   Yet Mother Hunn, who brought this hopeful cub into the world (without knowing who was his father), had £500 for the useful event, and her worthy daughters had also £500 each.'*   And in another part of his speech he is reported to have said: ' I know well the superiority of *mental* over *physical* force: while we have the power of exercising the *former*, we cannot be justified in resorting to the *latter*.' This might be construed into a sort of ' Don't nail his ear to the pump '—and was remembered as such on the 2nd of December.

Well, he made his Speech, and proposed some Resolutions which were cut and dried, and moved that they be embodied in a Petition to the Regent, which was to be personally presented to him.   This Motion was carried by acclamation, and it was afterwards moved that Mr. Hunt, and Sir Francis Burdett, should present it.   Hunt said he never had been to Court—that he never wished to go there, and, therefore, he requested that the meeting would not send him there.

The Meeting, however, adopted the proposition, and Hunt said ' That, having good health, with a willing heart, he should comply with the wish of the Meeting.   He should, to-morrow, in conjunction with Sir Francis Burdett, seek out the Regent wherever he was to be found, whether at Carlton House, the Stud House, the Brighton Pavilion, or Manchester Square† (*laughter and applause*); for, thank God, his horses had not yet been taken from him by the oppressive hands of the tax-gatherer.'

* Hunt must have known he was lying, for George Canning was born in London in 1770.   His family was originally of Foxcote, in Warwickshire, and one of his ancestors had emigrated to Ireland, at the commencement of the seventeenth century, as agent of a company of Londoners in the plantation of Ulster, and settled at Garvagh, in the county of Londonderry.   His father, George Canning, who had been educated for the bar, to which he was called by the Society of the Middle Temple, having offended his parents by marrying a lady inferior to him both in rank and fortune, was cut off by them with a pittance of £150 per annum.   Finding him-self thus discarded by his family, who possessed considerable property in Ireland, he left that country, and removed with his wife to London, where, after unavailing efforts to enlarge the means of sub-sistence, he died broken-hearted, in a year after the birth of his son.

† Hereford House.

The meeting then broke up in a very orderly manner.

On the 2nd of December another meeting was convened at Spa Fields to hear Hunt's account of his stewardship. He duly arrived, and went into ' The Merlin's Cave.' Addressing the Mob, he said that having found that Sir Francis Burdett was at Brighton, he determined to do their will by himself. ' I went, then, first of all, to Carlton House, where, being admitted, I inquired if I could have an audience of his Royal Highness the Prince Regent, for the purpose of presenting your Petition to him. I was told, there was no way of presenting that Petition, unless at the Prince's Levée, or by the Secretary of State for the Home Department, that is, Lord Sidmouth, you know. I then inquired when a Levée would take place, and was told it was quite uncertain, at least none would be for some time.'

He then thought he was entitled to use his own discretion, and waited upon Lord Sidmouth, which he did, having first written his lordship a letter, and enclosing the Petition. He was received by Lord Sidmouth most courteously, and afterwards spoke of his reception in terms of eulogy. His lordship assured him that what had been told him at Carlton House was perfectly true, and that he would present the petition to his Royal Highness without delay ; adding (to quote Hunt's speech), ' that since the present family had come to the throne, no answer had ever been given to any Petition, unless presented by the Corporation of London, or by the two Universities, that, when he, himself, as Secretary of State, presented a Petition, he made his bow, and went on, and if I went to the Levée, I could only do the same.—Ah ! Gentlemen, this is the Court Fashion. I told you I did not wish to go there.'

But, either the fact of his going to Court, or his subsequent knowledge of popular feeling, made him far quieter in his after speech ; and, although the Resolutions proposed were far too advanced to be accepted by the moderate Reformers there was not the same rancour in his speech, or the Resolutions, as in his previous speeches, and the meeting, as a whole, was very orderly.

But, as we have the unfortunate example in our own times —not so very long ago, in Trafalgar Square—the calling together of a Mass meeting does not always guarantee that the gathering shall consist entirely of persons interested in the object of the meeting—the thing is impossible. The gather-

ing of a crowd is the rough's opportunity, and the greater the
Crowd, the greater his chance.   If, to this, are added the
thousands of fools who go to look on, get mixed up in the
mob, and occasionally get a cracked head, broken arm, or are
trampled on, as a reward for their folly, we have the same
mob to-day as there was in 1816.

I cannot believe that Hunt, or any of those who were
absolutely around him, ever for a moment foresaw, or could
have conceived, the outcome of this Meeting.   The former
one, on November 15th, was marked by its order ; their
petition had been courteously received, and presented to the
Regent ; but the roughs only want a Cry and a Crowd, and
both were afforded them ; hence the subsequent riot.

In fact, it was before the business commenced that a
waggon drove up bedecked with tricolor flags and mottoes—
the same sort of thing that we could, if we were foolish
enough to go and look, see two or three Sundays in the year
in Hyde Park—where the leather-lunged patriots belch forth
their opinions—and in it was the typical Mob-orator, ' a young
man,' named Watson.   He was something in the Medical
profession, and not being successful in that branch of industry
tried, as needy patriots will do, to turn instructor of the
people.   He is reported to have made a very inflammatory
speech, and ' at the close he asked them if they would accompany him ?   There was a Cry on the part of some that they
would to any place.   "And will you protect me ?" he said.—
They replied, " As long as life remained."

' He jumped off the waggon, and headed the Mob, which
went from Spa Fields to Skinner Street, and whose disgraceful
conduct is detailed below ; but who appeared to have had no
other connection with the Meeting in Spa Fields than being
on the spot where it was held.   There is, indeed, no doubt,
from the circumstances that occurred, that the greater number
of those men who behaved so outrageously in the City, came
to Spa Fields with a premeditated design not to take any part
in the business of the Meeting, but to commit riot, as it
appears that about two hundred men, chiefly dressed like
sailors, had no sooner arrived there, than they found the man
above mentioned ready to lead them, and they immediately
followed him.   These formed the chief part of the Mob in the
City.   It is evident, therefore, that all this was the result of
some previous concerted plan, but it is equally evident that
the plan had no connection with the Spa Fields meeting, the

people who came to attend it remaining perfectly quiet, and taking no part in these outrageous proceedings. . . .

'The Lord Mayor, as on the former day of meeting at Spa Fields, took every precaution for the purpose of preserving the public peace ; but, serious apprehensions being entertained that on the present occasion mischief and outrage were contemplated by the misguided populace, additional measures were adopted. The Ward Constables, who had been considerably augmented, assembled at an early hour, and the following notice was posted on large boards, and not only fixed in conspicuous places, but carried about various parts of the City, by order of his Lordship :—

'" OUR SOVEREIGN LORD THE KING

Chargeth and commandeth all persons being assembled, immediately to disperse themselves, and peaceably depart to their habitations, or to their lawful business, upon the pains contained in the Acts of the first year of King George—for preventing Tumults and Riotous Assemblies.

" GOD SAVE THE KING."

'The Lord Mayor, who was actively engaged all the morning in devising his arrangements, suddenly received information that a body of rioters, headed by a young man (whose name was said to be Watson), and who addressed the multitude at an early hour in Spa Fields, was on its way, by Clerkenwell, to the City. They had, in fact, already reached Snow Hill, and it was impossible at the moment to stop their career. Upon their arrival at Snow Hill, three of the rioters marching some distance before the multitude, entered the shop of Mr. Beckwith, the gunmaker, and demanded arms. Their companions were not in sight, and their demand was opposed. This, however, so exasperated these desperate wretches, that one of them dressed in a sailor's habit, drew forth a pistol, and shot a Mr. Platt in the groin.

'Mr. Platt is a young man of respectability, and resides in Cateaton Street. He was a mere casual visitant at the shop, and the ruffians escaped, the mob coming up at the moment, and the former intermixing with it.

'After rifling the shop of all the arms it contained, they formed a new procession, and bent their way towards Cheapside, not forgetting, however, to lodge a few balls in the windows of a house in Newgate Street, on the way, where they fired for the purpose of annoying a gentleman who had retreated from the displeasure of the mob.

'The Lord Mayor, being apprized of their movements, set out, accompanied by a few officers, and came up with the party at the Royal Exchange. They were about three hundred in number, and fifty appeared armed with all kinds of weapons, viz., swords, pistols, musquets, blunderbusses, &c. Their leader (as we understand, Mr. Watson) carried before him a large tricoloured flag, on which were written the following sentiments :—

> '"Nature—Feed the Hungry.
> Truth—Protect the Distressed.
> Justice—Punish Crime."

'Upon their arrival at the Exchange, the name of the Lord Mayor was mentioned, as being very active, when he was instantly greeted with the shouts of the multitude. This ill-timed approbation had no effect upon his Lordship's conduct, and, seeing the mob turn into Sweeting's Alley, close to the Royal Exchange, he entered that place at the southern side, and, the mob not being able to retreat through so narrow a lane, they entered, of necessity, the Exchange by the eastern door. They were instantly summoned to surrender, and, after discharging a few pieces of musquetry, were overcome, and their arms seized. The leader only, and two others, were kept in custody.

'A proper force was then stationed at the Exchange, it being apprehended that the party would return to seek their arms, and to rescue their companions. At the Bank there was also a military guard, consisting of about two hundred of the Guards ready accoutred. Independently of this, the East London Militia were under arms, and numbers of persons, contiguously resident, applied to offer themselves to serve the temporary office of Constable, and were accordingly sworn in.

'About half-past two o'clock, an account reached the Mansion House, that the mob had risen in considerable numbers, in and about the Minories, had broken open the houses of two gunsmiths there (Messrs. Ray's and Brandon's), and robbed the place of every piece of firearms that could be found. With these, they again rallied a force, and commenced an attack on the soldiery at the top of the Minories, in Aldgate High Street. After a short delay here, however, they were completely beaten, and retired towards the Tower, where, to render the scene more ridiculous, some of the party actually proposed the surrender of that place. In the struggle between the soldiery and the mob, in the Minories, it was said that one of the Guards fell, but we could not trace the account to any authentic source.'

After doing this, the Mob dispersed in every direction, whooping and yelling, breaking a few windows, rifling a few butchers' stalls, robbing a few people of their purses and watches, and then the riot was all over.

Mr. Platt, the Gentleman who was shot, lingered some time, but eventually died of his wound, and, on the 12th of March, 1817, his murderer, Cashman, was hanged in front of Mr. Beckwith's shop. His end was not edifying. The Mob was howling at him, 'and Cashman joined his voice to the shouts, crying out, "Hurrah! my Boys, I'll die like a man." On his quitting the Cart, and mounting the Scaffold, the groans were redoubled; he seemed to enter into the spirit of the Spectators, and joined in their exclamations with a terrific shout. . . . He now turned towards Mr. Beckwith's house, in an angry manner, and, shaking his head, said : " I'll be with you,——there"; meaning that he would haunt the house after his death. The executioner having quitted the platform, the unfortunate wretch addressed the crowd nearest them, and exclaimed : " Now, you ——, give me three cheers when I trip." And then, calling to the executioner, he cried out : " Come, Jack, you ——, let go the jib-boom." He was cheering at the instant the fatal board fell.'

The fullest details of the King's life and illness are given us in January. After the usual bulletin, dated January 5th, *The Gentleman's Magazine* gives us as follows :—' The public bulletins which have been issued for some months past, have all stated that his Majesty's disorder remains undiminished ; and we understand that it is the opinion of the medical gentlemen attending him, that nothing far short of a miracle can bring about a recovery from his afflicting malady. At times, we are happy to learn, he is tolerably composed. The number of persons specially appointed by the doctors is reduced from six to two, and his principal pages are admitted, and have been for some time, to attend upon him, as when he enjoyed good health.—His Majesty dines at half-past one o'clock, and, in general, orders his dinner : he invariably has roast beef upon the tables on Sundays. He dresses for dinner, wears his orders, &c.

' He occupies a suite of thirteen rooms (at least he, and his attendants) which are situated on the North side of Windsor Castle, under the State rooms. Five of the thirteen rooms are wholly devoted to the personal use of the King. Dr. John Willis sleeps in the sixth room, adjoining, to be in readiness to attend his Majesty. Dr. John attends the Queen every morning after breakfast, about half-past ten o'clock, and reports to her the state of the afflicted monarch ; the Doctor, afterwards, proceeds to the Princesses, and other branches of the Royal Family, who may happen to be at Windsor, and makes a similar report to them. In general the Queen returns with Dr. Willis, through the state rooms, down a private staircase, leading into the King's suite of rooms, appropriated to this special purpose. Sometimes she converses with her Royal husband. The Queen is the only person who is admitted to this peculiar privilege, except the medical gentlemen, and his Majesty's personal attendants. In case of Dr. John Willis's absence, Dr. Robert Willis, his brother, takes his place. The other medical gentlemen take it in rotation to be in close attendance upon the King.

' The suite of rooms which his Majesty and his attendants occupy, have the advantage of very pure and excellent air, being on the North side of the terrace round the Castle ; and he used, occasionally, to walk on the terrace ; but, we understand, he now declines it, owing to the bad state of his eyes, not being able to enjoy the view.—The Lords and Grooms of the King's Bedchamber, his Equerries, and other attendants, are occasionally in attendance at Windsor Castle, the same as if the King enjoyed good health. Two King's messengers go from the Secretary of State's Office daily to Windsor, and return to London, as they have been accustomed to do for a number of years past. The messenger who arrives at noon brings a daily account of the King's health to the Prince Regent, and the Members of the Queen's Council.—His Majesty has never been left since his afflicting malady, without one of the Royal Family being in the Castle, and a member of the Queen's Council, appointed under the Regency Act.'

The monthly bulletins for the remainder of the year all tell the same story, that the King enjoyed good health, and was tranquil, but that his malady remained unaltered.

CHAPTER XXVI.

1817.

Visit of the Grand Duke Nicholas of Russia—Stones thrown at the Regent—Issue of the new Silver Coinage—Riots and arrests for sedition—First issue of Sovereigns—The Case of Abraham Thornton and appeal by battle—The Queen at Bath—Death of the Princess Charlotte—Richard Owen and his scheme—'The Fortunate Youth'—'Caraboo.'

THE Chronicle of this year opens with the record of a luckily rare visitation, namely, that a slight shock of earthquake was felt on January 8th at Mansfield, in Nottinghamshire. In 1816 a shock had been felt in several places in Scotland.

The Grand Duke Nicholas of Russia, afterwards Czar, was over here, and spent some months in this country, and those of us who remember the last war we had with Russia, will scarcely recognize the stern Nicholas of the Crimea, under the guise of the light-hearted Grand Duke, as exemplified in the following anecdote, which occurred early in January :—

'A LITTLE FROLIC OF THE GRAND DUKE NICHOLAS.—On his Imperial Highness leaving Chester for Montgomeryshire, he perceived one of the outriders to be mounted on a good horse; being a fine morning, his Highness felt disposed to take a ride, and requested to change place with the Courier ; it was a fourteen-mile stage, and, on descending a very long and steep hill, his Highness did not like to crawl down so slow as the others, and told his suite that he would ride on, and order some refreshment and horses for them. On his Highness arriving at the Inn, he desired the landlady to prepare some beefsteaks and mutton chops for the Grand Duke and his suite.

'The landlady observed that they should immediately be

got ready, and, taking his Highness for the Courier, asked him to accept of something, which he politely declined, observing that he would wait until the company arrived. She then showed him the room she had prepared for the Grand Duke, and asked him if he thought it would do? His Highness told her that it would do extremely well. The carriages shortly after arrived, and the hostess begged him to have the goodness to point out to her the Grand Duke; his Highness smiled, and said she would be sure to see him.' When Generals Kutusoff and Mansel alighted and saluted him, one can picture the landlady's astonishment. Nicholas was so pleased with the horse that he bought it. He left England at the end of March.

Far less popular was another Royal Highness, far nearer home. The Prince Regent went on the 28th of January to open the Session of Parliament, and was met with a storm of yells and opprobrious epithets, but he got safely to the House of Lords, and delivered his speech ; on his return, the clamour and insults had vastly increased. It is true that some few cried, ' God save the King,' but the majority hissed and hooted at, and called his Royal Highness naughty names; the climax was reached when the Regent's carriage was about the middle of the Mall. Some evilly disposed person threw a stone, or stones, at the Royal equipage, and made a hole in one of the windows. This hole remains a mystery, for the window on the opposite side was not broken, and no stone, nor other missile, was found in the carriage.

Lord James Murray, who was Lord of the Bed-chamber to the Regent, was in the carriage with him, and was examined shortly afterwards at the bar of the House of Commons, and he was of opinion that the hole in the window was made by two small bullets, about a quarter of an inch apart—but this must have been pure conjecture on his lordship's part. He went on to say that ' about a minute after the glass was broken, as I have described, a large stone was thrown against the glass of the carriage, which broke it, and three or four other small stones were thrown, which struck the glass, and the other part of the carriage.' And this is all that was found out about it.

The Lords and Commons united in an Address conveying their Abhorrence of this attack upon his Royal Highness— the Guards at the Palaces, the Parks, the Bank, and elsewhere were doubled ; the Lord Mayor was informed of the awful occurrence, and requested, if he thought necessary, to call in the aid of the Military power, and despatches were sent by the Mail Coaches to every part of the kingdom, to put the Magistrates in every place on their guard.   But there was no occasion for all this fuss : the event did not produce a ferment in the public mind, and we learn in next morning's paper, 'that by five o'clock in the afternoon the streets were perfectly clear of all mob, and no disposition to riot appeared in any part of the town.'

A man named James Scott was the only one arrested, although £1,000 reward was offered for the Criminals, and as somebody was wanted to be hanged, they accused him of high treason in throwing stones at the Vicegerent of the Lord's Anointed.   But, although they tried very hard for a conviction, it only wanted three examinations by a Magistrate to acquit the man of the charge of treason, but he was committed for a misdemeanour in aiding and abetting of the Riot.   He was admitted to bail in two Sureties of £100 each, and himself in £200.   Reading the evidence, I can see nothing to incriminate him, and as I can find nothing about his conviction, or acquittal, from any source, I presume he was never called upon to appear.   Peter Pindar satirised this event in ' R—lty Beset.'

On the 18th of January, a proclamation was issued 'from our Court at Brighton,' announcing the issue of a new Silver Coinage, which might be changed for old, at the Mint, between the 3rd and 17th of February : and another proclamation of the 12th of February, ' from our Court at Carlton House,' gave the date of the 13th of February as that of general issue, after which they were to be taken as lawful money.   On this date was published a Satirical print, called ' The New Coinage ; or, John Bull's visit to Mat of the Mint ! ! '* in which Wellesley Pole, ' Master and Worker of his Majesty's Mint,' is shovelling money into a sack, saying ' There, Johnny ! see how I have been working for you for months past ; you can't say I get my money for nothing.' John Bull replies, ' You be a very industrious man, Master Mat, and the prettiest *Cole*† merchant I have dealt with for many a day.'   The room, and the street, seen through an open door, are crowded with men, women, and children,

---

* Mat o' the Mint was a character in Gay's ' Beggar's Opera.'

† *Cole* or *Coal* is thieves' slang for money, and many people carry a piece of Coal in their pocket, under the belief that so long as they have *Cole* in their pocket they will never want for money.

anxious to get the new silver. That advantage was taken of
promptly changing old worn silver for bright new coin, is
shown that by the 19th the large Hall of the Bank, which

'THE NEW COINAGE; OR, JOHN BULL'S VISIT TO MAT OF THE MINT!!'

(*February* 13, 1817.)

was given up to its issue, was nearly empty, and the old
coinage had disappeared from circulation. They were counter-
feited immediately, which was a natural sequence, and there
were squabbles about their artistic merits, which was also

natural. Regarding the latter, as there are plenty of this issue now in circulation, my readers can judge for themselves. There was the usual epigram upon it.

'THE NEW COIN.

It is allow'd, throughout the town,
The head upon the new Half-Crown,
Is not the GEORGE we so much prize—
The Chin's not like—the Nose—the Eyes.
This may be true—yet, on the whole,
The fault lies chiefly *in the Pole* !'

Reform was being violently agitated all over the country, and, without wishing to give this book any political character, yet as a phase of social life it must be mentioned. There were riots late in February in Somersetshire, among the Colliers, who struck against a deduction of 10 per cent. in their wages. They did not do much damage, but a dangerous spirit was abroad, and the cry of ' Bread or Blood ; Hunt for ever !' was ominous of mischief. They were soon put down by a troop of the 22nd Lancers, from Bristol, and the North Somerset Yeomanry, without bloodshed.

On the 28th of February, the operation of the Act of *Habeas Corpus* was suspended, and was not resumed until the 31st of January, 1818.

Of the Spa Fields rioters, two others beside Cashman, whose execution has already been recorded, were hanged— and the others in custody respited during pleasure : but no severity could quell the unhappy feeling all over England. The people were restless and suffering, and were determined to make themselves heard : as, for instance, on the 10th of March, a meeting took place at Manchester for the avowed purpose of petitioning the Prince Regent for a redress of grievances, and a Reform in Parliament. It was recommended for the Reformers to proceed in a large body to London, which was attempted to be carried into effect by some hundreds, who had provided themselves with blankets and bundles ; but, by the activity of the Magistrates, aided by the military, their purpose was defeated, and several of the leaders were committed to prison.

On the 18th of March numerous arrests took place at Manchester, of persons charged with seditious practices ; and on the 25th of March the Bill to prevent seditious meetings passed the House of Commons by a large majority. High

20

treason had become so familiar that new regulations had to be adopted in the Tower, as to prisoners contained there. ' Each prisoner is kept in a separate apartment, and night and day, two yeomen, or warders, continue in the room, the door of which is locked, and on the outside a sentinel is placed to prevent the approach of any one, except those in the Governor's establishment. Their beds and board are provided by the Government. No person is allowed to see the prisoners, unless a special order is sent to the Lieutenant-Governor by the Clerk of the Council, and then they are restricted from holding any communication except in the presence and hearing of some persons appointed by the lieutenant, or his deputy.'

Let us pass to something pleasanter. The Custom House was opened for business on the 12th of May without ceremony, and as one newspaper says : ' This structure is, in fact, perfect in everything, as its inmates confess, and wants nothing but *business.*' But the building was not finished until the 2nd of August.

The only Social News between this date and July is the account of more riots at Nottingham and Leeds—together with State trials—which we will skip.

On the 1st of July was issued the new gold Coin ' the Sovereign,' and from that date the old Guinea was doomed, and only now survives in professional fees, and wherever any one can stick on an extra shilling to a Sovereign. They were taken very kindly to, only some exception was taken to the name, many thinking they ought to have been called a ' George.' The half-sovereigns soon got a nickname, that of ' Regents.' This is what a wicked wag thought of the ' New Sovereign ' :

> ' The Horse on the *Coin* is more fit for a Waggon,
> Than meet for *St. George* to encounter the *Dragon !*
> And, as for the *Effigy*, meant for the *Saint*,
> He appears like a *Sans Culotte*, ready to faint ;
> With his head hanging down o'er a lean hungry paunch,
> He has struck, with his spear, his poor horse, on the haunch ;
> While the *Dragon* in pity, looks at the incision,
> And cocks up his nose, at *St. George* in derision ! ! !'

One of the most famous Criminal Cases of modern times occurred this year—singular for the fact that it revived the old Ordeal, ' Appeal by battle,' which had been in abeyance since 1771, and which no one ever dreamed would be revived. One Abraham Thornton had been accused of murdering Mary Ashford by drowning her on the 27th of May. He was tried, and acquitted, but was subsequently arrested in October on an appeal. This was heard in the King's Bench on the 17th of November, and both Appellant and Appellee answered to their names. The first, William Ashford, brother of the deceased, is described as being a slight made lad, about seventeen years of age, and short in stature. Thornton stood about five feet four inches high, very stout and robust.

After the preliminary formalities were over, Mr. Leblanc, clerk to the Crown, read over the record against him, and asked him whether he was guilty or not. 'His Counsel, Mr. Reader, then put a piece of paper in his hand from which the prisoner read :

'"Not guilty ; and I am ready to defend the same with my body."

'Mr. Reader had likewise handed a pair of large gauntlets, or gloves, to the prisoner, one of which he put on, and the other, in pursuance of the old form, he threw down for the appellant to take up. It was not taken up, and

'Mr. Reader moved that it should be kept in the custody of the officer of the Court.

'Mr. Leblanc : Your plea is that you are not Guilty, and that you are ready to defend the said plea with your body ?

'The Prisoner : It is.

'Lord Ellenborough : Is the Appellant in Court ?

'Mr. Clarke (his Counsel): He is, my Lord.'

He appeared, but said nothing, and then Mr. Clarke addressed the Court with a counter plea for the Appellant. In the course of his speech, he said, 'It would appear to me extraordinary indeed, if the person who murdered the sister, should, as the law exists in these enlightened times, be allowed to prove his innocence by murdering the brother also, or at least, by an attempt to do so.

'Lord Ellenborough : It is the law of England, Mr. Clarke. We must not call it murder.'

Mr. Clarke then went on arguing that, surely the appeal must be discretionary with the Court, and urged the inferiority of his client's physique.

The Case was adjourned until the 22nd of November, when the Appellant pleaded that Thornton ought not to be admitted to wage battle with him, because both before and after the appeal there had been, and still were, proofs that he had murdered the Appellant's sister.   Case adjourned.

On the 16th of April, 1818, Abraham Thornton was discharged, without bail, the appellant declining the Challenge to combat, according to ancient usage.   But such a scandal could not long continue, and the law was repealed in 1819 (59 George III. cap. 46).

What became of him, I know not, but I find mention of him in *The Morning Chronicle* of the 26th of October, 1818. *The Liverpool Courier* says : ' We stated a few weeks ago, that the celebrated Abraham Thornton had arrived in this town for the purpose of emigrating to the United States.   He has experienced more difficulty than he anticipated in getting a passage thither.   It appears that he had engaged one in the *Independence,* but, when the other passengers became acquainted with his name and character, they unanimously refused to go in the same vessel with him ; and a new Muster roll was, in consequence, made out, in which his name was omitted.'

The Chinese Embassy sent out under Lord Amherst had returned, having failed in its object, his lordship refusing to kotoo to the Emperor : his ship, the *Alceste,* being fired into by the Chinese.

The health of that tough old lady, Queen Charlotte, was beginning to fail, and her physicians recommended her to go to Bath, for the waters, and, in November, she thither repaired, accompanied by the Duke of Clarence.

The illustration gives an extremely graphic idea of the effects of the Water upon the afflicted Queen.   It is called ' A PEEP into the PUMP ROOM ; or, the Zomersetshire folk in a Maze.'

The following anecdote of her sojourn is dated ' Bath, November 28th.—The Queen wishing to ride through Prior Park, the property of John Thomas, a very rich Quaker, a footman was sent forward to the house to ask leave for the gates to be opened.   Mr. Thomas received the Queen very respectfully at the park gate, and addressed her as follows : ' Charlotte, I hope thee is very well : I am glad to see thee in my park ; thou art very welcome at any time, and I shall feel proud in opening my gates for thy pleasure.   I hope thou receives benefit from the Bath waters.   I wish thee well.'

Early in the morning of the 6th of November, died the Princess Charlotte.   On the day before she had been delivered of a stillborn child, and was reported to be going on well, but within twelve hours she was a corpse. There really was

A PEEP INTO THE PUMP ROOM ; OR, THE ZOMERSETSHIRE FOLK IN A MAZE, OCTOBER, 1817.
(*Published February, 1818.*)

sorrow when she died. Her husband was inconsolable, and her father, bereft of his only, though somewhat wayward child, stayed at home and was ill. She was buried, with all pomp, at Windsor, on the 19th of November. There was no Lord Mayor's Show this year.

Before the end of the year there were more riots at Brighton and Worcester, and a Commission sat at Derby, upon thirty-five persons charged with high treason. Three of them, Brandreth, Ludlam, and Turner, were found guilty, and afterwards hanged and beheaded. The others, on withdrawing their plea of not guilty, were dealt with mercifully.

The Chronicle of this year must not be closed without mention of Robert Owen, a Cotton Spinner at Lanark, who was a Social Reformer of somewhat peculiar views. He had a Plan for the better support and government of the poor, the outlines of which are as follows :—He proposed to make the poor National, and to raise funds by mortgaging the poor's rate to the amount of five or six years of its annual value. The money so raised, in sums as required, he would have applied in purchase of land, in portions of different magnitudes, and erect establishments thereon for the accommodation of from five hundred to fifteen hundred people. Of these buildings he furnished a plan, on a scale for twelve hundred persons—men, women, and children. The buildings were to be surrounded by a regulated quantity of land for *spade* cultivation—say an acre for each person, including the site of erection—and they were designed for a pauper community, which was to supply everything for itself; and to be super-intended on the principle of combining moral culture, and reformation, with industry and frugality.

The occupants were both to farm and manufacture, and, consequently, to employ the faculties of each description of poor. Besides comfortable lodging rooms, the buildings were intended to contain a public kitchen, mess rooms, and all requisite accommodation attached to comfortable cookery and eating ; a chapel, infant schools, schools for adults, grounds for exercise and recreation, planted and beautified with trees. The lodgings for the married poor, each to be sufficient to accommodate two children with their father and mother : dormitories for children above three years of age ; manufactories and gardens ; a complete farming establishment ; malting, and brewing-houses, corn-mill, dairy, and, in short, all the constituents for self-support. To the men were assigned the labours of agriculture, and the heaviest part of the manufactures. To the women the care of their children

ROBERT OWEN, AUGUST 21, 1817.

and houses, the cultivation of vegetables, the making of clothes, and an attendance, in rotation, on the kitchen, mess-room, and dormitories.   The children were to be trained in the lighter occupations until fit for manly or womanly employ-ment, &c.   The expense of such an establishment for twelve hundred people, Owen estimated at £96,000

In the latter part of this year, a great deal was heard of 'The Fortunate Youth.'   The story told about whom was, that a young gentleman met with a very rich old one, who took a violent fancy to the youth, used often to have him at his house, without the knowledge of his parents, and finally, dying, left 'The Fortunate Youth' an immense fortune. This lad succeeded in humbugging people to an unlimited extent, and in obtaining money from them, until, in a News-paper of the 6th of December, appeared : ' Soi - disant Fortunate Youth.—We lament to wound the feelings of the friends of this young man, but we are bound by a painful duty to caution the public against an impostor, whose detected falsehoods, and disingenuous acts, authorize the assertion that there is not one word of truth in his whole story.'

This was pretty plain speaking, and brought forth a dis-claimer from 'The Solicitor and Confidential Friend of "The Fortunate Youth" and his family,' in which he says, ' I will venture to assert that this Youth has never defrauded, nor attempted to defraud, any one ; and that if any person has any just pecuniary claim upon him, the liquidation of it will be immediately provided for, on such claim being made known to me.'   Once again he wrote defending his client ; but alack, and well-a-day, a little time afterwards, in a letter to the same Newspaper, he writes (giving his own name, Weatherby) : ' I feel it now a duty I owe to the public to declare, that circumstances have since occurred, which induce me to think that I have been grossly deceived in my opinion of him, and that his pretensions to a large property are with-out foundation.'

The editor then gives the impostor's real story.

' This young man's name is Abraham W. Cawston.   His father is a farmer at Chippenham, near Newmarket.   The early promise of shining talents induced his father to send him to school, under the tuition of the eminent Dr. Butler, of Shrewsbury, and there his attainments and abilities gained him universal admiration.   He was not seventeen years of age when he paid his addresses to a young lady of fortune in that place, and from that time the strange artifice or imagination of this enormous fortune that had dropped to him, as it were, from the clouds, had birth.   He first opened his wonderful secret to his father ; and the story which he told was, that an aged gentleman had, at one of his journeys from home to school, fallen in with him in a stage coach going to Birmingham, and that he afterwards made him *a deed of gift* of his whole fortune !   It did not, in the first disclosure, swell to the magnitude which it afterwards attained ; but the first feeling that he manifested was to settle a part of his wealth on his parents and brother.   For this purpose he was introduced to Mr. Weatherby, to whom he gave instructions to make a will ; and, as his fortune was stated to be all personal, Mr. Weatherby saw no objection to the deed.   His distribution of wealth, though uncommon, did not strike Mr. Weatherby as improbable, so clear and consistent were the boy's statements in their different interviews, and so filial, and brotherly, were the bequests.

' From this time, nothing could equal the romance of his story, the unblushing effrontery with which he maintained it, and the ingenious stratagems he devised to keep up the delusion.   It would fill a volume to recount the history of the youth for the last two months ; and we are possessed of so many curious anecdotes, that we shall entertain our readers with the relation of a few of them, since the affair has afforded a striking example of the courtesy which is shown to appearance, and the eagerness with which a meteor is contemplated in the hemisphere of rank and fashion.   That tradesmen of all descriptions should crowd round his doors for the advantage of his orders, was natural ; but that Bankers should contend for his account—Duchesses for the honour of his acquaintance—and Ministers for his Parliamentary support— prove how much all conditions of Society are on the alert for gold and power.

' He prevailed on his father to enter his elder brother, who is twenty-four years of age, and had been brought up in the line of farming, as a fellow commoner of Emanuel College, Cambridge.

' He instructed one solicitor to enter into a negociation for the purchase of several estates, and surveys had actually been made.

' He applied to Government for a grant to take the name and bear the arms of Devereux, and the Heralds' College had begun to take steps to exemplify the arms, and waited only for information as to which branch of the house of Devereux his benefactor belonged.

'He instructed another Solicitor to insert an advertisement in the public papers, calling on the Creditors, if any, of Don Gaspar de Quintilla, deceased, to bring vouchers of their demands, in order that they might be immediately liquidated. (Meaning to couple him with Don Joachim de Quintilla, a rich Portuguese diamond Merchant.)

'He stated that it was his determination to purchase ten Boroughs, that he might have twenty Members of Parliament in the House of Commons, to procure him an Earldom.

'He said that his half-year's dividend, due on the 5th of January next, was £92,000, and that he held annuities from several of the crowned heads of Europe to the amount of millions.

'He was in the habit of suffering drafts on bankers for thousands, nay, at times for tens, and hundreds of thousands, to drop from his pocket-book, as if by accident, that they might be seen; and he talked of loans to persons of the highest distinction, on whose estate he had mortgages.

'When strongly pressed for an explanation as to the *Deed of Gift* by which the Legacy Tax had been evaded, he said that it was a secret which he was bound to conceal for a time, but it was in an iron chest, buried in the garden of his benefactor.

'So entire was the conviction of his friends, as to the certainty, and extent, of his wealth, that a consultation was held with two eminent Lawyers, to devise the means of making him a Ward of Chancery ; and, as his wealth was all his own, and, consequently, there was no ground for the interference of the Lord Chancellor, it was settled that he should present £30,000 to his father, and file a friendly bill, upon which application might be made to constitute him a ward.'

This is only a slight portion of the revelations made respecting him ; but, although highly amusing, the relation of them would occupy too much space. I have not taken the trouble to try and find out what became of him.

It is curious that this should have been the year of two notorious and historical impostors. One we have just heard of : the other was a hussey named Wilcox or Baker—who tried to ape the *rôle* of George Psalmanazar. Her story is on this wise. On the evening of 3rd April, 1817, the guardian of the poor brought a female, aged about twenty-five, clothed in ordinary costume, although it was somewhat fantastically put on, to Mrs. Worrall, of Knole Park, for advice. She had been found in the neighbouring village of Almondsbury (Gloucestershire), and had gone into a cottage, making signs that she wished to rest and sleep there : but as there was something uncanny about her, and she spoke no language they understood, she was taken to the Great House. Mrs. Worrall very kindly sent a maid with her to the village inn, where she slept that night. Next day she was interviewed, but all that could be got out of her was some gibberish no one could understand, and she kept pointing to herself, saying 'Caraboo,' by which it was inferred that such was her name. She was taken to Bristol and examined : many persons versed in Eastern languages trying to converse with her, but failing —her language being utterly unknown to them.

Mrs. Worrall then took her to her house at Knole, and afterwards, a Portuguese Malay appeared on the scene, un-doubtedly a confederate, who could talk to her, and then it came out that she was a Malayan princess, of Chinese origin, and that she came from *Javasu* (wherever that may be). One day she was walking in her garden attended by her women, when the crew of a pirate prahu landed, scaled the walls, gagged her, bound her and carried her off ! (*Red fire. Curtain falls*).—Act II. She is now discovered in a state of slavery—having been sold by the pirates to the captain of a brig, from which ship she was transferred to another, where she found company in the society of a few more female captives, who, after five weeks' cruise, were landed at another port. Caraboo, however, continues sailing the wild ocean for nearly three months, till, nearing land, and preferring death to slavery, she jumps overboard ! (*Soft music. Curtain falls.*) —Act III. A merciful Providence watches over her, and she swims ashore, borne to a land to which she is an utter stranger, wanders about for six weeks, and at last finds herself in this village of Almondsbury, clad like a respectable working woman, in stuff dress, bonnet, woollen socks, leather boots, a piece of soap, and other necessaries in a bundle, and a few halfpence and a bad sixpence in her pocket. Kind people befriended her, she composed a new language, and wrote some of it. Suspicion is aroused, other kind people take an interest in her, who trace different antecedents for her ; she is con-fronted with the friends of her youth, and (counterpart of

Rider Haggard's 'She') the Princess Caraboo ot Javasu crumbles into Mary Baker, or Wilcox, of Witheridge, in the county of Devon ! ! ! (*Tableau. Curtain falls, hisses and catcalls.*)

She afterwards went, still in 1817, to America, but a New York paper noticing her arrival at Philadelphia, remarked, 'That her personal charms will have their due weight here, we should be sorry in this age of gallantry, to doubt ; but as to any prospect of success which the fair adventuress may promise herself in the way of *hoaxing*, she will shortly discover, from the number of our *banking institutions*, our *stones in cotton*, and *wooden nutmegs*, that we are already adepts in her profession.'

In the year 1824 she returned from America, and took apartments in New Bond Street, where she publicly showed herself at a shilling a head. She finally settled down at Bristol, where she sold leeches, and died at the close of 1864.

CHAPTER XXVII.

1818.

Distress among discharged Seamen—Finding the Scotch Regalia—
Strathfieldsaye bought for the Duke of Wellington—The Kyrle
Society — Royal Marriages — Annoying the Queen — Riotous
school-boys—The Regent mobbed—Death of Queen Charlotte.

THIS year did not open as one of national prosperity. There
was one subject that especially appealed to the country's
benevolence. Of course, when the long, long war was over,
the Navy was reduced to a peace footing, and thousands of
men-of-war's men were paid off; and those who were obtained
with such difficulty, who, in spite of being pressed, and forcibly
taken from all that was dear to them, bullied by their officers,
flogged nearly to death for comparative trifles, yet fought like
lions, and laid the foundation of England's present prosperity,
were cast adrift to shift for themselves as best they might.
They were wanted no longer. Had trade been good, nothing
more would have been heard of it, they would have been
absorbed into the merchant navy, and the Government would
have had all the credit of retrenchment, and dutifully administering the funds of the Nation.

As it was, people could see for themselves, the streets
teeming with old sailors, unable to obtain employment, and
walking about almost in a state of nudity, and with empty
stomachs. I am not exaggerating. I go upon contemporary
authority. But, I need scarcely say, that Englishmen then,
as they ever do now, as soon as the distress was manifest to
them, met together and tried to alleviate the sufferings of
their fellow countrymen. On the 5th of January, a meeting
of gentlemen was convened at the London Tavern, and Wm.
Wilberforce, Esq., M.P., was elected chairman, and by the

14th of January nearly £7,000 had been collected, besides a
quantity of clothing, and gifts in kind. In a Newspaper of
January 10th, we find the following : ' We can confidently
inform our readers that the " Society for the Aid of Destitute
Seamen," are proceeding with much energy : Officers in the
Royal Navy are, with much patience, and unwearied assiduity,
examining the various objects as they present themselves.
The greater number are men-of-war's men. Near two hundred
and fifty seamen have been housed in a temporary lodging.
Yesterday morning they breakfasted on wholesome porridge.
It was a pleasant sight, and, already, these sons of distress
have an improved appearance, which is highly gratifying.
Many have been enabled to remove part of the filth which
had accumulated about them, and their sense of gratitude is
continually expressed by the pleasure they evince in their
greater comforts.   The *Abundance* store-ship is now off the
Tower, and the utmost activity is engaged in victualling, and
other preparations ; so that, when the other ships shall be up,
which Government have promptly granted (and they are daily
expected), the Seamen may, it is hoped, be all taken from the
Streets, and on board, by the end of next week.   Thus, the
humane purposes of the benefactors to these deserving men
are, with astonishing celerity, carrying into effect, by those
who have from morning till night, devoted their valuable
time, and their best energies to relieve distress, which had
nearly reached their highest pitch of endurance.   The applications were so numerous, yesterday, that the Committee,
with much regret, have been obliged to suspend granting
temporary relief for a day or two, to give time for investigation of the cases already before them.'   Thanks to private
Charity, this scandal was ended, and we hear no more of
distressed seamen.

This year's Chronicle is not so full of public interest as its
forerunners, and I am fain to be content with small things,
such as the finding of the Scottish Regalia—which had been
lost since the time of Queen Anne.   It seems that some years
before 1818 a Commission had been issued to open the
' Crown Room ' at Holyrood, and search for certain records.
They found dust about six inches deep lying evenly spread
over everything, a sign that nothing had been disturbed ; and
they searched in all the places, for which they had a Commission to search, and did not find what they wanted.   There
was one chest left unopened, and in January this year, a Com-

mission was appointed to open it, examine its contents, and report upon them. Another account points to a different room, in which was only one chest—but this is immaterial. No keys being forthcoming, the Chest was forced on Wednesday, February 4th (some say 5th), and it was found to contain the Crown, Sceptre, and Sword of State of Scotland, completely answering to their description in the Instrument of Deposition, March 26, 1707. With them was also found a silver rod of office, of which the peculiar use was not then known. I believe they are all now religiously preserved, and guarded, in Holyrood Palace.

In February the purchase of Strathfieldsaye was completed, being a National gift to the Duke of Wellington.

In turning to one of my sources of information for the above, I find the next paragraph to be : 'A Society is about to be formed at *Ross*, under the designation of the *Kyrlean, and Philanthropic*, the object of which is to celebrate the birthday of Mr. John Kyrle (already immortalized by Pope, as the " Man of Ross "), and to raise a fund for the improvement of the walks, and those public buildings which he erected, and, in imitation of that amiable philanthropist, to relieve honest merit in distress. The Members are to be elected by ballot, but not confined to distance.'

I do not know whether this Society was started, or whether it had a long life, but I do know that there is now a very praiseworthy ' Kyrle Society,' whose power of doing good might be largely increased, by their possessing a larger income. Their object is to bring beauty home to the people. The means employed are (1) The decoration of working men's clubs, hospitals, &c., by mural paintings, pictures, &c. (2) By laying out, as gardens, or recreation grounds, any available strips of waste land. (3) By a voluntary choir of singers, who give oratorios and concerts to the poor, singing in hospitals, workhouses, and carrying out a scheme for providing Choral Classes for the people.

This year, there was quite an epidemic of Royal Marriages. The Princess Elizabeth was married to the Prince of Hesse Homburg, the Duke of Clarence to the Princess of Saxe Meiningen, the Duke of Cambridge to the Princess of Hesse, and the Duke of Kent to the Princess Victoria of Saxe Cobourg, the mother of our present Queen, and as ' Sons and Daughters of England,' they were all dutifully provided for.

From Fetters Matrimonial to those of a baser, yet not more

material kind, is an easy transition, and it is pleasing, to record, as an advance in humanity, and civilization, that in April of this year, the disuse of fetters on the prisoners was commenced at Clerkenwell prison, and immediately followed by Newgate.

In May, a woman was arrested for trying to annoy the Queen, and she seems to have had a peculiar penchant for keys. 'On the sentinels being placed on duty on Tuesday night, in the Garden at the back of the Queen's Palace, the key of the garden, belonging to the watch house, could not be found, and it was ascertained she had stolen it. She had been at Carlton House, York House, most of the Courts of Justice, and, in all the places where she gained admittance, she stole keys, or trifling articles. She had stolen, in the whole, 146 keys.'

Schoolboys, now that grown-up men had ceased from rioting, took to it. First of all the Winchester boys caught the disease, and on May 7th, on returning from a ramble on the hills, 'they suddenly attacked the porters, forced from them the keys of the College, and locked out all the Masters. Having thus obtained full possession of the building, they proceeded to take up, with pickaxes, &c., the large stones with which the Court was paved, and soon conveyed upwards of a cart-load of them to the top of the building, threatening any one who approached the gates. In this barricaded state, they kept possession all the night, deaf to the remonstrances of their friends, and bidding defiance to their Masters. On the following morning, after many admonitions were in vain given them to return to their duty, it was found necessary to call out a party of Military, some Constables, &c., who procured crowbars and other instruments to force the gates. Upon observing these preparations, the young gentlemen opened the gates, came out in a body, and many of them went to their respective homes. Twelve ringleaders were expelled ; and about forty of the Gentlemen Commoners have been allowed to resign. There were only six out of 230 who did not join in the revolt.'

Again we read, 'Nov. 14.—During the last week, the boys at Eton College were in a state of rebellion, and offered the grossest indignities to Dr. Keate, the head of the College. By his firm and judicious conduct, however, aided by the other masters, peace was restored on Saturday. Seven of the boys have been expelled.'

The poor Prince Regent could not get popular. On the

7th of July his carriage broke down in South Audley Street, on his way to, or from, the Marquis of Hertford's.   A mob instantly collected, as the carriage was known to be the Prince's.   The blinds were all drawn up and he could not be seen, but they called him naughty names, and said naughty things about him, begging him, not very politely, to show himself.   He endured this for some time, but, afterwards, emerged, and, making his way through a Mews, he took shelter in General Cradock's house, followed, and grossly insulted by the populace.

In October, this year, was issued the Noble Crown piece by Pistrucci, which completed the series of the Silver Coinage. It is remarkable, not only for its beauty, but for the fact that it was the only Crown-piece coined during the long reign of George III.   It had on the reverse St. George and the Dragon, surrounded by the Garter, and excited much controversy, because the Moneyer had introduced his name on the coin.   It was classed with Cardinal Wolsey's famous 'Ego et Rex meus.'

On 10th of November, Capt. Ross and Lieut. Parry returned from their voyage of discovery in the Northern Seas, after a fruitless attempt to pass through Behring's Straits.   They brought home some live Esquimaux dogs, sledges, &c., with specimens of mineralogy, botany, &c., which were deposited in the British Museum for public inspection.

On 17th of November, at Kew Palace, died her Majesty Queen Charlotte ; she had been ailing ever since the previous year, when we have seen her at Bath, latterly she got much worse, but she bore up well against her fatal illness.   She was buried, with great pomp, at Windsor, 2nd of December.

The Queen's Income, latterly, was very good ; by 52 Geo. III., it was settled (independent of the King's establishment at Windsor) at £58,000 a year, with an allowance of £10,000 a year for travelling and other contingent expenses. She had other pickings besides, so that we can scarcely understand her only having left behind her personal property valued at £140,000, of which the greater part consisted of jewels given her by Geo. III. and the Nawab of Arcot.   Those given by the King she left to the House of Hanover as an heir loom.

The Nawab's jewels were to be sold, and the proceeds divided between her four daughters, the Queen of Wurtemburg being excepted, as being sufficiently well provided for.

Her other jewels she desired should be valued, and equally distributed between the said four daughters.

Her landed property she gave away, and directed that her books, plate, house linen, china, pictures, drawings, prints, all articles of ornamental furniture, and all other valuables and personals, should be divided in equal shares among her four youngest daughters.   These are the principal heads of her will.

Of her death, the King, of course, knew nothing, and it was lucky for him that it was so, for he dearly loved his wife, and the homeliness of their natures eminently fitted them for each other.

The last bulletin for this year will as well describe his Majesty's state for the whole twelve months, as if I transcribed every one.   ' *Windsor Castle*, December 5.   His Majesty's tranquillity has been undisturbed throughout the last month, and his Majesty's health has been good ; but his disorder continues in the same state.'

CHAPTER XXVIII.

1819.

Sale of the Queen's effects—Duke of York has custody of the King
—The 'Dandy horse'—Loss of, and finding the King's jewellery
—A public dinner—A Royal freak—Unqualified medical practitioners—Emigration to America—'The fair Circassian'—Birth
of Queen Victoria—Napoleon's carriage—An Irish witness.

'THEY of the household divided the spoil' very shortly after
the old Queen's death.   On the 4th of January, her horses
and carriages were sold at Tattersall's.   Several of the old
horses were shot to prevent them going into abject slavery,
and the fifty-five that remained, sold for £4,544, and eighteen
carriages fetched £1,077.   Messrs. Rundle and Bridge, the
Royal Goldsmiths, apportioned the jewels into four equal lots.

   'January 12.—Part of the Queen's property, consisting of
pieces of silk and satin, gold and silver, figured and plain, not
made up, were measured on Friday, at the Queen's House,
St. James's Park, amounting to 2,140 yards.   They were
presents to her Majesty, or purchases made by her for the
encouragement of the manufactures.   They are of various
prices, from one guinea to five guineas per yard, and many of
them of the most beautiful workmanship—one of them, a
piece of green silk shot with gold, is of the most exquisite
beauty.   This valuable collection the Princesses have, with
their characteristic kindness and generosity, presented to
Madame Beckendorff, as a mark of their esteem for the
favourite of their deceased Royal Parent.   In another apartment was a large store of the most superb shawls, Oriental
presents to her Majesty, but many of them nearly consumed
by moths.'

A great many things were sold privately, but her Oriental

curiosities, &c., were sold at Christie's early in May.   Among
the other things that were to be sold on the 25th of May
were :—
   1. 44 Shillings and 66 Sixpences, chiefly of the present
reign, 5 Crown-pieces, a well-preserved Half-Crown of 1817,
ditto 6 Sixpences 1816, and 11 Bank Tokens.
   2. 170 Silver Groats.
   3. 170 Threepences.
   4. 200 Twopences.
   5. 18 English and foreign Dollars, Crowns, and Bank Tokens,
and 8 English Half-Crowns, 28 Smooth Shillings, 22 English
and foreign Sixpences.
   6. 209 Provincial Tokens.
   These items bear witness to the Queen's saving qualities,
and also to the meanness which prompted the sale of such
comparative trifles—only those were sold which were not
Current Coin—because it was an offence against the law to
sell money that was in use.   Her veriest trifles were sold.
'Among the articles of *vertu* in the last sale of her late
Majesty's Curiosities, were a number of *paper* portraits *cut in
profile* of the members of the illustrious Houses of Brunswick
and of Mecklenburgh Strelitz, both male and female : the
ladies in the costume of 1770, with the head-dresses three
stories high, and with elegant flowing lappets.   Of the same
subjects, the most remarkable was the Lord's Prayer, cut
in paper with a pair of scissors, by an artist born without
hands.'*
   A Satirist brought out an Engraving, ' SALES by AUCTION !
or, Provident Children disposing of their deceased Mother's
effects for the benefit of their Creditors !'   The Regent, gouty
as usual, is the Auctioneer, and his remarks upon the lot he
has for sale, an Indian Shawl, are: ' Here are some genuine
Articles, a present from an Indian Prince to the deceased
owner, and saved entirely for the *Moths,* as they were *never
worn,* given away all her MONEY IN CHARITY.   So, pray, good
people, Bid liberally, or the Children will be destitute.'   The
Princesses are pleading in the same strain, and the Duke of
York is sale Clerk.   A short time previously he had a fall,
caused by one of his spurs catching in a carpet, at Windsor,
and he broke his arm ; he sits comfortably on £10,000 which
was the sum paid him annually, for paying a monthly visit to
his father, to whom he acted as Custodian, after his mother's

* Probably Matthew Buchinger, who died 1722.

'SALES BY AUCTION! OR, PROVIDENT CHILDREN DISPOSING OF THEIR DECEASED MOTHER'S EFFECTS FOR THE BENEFIT OF THEIR CREDITORS.'

death. In January a Bill was brought in, with this provision, but it met with strenuous opposition, as far as the monetary portion went, as it was felt that no son, with any remnant of filial affection left, would, or ought to, take such a sum for occasionally visiting an aged and sorely afflicted parent ; but it finally passed into law. Of course, the Duke of York must have expected, and he certainly got, censure for his greed,

'MAKING MOST OF £10,000 PER AN.'

and we find him pictorially satirised as using one of the then newly invented, and fashionable ' Dandy,' or ' Hobby ' horses —by means of which he could visit his poor old father at Windsor. This engraving is called ' MAKING MOST of £10,000 PER AN., by SAVING TRAVELLING EXPENSES (that is) going on *Monthly* visits to WINDSOR ! as appointed by . . . . having only the small sum of Ten Thousand Pounds per year, granted for

'THE HOBBY HORSE DEALER.'

that arduous task, has wisely procured a pedestrian Hobby Horse.' The Duke comforts himself by saying, 'Every Man has his Hobby Horse, mine is worth Ten Thousand ! ! !'

This parent of the bi- and tri-cycles was only introduced into England early this year. It is said to have been the invention of the Baron Charles de Drais, Master of Woods and Forests to H.R.H. the Grand Duke of Baden. In English it was called the 'Dandy Horse,' because the word Dandy as applied to a fashionably dressed man, had only just been coined ; and Hobby Horse, although it had nothing in common with the barded horse with which jesters used to caracole in mimic jousts with one another. The Germans called it either the German horse, or *Drais Laufmashin ;* the French, *Drais ena.* They were obtainable at Johnson's Repository in Long Acre, and cost about eight pounds each, weight about fifty pounds each, and it was reckoned that, by their means, a man could travel at a speed of eight to ten miles an hour.* The pedestrian sat astride, leaning against a pad in front, and holding the steering cross-bar with his hands, then with his feet alternately, he spurned the ground. For a short time they were very popular, and there are many specimens of them now in existence. The Police were very opposed to them, and gave as a reason that the crowded state of the Metropolis did not admit of this novel method of travelling, and they put a stop to their use.

We get an excellent view of one in 'The Hobby Horse Dealer.' Here we see the poor starved horses looking hungrily out of the Stable windows, and the groom in rags, his occupation gone. Of the Dandies, one critically examines it, and says, ' It seems to me, Jack, not to have quite barrel enough.' His quizzical friend, thinks it has a ' Fine forehand, by Jove.' The dealer, of course, vaunts his goods. ' I'll warrant him sound, and free from vice.' But the would-be purchaser decries it, saying, ' I can see he has been down, once or twice, though, my lad.'

I don't think 'the Lady's Accelerator' ever came into vogue, even among the ' Dandizettes.'

It was a lucky thing that there was a regular clear out of the old Queen's things; for many of the poor old King's jewels had been missing for a long time, and their disappearance had caused much uneasiness. Messrs. Rundle and

* A trip to Brighton, say a little over fifty miles, is recorded to have been done in nine hours.

'THE LADY'S ACCELERATOR.'

Bridge had been for several days examining and estimating
the value of the Queen's jewels, preparatory to their being
divided between the four princesses. When this was satisfactorily accomplished, the Prince Regent came to see the
division, and the Princess Augusta also was present. On the
jewels being apportioned into four several heaps of equal
value, a question arose about the manner in which they were
to be packed, until it should be necessary to reproduce them.

One of the female attendants suggested that, in a lumber
room, not very far distant from her late Majesty's apartments,
a number of empty boxes were stowed, which had been used
on former occasions, as cases, in which the Royal Jewels had
been carried to and from the Bank of England (where they
are usually deposited) to Buckingham House ; and 'perhaps,'
said she, 'these may serve the purpose for which they are
wanted, without troubling Messrs. Rundle and Bridge to send
for fresh packages from their house in town.' The suggestion was thought good ; and the boxes were accordingly
ordered to be produced before the Royal Company. In
examining one of them, which at first sight appeared to be
filled with nothing more than the lawn, or silver paper, in
which jewellery is usually enveloped, the King's sword
handle, star, loop, garter, and other jewels were unexpectedly
discovered.

It is well, sometimes, to read what other nations think of
us, and our customs, even if it be Max O'Rell and water, and
we find in a Newspaper of Feb. 13th, the following. It will
create a smile to read the account of English Manners given
by a Frenchman, who, on the authority of a short residence,
takes upon himself to describe, and expose our peculiarities.
A little volume, entitled 'A Year in London,' gives the following account of a public Tavern Dinner :—

'Few days pass in London without public Dinners. Our
traveller acquainted a Portuguese Jew, long resident in
London, with the desire he had to make one at this kind of
entertainment. " Nothing is so easy. How do you go to the
play ?" " I pay for a ticket at the door." " How do you see
Westminster Abbey ?" " I pay a shilling at every door they
open for me." " How do you see St. Paul's, the Tower, the
Crown Jewels ?" "The same way, I pay." " You see, then,
in London, you have only to pay ; you must, however, take
care to have your name put down two days before, for
decency's sake, that you may not have the appearance of

going to a Table d'Hôte ; but I will put you down for one
that is to take place to-morrow."

'Each having paid 15s. entrance,' says our traveller, ' we
were introduced into a large dining-room, surrounded by
tables, where, already, were seated about two hundred guests,
though the tables were only covered with a cloth ; there were,
at the top of the room, about six vacant places, but we were
told they were for the singers ; twelve or fifteen persons, who,
like ourselves, had arrived a little too late, walked about in
the middle of the room. At length we were invited into
another room, much less than the first, and where tables were
set in the same manner to accommodate about forty persons.
A waiter brought soup, and a heap of plates ; he who was
nearest took possession, and distributed it to those nearest
him, before a second tureen was placed at the other end of
the table, and that, also, disappeared, before the arrival of a
third. This soup is called mock turtle, that is, pieces of
Calves' head, and Oxtails floating in the water in which they
are dressed, and has no flavour but pepper, which had not
been spared.

'Soon afterwards, the table was covered with a profusion of
roast and boiled meat, that everybody began to hack at the
same time—and vegetables, boiled in *water*, the only sauce
given to them in this country. I had hardly finished my
plate of mock turtle, when it was loaded with a wing of boiled
fowl, an enormous piece of roast beef, a slice of hot ham, a
potato, two carrots, and leaves of boiled, not chopped spinach,
completed the pyramid. No one thought of drinking, for the
English, in general, are not thirsty till no longer hungry ; in
about a quarter of an hour, they cleared away, and put down
apple tarts, in comparison with which, our village pastry are
models of excellence, some salads eaten without seasoning,
and cheese, to which some added mustard and salt : they then
placed before each guest a bottle of red wine, or sherry, as he
preferred ; hardly was this done, when five or six persons rose
from the table, carrying in one hand their glass, in the other,
their bottle : every one imitated them ; I followed and did as
the others, and we found ourselves in the great room, standing
between the tables, shoved by a crowd of waiters, who were
clearing away. Oranges and nuts were brought, which my
companions below often pillaged before they arrived at their
destination. At last, after having been squeezed, pushed, and
elbowed, for half an hour, we succeeded in obtaining some

seats in the middle of the room, each having his bottle between his knees, and glass in his hand. After every health, one of the singers amused the Company with a song ; a pause of some minutes ensued, and the same thing was repeated.'

Doubtless, but for the finding of oxtails in Mock Turtle Soup, this is a very accurate sketch of a Charity dinner of the time, and it bears the impress of truth upon it.

Apropos of feeding, we may read the following travesty of the 'mad young prince,' afterwards the wise Henry V. ' Brighton, March 13, ROYAL FREAK.—We are assured, that a few nights ago, the REGENT, in a merry mood, determined to sup in the kitchen of the Pavilion. A scarlet cloth was thrown over the pavement, a splendid repast was provided, and the good-humoured PRINCE sat down, with a select party of his friends, and spent a joyous hour. The whole of the servants, particularly the female part, were, of course, delighted with this mark of Royal condescension.' Of this supper there were numerous Satirical prints, and I have chosen the least offensive of them, which is really laughable, the Prince being so ' royally drunk.' It is called ' HIGH LIFE BELOW STAIRS ! ! a new Farce, as lately performed at the Theatre *Royal*, Brighton, for the edification and amusement of the Cooks, Scullions, Dish-Washers, Lick-Trenchers, Shoe-Blacks, Cinder-Sifters, Candle-Snuffers, &c., &c., of that Theatre, but which was unfortunately Damn'd the first night, by Common Sense !'

When ill, the good folks of that time, must, especially in the country, have been very much at the mercy of quack practitioners. It is true that both the Apothecaries' Company, and the College of Surgeons were in existence, and had been, the former since 1670, the latter since 1745, but their diplomas were not considered absolutely necessary in order to practise Medicine. I give an instance early in April. ' At the Stafford Assizes a cause was brought on at the suit of the Apothecaries' Company, against the son of a man who had been originally a gardener, but who had long exercised the business of a *cow-leech*, and *quack doctor ;* the son claiming a right of following the profession of an apothecary, through having studied under his renowned father.

' In the cross-examination of the father by Mr. Dauncey, he was asked if he had always been a surgeon. The witness appealed to the Judge, if this was a proper *answer !* and whether he must reply to it ; and, at last, said : " I am a

'HIGH LIFE BELOW STAIRS!!'

surgent." Mr. Dauncey asked him to spell this word, which he did at several times, viz., " Syurgunt, surgend, surgunt, sergund." Mr. Dauncey said, " I am afraid, Sir, you do not often take so much time to study the cases which come before you, as you do to answer my question."—" I do not, Sir."— Witness said he never employed himself as a gardener, but was a farmer until he learnt his present business. Mr. Dauncey asked, " Who did you learn it of ?"—" I learnt it of Dr. Holme, my brother-in-law ; he practised the same as the Whitworth doctors, and they were regular physicians."—Mr. Dauncey : " Where did they take their degrees ?"—Witness : " I don't believe they ever took a degree."—" Then were they regular physicians ?"—" No, I believe they were not ; they were only doctors."—" Only doctors ! were they doctors in law, physic, or divinity ?"—" They doctored cows, and other things, and *humans* as well."—Judge to witness : " Did you ever make up any medicine by the prescriptions of a physician ?" — " I never did." — " Do you understand the characters they use for ounces, scruples, and drachms ?"— " I do not."—" Then you cannot make up their prescriptions from reading them ?"—" I cannot, but I can make up as good medicines in my way, as they can in theirs."—" What proportion does an ounce bear to a pound ?" (a pause).—" There are sixteen ounces to the pound ; but we do not go by any regular weight ; we mix ours by the hand."—" Do you bleed ?" —" Yes."—" With a fleam, or with a lancet ?"—" With a lancet."—" Do you bleed from the vein, or from the artery ?" —" From the vein."—" There is an artery somewhere about the temples ; what is the name of that artery ?"—" I do not pretend to have as much learning as some have."—" Can you tell me the name of that artery ?"—" I do not know which you mean."—" Suppose, then, I was to direct you to bleed my servant, or my horse (which God forbid), in a vein, say, for instance, the jugular vein, where should you bleed him ?" —" In the neck, to be sure."—The Jury, almost instantly returned a verdict for the plaintiffs.'

Over-population, coupled with distress, was beginning to be felt ; and the tide of emigration began to flow, naturally to America, because of its proximity, and consequent cheapness of Carriage : but Australia and New Zealand, also had their attractions—the flax (*Phormium tenax*) of the latter place having already been experimented upon at Portsmouth Dockyard, and favourably reported on as a good material for rope-making, and its cost, delivered here, was put down at £8 a ton, or a seventh of the then price of Hemp.

Yet America was the favourite place of emigration, and we read, under date of April 14th : ' The spirit of emigration from Portsmouth continues unabated. Every packet for Havre, conveys numerous passengers destined for America ; and not less than five hundred Englishmen are supposed to be now at Havre, waiting for a fair wind, many of whom have been there upwards of a month. About seventy persons, chiefly artisans and mechanics, with women and children, amounting in the whole to at least two hundred, have embarked during last week, intending to proceed from Havre in an American brig belonging to Baltimore, which has been taken up expressly for the purpose. The expenses of the voyage are to be defrayed out of a fund which has been accumulating for some time past, by a small weekly subscription, and the total charge for each passenger, is said to be less than £4.'

A foreign Embassy was something unusual in those days, and when they came two at a time, it gave people something to talk about. First to arrive was an Ambassador from Algiers ; and then came the Persian Ambassador, who created almost as great a sensation as did the Shah when he came here in 1873. This ambassador was accompanied by a ' fair Circassian,' whom people raved about, although no one ever saw her face. Here is the contemporary account of their arrival :—

' DOVER, *April 25th.*—About three this afternoon, his Majesty's schooner *Pioneer* arrived in the roads, and very shortly after, the boat belonging to the Customs put off under a salute. She had on board the Persian Ambassador and suite, who, on landing, were greeted with another salute from the guns on the heights. As the schooner had been seen for some time before her arrival, there was an amazing concourse of people assembled on the beach, and the novel nature of the arrival of ten or a dozen persons, habited in silks and turbans, with daggers, and long beards, in no small degree attracted the attention of the inhabitants, whose curiosity had been raised to the highest pitch by the different accounts of the beauty of the fair Circassian ; and, had not a coach been provided at the water's edge, I much doubt if his Excellency and suite would have reached the Inn without considerable difficulty.

' The crowd followed to Wright's Hotel nearly as fast as

the Carriage, it being reported by some, that the fair female was in a mask, under the habit of a male attendant, whilst others stated she would not be landed till the middle of the night.   In about half an hour, however, from the arrival of the first boat, a second boat came into the harbour, and landed the Circassian Beauty !   She was attended from the schooner by Lieutenant Graham of the Preventive service, and two black eunuchs.   She was scarcely seen ; for the instant she landed, she was put into a Coach which conveyed her to the Inn.   She had on a hood, which covered the upper part of her head, and a large silk shawl screened the lower part of her face, across the nose, from observation ; therefore her eyes, which are truly beautiful, and part of her forehead, were the only parts of her beauties that could be seen.   She is of middle stature, and appeared very interesting.   Her look was languid from illness, arising from a rough passage.   She was conducted to a bedroom on reaching the inn, but no one was allowed to attend her but the eunuchs.'

They gave the Ambassador plenty of time to recover from his sea voyage, for he did not have an audience of the Regent, until the 20th of May, when he had a magnificent reception. All the Royal Servants put off their mourning for the Queen, and appeared in their State liveries.   The thing was done in style.   ' The procession of his Excellency was preceded by a numerous detachment from the Corps of Lancers, followed by six of the Prince Regent's Carriages, with servants in their State liveries, five of them drawn by six bays, and the sixth by six superior black horses, surrounded by a numerous detachment of the Royal Horse Guards.   The Arabian horses brought by his Excellency to England, as a present to the Prince Regent, were drawn up in the front of Carlton House in the Courtyard at the time of the arrival of his Excellency. In five of the Carriages were four of his Excellency's attendants dressed in the Costume of their Country, Mr. Morier, the Mehmander, and Captain Willock ; two of the Carriages contained presents brought for the Regent ; among them were a most magnificent, costly sword, the sheath ornamented with emeralds, rubies, and diamonds, also two large silver salvers, on one of which was a splendid Cabinet, and on the other, a numerous collection of large pearls, besides other valuable articles.

' His Excellency was attended in his Carriage by the Marquess of Headfort, who was specially appointed, with

Sir Robert Chester, to conduct the Ambassador into the presence of the Regent. His Excellency was dressed in a rich embroidered robe; his turban ornamented with jewels, carrying a silver stick or staff, his Excellency leaning on the arm of Sir Robert Chester, being a little lame from a kick he received on Tuesday from one of his horses. . . .

'At half-past three the Algerine Ambassador, attended by Mr. Salame, his Excellency's interpreter, arrived at Carlton House in one of the Regent's Carriages, the servants in their State liveries, with the six beautiful horses brought by his Excellency as a present to the Regent; three of them light greys, one iron grey, one black; one of the light greys had been ridden by the Dey of Algiers, and was most richly, and costly caparisoned, with a saddle, shabrac, bridle, winkers, and holsters most richly embroidered with gold, with wide silver stirrups, made according to the fashion of that Country, with filigree ornaments. The other numerous and costly presents were sent to Carlton House in the course of the morning.'

'The fair Circassian' was once, if not oftener, interviewed by some ladies of 'the upper ten.' 'May 13. THE FAIR CIRCASSIAN.—The above much-talked of female, was, by permission of her keeper, his Excellency the Persian Ambassador, introduced on Monday last to upwards of twenty ladies of fashionable distinction, friends of his Excellency. The introduction took place between one and two o'clock, in the front drawing-room at his Excellency's residence in Charles Street, Berkeley Square. The fair stranger was elegantly attired in the costume of her country; her dress was a rich white satin, fringed with gold, with a bandeau round her head, and wreaths of diamonds. She received her visitors with graceful affability, and they were highly pleased with her person and manners. She is not, as has been represented, short and slender, she is of the middle stature, of exquisite symmetry, rather *en bon point*: her complexion is of a brownish cast, her hair of a jet black, with beautiful arched black eyebrows, handsome black, penetrating eyes, her features regular, and strikingly handsome. The Ladies were highly gratified, and passed great encomiums on the elegance of her person. Lady Augusta Murray presented the fair Circassian with a beautiful nosegay, with which she seemed highly pleased.'

She returned before the Ambassador, who stayed in England about a year, going through England, Ireland, and Scotland. She sailed for Constantinople on the 31st of August.

22

On the 1st of May Lieutenant Parry sailed from England, having under his command the *Hecla* and *Griper*, being bound for another voyage of discovery in the Arctic regions.

On the 24th of May was born our beloved Sovereign Lady, Queen Victoria. About that time, her father, the Duke of Kent, who, like all his brothers, was deeply in debt, although he claimed to have reduced his liabilities down to £60,000, applied to Parliament (July 2nd) for leave to dispose of his house at Castlebar Hill, and its furniture, by lottery, for a sum of £50,000. His case was warmly pleaded by Alderman Wood, who said that out of an income of £24,000, he put by £17,000 for liquidation of his debts. This assertion was, however, traversed by Sir Charles Burrell, who showed that his Royal Highness at that moment had an income of above £31,000, made up thus — Out of the Consolidated Fund £18,000 ; £7,000 from the Government of Gibraltar ; £6,000 on his late marriage ; and the revenue of the Colonelcy of the Scots Royals, with the usual allowance for clothing that regiment. In the face of these facts, it was no use going on with the motion, and it was withdrawn.

Both Queen and Princess Charlotte being dead, and the Princess of Wales not being received at Court, and, besides, being abroad, the holding of a Drawing-Room, so necessary for launching Society young ladies into life, and for their admission into Foreign Courts in after-life, seemed rather problematical ; but the Board of Green Cloth, or whatever other authority had it in hand, was equal to the occasion, and a precedent was found in the case of George II., who was accustomed to hold drawing-rooms after the death of Queen Caroline. Therefore the Regent held a Drawing-room all by himself, and we read that 'the Court was a very crowded one, and the presentations were very numerous.'

The following paragraph may interest some of the millions of people who have visited the ever-popular exhibition of Madame Tussaud : 'July 16. BONAPARTE'S CARRIAGE, &c.—At the late sale of the contents of Mr. Bullock's Museum, the articles brought a much higher price than was originally expected. Bonaparte's Carriage, and the different dressing materials it contained, and which were taken by the Prussians at Waterloo, were sought with great avidity. The following are the prices they brought :—

'For the Carriage, which had been exhibited in every town of the Empire, and was quite worn out in the service, there

were several bidders.   It was originally built at Brussels, and
had been used by Bonaparte in the last Russian Campaign, and
subsequently at Elba, and finally in Flanders—

It was knocked down for ...	...	£168	0	0
The Opera Glass	...	...	5	5	0
Tooth brush	...	...	...	3	13	6
Snuff-box	...	...	...	166	19	6
Military Stock or Collar	...	...	1	17	0
Old Slippers	...	...	...	1	0	0
Common Razor ...	...	...	4	4	0
Piece of Sponge ...	...	...	0	17	6
Shaving-brush	...	...	...	3	14	0
Shirt ...	...	...	...	2	5	0
Comb ...	...	...	...	1	0	0
Shaving box	...	...	...	7	7	0
Pair of Gloves ...	...	...	1	0	0
Pocket Handkerchief	...	...	1	11	6.'

In my search through newspapers of this time I came
across the following—which belongs to no section of this book,
and yet is too good to leave out : ' IRISH EVIDENCE.—During a
trial at the Carlow Assizes, on the 29th ult. (July, 1819), on
an indictment for stealing 30 lbs. of tobacco, the following
confessions were extracted from an accomplice in the robbery,
who was admitted King's evidence—

'Q. How many robberies have you been at altogether?

'A. Together! (laughter.) Why, sure I could not be at
more than one at a time.

'Q. You certainly have knocked me down by that answer
(loud laughter in Court). Come, now, tell us how many you
have been at?

'A. I never put them down, for I never thought it would
come to my turn to give an account of them.

'Q. By virtue of your oath, Sir, will you swear you have not
been at fifteen?

'A. I would not (witness laughing).

'Q. Would you swear that you have not been at twenty?

'A. I would not (still laughing).

'Q. Do you recollect robbing the Widow Byrne in the
County of Wicklow?

'A. The Widow Byrne—who is she? May be it is big Nell
you mean? Oh! I only took a trifle of whisky from her,
that's all.

' Q. Was it day or night ?

' A. (*laughing*). Why it was night, to be sure.

' Q. Did you not rob the poor woman of every article in the house ; even her bed-clothes, and the clothes off her back ?

' A. I took clothes, but they were not on her back.

' Q. Do you recollect stealing two flitches of bacon from Dovan, the Wexford Carman ?

' A. Faith ! I do, and a pig's head beside ! (*loud laughter in Court*).

' Q. Do you recollect robbing John Keogh, in the County of Wicklow, and taking every article in his house ?

' A. You're wrong there ; I did not take everything ; I only took his money, and a few other things ! (*Witness and the Auditory laughing immoderately.*)

' Q. Why, you're a mighty good-humoured fellow?

' A. There isn't a better-humoured fellow in the County— there may be honester.'

CHAPTER XXIX.

Reform Meetings—Peterloo—Orator Hunt's entry into London—
The King's last illness and death.

But I must return to my Chronicle. There were Reform
Meetings everywhere. The evils in the Representation of the
people were patent to everybody who would see, but the
Regent was not gifted with that perspicuity of vision that is
suitable to a Ruler of Men, and his blindness led to deplorable
results, which, after all, were probable benefits, inasmuch as
they hastened the passing of the Reform Bill. Things were
beginning to look ugly. In some districts the people were
beginning to drill, and they were not of the best class. *Vide*
the following—

'MANCHESTER, Aug. 15.—The circumstances of parties going
out to drill, having been much talked about here, *viz.*, John
Shawcross, of Blossom Street, Salford, and James Murray, of
Withy Grove, Manchester, set out this morning, about one
o'clock, for the purpose of ascertaining this fact. On their
way towards Middleton, these two persons passed several
squads who were in regular Marching Order, and they heard
a great many more parties calling to each other, and, from the
answers being more distant, every time they were repeated,
suppose the fields for some extent, contained different parties.

'The place appointed for a general muster was Whitemoss,
betwixt Middleton and Oldham. When Murray and Shawcross arrived at this spot, there were at least five hundred men
at drill; the greater part were drilled in a body; there were
also detached squads of fifteen or twenty each.'

The two men were found, pounced upon as spies, and nearly
kicked to death.

I give this passage, as it shows that armed men were preparing themselves for a conflict with the civil power, which

they certainly thought imminent, yet like all cowardly English Mobs, they howled most valiantly, and complained of the butchery, when they came into conflict with even Citizen Soldiery. There are some people still who regard ' Peterloo ' as a massacre of the innocents : they must be either very wrong-headed, or very badly informed. Let me give the shortest, and most succinct, contemporaneous account of that memorable day.

' Aug. 16. A meeting of Reformers took place at Manchester, on a vacant piece of ground, on the north side of St. Peter's. The number of persons from Oldham, Saddleworth, Royton, and other places, were supposed to be at least 50,000, bearing banners inscribed " Hunt and Liberty "— " Universal Suffrage "—" Annual Parliaments," &c., and a Club of female Reformers also joined the group. Mr. Henry Hunt was called to the Chair, and commenced an harangue on the usual topics of public grievances, during which, the Manchester Yeomanry Cavalry, aided by the Cheshire Yeomanry Cavalry, and the 15th Hussars, advanced to the crowd, and rode through them, sword in hand ; and having arrived at the waggon, from which the orator was declaiming, Mr. Nadin, the police officer, arrested Hunt and Johnson, on a warrant. They submitted quietly and were taken to gaol. The Cavalry then rode through the mob, and seized their banners, in doing which, several persons were killed and wounded ; bricks and other missiles were thrown at the Cavalry, who, however, succeeded in dispersing the mob : several other persons were taken into custody in the course of the day.'

Such is an unvarnished tale of Peterloo, and the student of history must ever bear in mind, that at this period, there were no police, as we know them, and that in case of riot the Military were always called out, and that they had but to obey orders.

The Radical papers held it, of course, to be a brutal massacre, and I give one print which takes a highly poetical view of it. It is called ' The Massacre at St. Peter's ; or, " Britons, strike home ! ! !" ' The officer on extreme left calls out to his corps of butchers, ' Down with 'em ! Chop 'em down ! my brave boys ! give them no quarter. They want to take our Beef and Pudding from us ! And, remember, the more you kill, the less poor's rates you'll have to pay ; so, go it, lads, show your Courage, and your Loyalty !' This is about as

THE MASSACRE AT ST. PETER'S; OR, 'BRITONS, STRIKE HOME!!

truthful as nine-tenths of what has been written about ‘ Peterloo.’

This was the occasion, of which I have written, that Hunt got fined. When he was bailed, he made a ‘ triumphal entry ’ into London. Of course, like all his class, he was nothing except he was *en évidence*. It was well organized : there was the young man from Manchester, who had got hurt at ‘ Peterloo,’ there was a huge dog with a large white collar, bearing thereon, ‘ No dog tax,’ and at last came the procession itself.

Horsemen.

Footmen bearing a bundle of Sticks, the emblem of Unity.

Horsemen.

Six Irish footmen, bearing a green flag, with the inscription, ‘ Universal, Civil and Religious Liberty.’

Horsemen.

Footmen, bearing a flag of mourning—Inscription, ‘ To the immortal Memory of the Reformers . . . at Manchester.’

Horsemen.

Footmen bearing a flag — Inscription, ‘ The Palladium of Liberty—Liberty of the Press.’

Carriages for Gentlemen connected with the Press.

Horsemen.

Footmen, bearing a Red flag—Inscription, ‘ Universal Suffrage.’

A Landau, containing Mr. HUNT, preceded by a flag, with this inscription, ‘ Hunt, the heroic Champion of Liberty,’ and surrounded by six horsemen, and Members of the Committee.

Carriages and Footmen.

A Landau, with Watson, Thistlewood, and Preston, and their Friends.

Flag—‘ Trial by Jury.’

Horsemen and Footmen.

Flag—‘ Liberty or Death.’

Carriages, Horsemen, and Footmen.

Flag—‘ Liberty or Death.’

Closed by Horses, Carriages, and Footmen.

There! does not that read like a modern Irish Procession to the Reformer's tree in Hyde Park? It had the same value and the same result—somebody got paid something. There were also riots in Scotland, both in Paisley and Glasgow.

I am approaching the end of my Chronicle of the Regency. In November, it could not be concealed that the poor old King was very bad; in fact, now and then it was rumoured that he was dead. And so he was to himself, and to the world. Nature was having its grand and final fight; and in a few weeks the mortal life of George III. would be closed. How well the following description of the old King tallies with the scarce portrait which forms the frontispiece to this volume: ' His MAJESTY.—A gentleman who has been in his presence a short time ago, states, that the appearance of our aged Monarch, is the most venerable imaginable. His hair and beard are white as the drifted Snow, and the latter flows gracefully over a breast which now feels neither the pleasures nor the pains of life. When the gentleman saw him, he was dressed in a loose Satin robe, lined with fur, sitting in an apparently pensive mood, with his elbows on a table, and his head resting on his hands, and seemed perfectly regardless of all external objects ' (*Bath Journal*).

Still they hoped when there was no hope, for, under date November 26th is the following : ' The examination of his Majesty's Physicians by the Members of the Council, at Lambeth Palace, has made a strong sensation on the public mind, as they conceive that it could only be occasioned by the conviction in the breast of his Royal Highness the Duke of York, that the inquiry became necessary. The result of the examination has not transpired. Report says that his Majesty has shown symptoms of decay, by the wasting of his person, and general weakness, which, at the advanced age of eighty-two, are signs not to be overlooked : but we believe, that immediate danger is not apprehended.'

On the 23rd of January death claimed the Duke of Kent, the father of our present Queen; and on the 29th God took to Himself the poor old King—which event necessarily brings to a close my Chronicles of the

REGENCY.

CHAPTER XXX.

A foreigner's view of England—The packets—Roads—People—
Posting — Mail and Stage Coaches—Amateur coachmen — Fast
driving—Perils of travelling—A lioness attacks the Mail—Dog-
carts and donkey-riding—The Streets and Houses.

WHAT was England like at this time? I have notes enough,
and to spare, *de omnibus rebus,* for a volume upon it; but I
withdraw, and allow a foreigner to give his impressions, and
we shall have the advantage of viewing England with other
spectacles.* I extract from a book by 'M. de Levis, Duke
and Peer of France,' an English translation of which was
published in 1815.

Of course steamboats were not, and that 'silver streak'
between France and England, was even more of a bugbear
than it is at present. 'Foreigners who visit England in time
of peace, usually pass through Dover; this port being the
nearest point of land to the Continent of Europe. The
distance is only seven leagues, but the passage is not the less
uncertain; it varies from two hours to thirty-six, when it
becomes excessively fatiguing; obliged to struggle against
the wind in a narrow sea, and in which it is impossible to
make long tacks. . . . The cabin is so low that you cannot
stand upright; it usually contains eight beds placed two by
two upon one another, like drawers, in a bureau. The disagreeable smell of the bedding, and of the whole furniture,
increases the sickness which the horizontal position would
tend to alleviate. This sickness is not dangerous, but it is
very severe, and sometimes persons of a delicate habit ex-

* 'O wad some Pow'r the giftie gie us,
   To see oursels as others see us!'
               BURNS, 'To a Louse, on seeing one on a
                         Lady's bonnet, at Church.'

perience the effects of it for several days. However, if this passage be often painful, and always disagreeable, it is, at least, very safe. *In times of peace, few days pass without packet boats crossing the Channel,** and we never hear of shipwrecks. The usual price for the passage is one guinea for gentlemen, and half for servants; the hire of the whole vessel costs from five to ten guineas, according to the condition of the travellers.'

On landing, next to the comeliness of the women and children, the men's dress seems to have struck him. 'Their dress is equally remarkable for its fulness, uniformity, and neatness. Those scanty clothes, so mean, and strangely absurd, which we meet with, on the Continent, are never found in Britain, still less are the worn-out and dirty clothes, which, preserving the traces of a luxury, unsuitable to the condition of those who wear them, appear to be the livery of wretchedness: on the contrary, all the apparel here seems at first sight fresh from the manufactory, and the same taylor appears to have cut the Coats of the whole nation. . . .

'Large scarlet cloaks, black silk bonnets, which preserve and heighten the fairness of their Complexion, distinguish the country women who come to market. When a class, so inferior, is so well dressed, we cannot doubt of the prosperity and comfort of the nation to which it belongs.'

Of course there were no railroads, and people had the choice of three conveyances, as they now have the choice of three classes. For people of very slender purses, there was the Waggon—very slow, but bound to get to its destination safely—with many horses, having bells, and yokes to the hames of their Collars; broad-tyred wheels, which could not even sink in the mud of a country lane. But M. le Duc de Levis could not patronize such a vehicle—he, of course, must go post. 'The Post is not, as on the Continent, an establishment dependent upon the Government; individuals undertake this business; most of the inns keep Post Chaises; they are good Carriages with four wheels, shut close, the same kind as we call in France "*diligences de ville.*" They hold three persons in the back with ease; are narrow, extremely light; well hung, and appear the more easy, because the roads are not paved with stone. The postillions wear a jacket with sleeves, tight boots, and, altogether, their dress is light, and extremely neat; and they are not only civil, but even respectful.

'On your arrival at the Inn, you are shown into a good

* My italics.—J. A.

room, where a fire is kept in winter, and tea is ready every hour of the day. In five minutes at most, another Chaise is

MARKET WOMEN.

ready for your departure. If we compare these customs with those of Germany, or particularly in the North, where you

must often wait whole hours to change horses, in a dirty
room, heated by an iron stove, the smell of which is suffo-
cating; or even those of France, where the most part of the
post-houses, not being Inns, have no accommodation for
travellers, it is evident that the advantage is not in favour
of the Continent. The only inconvenience attached to the
manner which I am describing, is being obliged at almost
every stage to untie and pack up baggage and parcels; but
English gentlemen (which will appear very extraordinary to

THE WAGGON.

French ladies) and English ladies carry so little with them,
that this inconvenience is little felt. By this manner of
travelling we avoid *ennui*, and immense expense, and delays
caused by frequent mending of Carriages, which sometimes
occasion the loss of rest on the road.

'Competition is, of course, established, and the interest of
the postmasters obliges them to keep good carriages: there
are many that for their neatness may excite the envy of the
foreigner. The price of travelling is the same throughout
England, one shilling a mile for horses and carriage, without

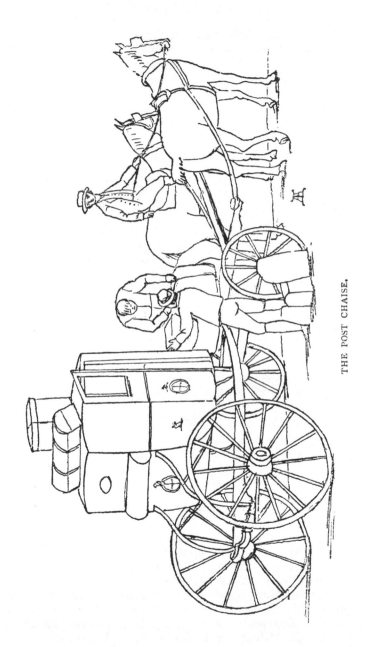

THE POST CHAISE.

reckoning what is given to the postillion; this is extremely cheap, considering the high price of every article, and even in proportion to other Countries; at those times when forage is dear, a few pence are added, but this is never done without the concurrence of the principal postmasters of the Country. When quick travelling is desired, four horses are provided, driven by two postillions, and then travelling is performed with a rapidity known only in Russia and Sweden in the winter season.

'The Mail Coaches also afford means of travelling with great celerity into all parts of England. These are Berlins, firm and light, holding four persons; they carry only letters, and do not take charge of any luggage. They are drawn by four horses, and driven by one Coachman; they travel never less than seven to eight miles an hour.

'Stage Coaches are very numerous, they are kept in every City, and even in small towns; all these Carriages have small wheels, and hold six persons, without reckoning the outside passengers. About twenty years ago a carriage was invented in the form of a gondola; it is long, and will hold sixteen persons, sitting face to face; the door is behind, and this plan ought to be generally adopted, as the only means of escaping a great danger when the horses run away. What adds to the singularity of these carriages is, that they have eight wheels; thus dividing equally the weight, they are less liable to be overturned, or cut up the roads; they are, besides, very low and easy.

'When these long coaches first appeared at Southampton, a City much frequented in summer by the rich inhabitants of London, who go there to enjoy sea bathing, they had (as every new thing has) a great run, so that it was nearly impossible to get a place in them.

'One of the principal Innkeepers, jealous of this success, set up another, and, to obtain the preference, he reduced the fare to half-price, at that time a guinea. In order to defeat this manœuvre, the first proprietor made a still greater reduction, so that, at last, the receipts did not cover the expenses. But the two rivals did not stop here; for one of them announced that he would take nothing of gentlemen who might honour him by choosing his Coach, but he would beg them to accept a bottle of Port before their departure.'

After this, I think I must, for a while, leave my French Duke, and follow my own Notes, on the road.

This was a transition age.   Sedan Chairs were still used,
especially for State occasions.   March 26, 1814: 'The Queen
and Princesses went in Sedan Chairs on Thursday evening, in
the same order as on Wednesday evening, to dine with the

THE MAIL COACH.

Prince Regent at Carlton House.' Nor is this the only
example that could be adduced.

   Then, as now, there was among a certain class, an ambition
to do something, if only to drive a Coach.   By the way there

is no ambition among 'Noble Swells' to drive Omnibuses.
Like 'Tommy Onslow,' who could not only drive a Coach and
two, but a Coach and four, the gilded youths of that time
sought a cheap renown, as do our modern bankers and linen-
drapers, by driving public coaches!! *Chacun à son gout.* As
Artemus Ward said : ' It isn't my fort,' but it gives pleasure to
somebody else, and nobody ought to grumble at it. It may
give amusement to some noble lords, or otherwise, to ape the
fashion of the late James Selby, or some other professional
Jehu, or for a barber's Clerk to pay a trifle extra to sit on the
box seat by the side of My Lord ; but, in the old days they
took things at a better value, and pointed out its folly.
January 26, 1811 : ' The education of our youth of fashion is
improving daily ; several of them now drive Stage Coaches to
town, and open the door of the Carriage for passengers, while
the Coachman remains on the box. They farm the *perquisites*
from the Coachman on the road, and generally pocket something into the bargain.'

January 30, 1811 : ' The prominent figure cut by our *young
men of fashion* on the Coach box makes them a fit subject for
ridicule on any stage.'

They used to drive fast in those days. ' Mr. Milton, the
Horse-dealer, has made a match for seven hundred guineas to
drive four-in-hand, 15 miles in 48 minutes, to start the week
before the Epsom races commence, and to be done within 20
miles of London. Betting is against the undertaking.' One
more Newspaper cutting *re* fast driving, and I have done.
May 16, 1815 : ' We have been much shocked by reading in
some papers accounts of the extraordinary expedition of the
several Leeds Coaches, occasioned, we suppose, by opposition
among themselves. One Coach boasts of having reached
Newark from London in 12 hours, a distance of 124 miles,
and which takes the Edinburgh Mail 17 hours to perform.
Another is said regularly to reach Leeds from London (194
miles) in less than 21 hours ! This is certainly most astonishing velocity, but how great must be the sufferings of the poor
horses thus unnaturally urged.'

Brighton was not only the abode of the Regent, but,
naturally, everyone who wanted to be somebody, went there,
to pay their Court. As we know it now, it is the promised
land of the Hebrew, and the delight of 'Arry and 'Arriette,
shrimps, winkles, and the small half-quartern glass bottle.
But, dear me ! Brighton had fast Coaches then, as now—when

fools and professionals drive them, and are cheap heroes; and they gloried in publishing the fact that a horse could go quicker than a man! A noble Ambition! Put this and that of our times together, and how do we—in Australian language —'pan out'? We, nationally, do not seem to get wiser as we get older.

Under date October 17, 1816, we read : 'A new coach was started by some Jews in the Spring to run to Brighton, a distance of 52 miles, in six hours, with a pledge, that if they did not accomplish the journey in that time, they would carry the passengers gratis; to accomplish which the horses were kept upon a gallop all the way; and, notwithstanding this great risk, the coach was always filled with passengers. In one of the journeys the Coachman broke three whips. In one week 15 horses died.' The authorities had, however, to interfere, as they considered this speed both dangerous and cruel. On July 14, 1888, a professional coachman, named James Selby, who had accepted a bet of £1,000 that he could not drive from White Horse Cellars, Piccadilly, to Brighton and back to the same place, within eight hours, did it, and had ten minutes to spare. In 1818 there were thirty-seven coaches which left and returned to Brighton daily.

There were perils in travelling then, as now, only perhaps for the percentage of travellers, rather more so. There were highwaymen, though they were getting somewhat scarce. But the wheels came off, horses kicked over the traces, reins broke; and there are a thousand and one little accidents arising from man's subjugation of the horse, which are almost inseparable from their mutual positions; but we hardly expect to hear that on October 27th, 1812, one of the Hampstead stages got blown over by the wind. We have already heard that passengers were occasionally frozen to death outside a Coach. But there is one peril one would scarcely have discounted. In Railway travelling, if a cow gets on the line, and tilts with dire onslaught at the train, Stephenson's grim speech, 'So much the worse for the Coo,' is verified; but when a lioness breaks loose, and attacks the horses of a Stage Coach, it strikes me that the 'Coo' is the passenger thereby.

This was a little item of news which enlivened the good folks of 1816, for on October 20th of that year the Exeter Mail Coach, on its way to London, was attacked, at Winterslow-hut, seven miles from Salisbury, by a lioness who had escaped from a passing menagerie; she sprang at one of the leaders, and for some time things were rather mixed. Two inside passengers hurriedly got out, rushed into a house close by, and locked themselves in. The driver wanted to get down and emulate the old Roman gladiatorial feats, by attacking the lioness with his pocket-knife, but the wiser counsels of his Guard restrained him. Then appeared a *Deus ex Machina*, in the shape of a large Mastiff dog, who 'went for' *Madame la Lionne,* and made her retreat, her keepers afterwards capturing her. I believe the horse attacked afterwards died. But the incident, although ending fairly happily, created a great sensation at the time.

Among the minor scenes of the road, with which people were then familiar, were little carts drawn by dogs, as are the milk carts at Brussels at this day. I even recollect them, and their being put down. There is no doubt but it was in the power of a Costermonger (for they even existed in those days) to overload and ill treat his dog; but I believe the same liberty is even now accorded to him with respect to his donkey.

Apropos of these useful animals, my readers may not be aware of a highly important historical fact, which my researches have unearthed. 'August 21, 1817 : *Donkey-riding* is introduced on Hampstead Heath, and the Ladies of the neighbourhood, notwithstanding the vicinity of the Metropolis, enjoy the mode of taking the air without interruption. About a dozen donkeys stand for hire on the Heath every morning, most of them with side-saddles. There are also donkey carts, and whiskies with ponies.'

From the Road to the Streets, and from the Streets to the Houses, are only graceful and legitimate transitions, and here we can again learn something from the Duc de Levis, by using his eyes, and he thus writes of the general aspect of London, as he saw, and judged it. It may not be flattering to us, but we must remember, that in the Georgian era, especially in the long reign of George III., domestic architecture had reached its lowest depth. Mean frontages to houses, oblong windows, small panes of bad glass ; no sanitary arrangements to speak of; a bath almost unknown ; it was a time of the dullest mediocrity. It has been reserved to the last twenty-five years of our time to make things architectural more truly beautiful, and to restore, with some degree of knowledge, the legacies which our veritable art-loving ancestors left to our care.

M. le Duc says, 'At length arrived in London, I should like

23—2

to be able to give an idea of this immense city, by comparing it with other great capitals, a method which I prefer to all others ; on this occasion, unfortunately it is not. In vain have we visited Paris, Vienna, Rome, Venice. Should you have even been at St. Petersburg or Moscow, none of these cities can give you a just idea of the English Capital. The greater part of large cities offer a collection of irregular hotels, palaces, and buildings ; others, like Turin, are distinguished by long arcades. Amsterdam, Dantzic, contain a multitude of Canals ; but nothing of all this resembles London. I must therefore have recourse to a particular description of it.

' First of all, represent to yourself wide streets running in a straight line, with good foot-paths ; iron rails, upwards of five feet in height, are placed the whole length, which separate the houses from the footway, by an area, narrow, and of little depth, which lights the under stories ; there are the kitchens, and the offices ; a flight of steps serves at the same time for a communication out of doors. Over this kind of under storey is the ground floor, then the first and the second floor, but seldom a third, and never an elevated roof ; neither is there any architectural decoration.

' But every house, which has seldom more than three windows in front, has the door ornamented with two wooden pillars, painted white, surmounted by a heavy pediment ; a small glass window gives light to the passage ; in the front is the dining parlour ; underneath a room, almost dark, because it looks only into a small opening, a few feet wide, which does not deserve the name of a court-yard. The staircase is some-times of stone, but mostly of wood, and always covered with a Carpet.

' The first storey contains the drawing-room, and a tolerably large closet behind, where sometimes a bed is placed, but the proper bed-chambers are in the second floor. Under the roof are garrets for the servants. The furniture agrees with the simplicity of the building ; it is much the same among all the opulent classes. The mantelpieces are usually of wood ; no time-pieces ; vases, candelabras, brackets, bronzes, are hardly known ; and of all the arts, gilding is the least advanced. The only thing which shines is the *Grate*, in which Sea coal is used ; the front is polished steel, and kept extremely bright ; the tables, and the rest of the furniture being mahogany, take a fine polish. The paper-hangings are of an insipid colour, and insignificant design ; the dining parlour and the halls are painted in fresco, mostly of a pale blue colour.

'The bed-chambers are still more plainly furnished than the drawing-room; true it is that they are made use of only for sleeping in, as they never use them for sitting-rooms; and the bed-chambers of the women are as inaccessible to the men as the Harems of the East. The beds are of white dimity or calico, with mahogany posts; and their form is simple, and does not vary. The beds, in the best houses, are but indifferent, especially the feather beds, which they usually cover with a blanket, and which, being placed immediately under the sheet, is not agreeable to foreigners, particularly in the summer season. The boudoir is unknown in England. This is, however, the manner of living even among the most wealthy. The progress of luxury has only lately induced them to adopt chimney-pieces of marble, and mirrors have become more frequent. . . . .

'It is impossible to invent anything better adapted for walking the streets of a great city than the footpaths of London; too seldom imitated elsewhere, and always imperfectly. They are paved with broad flag-stones, brought more than a hundred miles, and with a magnificence that reminds us of antiquity. If the whole were put together, they would cover the space of several square miles. They are so even, that you walk without fatigue; and we endeavour to forget the rough and slippery pavement on the Continent. These footpaths are kept constantly swept, and free from dust and dirt; and, as they are on a gentle slope, the wind and the sun soon dry them.

'Neither is here experienced the inconvenience of gutters, which, elsewhere, inundate passengers; and in storms, heavy rains, and floods, stop the way. The English have an ingenious method of getting rid of these rainy torrents; their roofs are almost flat, and the front wall, rising above the upper floor, forms a double slope like our terraces. The waters, being thus collected, descend by a spout into the drains, and are lost in the great common sewer under the middle of the streets. Sometimes they are led into cisterns. It is not that London is destitute of this precious element; a small river, brought at an immense expense, from a great distance; and immense engines, worked by the Thames, distribute the water in all quarters.

'Sea coal, whose black dust attaches so easily to furniture and clothes, is kept in cellars under the footway. In a word, Stables, and, with them, dunghills, with the smells inseparable from them, occupy back streets, and have no communication with the inhabited houses. The lamps are placed on both sides of the street, upon posts a little elevated ; they are very numerous, and are always lighted before sunset. . . . .

'They have even gone so far as to pave, with flat stones, those places where you cross the street, to make an easier communication from one side to the other, and these paths are swept. Carriages are not driven at a dangerous pace in the interior of the city ; lighter equipages go the same pace as the humblest coach. The horses—so swift on the road, that they seem to fly rather than run—forgetting their rapid pace, only go a gentle trot ; and we never see Coachmen endeavouring to pass by and break the line at the peril of the passenger.'

If I want to give a living touch to this book, I must still quote, because, to be honest, I must do it. Others assimilate bodily, or paraphrase facts : then, they are 'men of genius,' and they call me, in reviews, 'a mere compiler.' Granted ; I take the latter as a compliment, for I give the very living age, and sink myself ; because the quotations are better than can now be written—they are *of the time*. We have novels— we have plays—mostly imaginative, because of the ignorance of the writer ; but an honest historian ought only to give the history of the times as he has found it, and, to any one who has conscientiously worked, the crass ignorance, and superficial knowledge, of the present time is stupendous.

The suburbs of London were still being built, and it is pleasant to read an *outside* criticism upon them.

'Scarcely a year passes without hundreds of houses being built ; and even thousands, on the North East side of London ; the most healthy part of the City, on account of its elevation : besides, the parks hinder any increase on the west. Many of the new houses are inhabited by bankers, and rich merchants, who establish themselves there, with their families ; they, however, keep their counting houses in the city, where they transact business till Change-time. These daily journeys (for the distance is sometimes several miles) would appear insupportable in any other country ; but it agrees very well with the active habits so common to all classes of the English nation. Besides, the women, who possess, here, more influence than is generally imagined, and who are as much afraid of damps as they dislike noise and dirt, persuade their husbands to keep these separate establishments, as soon as their circumstances will permit.

'The shops are regularly distributed in all parts of London, yet without being anywhere *en masse*, as they are at Petersburg, and at Moscow. The finest are in the environs of St. James's, because it is here that the most money is spent. The English are unrivalled in the art of displaying their goods to the greatest advantage ; they dispose their various kinds of merchandise with the most fascinating effect ; and, even, with an elegance quite uncommon ; they thus find means to give them an appearance far beyond their value. . . . The English ladies often tax the patience of shopkeepers by making them take down a multitude of goods, without even intending to buy anything. Without being obsequious, these tradesmen are civilly officious, and an air of urbanity is visible in their manners. One might suppose, from their grave and serious deportment, that they had determined to abate nothing from the price demanded. They are, however, like their fellows in other countries : it is, therefore, necessary to bargain with them.

'Foreigners act very imprudently when they speak French to each other in shops. There are, perhaps, ten thousand shops in London, where the French language is understood ; and this number increases daily. This is not suspected. Instead of the officious eagerness, always blended with vanity, with which the people of the south of Europe begin to speak a foreign language, as soon as they know a few words of it ; English sensibility is afraid of committing itself, in the use of a language which is not their own : necessity only forces it upon them. It is as much owing to the curiosity continually excited by the novelties of these shops, which, each in their way, are taking to the eye, as well as to the conveniences afforded by the foot-paths, that we are to attribute the preference given by the idlers of London to certain streets, instead of the public walks and parks.

'That which has been the most fashionable, for a long time, is called Bond Street, and communicates with St. James's Street and Pall Mall, by Piccadilly on one side ; and Oxford Street on the other. When the weather is fine, it is the rendezvous of good company ; thus, in novels, and in plays, coxcombs are all called *Bond Street Loungers.* This latter appellation comes from the pastrycooks' shops, where they find means to wait with some patience for dinner ; by taking some slight refreshment, which the English call *a lunch.* This happens between one and two o'clock. These shops are always supplied with a great variety of pastry, in which currants are most used. The refreshments consist of lemonade, or orgeat; and, in summer, very inferior ices. At other shops forced fruit is sold at a high price.

'The public squares are almost all regularly built; their form is oblong, from whence they take their name (?). The centre of the greater part of the squares is laid down in grass, planted with shrubs, and divided by gravel walks; these grounds are surrounded by iron rails, like the Palais Royal at Paris; they are always kept shut. The neighbouring houses only, have keys, which they make use of for an airing for children and sick persons.'

Speaking of St. James's Park he says that ' In the centre is a meadow, with cattle grazing, watered by a canal, and surrounded with wooden rails.' The Green Park he dismisses in a few words, and of Hyde Park he says that it is 'the general rendezvous of all classes, who parade here in great numbers, on foot, on horseback, and in carriages. It is supposed that sometimes a hundred thousand persons assemble there. This assertion seems, at first, spoken at random; but it is grounded on probability, and even on calculation.'

Then, after treating of Kensington Gardens, he says: ' There are no other gardens in London that deserve notice, except those at Buckingham House, the usual residence of the Queen; and a few, attached to the houses of the great. There are two or three other gardens in the City, the access to which is not difficult, belonging to public bodies, but they are neither large nor pleasant: besides, the streets are so convenient and straight, that this deficiency is less felt than elsewhere. In the suburbs, on every side, are numerous tea gardens, where tea and other refreshments are provided. Here bowls are played on a green as level as a billiard table ; indeed they are called bowling-greens; from whence we get our word *boulingrin*. These public places are frequented by citizens, and their families, on Sundays; the tranquillity, and decency, which is observed at these places is surprising to foreigners, who recollect the turbulent gaiety of the *Ginguettes* of Paris, and other capitals of Europe.' I may be wrong, but, personally, I lament over the loss of the London ' Tea Gardens': they were places of innocent enjoyment, and their popularity may be estimated, by this generation, by the open-air gatherings at the various exhibitions at South Kensington.

CHAPTER XXXI.

London improvements—The Country—Gleaning—Dairying and out-door Washing—The Gipsy.

In writing a book like this, it is manifestly impossible to give an account of all the public works and improvements all over the country—perforce, they must needs be confined to the national heart—the Metropolis. And we, who have reaped the benefit of the large-hearted, and open-handed policy which was then just being inaugurated, may just as well be reminded of what our grandfathers did for us.

In January, 1811, the New Kent Road was suggested, and afterwards carried out, which was the means of purifying a not particularly savoury neighbourhood, called St. George's Fields. In the same year, was a proposition to convert certain dairy farm lands at Mary le bone, into a park for public recreation. We now reap the benefit of it in Regent's Park, or, as it was first named, Mary le bone Park. The first stone of the Strand Bridge, ' Waterloo Bridge,' as it was afterwards called, was laid in this year. Perhaps the first cast-iron bridge ever built was, in this year, an aqueduct over the Ouse, at Wolverton.

In 1812 the Regent's Canal was commenced, and the first stone of Plymouth Breakwater was laid. Vauxhall Bridge was also begun. Millbank Prison was also started this year, and in 1813 Whitecross Street Prison was commenced. Both these have ended their existence. To show how far in advance of their times they were, there was a proposition in 1814 to remove Smithfield Market to Islington, which has come to pass. In 1815, when Napoleon was supposed to be chained at Elba, home affairs again attracted attention, and we find Burlington Arcade in contemplation, Bethlehem Hospital, as we now know it, opened, and the first stones of Southwark

Bridge and the London Institution were laid. So, also, the Post Office in Aldersgate Street was inaugurated.

In 1816 Regent Street was being built, and '*Mr. Nash's Positive Order*' was duly discussed, and, I am afraid, a wee bit ridiculed.

> 'Nash draws designs ; but, honest Master Nash,
> Tho' you may draw—who answers with the cash ?'

Perhaps it might have been that he was architect to the Prince of Wales, and was thought very much of by the Regent.

> 'Master Nash, Master Nash,
> You merit the lash,
> For debauching the taste of our Heir to the Throne,
> Then cross not the Seas,
> To rob the Chinese,
> But learn to grow wise from Vitruvius and Soane.'

We, who are accustomed to our modern London, will read, almost with astonishment, that in October, 1816, 'It is said that Oxford Road is to be continued as far as Bayswater Brook, which, when completed, will make the longest street in Europe. When the New Post Office is finished, the Western Mails are to go out direct, along Holborn, instead of through the narrow streets, Charing Cross, Piccadilly, &c. ; and it is said that a short cut is to be made into the other western road, angular from Shepherd's Bush to Hammersmith, which, certainly, would save a mile of ground.' This ' Bayswater brook ' was that which now feeds the Serpentine, running from Hampstead, by Kilburn, and entering Hyde Park at its Northern part.

On the 18th of June, 1817, the anniversary of the battle of Waterloo, the new Bridge over the Thames, previously called the Strand Bridge, was opened as Waterloo Bridge, which name it now bears. In this year there is a little bit of gossip anent Marlborough House which may be interesting to some readers, especially as its use was foreshadowed : ' The tenure of the magnificent house near St. James's Palace, which was granted to the first Duke of Marlborough, about a hundred years ago, expired, it is said, with the death of the last Duke ; and now reverts to the Crown. This was the house in which Queen Anne resided before she ascended the throne, and it has been observed, that it would scarcely be possible to find a town mansion more suitable to the Heiress of the British Throne.'

In 1818, Regent Street was still being built, and we also

learn—'Dec. 7. The new street from Carlton House to the
Regent's Park is making rapid strides to its completion, almost
the whole of the ground on the intended line of it, being now
let. The part of it which forms a square, in front of Carlton
House, is called "Waterloo Place"; from thence to Piccadilly,
it is called Waterloo Street, and, from Piccadilly, the street,
which will form a grand approach to the Regent's Park, is to
be called the Regent's Parade.'

On the 20th of March, 1819, Burlington Arcade was opened,
and on the 24th of March, Southwark Bridge followed suit.
On the 10th of August the first stone of Telford's bridge
across the Menai Straits was laid: and in November the
arrangements for rebuilding Buckingham Palace were com-

THE PLOUGH.

pleted, Carlton House being too small for ' George the Magnificent.'

In the Country, things were somewhat primitive, to our
thinking, see, for instance, this heavy cumbrous plough drawn
by four long-legged hairy-hocked horses, with their fringed
leather yokes, attached to the hames (which, by the way were
very useful, as they let down, backward, in wet weather, and
protected the horse's withers).

There were no drilling machines, so wheat, and other crops
had to be sown broadcast, an operation which required a
peculiar, and deft turn of the hand, and, as thrashing machines
were only just being dreamed of (a few having been made),
we see the old flail at work.

The agricultural labourer did not receive so much nominal
pay as now, but he had much more in kind, and was strong
and healthy, although dressed in a more homely fashion than

at present.   In those days a man was not ashamed of showing himself to be what he was, a farm labourer, and he wore that most seemly of garments, now dying out fast—a smock frock— good home-made stockings, and strong *ankle jacks.*

In those days, it was like the times of Boaz and Ruth, and women went gleaning in the fields : a sight we seldom see now, in these days of machinery, when the plough follows swiftly after the reaping machine.   The practice of gleaning

SOWING BROADCAST.   USING THE FLAIL.

was a kindly privilege granted by the farmer to his labourers' wives and children, and to the poor women of the parish ; one which he had no need to give, but had been so practised from early ages, that it was looked upon as a right, and consequently abused : see the following : ' Oct. 18, 1813.   At the Nottingham County Sessions, William Pearson and John Sprey were convicted of felony, in stealing wheat in the ear, from shocks standing in the field, and sentenced to fourteen days' im-

THE FARM LABOURER.

prisonment, in the county gaol. The Chairman told them the Court would not have been so lenient, but for their youth, and having been already *five weeks** in prison. He remarked, " that this species of depredation was become so prevalent, as to be loudly, and justly, complained of. He wished it, there-fore, to be understood, that no person has a right to enter the field of another, for the purposes of gleaning, without the owner's permission." '

GLEANERS.

Old phases of English country life are dying out very fast, and it is as well that some one should record them, and that needs both pen and pencil. Take, for instance, the pictures of dairying. In these days of cheese factories and thermo-meters *versus* dairymaids' thumbs, these rough out-door dairy

* Italics are mine.—J. A.

DAIRY FOLK.

WASHING CLOTHES.

arrangements, although they do exist, are not particularly scientific, and do not yield the most paying results.

Even now may be seen in some parts of Scotland, and, possibly, of Wales, the 'Clapping of claes in the burn'—a process of destruction to the linen which may be, perhaps, on a par with the chemicals of a London laundress.

Take another type, fast dying out, absolutely gone in London, the mounted butcher boy, who had but one stirrup, and who used always to ride at racing pace : here, overleaf, we have him perfect ; his peculiar saddle, and the way his tray was strapped on.

Then there is a race of people rapidly dying out—the gipsies ; it is impossible they can exist much longer, in their old nomadic life, and the Lees, Coopers, &c., will be quietly absorbed into the general population. County police and school boards are bound to improve them out of the land.

But at the time of which I write Addison's description* of them would answer very well. 'If a stray piece of linen hangs upon a hedge,' says Sir Roger, 'they are sure to have it ; if a hog loses his way in the fields, it is ten to one but he becomes their prey ; our geese cannot live in peace for them ; if a man prosecutes them with severity, his hen roost is sure to pay for it. They generally straggle into these parts about this time of the year ; and set the heads of our servant maids so agog for husbands, that we do not expect to have any business done as it should be whilst they are in the Country. I have an honest dairymaid who crosses their hands with a piece of silver every summer, and never fails being promised the handsomest young fellow in the parish for her pains. Your friend the butler has been fool enough to be seduced by them ; and, though he is sure to lose a knife, a fork, or a spoon every time his fortune is told him, generally shuts himself up in the pantry with an old gipsy for above half an hour once in a twelvemonth. Sweethearts are the things they live upon, which they bestow very plentifully upon all those that apply themselves to them. You see now and then some handsome young jades among them ; the sluts have very often white teeth and black eyes.'

There are one or two stories told of gipsies about the time of the Regency, which will show what manner of men they then were. 'May 17, 1815. The *Hereford Journal* of last week states, that early in March, a gang of gipsies pitched

* *Spectator*, No. 130.

24

MOUNTED BUTCHER BOY.

their tent on a waste piece of ground in the parish of Stretton Sugwas in Herefordshire, and an old woman, one of the party, persuaded a man of the name of Gritton, that an immense quantity of gold coin lay concealed on the premises he occupied, and that it was necessary that a large sum of money should be made into a parcel, and, after being endowed with a charm, it was to be sewed into the side-pocket of his coat, and the more money the parcel contained, the more considerable would be the treasure he should find. A sum of £70 in gold, bills, and silver, was, accordingly, made up in a parcel,

THE GIPSIES.

and, after some preparations, sewed by the Sybil into the pocket of Gritton's coat, where it was to remain nine days ; at the end of which time she promised to return, and a coffer of guineas was to arise from the ground. When the day arrived, she, of course, did not make her appearance, and, on his opening the parcel she had sewn up, he discovered that the witch had managed to turn gold, silver, and bills into halfpence, stones, and waste paper ; leaving them in exchange for his cash, and as a reward for his folly.'

' July 18, 1816. *The Gipsies.*—Of late years some attempts have been made to reduce the numbers, or at any rate to civilize the habits, of that vagabond and useless race, the gipsies. In pursuance of such purpose, a society of gentlemen have been making all the preliminary inquiries requisite to a proper understanding of the subject. A series of questions have been proposed to competent persons in the different counties in England and Scotland. Reports in answer to these questions have been received, and their contents are thus briefly stated.

' 1. All Gipsies supposed the first of them came from Egypt.

' 2. They cannot form any idea of the number in England.

' 3. The Gipsies of Bedfordshire, Hertfordshire, parts of Buckinghamshire, Cambridge, and Huntingdonshire, are continually making revolutions within the range of those counties.

' 4. They are either ignorant of the number of Gipsies in the counties through which they travel, or unwilling to disclose their knowledge.

' 5. The most common names are Smith, Cowper, Draper, Bosswell, Lovell, Loversedge, Allen, Mansfield, Glover, Williams, Carew, Martin, Stanley, Buckley, Plunkett, and Corrie.

' 6 and 7. The gangs in different towns have not any regular connection or organization; but those who take up their winter quarters in the same city or town, appear to have some knowledge of the different routes each horde will pursue; probably with a design to prevent interference.

' 8. In the county of Herts it is computed there may be sixty families, having many Children. Whether they are quite so numerous in Buckinghamshire, Bedfordshire, and Northamptonshire, the answers are not sufficiently definite to determine. In Cambridgeshire, Oxfordshire, Warwickshire, Wiltshire, and Dorsetshire, great numbers are calculated upon. In various counties, the attention has not been competent to the procuring data for any estimate of families or individuals.

' 9. More than half their number follow no business; others are dealers in horses and asses; farriers, smiths, tinkers, braziers, grinders of cutlery, basket-makers, chair-bottomers, and musicians.

' 10. Children are brought up in the habits of their parents, particularly to music and dancing, and are of dissolute conduct.

' 11. The Women mostly carry baskets with trinkets and small wares; and tell fortunes.

' 12. Too ignorant to have acquired accounts of genealogy, and, perhaps, indisposed to it by the irregularity of their habits.

' 13. In most counties there are particular situations to which they are partial. In Berkshire is a marsh, near Newbury, much frequented by them ; and Dr. Clarke states, that in Cambridgeshire, their principal rendezvous is near the western villages.

' 14. It cannot be ascertained, whether, from their first coming into the nation, attachment to particular places has prevailed.

' 15, 16, and 17. When among strangers they elude inquiries respecting their peculiar language, calling it gibberish. Don't know of any person that can write it, or of any written specimen of it.

' 18. Their habits and customs in all places are peculiar.

' 19. Those who profess any religion represent it to be that of the Country in which they reside ; but their description of it seldom goes beyond repeating the Lord's prayer ; and, only few of them are capable of that. Instances of their attending any place for worship are very rare.

' 20. They marry, for the most part, by pledging to each other, without any ceremony. A few exceptions have occurred, when money was plentiful.

' 21. They do not teach their Children religion.

' 22 and 23. Not *one* in a *thousand* can read.

' 24 and 25. Some go into lodgings in London, Cambridge, &c., during the winter ; but it is calculated three-fourths of them live out of doors in winter as in summer.'

WALKING COSTUME. 1812.

LADIES' HEAD-DRESS.

NOS. 1 AND 2, 1811; NO. 3, 1812; NOS. 4 AND 5, 1813.

NOS. 1 AND 2, 1814; NOS. 3 AND 4, 1815.

CHAPTER XXXII.

For the limits of a book like this, I have spent enough time
on the Roads, Streets, Country, and even Gipsies, so let me
turn to the men and women of the time. *Place aux dames*
of course—so we will begin with the ladies first. And in
the next few engravings which I give are culled specimens of
women's dresses from 1811 to 1820.

Of course there would be caricatures—some rather *outrée*,
others very moderate — I give two of the *Dandizette* or
Dandyess as she was indifferently called, one true, the other,
as with her concomitants, perhaps, a trifle exaggerated—but
not a great deal. Perhaps it is most so in 'the Fashionables
of 1816,' where, I must own, the feathers in the bonnets, the
large Muffs, and the short skirts are, doubtless, slightly in
advance of the fashion, but it is an amusing picture, with no
harm in it, and I give it. Of course, I cannot vouch for its
truth, but the following little story is as I find it: 'June 8,
1812. A young lady of rank and high Condition, in the
warmth of her dancing heart, thus addressed her partner
at the late Lord Mayor's ball.—"God bless you—take care
and don't tread upon my muslin gown, for you see that I have
nothing under it."'

And, when we look at a really sensible picture of a dance
(Waltzing), I do not think it is very much exaggerated.
Waltzing was considered by some as awfully wicked. It may
be. Personally, my dancing days are over, but I never felt
particularly sinful when waltzing—Mrs. Grundy is another

FASHIONABLES OF 1816 TAKING THE AIR IN HYDE PARK.

BELLES AND BEAUS; OR, A SCENE IN HYDE PARK, AUGUST 12, 1817.

A DANDYESS, 1819.

WALTZING.

name for nastiness. For instance, take two separate verses in the same paper :—

> ' What ! the girl of my heart by another embrac'd ?
> What ! the balm of her lips shall another man taste ?
> What ! touch'd in the twirl by another man's knee ?
> What ! panting recline on another than me ?'

Very properly rebuked thus :—

> ' Sir H. E. thinks each waltzing Miss
> From every partner takes a kiss ;
> Then O ! how natural the whim
> That makes them loath to dance with him.'

Read ' The Waltz,' by Lord Byron, and see what was thought of this dance. On June 9, 1817, we read : ' *Quadrilles* have had but a short run. They have now had a lamentable descent, not from the drawing-room to the kitchen, to supersede the *Contre Danse,* but from Almack's to Hockley in the Hole. Though they have not yet fallen into the kitchen, the kitchen has risen to them. Some days ago the Lady of a Noble Admiral, lately returned from the Mediterranean, happened to come home from a Ball unexpectedly, when her Ladyship found all her domestics busily employed in a *quadrille* in the drawing-room, with the chandeliers lighted up, and a regular band of two violins, a bass, and a harp. Her Ladyship owns that they danced them with as much grace and spirit as is visible elsewhere.' And they did dance in those days—there was no languid walking through a quadrille. All the steps were properly and accurately performed. I have before me engravings of a set of all the figures—1 *Le Pantalon,* 2 *L'Eté,* 3 *La Poule,* 4 *La Trenise,* or 4 *La Pastorale* and *La Finale,* which are delicious, but are too large for reproduction in this book.

Of course, the *Crême de la crême* went to Almack's, but numberless were the Peris who sighed to enter that Paradise, and could not. Capt. Gronow, writing of 1814, says : ' At the present time one can hardly conceive the importance which was attached to getting admission to Almack's, the seventh heaven of the fashionable world. Of the three hundred officers of the Foot Guards, not more than half a dozen were honoured with vouchers of admission to this exclusive temple of the *beau monde ;* the gates of which were guarded by lady patronesses, whose smiles or frowns consigned men and women to happiness or despair. These lady patronesses were the

Ladies Castlereagh, Jersey, Cowper, and Sefton, Mrs. Drummond Burrell, the Princess Esterhazy, and the Countess
Lieven.'

In a Newspaper of May 12, 1817, we read—' The *rigorous
rule* of entry established at Almack's Rooms produced a
curious incident at the last Ball. The Marquis and Marchioness of W——r, the Marchioness of T——, Lady Charlotte
C——, and her daughter, had all been so imprudent as to
come to the rooms without tickets ; and, though so intimately
known to the Lady Managers, and so perfectly unexception-
able, they were politely requested to withdraw, and accordingly they all submitted to the injunction.'

Again, at the beginning of the season of 1819 we find these
female tyrants issuing the following *ukase :* ' An order has
been issued, we understand, by the Lady Patronesses of
Almack's, to prevent the admission of Gentlemen in *Trowsers*
and *Cossacks* to the balls on Wednesdays—at the same time
allowing an exception to those Gentlemen who may be *knock-
kneed,* or otherwise deformed.' But the male sex were equal
to the occasion, as we find in the following lines :—

'TO THE LADY PATRONESSES OF ALMACK'S.

Tired of our trousers are ye grown ?
But, since to them your anger reaches,
Is it because 'tis so well known,
You always love *to wear the breeches ?*'

I have collected a quantity of *ana* respecting ladies' dress
of this period, but some would take too long to explain their
point, and others are too *risqué* for the modern Mrs. Grundy.
However, here is one which can offend no one : ' August,
1814. The Wife of a respectable citizen has excited a good
deal of curiosity at Margate. She bathes in a green dress,
without a cap ; and, attached to the shoulders of the dress is
something resembling fins. She swims remarkably well, and
the peculiarity of her paraphernalia, together with her long
black hair, have occasioned many to believe that she was a
mermaid.'

Women were not, as a rule, what we should now term,
highly educated : they knew very little of the ' ologies,' but
they were good women, and true. Their music had not
reached the sublime height of the weird discord of Wagner,
and they knew nothing of the ' Higher Cult ;' but they had
as pretty ballads to sing as ever were sung, from which we are

glad to borrow, and which are refreshing to hear. They did
beautiful needlework, and vied with each other in this
respect; they painted a little on velvet and satin—sometimes
did a little mild water colour on paper—but their efforts were
hardly commendable as works of art, according to our modern
standard.   But they were notable housewives, and there were
female servants in those days who were not above their
position, but knew their work, and did it.   There were no

AT THE SPINNING-WHEEL.

five o'clock teas, no reception days; all had their circle of
acquaintances, who were welcome to call whenever they
chose, and were received without fuss: in fact, as a rule, the
women were helps-meet for their spouses—thrifty, caring for
their husbands and children, and were, essentially, home
makers.

In the Country, the whir of the spinning-wheel might be
heard—but such a thing is not to be seen in use now except

in dilletante hands, like those of Her Most Gracious Majesty. Then, too, at a Cottage door might be seen a woman making pillow lace, now getting rarer and rarer, and it is not an occupation much taken up by the higher classes, as it shows

MAKING PILLOW LACE.

small results for much hand-and-brain work. Straw-plaiting in some districts, glove sewing in others. Now we get straw plait from China, and the gloves are machine sewn. Then all the milk carrying, especially in London, was done by a hardy

MILK WOMAN.

25—2

race of women, principally Welsh, carrying yokes and pails; now the Milk Cart and Perambulator have superseded them.

And there must have been women of thews and muscle, with plenty of pluck, or we should not hear of so many female sailors, and soldiers, during this period. In May, 1813, one was taken on board an American prize, and her sex was only discovered on her being sent to prison. In September of the same year, the master of a Collier, belonging to Ipswich, had reason to believe that one of his apprentices who had made two voyages, was a girl, and so it proved, and, as in the former case, the girl appeared to be a respectable, steady young man, so in this latter, whilst she was on board, she conducted herself with great propriety, and was considered a very active clever lad. Again, in September, 1815, when the Crew of the *Queen Charlotte*, 110 guns, was paid off, one of the Crew, an African, was discovered to be a woman. She 'had served as a seaman in the Royal Navy for upwards of eleven years, during several of which she had been rated able on the books of the above ship, by the name of William Brown, and had served for some time as Captain of the foretop, highly to the satisfaction of the officers.'

But the ladies did not confine themselves to 'ploughing the main.' We know what an attraction a red coat has for them, and therefore no surprise need be manifested, if some of them tried the army. In January, 1813, was a rather romantic case : a girl, in man's clothes, was enlisted in the 53rd Regiment. Her sex was afterwards discovered when she said her lover was in the 43rd Regiment on foreign service, and she wanted to be near him. In 1814, Old Phœbe Hassel was alive, and at Brighton, aged 99. She had served in the army for seven years. I do not know when she died, but there is a portrait and biography of her in Hone's 'Year Book,' ed. 1838, pp. 209, 210, 211, 212, in which she is spoken of as being 106 in 1821. The Regent, after seeing her in 1814, allowed her half a guinea a week, and at her death ordered a stone to be put up to her memory. Another woman who had served five years in the German army, applied for relief to the German Committee at Baker's Coffee-house— she had been several times wounded, but was so badly hit at Leipsig, that she had to be taken to hospital, where her sex was discovered.

Women were then even as now, they aped the manners of the stronger sex. Now as we know, they invade the Smoking and Billiard Rooms, which used to be considered Man's

strongholds ; they won't let him alone even when shooting
—for, so solicitous are they after his welfare, that they will
bring him lunch : they run him hard in School Board,
and County Council, and his last refuge is his Club, where,
in some instances, he is not safe. We have seen how (p. 49)
they played Cricket publicly—a practice lately revived by
' Actresses' and others. We know them well on the river,
but I do not know of a revival of professional boat racing by
them, so I give the following :

'FEMALE ROWING MATCH.—A rowing match took place on
Monday (September 29, 1817), on the river, between Chelsea
and Battersea, which excited great interest. Six watermen's
wives started in six scullers, to row a given distance for a
wherry. The ladies were dressed in appropriate trimmings,
and the boats were discriminated by different colours waving
gracefully in the wind, at the stern. In the first heat two of
the Candidates were distanced. The remaining four then
started, and the prize was won, at two heats, by a strapping
woman, the mother of four children. At the moment of her
arrival at the goal, her victory was proclaimed by the discharge
of a pistol by the Judge on shore, and she was carried in
triumph into a public-house on the beach. No jolly young
waterman could handle his oar with more becoming dexterity
than this dashing female. Her numerous friends crowded
after her, and drank her health in copious libations.'

They were equal to us even in ' FEMALE PEDESTRIANISM.'
Esther Crozier, who commenced on Wednesday (29th of
October, 1817) morning, on the Croydon road, to walk 1000
miles in 20 days, completed 50 miles that evening, at 35
minutes past 9. She commenced her second day's journey
yesterday morning (October 30th) at a quarter before 7 o'clock,
and, at a quarter past 4 she had gone $32\frac{3}{4}$ miles.' She is
mentioned again and again in the papers as going on with her
task ; but I do not think she accomplished it, as I find no
triumphal record of it.

I suppose the proudest day of a woman's life is her Marriage
day, and so we will talk about Marriage in these times. A
trip over the border was a common event, but the smith who
forged the matrimonial fetters at Gretna Green, was not
always a common individual. Early in January, 1811, one of
them, Joseph Paisley, died, at the ripe age of seventy-nine.
He was by vocation a salmon-fisher, and a brandy drinker of
such capacity, that he could drink a pint of brandy at a
draught, without its having any appreciable effect upon him :

he and a brother toper, between them, drank ten gallons of brandy in three days.   He was a foul-mouthed blackguard, but he served his purpose of marrying runaway couples, as well as a better man, and his marriages were just as valid. He obtained the honour of an obituary notice in the London Daily Papers, the *Annual Register,* and the *Lady's Magazine,* in which he is also perpetuated by a copper-plate portrait—so that he must have been considered somebody.

These were not the only curious marriages of that time ; take this as a sample (August 23, 1815) : ' THE NAKED TRUTH. —A scene of a singular and disgraceful nature took place a few days ago at Grimsby.   A widow, under the impression of indemnifying her *second,* from the debts of her *first* husband, proceeded out of the window, in a state of nudity, where she was received into the arms of her *intended,* in the presence of two substantial witnesses.'   This is a curious old tradition— the origin of which I must quote from myself.*   ' This is not uncommon, the object being, according to a vulgar error, to exempt the husband from the payment of any debts his wife may have contracted in her ante-nuptial condition.   This error seems to have been founded on a misconception of the law, because it is laid down (*Bacon's Abridgement,* Tit. Baron and Feme) that "the husband is liable for the wife's debts, *because* he acquires an absolute interest in the personal estate of the wife," &c.   An unlearned person, from this, might conclude, and not unreasonably, that, if his wife *had no estate whatever,* he could not incur any liability.'

One more little story about Matrimony in those times, and I have done.   ' A young man, having long wooed a buxom damsel, at last found a moment so favourable, that he persuaded her to accompany him to a Scotch Justice of the Peace, to have the ceremony performed between them. They stood very meekly under the operation until the Magistrate was laying the damsel under obligations to obey her husband.   " Say no more about that, Sir," said the half-made husband, " if this hand remains upon this body, I'll make her obey me !"—" Are we married yet ?" said the exasperated maiden to the ratifier of Covenants between man and woman.   " No," said the wondering Justice.   " Ah ! very well," cried she, enraptured, " we will finish the remainder to-morrow !" and away skipped the damsel, congratulating herself on her narrow escape.'

* ' Social Life in the Reign of Queen Anne,' by John Ashton.

CHAPTER XXXIII.

The Man of the period—Drinking habits—Dandies—Lord Petersham
—A Dandy's diary—Gaming—Prize fighting—Country Sports.

AND what was the man of the period like? Well! there is
no concealing the fact that he was narrow-minded—because
he had no opportunity of mixing much with his other fellow
creatures either abroad or at home—war stopping the former
and means of communication the latter, and so, the necessary
rubbing off of his angles did not take place. The Middle
Class gentleman was not too well read. Latin, of course, he
knew, or had learnt. Perhaps a little Greek—his French was
very 'Stratforde at yᵉ Bowe,' and German was to him
'unknowe.' His English, too, was shaky. The Peninsular
War over, the Officers brought back with them a smattering
of Spanish, the Guitar, and the Cigar. Personally, he had
plenty of Courage which found its vent in the Army and Navy
and, in Civil life, in duelling and boxing. As to duelling, it
was so common that you can scarcely take up a London Newspaper of the time without some 'affair of honour' being
chronicled; and, as to boxing, every man learnt it, put his
teaching into practice, and talked it. It was, except
pedestrianism, the only athletic sport known. Rowing was
not; of riding there was plenty, with a good breed of horses
fit to carry a man. Cricket was played—but there was no
football, nor cycling, if we except the short-lived dandy horse.

They worked longer hours at their divers businesses than
we do, but they did far less work; they dined early, and had
suppers, and, for evening amusements there were the theatre,
and the social meeting at the Inn, where much Rum Punch
and Brown Brandy was drunk, and the affairs of the Nation
duly discussed, among a select Coterie. Those old boys could
drink, too. A three- or four-bottle man, then common, would

now be a phenomenon—and, mind you, it was not Claret or other light wines they drank—the war with France made that too great a luxury ; but it was the stronger wines of Portugal and Spain, well fortified with brandy. I wonder how many died in 'making their heads,' and whether it was always ' the survival of the fittest '!

They were of Convivial habits, and did not ' join the ladies ' after dinner, or, if they did, they were slightly inebriate, and the accompanying illustrations are no caricature of an advanced stage of a *symposium*. No. 1 is, ' Are you all charged, Gentlemen ?' No. 2 is, ' A Song, Gentlemen, if you please.' No. 3 is, ' Sing Old Rose, and burn the bellows.'* No. 4 says, ' I humbly move to throw the waiter out of the window, and charge him in the bill !'

Very little need be said about their dress, the illustrations throughout the book show its different phases. The Regent, of course, set the fashions, for tailoring, and building, were his hobbies ; but even he could not do anything against the dictum of George Bryan Brummell. When he retired in poverty to Calais, in 1816, he left the field entirely to the Regent. There were some who gained a nickname from some eccentricity in costume, as ' Blue Hanger ' (Lord Coleraine), or 'Peagreen Haynes '—but they were not many.

The principal variation in men's attire, at this period, was

* *Izaak Walton* says, ' Now let's go to an honest alehouse where we may have a cup of good barley wine, and sing " Old Rose," and all of us rejoice together.' And we get a presumed explanation of the Song in *The British Apollo* (1708-9).

> ' In good King Stephen's days, the Ram,
> An ancient inn at Nottingham,
> Was kept, as our wise father knows,
> By a brisk female call'd *Old Rose ;*
> Many, like you, who hated thinking,
> Or any other theme than drinking,
> Met there, d'ye see, in sanguine hope
> To kiss their landlady, and tope ;
> But one cross night, 'mongst twenty other,
> The fire burnt not, without great pother,
> Till *Rose*, at last, began to sing,
> And the cold blades to dance and spring ;
> So, by their exercise and kisses,
> They grew as warm as were their wishes ;
> When, scorning fire, the jolly fellows
> Cry'd, " *Sing Old Rose, and burn the bellows.*"

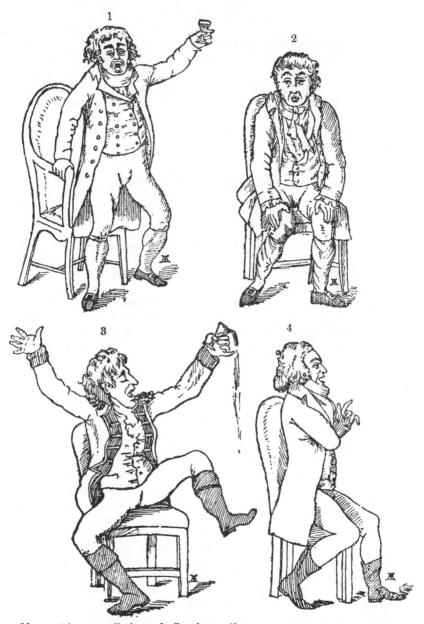

No. 1. 'Are you all charged, Gentlemen ?'
No. 2. 'A song, Gentlemen, if you please.'
No. 3. 'Sing Old Rose, and burn the bellows.'
No. 4. 'I humbly move to throw the waiter out of the window, and charge
     him in the bill !'

the way in which they clothed their legs. Breeches and boots were now eschewed by fashionable men, and their place was taken by the pantaloon, made of some elastic stuff, generally 'stockinette,' fitting tightly to the leg, and after 1814 by the Cossack trouser: an example of both being given in two pictures of Lord Petersham, a distinguished leader of fashion, who married Miss Foote, the actress, and afterwards became Earl of Harrington. Over the trousered picture are these lines :—

> 'I'll prove these Cossack pantaloons
> (To one that's not a Goose)
> Are like two Continental towns
> Called Too-long and Too-loose.'

This was that Lord Petersham who never went out of doors till six p.m., and whose horses, carriage, and harness, were all of the same shade of brown. He had other foibles which are amusingly told by Capt. Gronow. 'The room into which we were ushered was more like a shop than a gentleman's sitting room ; all round the walls were shelves, upon which were placed the canisters, containing Congou, Pekoe, Souchong, Bohea, Gunpowder, Russian, and many other teas, all the best of their kind ; on the other side of the room were beautiful jars, with names, in gilt letters, of innumerable kinds of snuff, and all the necessary apparatus for moistening and mixing. Lord Petersham's mixture is still well known to all tobacconists. Other shelves, and many of the tables were covered with a great number of magnificent snuff-boxes ; for Lord Petersham had, perhaps, the finest collection in England, and was supposed to have a fresh box for every day in the year. I heard him, on the occasion of a delightful old light blue Sèvres box he was using, being admired, say, in his lisping way—"Yes, it is a nice summer box, but would not do for winter wear." In this museum there were also innumerable canes of very great value. The Viscount was likewise a great Mæcenas among the tailors, and a particular kind of great coat, when I was a young man, was called a Petersham.'

These trousers later on (see illustration, p. 398) were worn, instead of breeches and boots, on horseback, but this was only affected by the 'Dandy,' a term which came into vogue two or three years before this time, and which, according to Webster, is derived from the French *dandin,* 'a ninny, a silly fellow.' The Dandy at his toilet is of the same date,

A PORTRAIT (LORD PETERSHAM).
(*Published January 10, 1812, by H. Humphrey.*)

LORD PETERSHAM. 1815.

and here we see him in his evening dress. The huge cocked hat is exaggerated, but it was the shape of the *chapeau bras,* which folded flat, and was carried as we now do a *Gibus.* The

A DANDY.
(*December* 8, 1818.)

looking-glass, wash-stand, &c., are very meagre according to our ideas, but much ornament was not lavished on bedroom furniture.

Here is the Diary of a Dandy (Sept., 1818):—

'SATURDAY.—Rose at twelve, with a d——d headache. *Mem.* Not to drink the *Regent's Punch* after supper.—The green tea keeps one awake.

'Breakfasted at one.—Read the *Morning Post*—the best Paper after all—always full of *wit, fine writing,* and *good* news.

DANDY ON HORSEBACK.
(*November* 2, 1818.)

'Sent for the tailor and staymaker—ordered a morning *demi surtout* of the last Parisian cut, with the collar *à la Guillotine,* to show the neck behind—a pair of *Petersham Pantaloons,* with striped flounces at bottom—and a pair of *Cumberland corsets* with a whale-bone back.—*A caution to the unwary.* The last pair gave way in stooping to pick up Lady B.'s glove.—The Duke of C——e vulgar enough to laugh, and asked me in the *sea slang,* if I had not *missed stays in tacking.* Find this is an old joke stolen from the *Fudge Family.*—Query. Who is this Tom Brown? Not known at *Long's* or the *Clarendon.*

' Three o'clock. — Drove out in the *Dennet*—took a few turns in Pall Mall, St. James's Street, and Piccadilly.—Got out at Grange's—was told the thermometer in the *ice cellar* was at 80. *Prodigious!* Had three glasses of *pine* and one of *Curaçoa*—the *Prince's Fancy,* as P—— calls it.—P. is *a wag in his way.*

' Five to seven.—Dressed for the evening—dined at half-past eight, " nobody with me but myself," as the old Duke of Cumberland said—a neat dinner, in *Long's best style,* viz., A tureen of turtle, a small turbot, a dish of Carlton House Cutlets.—*Remove*—a turkey poult, and an apricot tart.— *Dessert*—Pine apple and brandy cherries.

' Drank two tumblers of the Regent's Punch, iced, and a pint of Madeira.—Went to the Opera in high spirits—just over—forgot the curtain drops on Saturdays before twelve.— *Mem.* To dine at seven on Saturdays.

' Supped at the Clarendon with the *Dandy Club*—cold collation—played a few rounds of Chicken Hazard, and went to bed quite cool.

' SUNDAY.—Breakfasted at three—ordered the *Tilbury*—took a round of *Rotten Row,* and the *Squeeze,* in Hyde Park— cursedly annoyed with dust in all directions—dined soberly with P——m and went to the Marchioness of S——y's *Conversatione* in the evening—dull but genteel—P. calls it the *Sunday School.*

' N. B. P——m, who is curious in his snuff as well as in his snuff boxes, has invented a new *mixture,* Wellington's and Blücher's, which he has named, in honour of the meeting of the two heroes, after the battle of Waterloo—*La belle Alliance* —a good hit—*not to be sneezed at.*'

'A DANDY.

I do remember me in Hertford streets
Walking at noon, I met an exquisite,
A thing, whose neck in Oriental tie,
Where not a crease is seen, so stiff withal
The powers of starch had rendered it, tho' made
Of finest muslin, that to my wondering gaze,
(Unlike the ease of Nature's masterpiece),
It seem'd as 'twere a mere automaton ;
And then its shape, so all unlike a man,

So tightly laced that 'twas self-evident
He walk'd in pain, if walking 't could be call'd,
Since from the earth to raise his languid foot,
It seem'd a labour too Herculean ;
But, still, thus mincingly, he reached the Bell—
There stopped.   I, being anxious to o'erhear
The sounds this creature, nicknam'd man, would utter,
Entered the room apologizing to it ;
No answer I receiv'd, save a low murmur,
For too fatiguing 'twas to articulate.
Finding it useless farther to intrude,
I asked the waiter who and whence he was ?
" One of our College* Dandies," he replied.
No longer wondering, straight I left the Inn.'

Naturally, the tight-fitting pantaloon required a well-made leg, so those gentlemen to whom Nature had not been bountiful, used false calves, and thus passed muster.   They took snuff in quantities, but very rarely smoked.   When Lord Petersham's Collection of Snuff was sold, it took one of the partners in the firm of Fribourg and Treyer, of the Haymarket, and two assistants three days to weigh it—and the same firm, when they bought George IV.'s collection, at his death, set a room apart, entirely for its sale.

They gambled terribly, not perhaps as much as now, but still large sums were won, and lost, on the cast of a die. March 28, 1811 : 'The brother of a Noble Marquis, is said to have lately won at *hazard* upwards of £30,000, all in one night!' April 3, 1811 : 'A young gentleman of family and fortune lost £7,000 on Sunday Morning at a gaming house in the neighbourhood of Pall Mall.'   But, although the Turf was an Institution of the day, there was but very little betting, compared to what goes on in that gigantic Cancer which so grievously afflicts England in the present day.   Nor had they such a stupendous gamble as our Stock Exchange.   There was plenty of betting on Cock fighting, which was a very fashionable amusement, even patronized by our Imperial Guest, the Grand Duke Nicholas, who, on February 10, 1817, accompanied by the Duke of Devonshire, the Russian Ambassador, Sir William Congreve, Baron Nichola, General Kutusoff, &c., &c., went to the Cockpit and saw five Cock fights.   'His Imperial Highness remained an hour and a half, and appeared much amused, never having seen Cock fighting before.'

* The East India College.

But then he was here to study our manners and customs, and even went to a prize fight. February 14, 1817 : 'An Imperial Boxing Match, to use the general term of the ring, took place yesterday at Coombe Warren, for a subscription purse of twenty guineas, between Croxey the Sailor, a *bustling* second rater, and a candidate for *milling* notoriety. . . . The Grand Duke Nicholas, desirous of viewing the British character throughout, signified his wish to see the method of English boxing. . . . His Imperial Highness arrived at the ring in a carriage and four, at one o'clock, accompanied by his own suite, and some English Noblemen, admirers of gymnastics. A waggon was reserved for the Grand Duke's reception, and he ascended it with a hearty laugh. Under it were placed the bull dogs and *bull hankers* for the last sports of the day. Bill Gibbons introduced his trusty bitch to the Patricians in the waggon as the favourite for the *Bull* prize.'

The fight, or rather the fights, for there were two of them, took place, but they were stigmatized as very poor and tame affairs. 'The Bull was the next object of attack, for a silver collar, and all the fancy buffers the town could produce were let go from the Royal waggon, which was decorated with purple flags. Gibbons' fancy dog was lamed early, but the best of the fun was, after the bull had broken a horn, he began to snort up on end, and went and got loose. Helter skelter was the consequence, and the bull, as regardless of men as dogs, made play through the ground, reclining his head, and tossing mortals before him, until he got clear off, upsetting carts, &c., that impeded his way. The fun concluded just before dark, and the whole sport went off with *éclat.*'

Apropos of prize fighting the last sentence in the following paragraph is worthy of note. Feb. 28, 1817 : 'Carter next asked to be backed to fight any man, when Cribb mounted the table, and challenged to fight anything in being, from *three* to *twelve* hundred, observing he had fought so often that he should not again prostitute his talent for a trifle. Carter said he thought the Carlisle people would back him for £300, and he would ask them. After devouring about twenty dozen of wine, the lads departed *to spend the evening,* and amuse themselves at the expense of lamp contractors and watchmen's rattles.'

Although we may think all this very brutal, yet, with the exception of the bull baiting, which was only made illegal in

26

1835, I fancy that things go on very much now, as they did then, only they are done more quietly. In the country, men had their hunting, shooting, and fishing to amuse them, and

PLAYING AT BOWLS AND QUOITS.

they were as keen then as in our time. True, they did not rent deer forests in Scotland, at fabulous prices, nor did they take salmon rivers in Norway; but although they did not enjoy breechloaders, with spare gun ready loaded handed as soon as the other is discharged, and though they were innocent of the cruel slaughter of a *battue*, yet they had good sport both in wood and stubble, and the old flint gun, if held straight, would make a respectable bag to carry home. Then they played cricket, but they did not armour themselves, because there was no necessity for so doing, the ball then being bowled and not hurled as if from a cannon. Then for the quieter and middle-aged there were the healthy out-door games of bowls or quoits.

Among the younger men the manly sports of wrestling, quarter-staff, and back-sword, had not died out, but then they had not the advantage that we have of football and Rugby rules.

CHAPTER XXXIV.

Eating and drinking — Recipe for punch — The stage — Baron
Geramb—Romeo Coates—Actors and actresses—Mrs. Jordan.

PERHAPS they ate more solid food than we do, and it was a
point of honour, at a dinner, to provide and display vastly
more food than could possibly be eaten. As an example.
On Jan. 1, 1811, General Grosvenor, Mayor of Chester, gave
a dinner to his friends and two hundred sat down. Here is
the bill of fare : 'Sixteen tureens of soup, eight boiled turkeys,
three hams, four dishes of *à la mode* beef, five pigeon pies,
three saddles of mutton, thirteen plum puddings, six dishes of
murinade pork, eight French pies, four roasted turkeys, eight
dishes of rabbits, three legs of mutton, four geese, two fillets
of veal, ten dishes of chickens, four dishes of veal surprise,
three beef-steak pies, three dishes of sweet-breads, six hares,
six venison pasties, eight dishes of ducks, six oyster patties,
six dishes of mutton casserole, six dishes of pig, six lemon
puddings, eight dishes of haricoed mutton, four neat's
tongues, three dishes of collared veal, and a round of beef.

'*Removes*—Ten haunches of venison, ten necks of venison.

'*Sweets*—Thirty salvers of whips and jellies, twenty moulds
of jelly, forty moulds of blanc mange, tarts, cheese cakes,
mince pies, puffs, &c., &c.'

The guests must have needed appetites such as were
possessed by the gentlemen chronicled in the two following
paragraphs. Sept. 9, 1812 : 'On Wednesday last, two gentlemen, in the neighbourhood of Ratcliffe Highway, had a wager
of £5 upon a man named *Leurnen*, a coal-heaver, that he
should devour, in the space of three-quarters of an hour, nine
pounds of bullock's heart roasted, three pounds of potatoes,
half a quartern loaf, and drink a pot of porter. The parties
met at the Queen's Head public-house, Broad Street,

Ratcliffe Highway, and the spectators, of whom there were a considerable number, paid sixpence each to be admitted. He completed his task, and drank three or four glasses of rum besides, within the time allowed him, without producing the smallest apparent inconvenience.'

Aug. 2, 1816: 'Yesterday morning a young man, of the name of Robert Hunt, better known by the name of *Rob-the-Grinder*, he being a knifegrinder by trade, undertook, for a wager, to eat three quarts of peas, three pounds of fat bacon, half a quartern loaf of bread, and drink two quarts of porter, and a pint of gin in the space of one hour. He sat down to his meal at eleven o'clock in the forenoon, and he devoured the whole in fifty-two minutes, with seeming ease, saying it was only a good lunch, as his appetite would serve to a good dinner by two o'clock.'

But there was luxury in eating, as well as gross feeding. Green peas sometimes fetched several guineas a quart— the following is very mild. May 22, 1811: 'This is the earliest season known for many years. In Covent Garden Market, green peas were sold at eight shillings per quart on Saturday last, and moss roses which had blown in the open air at one shilling each.'

And, being connoisseurs, those old gentlemen knew good wine, and would pay a long price for it. At the sale of the Duke of Queensberry's effects, in 1811, some Tokay fetched £84 a dozen quarts, or £7 a bottle! The prices fetched at the sale of the Duke of Cumberland's wine pale into insignificance before this, but then he had no Tokay for sale.

Champagne 11 to 12 guineas the dozen
Hock   about 11   „   „
Hermitage   „   14   „   „
Madeira   „   7   „   „
Claret   „   7   „   „
Port from £4 10s. to £5 5s.   „

A sale is chronicled May 13, 1817: 'Friday, the cellars of Alexander Davison, Esq., were emptied to the best bidders. The prices, at which the several lots were knocked down, were unusually high. Three dozen of red Madeira, bottled in 1801, were knocked down at *eighteen* guineas per dozen, it was supposed, for a distinguished member of the Royal Family. One lot of Hock, a hundred and seventeen years old, sold at ten guineas per dozen, and very little of the Sherry went at less than five and six guineas per dozen.'

The middle classes could not, of course, afford these wines, but they drank sound Port, Sherry, and Madeira, brown Brandy and Gin—Whisky was almost unknown.   But for conviviality, Punch, in bowls, was the drink.   Green tea was introduced into the manufacture of Rum Punch—and may be now, for aught I know, if there is anybody living who knows how to make it—but here is a metrical recipe for Milk Punch, of the year 1815, which reads remarkably well.

> ' Take seven large lemons, and pare them as thin
> As a wafer, or, what is yet thinner, your skin ;
> A quart of French Brandy, or Rum is still better,
> (For you ne'er, in Receipts, should stick to the letter.)
> Six ounces of sugar next take, and pray mind,
> The sugar must be the best double refin'd ;
> Boil the sugar in as near half a pint of spring water,
> In the neat silver saucepan you bought for your daughter ;
> But be sure that the syrup you carefully skim,
> When the scum, as 'tis call'd, rises up to the brim.
> The fourth part of a pint you next must allow
> Of New Milk, made as warm as it comes from the Cow,
> Put the rinds of the lemons, the milk, and the syrup,
> With the rum in a jar and give them a stir up ;
> And, if you approve it, you may put some perfume,
> Goatstone, or whatever you like in its room.
> Let it stand thus three days, but remember to shake it,
> And the closer you stop it the richer you make it.
> Then, filtered through paper, 'twill sparkle and rise,
> Be as soft as your lips, and as bright as your eyes.
> Last bottle it up . . .'

It seems wrong to chronicle good living when bread was so dear—especially in the early years of the Regency where receipts for rice bread, and cheap adulterants of wheaten bread, were pressed upon the notice of the middle classes. One article of food they had which we should like at the same price—the very finest Native Oysters at 9s. and 10s. a barrel.

It was a brilliant period for the Stage.   Kean was to make his appearance on the boards, but then Mrs. Siddons and Kemble retired.   Death, too, was busy with some old dramatic favourites, and people connected with the Stage. In these nine years were called away—R. Cumberland,

W. T. Lewis, Malone, G. F. Cooke, Chas. Dibbin, Chas.
Burney, Mrs. Abingdon, H. Siddons, Mrs. Jordan, Sheridan,
Signora Storace, and Miss Pope.

In 1811 there were but three regular theatres in London—
Drury Lane, Covent Garden, and ' The Little Theatre ' in the
Haymarket—and they all did a good business, although the
prices charged their audiences were very moderate, so were
the salaries of the actors.   The pit was all pit, and the
pittites were a discriminating audience, who were neither
ashamed nor afraid to applaud, or censure, as their judgment
led them.   The plays were frequently changed.   There were
no runs of hundreds of nights, and the consequence was that
the actor, ' playing many parts,' could not acquire mannerism,
and gained greater experience in his profession.

In 1811 there were two persons, amateurs, who mightily
affected theatrical company, namely, the Baron Geramb and
Romeo Coates.   The Baron was principally known for his
enormously long whiskers—so feelingly alluded to by the
Regent (p. 274), and there is a very good account of him in
The Annual Register, April 6, 1812 :—

' The much talked of Baron Geramb, who has, for a year or
two past, made so conspicuous a figure in this metropolis, is,
at last, ordered out of the country.   This singular person
ushered himself into public notice by publishing a most
inflated and ridiculous letter, which he dedicated to the Earl
of Moira ; in which he described himself as a Hungarian
baron who had headed a corps of volunteers in the cause of
Austria against France, and stated that, after the peace, he
went to Spain to give the benefit of his courage and profound
military experience to the oppressed patriots of the Peninsula.   He accompanied this production with every other
mode of obtaining notoriety, such as filling print shop
windows with three or four different engravings of his person,
which few fools bought, in various costumes ; a star, a death's
head and cross-bones, and other terrific emblems, adorned the
person of the baron.   Nobody has walked the public streets
for some time past who does not know this redoubtable
nobleman.

' Wherever notoriety could be acquired, there was the
Baron Geramb.   At the funeral of the late Duke of
Albuquerque he exhibited himself in all the parade of grief,
in a jet black uniform.   Where money alone could not gain
admittance, the magnificent exterior of this seeming magnate

of Hungary was sure of procuring an introduction. At the Opera, at the Theatres, and the Park, his furred mantle and resplendent stars were seldom missed. When that wonderful master of histrionic art, Mr. Coates, played, or rather attempted to play, Lothario, last winter, at the Haymarket, the Hungarian baron sat with indescribable dignity in the stage box, and appeared the patron of the absurdities of the night, consoling the white-plumed Lothario with his nods, and bows and cheers, for all the coarse and severe, but justly merited, raillery which was unsparingly dealt out to him from the pit and galleries.

'But the baron was formed to embellish a Court as well as to dignify a playhouse. He was frequent in his inquiries after the health of the British Sovereign at St. James's ; and appeared with more than usual splendour at the celebrated *fête* of the Prince Regent at Carlton House. The fascinations of that scene of courtly festivity and princely elegance became the subject of the Baron's pen ; and he accordingly published a letter to "Sophie" describing, in the most romantic language, all the splendid objects of the night. . . . The Baron, it is reported, has had uncommon success in certain gaming houses. He is now at Harwich, on his way to the Continent. He is said to be a German Jew, who, having married the widow of a Hungarian baron, assumed the title by which he passed.'

Robert Coates, generally known as Romeo, was the son of a merchant and sugar planter at Antigua ; he was educated in England, and then returned to his father. At his death, in 1807, young Coates came back to England not only very wealthy, but with a large collection of splendid diamonds. He settled at Bath, which town he soon made lively by his vagaries. He drove about, drawn by white horses, his curricle being shaped like a kettledrum, in front of which was a large gilt cock, and its motto was, 'While I live I'll crow.' He developed a curious craze for theatricals, and on the 9th of February, 1810, he appeared at the Bath Theatre as Romeo. Let Capt. Gronow tell the story of that night :—

'His dress was *outré* in the extreme ; whether Spanish, Italian, or English, no one could say ; it was like nothing ever worn. In a cloak of sky blue silk, profusely spangled, red pantaloons, a vest of white muslin, surmounted by an enormously thick cravat, and a wig *à la* Charles II., capped by an Opera hat, he presented one of the most grotesque spectacles ever witnessed upon the stage. The whole of his garments were evidently too tight for him; and his movements appeared so incongruous that every time he raised his arm, or moved a limb, it was impossible to refrain from laughter.

' But what chiefly convulsed the audience, was the bursting of a seam in an inexpressible part of his dress, and the sudden extrusion through the red rents, of a quantity of white linen, sufficient to make a Bourbon flag, which was visible whenever he turned round. This was at first supposed to be a wilful offence against common decency, and some disapprobation was evinced; but the utter unconsciousness of the odd creature was soon apparent, and then unrestrained mirth reigned throughout the boxes, pit, and gallery. . . .

' In the midst of one of Juliet's impassioned exclamations, Romeo quietly took out his snuff-box, and applied a pinch to his nose; on this a wag in the gallery bawled out, "I say, Romeo, give us a pinch," when the impassioned lover, in the most affected manner, walked to the side boxes, and offered the contents of his box, first to the gentleman, and then, with great gallantry, to the ladies. . . .

' But how shall I describe his death? Out came a dirty silk handkerchief from his pocket, with which he carefully swept the ground; then his Opera hat was carefully placed for a pillow, and down he laid himself. After various tossings about, he seemed reconciled to the position; but the house vociferously bawled out, "Die again, Romeo!" and, obedient to the command, he rose up, and went through the ceremony again. Scarcely had he lain quietly down when the call was again heard, and the well-pleased amateur was evidently prepared to enact a third death; but Juliet now rose from her tomb, and gracefully put an end to this ludicrous scene by advancing to the front of the stage and aptly applying a quotation from Shakespeare—

" Dying is such sweet sorrow,
That he will die again to-morrow." '

He came before a London audience, and played Lothario at the Haymarket on the 9th of December, 1811, and I give an illustration of him in that character. He ran through all his money, and had to go to Boulogne: there he married, came over to England, and lived in Montague Square. He met with an accident, and died, aged seventy-six, in 1848.

LOTHARIO, AS PERFORMED BY MR. COATES AT THE HAYMARKET
THEATRE, DECEMBER 9, 1811.

On the 29th of June, 1812, Mrs. Siddons took her leave of the public. The scene was Covent Garden Theatre, and the play 'Macbeth,' in which, of course, she played Lady Macbeth. After the sleep scene, she came forward and recited a farewell address written for her by Horace Twiss. She then retired amid a storm of applause. Kemble afterwards came forward to ask the sense of the house whether they would hear the remainder of the play, but the universal consensus was that they *could* not, and the audience retired.

On the 30th of September the new Drury Lane Theatre was ready for opening. The building cost £112,000 ; the fittings, £13,000 ; wardrobes, scenery, &c., £25,000 ; in all, £150,000. It was honoured next day with a visit from the Queen, the Princesses Augusta and Mary, the Princess Charlotte of Wales, the Prince Regent, and the Dukes of Sussex, Kent, and Clarence. On this occasion the theatre was darkened, and the interior brilliantly lit up, in order to show it at its best advantage to its distinguished visitors. Elliston opened it on the 10th of October with ' Hamlet.'

In November Betty, better known as the ' young Roscius,' reappeared on the Stage at Covent Garden. But his boyhood's charm was broken, and, as a man (he was 22), he was a failure as an actor.

In 1813 Miss Stevens made her *début*, and so did Kean, at Drury Lane on January 26, 1814, and by his acting Shylock took the town by storm. ' For voice, eye, action, and expression, no actor has come out at all equal to him. The applause, from the first scene to the last, was general, loud, and uninterrupted.' Next month he appeared as Richard III., and, if possible, his acting was more belauded. People, including Coutts the banker, sent him cheques, one for £50, and the Managers of Drury Lane increased his salary.

The first mention I can find of Miss O'Neil, is March 24, 1812 : ' A Miss O'Neille, of whom report speaks very highly, at the Dublin Theatre, is engaged for Covent Garden Theatre the next season. She is said to be a good actress, a very great beauty, and a Roman Catholic, so there is something for all tastes.'

August 18, 1815 : ' Among the improvements making at Covent Garden Theatre, preparatory to opening for the ensuing season, backs are fixing to the seats in the pits, so that each person will sit at ease as in a chair.'

September 1, 1815 : ' The Managers of the Winter Theatres

have already, it seems, received no less than *Ninety-seven* Tragedies, Comedies, Operas, Farces, Melodramas, and Panto-mimes, intended by the *Authors*, for representation, during the ensuing season.'

We sometimes see very realistic effects produced on the Stage, but we have not yet arrived at this pitch. August 30, 1815 : 'A strolling company of Comedians in the County of York, in performing the tragedy of " George Barnwell," advertised that " Milwood would be hanged upon the Stage "; and, in consequence, the curtain dropped on a figure of Mil-wood suspended from a gibbet, to the great entertainment of the audience assembled.' By the way, every theatre at these times, invariably played 'George Barnwell' on Boxing Night, a practice which has not so very long been discontinued at some of the minor London Theatres.

Charles Bannister, who had been before the public upwards of thirty years, took his leave of them, June 1, 1815.

On February 17, 1816, the audience at Drury Lane were startled by a pistol shot. A farce called the ' Merry Mourners ' was being played ; a young man in the third row of the pit produced a pistol, and deliberately shot at Miss Kelly—luckily without hurting her. He was, of course, at once captured and locked up. He had been pestering her with his addresses.

Mrs. Jordan, wife of William IV., died July 5, 1816. She had been acting this year, but had grown stout, and had lost much of her vivacity. Here is the last record of her. July 13, 1816: ' Our correspondent from Paris informs us that Mrs. Jordan was buried in the cemetery of St. Cloud. She had resided in the village for some time with great privacy, under the name of Mrs. James. She was buried in a thin shell, stained black, but uncovered with cloth or ornament of any kind. Mr. Thomas Greatorex, an hotel-keeper in Paris, and Mr. William Henshall, statuary, of Mortimer Street, Cavendish Square, were by accident passing, and saw her interred. They were the only Englishmen present.' This account was afterwards confirmed in the same newspaper, date the 22nd of July. Such was her sad fate, after having borne the Duke of Clarence ten children, of whom those that survived came to great honour on his accession to the throne.

How different was Sheridan's funeral on the 15th of the same month ! His mortal remains were interred in Poets' Corner, Westminster Abbey, with all honour, the pall-bearers being the Duke of Bedford, Earls Mulgrave and Lauderdale, Lords Holland and Robert Spencer, and the Bishop of London. The Dukes of York and Sussex, the Duke of Argyle, the Marquess of Anglesea, and many other noblemen, all followed to do honour to his corpse.

The Lyceum Theatre, which had sheltered the Drury Lane Company after that theatre was burnt down, was again opened on the 15th of June for English Opera.

The following anecdote will show how sometimes the audience thoroughly enter into the play. August 13, 1816: 'Mrs. Mardyn and Mr. Oxberry have been performing at the Windsor Theatre. Oxberry, as the Jew, instead of taking the pound of flesh from the Merchant, by accident cut off the top of his own *finger* in placing the knife in his belt. This, however, did not prevent him from finishing the scene, although his blood dyed that part of the stage he occupied. When Portia requests Shylock "*To have some surgeon lest Antonio do bleed to death*," a man in the pit, thinking she alluded to the accident, exclaimed, "Here, mate, take my handkerchief, and I'll go for the Doctor."'

Kemble took his farewell of the stage on June 23, 1817, playing Coriolanus at Covent Garden. He spoke a short valedictory address, and of course was rapturously cheered. As he hurried off the stage, a gentleman in the pit handed Talma, the celebrated French actor, who was in the orchestra, a white satin scarf, embroidered with a laurel wreath, begging that he would throw it on the stage, which he did. The manager was called for, and came, went through the farce of asking whether it was intended for Mr. Kemble, and assured the audience that he would give it to the great tragedian 'with heart-felt gratification.'

Clowns are not responsible beings, at least on the stage, or, according to the following anecdote, off it. July 2, 1818: 'Usher, the Clown of the Coburg Theatre (opened on the 9th of May), in consequence of a wager, set off in a machine like a washing-tub, drawn by four geese, at half-past twelve o'clock from below Southwark Bridge, and passed under four bridges, and arrived at half-past two at Cumberland Gardens. A pole extended from the machine in which he sat, to which the geese were harnessed. For some time they were quite tractable, and he went on swimmingly, but, at times, they were quite restive, and not easily managed. A great number of persons accompanied him in boats, and several viewed the

whimsical expedition from the bridges.　After completing it
he offered, for a wager of one hundred guineas, to return
thence through the centre arch of London Bridge ; but no
person would accept the challenge.'　A Clown named Barry
did the same about thirty-five or forty years ago, I think.

A CLOWN AND A GRASSHOPPER.

Clowns did not dress then as they do now, as we see in the
illustration of a Clown and a Grasshopper in the pantomime
of ' Jack and Jill,' performed at the Lyceum in 1812.

CHAPTER XXXV.

The Italian Opera—An uproar—Catalani and her terms—Vauxhall —Musical prodigy—Painters, Sculptors, Art exhibitions—Literature and writers—Bibliomaniacs—George Bidder, the Calculating boy—Musicians—Medical men—The Clergy—Roman Catholic emancipation—Joanna Southcott.

THE Italian Opera flourished. Madame Catalani, undeterred by her reception by the public, at the time of the O. P. Riots, was prima donna ; for Mrs. Billington retired from the stage in May, 1811.

There was a pretty little riot on 2nd of May, 1813, at the Opera at the King's Theatre.

' We are indebted to a correspondent for the following particulars of what, we are told, for we were not present, was, in its progress, one of the most disgraceful scenes that the walls of that, or any other Theatre, ever witnessed.

' Much disapprobation had prevailed throughout the performance of the Opera on Saturday night, and, at its conclusion, cries for the Manager, and Catalani, resounded throughout the house. The Ballet was, however, suffered to commence, but had not proceeded many minutes, when, from behind the scenes—' a band of fierce barbarians rushed upon the stage ; the dancers flying for safety and for succour.' The dropscene in vain descended, for an irruption was made through the body of it, and, on its being drawn up, there was discovered a motley group of men and women, the latter shrieking and the former shouting, and most destructively active in the demolition of all that came within reach of their canes.

' Mr. Masterson, Secretary to the Theatre, made his appearance, to the interruption of the pleasing interchange of shouts, which alternately rang out from the audience before the stage, and the company of new performers upon it. The Secretary bowed, and silence ensued—when a gentleman, from the front of the pit, and not long from Ireland, made a speech on the occasion demanding the Manager. The Secretary expressed himself ready to convey their pleasure to Mr. Taylor, but said he, himself, was unauthorized to answer any questions. Catalani's name was immediately vociferated in one quarter, that of Angiolini in another ; and, in a third, a rise of salary was demanded for them as well as Tramezzani ; but the sums were so large, being £10,000 for one, £5,000 for another, that, whether intended, or not, it had the effect of changing the tone of this clamour, and the Secretary was not honoured with any further commands.

'The audience appeared now to be satisfied ; no further noise was heard, and the multitude on the stage were beginning to disperse, when, unfortunately, an order for the soldiers to clear the stage as usual, produced a most alarming scene. Three or four soldiers, and a sergeant, were most manfully assailed, and disarmed by the disappointed lovers of music and Catalani. The firelocks were brought as trophies to the front of the stage, and precipitated into the Orchestra. The pit, which contained the sober and orderly part, only, of its former contents, gave strong signs of disgust, which were received and returned by one of the disarming heroes in a manner only to be described as the utmost stretch of *black-guardism*. Our Correspondent says that he dares not describe the impudent species of insult which he offered to the spectators.

'The officer of the guard, the moment that he saw the unbecoming attack made on his small party, hurried to the spot, with the avowed intention of drawing them off ; but the moment he appeared, he also was hustled, his sword violently seized, and his person insulted, until Major Mellish came forward, and assured the house that his friend, Lieutenant White, had only presented himself to call off his party from the scene. The vengeance of the whole house was now directed against the man who had acted in so brutal a manner in face of the Ladies assembled in the Boxes. He was collared, dragged to the front of the stage, tweaked by the nose, and called on, after many other ingenious indignities, to make an apology to the house. But he was most stubborn, and fought about him ; till, at last, it was discovered that he was too inebriated for utterance. This was satisfactorily explained to the audience by a gentleman near him.

' Peace would have been now restored, but Mr. Coates—the tall Mr. Coates — made his appearance, and insisted on making a speech. He was almost equally impetuous, but he also was manœuvred off the stage. Much mischief was done, both to the musical instruments in the Orchestra, and to the scenery. It was most providential that a scene of bloodshed had not been the result; for the detachment of Guards in the street, hearing that their comrades had been assailed, and their officer insulted, rushed into the Theatre, and it was by a miracle that they were stopped from making their way to the stage. In fact, the practice of employing soldiers to clear the stage is most unbecoming. It puts the troops in a most embarrassing position, and is sure to raise the indignation of the spectators. It was intimated, we hear, that, in consequence of the dreadful scene of Saturday night, the Lord Chamberlain has issued an order, that no person shall be admitted behind the scenes, under the penalty of withdrawing the License from the Theatre.'

The managers of Theatres used to make large sums by allowing people behind the scenes, and it was said that the Lord Chamberlain's prohibition meant a loss of £3,000 a year to the Opera. I cannot, exactly, trace the cause of this riot. I know that Catalani broke her engagement, and can only suppose that it was something about Money, for she was as greedy as a certain modern Prima Donna. She had already received £1,275 for ten weeks, and would be paid at the same rate for the remaining twenty weeks of her engagement. Take a newspaper paragraph, 25th of March, 1814 : ' Madam Catalani has been offered two thousand guineas, and a free benefit, for thirty nights' performance at the Opera, which offer she has declined, asking three thousand.' So she did not sing that year.

Here is another little story. May 23, 1814 : ' Dr. Busby intends giving two Concerts at the Opera House. The Doctor consulted Mr. Braham in the first instance, requesting his advice what vocal performers he should engage. Mr. Braham immediately recommended Catalani, Dickons, Salmon, &c. &c. The Doctor, in consequence, waited on Monsieur Vallabrique, and begged to know Madame Catalani's terms. The answer was, 500 guineas each day; or half the gross receipts ; and Monsieur said, if the Doctor would agree to the latter proposal, that he, himself, would engage the singers at a great expense, and pay them liberally out of his

27

own portion. "Well," says the Doctor, "what would you offer them?" "Why," says Monsieur, "my wife 500 guineas each morning; Mrs. Dickons ten guineas each morning; Mrs. Salmon ditto, and Mr. Braham——" "Stop!" says the Doctor, "I have already engaged that gentleman. He is to have thirty guineas each morning; or if——" "Ha! ha!" interrupted the astonished Frenchman, with a long tragic groan. "*Thirty* guineas every morning? He is a Jew!!!" On which the Doctor made his bow and engaged Grassini.'

People were very fond of music, and there were plenty of good Concerts, and singers, with oratorios for the more seriously disposed. Did you object to the heat of a Concert room, you could have very good vocal music, with an excellent band, *al fresco*, at Vauxhall, with the very best of company to rub shoulders against. Take, for instance, only one day—and from my notes I could give many—July 12, 1819:

'VAUXHALL.—A more brilliant scene has scarcely ever presented itself than that which these gardens exhibited on Friday evening last. The walks were thronged with company of the first description, among whom we noticed the Duke of Argyle, the Duchesses of Richmond, Bedford, and Rutland; the Marquess of Worcester, the Marquess and Marchioness of Tavistock; their Excellencies the French and Spanish Ambassadors, Viscount and Lady Castlereagh; Lords George Cavendish, Petersham, Foley, Clare, Grantham, Harrington, Forbes, Clifford, and Kier; Ladies Brownlow, Warburton, and Otway; Sir Harry Hotham, Sir William Elliot, and Mr. Holme Sumner, M.P.'

Of course there was the usual musical prodigy, no age could do without that, and here it is, 10th of September, 1814: '*The Plymouth Chronicle* of Tuesday last (September 6th) contains the following singular statement, respecting a boy, living in Plymouth, only *eleven years and a half old*. Of Master *Whitcomb*, for such is the name of this prodigy, it is asserted that "unassisted in musical composition, this child has produced to the musical world several pieces in *score*, dedicated, by permission, to the inimitable Catalani"; but what we chiefly allude to, is, a challenge he received a few days since, viz., to compose a *full orchestra*, musical parts to accord in harmony with a given bass!! Thus taken by surprise, he accepted the challenge, and was locked up in a room, with only pen, ink and paper, the given bass was produced, and without any assistance, this child of nature produced, in about an hour, a complete musical score, viz., two violin parts, two flute parts, two horn parts, a tenor part, and oboe part !'

From Music to Art is but a short, and legitimate transition, and that period was no mean one in the history of Art, which could produce such a list of names as the following, which does not pretend to be exhaustive : Sir George Beaumont, Sir William Beechey, R.A., Henry Bone, R.A., the celebrated enameller, A. W. Callcott, R.A., A. W. Chalon, R.A., R. Cosway, R.A., I. Constable, P. de Wint, W. Etty, W. Finden, the engraver, Henry Fuseli, R.A., G. Hayter, W. Hilton, R.A., E. Landseer, Sir Thomas Lawrence, R.A., C. R. Leslie, J. Linnell, P. I. de Loutherbourg, R.A., W. Mulready, R.A., P. Nasmyth, J. Northcote, R.A., H. W. Pickersgill, W. H. Pyne, P. Reinagle, R.A., H. Raeburn, R.A., R. R. Ramsay, A.R.A., M. A. Shee, R.A., H. Sass, T. Stothard, R.A., J. M. W. Turner, R.A., W. Varley, C. H. Weigall, B. West, R.A., D. Wilkie, R.A., and W. Wyon the medallist.

Then among Sculptors were some glorious names — W. Behnes, F. Chantrey, R.A., J. Flaxman, R.A., J. Nollekens, R.A., W. Theed, P. Turnerelli, and R. Westmacott, R.A.

There were, besides the Exhibition of Pictures of the Royal Academy, which was held at Somerset House, or Somerset Place, as it was then called, two Water Colour Exhibitions— ' The Society of Painters in Water Colours,' and the ' Associated Painters in Water Colours.' And, occasionally, there were, as now, collections of the works of some one artist to be seen, as, for instance, in March, 1811, West's pictures were shown ; in May, 1812, Wilkie's pictures were exhibited ; and in May, 1813, a collection of Sir Joshua Reynolds' works was made, and there was a supplementary exhibition for the sale of pictures, called ' the European Museum.'

There was a craze for large Panoramas, and they generally followed the progress of the war : thus in 1811 we find them of Malta, of Cadiz, the Siege of Flushing, and a Panorama of Messina. In 1812 we have one of Lisbon, and in 1815 we are treated to a view of Elba.

Miss Linwood ought to rank as an artist, and her exhibition of Needlework was most popular, as may be judged by the fact that it was on show at Saville House, Leicester Square, from 1800 till 1844, when she died. It then filled up the place in public amusement now occupied by Madame Tussaud's

Exhibition. (By the way, Mrs. Salmon was the wax-work woman of those days.)

Miss Linwood's work, although done with coloured wools, was as like that awful Berlin wool-work of our day, as a picture by the President of the Royal Academy would resemble a coloured wall-poster. They were large and most faithful copies of some of the finest specimens of art, both British and foreign. The South Kensington Museum possesses some of them, notably a portrait of Napoleon. For one of her pictures, the *Salvator Mundi*, after *Carlo Dulci*, she refused three thousand guineas, and at her death left it as a legacy to the Queen; but, when her collection was sold, it fetched very little, somewhere about £1,000.

There was very little done in public statuary at this time, but the monument to the memory of Nelson, in the Guildhall, was uncovered on April 27, 1811 (Sheridan composed the inscription); and on March 27, 1813, that to Pitt, in the same building, was inaugurated, Canning being responsible for the inscription.

In literature we have a strong list of names, but in the one I give I do not pretend that it includes every one laying claim to literary merit — it is merely a representative catalogue :—Joanna Baillie, Mrs. Barbauld, Robert Bloomfield, Lord Byron, Thomas Campbell, Thomas Carlyle, G. Chalmers, S. T. Coleridge, George Crabbe, Alan Cunningham, Madame D'Arblay, Isaac D'Israeli, Sir Philip Francis, William Godwin, George Grote, Henry Hallam, William Hazlitt, Mrs. Hemans, James Hogg, Thomas Hood, Theodore Hooke, Leigh Hunt, Mrs. Inchbald, Mrs. Jameson, J. Keats, Charles Lamb, W. S. Landor, J. Lemprière, M. G. (or Monk) Lewis, Lord Lytton, Edward Malone, Miss Mitford, James Montgomery, Hannah More, Thomas Moore, Lady Morgan, Lindley Murray, Mrs. Norton, Mrs. Opie, Jane Porter, Anne Radcliffe, Samuel Rogers, Sir Walter Scott, R. B. Sheridan, Percy Bysshe Shelley, John and Horace Smith, Robert Southey, J. Horne Tooke, Henry Kirke White, William Wordsworth.

Death claimed, during these nine years, some of the older *littérateurs*, as the Right Rev. Thomas Percy, D.D., Bishop of Dromore, whose ' Reliques of Antient English Poetry ' is well known. He died Sept. 30, 1811. On March 18, 1812, died John Horne Tooke, who will always be remembered by ' The Diversions of Purley.' John Philpot Curran, the celebrated Irish lawyer and orator, died at Brompton, October 14, 1817 ; and Samuel Lysons, the eminent Antiquary, who was Keeper

of the Records when they were in the Tower of London,
whose 'Environs of London' is still a standard book of
reference, expired June 29, 1819. On August 25th of the
same year, died James Watt, whose name is so well known in
connection with the steam engine.

It was a dilettante age for books. It was the first wake up
after a long, long sleep. Men were only just beginning to
understand the value of the treasures they possessed, and the
mysteries of first editions, tall copies, &c., were just coming to
light. Old libraries were searched, and their secrets were
exposed. I think they over-valued their old books ; as a proof,
they do not fetch so much now. For instance, take the
'Valdarfer Boccaccio,' printed in 1471. This book was in the
library of the Duke of Roxburghe, and at the sale thereof
fetched, on June 17, 1812, the enormous sum of £2,260. It
was purchased by the Marquis of Blandford. He afterwards
sold it, on June 16, 1819, to Messrs. Longman and Co., at the
reduced price of £875, and on December 7, 1881, Mr. Quaritch
bought it for £585. At the same sale the Duke of Devonshire bought a Caxton, 'The Recuyell of the historyes of
Troye,' for £1,060. People other than those infatuated called
it bibliomania, and so I think it was.

The foundation of the celebrated Roxburghe Club took
place on that *dies mirabilis*, the 17th of June, when the
number was limited to twenty-four, and they dined annually
afterwards, the great toast of the evening being always, 'The
memory of the immortal Valdarfer.'

Here is a curious Advertisement, May 11, 1814 : 'A SHABBY
OLD MANUSCRIPT, to be seen at No. 15, Noel Street, Berwick
Street, Soho, is, perhaps, one of the greatest Curiosities now
existing; not so much for its Antiquity, though conjectured
to be of the 13th or 14th Century, for it has no date, or any
striking peculiarity either in the Character or spelling, as on
account of the subject, and the extraordinary nature of its
contents. The Proprietor of this singularly curious and
interesting document, a gentlemen of high literary attainments, would, under certain limitations and restrictions,
dispose of a Correct COPY for 200 guineas. Mere curiosity
may, however, be gratified with a sight of the original, and of
the heads of its principal contents, for a One Pound Bank of
England Note, or twenty shillings good and current money.'

In Science great strides were being made ; they were
emerging from the slough of ignorance, and treading the
right path at last ; and, although they cannot boast either of

the scientists, or the discoveries, of the Victorian era, yet an age that could produce a Humphry Davy and a David Brewster brought forth two famous men.

About this time there was a wonderful boy, who, since, developed into a good Civil Engineer. The earliest notice I can find of him is in a Newspaper of March 4, 1814. 'There is now at Moretonhamstead, Devonshire, a boy only seven and a half years old, of a most astonishing genius ; indeed, as a Calculator, quite a prodigy. A gentleman asked him how many eyes and toes six score of bullocks had, and how many minutes in a year, each of which questions he answered with the same ease and quickness. Another person put many difficult questions to him in arithmetic, to the whole of which he immediately replied correctly. The boy cannot account how he does it, and, till within a few weeks, did not know a figure. His name is Bidder, and his father is a mason at the above place.'

We hear of him again in October, 1819. 'A singular phenomenon appeared in the metropolis this month. A boy of the name of George Bidder solved the most difficult questions in arithmetic by mental calculation, in less time than could be accomplished by the most skilful by the ordinary operation ; and what was more remarkable he did not work by common arithmetical rules, but by a process entirely his own.'

Among the musical composers who were then living may be named Sir Henry R. Bishop, Dr. Callcott, Muzio Clementi, Dr. Crotch, Charles Dibdin, Thomas Greatorex, Thomas Kelly, Vincent Novello, John Parry, Cipriani Potter, and Samuel Wesley.

Medical Science had emerged from the empiricism in which it had so long been shrouded : and to this era belong some great names, both in Medicine and Surgery. Still, the Pharmacopœia was a great deal too redundant, and the family doctor was pompous, and not too learned. Doctors and Clergymen still stuck to their wigs—Barristers and Judges still do to theirs—and he could not be worth his salt as a physician, unless he carried a gold-headed cane, often with a round ball a-top, which was a relic of the time when it contained some aromatic mixture, which he smelt, in order to guard himself against contagion.

Among eminent medical men and surgeons of those days, first in alphabetical order is that clever old bear, John Abernethy, whose brusque sayings have been so often quoted.

Joseph Constantine Carpue, who distinguished himself by making false flesh noses, which he covered with skin let down from the forehead.   Sir Richard Croft, who attended the Princess Charlotte in her confinement, and whose death so preyed upon his mind that, about three months afterwards, he committed suicide by shooting himself.   Sir Henry Halford, who was physician in ordinary to George IV., and whom we

A PHYSICIAN.

have seen, in conjunction with that illustrious monarch, examining the bodies of Henry VIII. and Charles I.; and Dr. Jenner, whose connection with Vaccination everyone knows.

   In the Church of England there were no particular luminaries.   No doubt every Clergyman, from a Curate to an Archbishop, worked sincerely, according to his lights; but there was not the zeal, hard work, and self-abnegation which

are now the characteristics of our Anglican Clergy. Nor of
them only ; all sects are striving hard to win souls, and it
would be invidious, in this matter, to make a distinction. I
give an illustration of two opposite characters, the dear, suave
old Bishop, and the Charles Honeyman of the period, of the
diamond ring and pocket-handkerchief religion. Says the
Bishop, 'I shall endeavour, in a short, but eloquent discourse,
to remove the vulgar prejudices imbibed by a narrow
education.' The other commences his sermon thus : 'With
all the diffidence natural to my situation, I shall, for the first
time, venture to address this polite and discerning audience.'

In matters religious, men had not the breadth of thought
which we, now, happily possess. For instance, on May 5, 1813,
was introduced into the House of Commons a Bill, which, afterwards, became law, ' For the further relief of persons impugn-
ing the doctrine of the Trinity.' The Acts of 9 and 10
William III. had not been repealed, and by them, persons
who, in writing or in conversation, denied the existence of
any of the persons of the Trinity, were disabled, in law, from
holding any office, civil, ecclesiastical, or military, on conviction ; and, if a second time convicted, they were disabled to sue
or prosecute in any action or information, or to be the guardian
of any child, and liable to be imprisoned for three years.

This may appear extremely intolerant, but it must be borne
in mind that, well within every one's memory, an atheist,
avowing himself to be such, could not give testimony in a
Court of Justice, nor sit in the House of Commons. Tardily,
nous avons changé tout cela.

The Roman Catholics, too, felt the yoke that galled them,
and made strenuous efforts to obtain its removal. On April 30,
1813, Mr. Grattan presented to the House of Commons his
Bill ' to provide for the removal of the Civil and Military Dis-
qualifications, under which his Majesty's Roman Catholic
Subjects now labour.' At that time a Roman Catholic had
no vote for Members of Parliament, nor could he sit in the
House, and he could not hold any office, either civil or military.

On May 24th, the House of Commons having resolved
itself into a Committee on Mr. Grattan's Bill, the Speaker
protested against the admittance of Roman Catholics into
Parliament, the Privy Council, and the Judicial Bench ; and
concluded with moving that the words, ' to sit and vote in
either House of Parliament,' in the first clause, be left out of
the Bill. After a long debate, a division took place, the

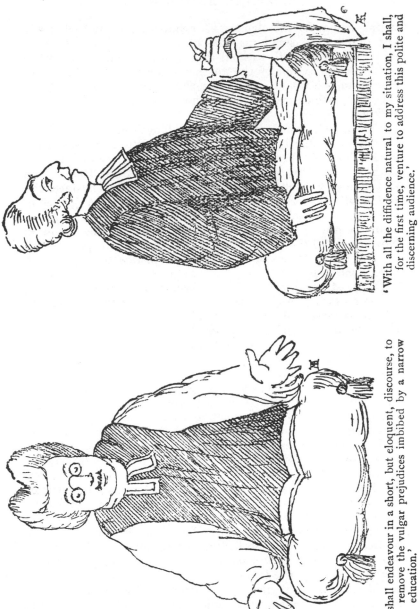

'I shall endeavour in a short, but eloquent, discourse, to remove the vulgar prejudices imbibed by a narrow education.'

'With all the diffidence natural to my situation, I shall, for the first time, venture to address this polite and discerning audience.'

voting being, for the clause 247, against it 251, so that it was lost only by the small majority of four. Mr. Ponsonby then said that, as the Bill, without this clause, was neither worthy of the Catholics, nor of the further support of the friends of concession, he would move that the Chairman do now leave the Chair, which was carried without a division, and thus the Bill was lost.

The Catholic Emancipation Bill did not receive the Royal Assent until April 13, 1829. Cardinal Wiseman was made Archbishop of Westminster, September 30, 1850. Roman Catholic Chaplains were permitted in gaols July, 1863. The first Roman Catholic Judge that sat on the Bench since the Reformation, was Sergeant Shee, who was made a justice of the Queen's Bench, December, 1863. We have even had a Roman Catholic Lord Mayor, Sir Polydore de Keyser ; and on November 3, 1884, Lord Petre, a Roman Catholic priest, took his seat in the House of Lords, so that justice seems to have been done at last.

Of the strength of the Nonconformists we gather something in the following, August 28, 1815 : ' At the annual conference of the *Wesleyan* Methodists, held at Manchester, it appears that the number of persons in the Connection amounted to nearly *One hundred and ninety thousand.*'

On December 29, 1814, died a remarkable religious impostor, one Joanna Southcott, who was born, of humble parents, in Devonshire, somewhere about 1750. In the year 1790, she was employed as a work-woman at an upholsterer's shop in Exeter. The shopkeeper being a Methodist, his shop was frequently visited by Ministers of the same persuasion, and Joanna, possessing what is termed ' a serious turn of mind,' did not pass unnoticed. She had frequent discussions in the shop with these Ministers, and was regarded as a prodigy. Indeed, so sensible was she of her own importance and superiority, that, with the aid of a few dreams, and some extraordinary visions, she began to think herself *inspired.*

But what confirmed her in this belief, was the realization of a circumstance which she had been forewarned of, in a dream —it was finding the *Miraculous seal.* One morning, in sweeping out the shop, she found a seal, with the initials I.S., which could mean nought else but Joanna Southcott. From this moment she bid adieu to the upholstering trade, and set up in business for herself as Prophetess. In her first prophecies she states that in 1792 she was visited by the Lord, who promised to enter into an everlasting covenant with her, and told her that a vision would be shown her in the night. It accordingly appeared, sometimes in the shape of a cup, then like a cat, which she kicked to pieces, but was very uneasy, until she was told that it was nothing more than a trick of Satan, with a view to torment her.

On the appearance of her first prophecies, the Methodist preachers, already adverted to, endeavoured to convince her of the *diabolical* nature of her doings, and attributed them to Satan himself. She then appointed an interview with as many as might choose to attend, in order to put the question at rest. The discussion was warm, but it ended in all present signing the following document :—

' I, Joanna Southcott, am clearly convinced that my calling is of God, and my writings are indited by His Spirit, as it is impossible for any Spirit, but an All-wise God, that is wondrous in working, wondrous in power, wondrous in truth, could have brought round such mysteries, so full of truth, as is in my writings ; so I am clear in whom I have believed, that my writings came from the Spirit of the most high God.
' JOANNA SOUTHCOTT.'

From this time her converts increased surprisingly, so that she could not furnish seals sufficient to answer all demands. The sealed papers contained a text of Scripture (not uniformly the same), promissory of beatitude hereafter, and the envelope was stamped with the seal found in the upholsterer's shop. The *sealed* person was forbidden to open the paper, lest the charm should be destroyed.

She came to London, at the invitation of Sharp the engraver, and then she began deluding her followers that she was the destined mother of the Messiah, who would be born on October 19, 1814. Her personal appearance favoured the opinion that she was in an ' interesting condition,' but after her death it was found she was suffering from dropsy. Large sums of money were subscribed towards the expense of her accouchement, and a most expensive cradle was provided. The time passed by, but no Messiah appeared ; and she died on December 29, 1814, and was buried in the churchyard attached to St. John's Chapel, St. John's Wood ; her deluded followers believing for long after that she would rise again, and come among them.

There are many satirical prints respecting this impostor, but I do not care to reproduce any of them, as they are either too silly or too coarse.

INDEX.

BILLING AND SONS, PRINTERS, GUILDFORD.